SOCIAL WORK PRACTICE

SOCIAL WORK PRACTICE

CASES AND PRINCIPLES

CYNTHIA BISMAN
BRYN MAWR COLLEGE

1994

BROOKS/COLE PUBLISHING COMPANY
PACIFIC GROVE, CALIFORNIA

I(T)P™ The trademark ITP is used under license.

A CLAIREMONT BOOK

Brooks/Cole Publishing Company
A Division of Wadsworth, Inc.

Printed in the United States of America
10 9 8 7 6 5 4 3 2 1

Library of Congress Cataloging-in-Publication Data
Bisman, Cynthia.
  Social work practice : cases and principles / Cynthia Bisman.
    p.   cm.
  Includes bibliographical references and index.
  ISBN 0-534-22230-7
  1. Social service.   I. Title.
  HV40.B543   1993
  361.31'2—dc20   93-23213

Sponsoring Editor: Claire Verduin
Marketing Representative: Ronald Shelly
Editorial Associate: Gay C. Bond
Production: Merrill Peterson, Matrix Productions
Production Coordinator: Joan Marsh
Manuscript Editor: Victoria Nelson
Permissions Editor: Elaine Jones
Interior Design: Nancy Benedict
Cover Design: E. Kelly Shoemaker, Laurie Albrecht
Cover Illustration: Diana Ong/Superstock
Typesetting: Kachina Typesetting, Inc.
Printing and Binding: Arcata Graphics/Fairfield

CONTENTS

Chapter One

INTRODUCTION: THE DOMAIN OF SOCIAL WORK

Chapter Two

BECOMING A SOCIAL WORKER: MAJOR CONCEPTS OF THE PROFESSION

Chapter Three

PROFESSIONAL VALUES AND SOCIAL WORK ETHICAL CODE   45

Chapter Four

RELATIONSHIP: THE BELIEF-BONDING   73

Chapter Five

ASSESSMENT: THE CASE THEORY   111

Chapter Six

COMMUNICATION: THE METHODS AND SKILLS   177

Chapter Seven

PRACTITIONER OBSERVATION: THE SELF-MONITORING OF PRACTICE   209

Chapter Eight

INTERVENTION: PLANNING, CONTRACTING, EVALUATION 247

PREFACE

While most educators probably perceive their own teaching areas as the most fraught with difficulty, the social work practice classes do present pedagogic quandaries. Accompanying lack of clarity about the substance is the absence of agreement about the best methods for conveying the material to students. At the same time, those teaching these classes consider them the foundation on which the rest of the curriculum depends.

Related to the profession's continuing struggle for greater legitimacy, in many programs the practice classes are viewed as "soft," deficient as they are in the kinds of theories presented in human behavior and the historical and legislative data of policy courses. Some schools have attempted to "strengthen" practice courses by integrating them with research content. Yet, human behavior, policy, research and yes, even field and the range of electives, can not hold together without the practice courses to explicate what it is that social workers do when they engage in the execution of their discipline.

Claiming to cover the breadth of social work practice, most of the available practice texts give short shrift to communities, the organization and policies, and primarily focus on change of individuals. In this book, the acknowledged emphasis is on practice with individuals. Offering in-depth case material accompanied by definitions and the current professional literature, social casework, or practice with individuals, is explained and illustrated as it is practiced in the public and private sector.

Drawing upon my over twenty years of practicing social work and greater than fifteen years of teaching it, I have developed the components of practice including relationship, assessment, communication, self-awareness/use of self and intervention into a coherent theory of social casework practice. There are general principles that all practitioners follow, regardless of their particular theoretical approach or specialized training and it is these principles that this book covers.

We have become accustomed to thinking of theory as increasing our understanding of client behaviors, such as the psychoanalytic interpretation of the borderline personality. Or theories are to prescribe particular interventions such as cognitive theory and its emphasis on altering the thoughts people have ascribed to events. The social work practice theory developed in these pages provides a context and content for use of these other theories; understanding of social work is the thrust rather than the rote application of a set of concepts.

Although no one theoretical model is favored, a wide range of the theories of intervention and human development are presented as over twenty-five case studies are discussed and analyzed. Contrasts are provided when similar problems are approached quite differently by various social workers in disparate settings. A model is provided for the utilization and integration of the professional literature with practitioner decision-making and interventions. Students are taught that theory is a necessary ingredient of social work practice and they learn how to inform and shape their practice with contemporary knowledge and thinking. Bibliographies at the end of each chapter provide source material to expand understanding about each of the cases and problem areas discussed in the text.

While my primary educational background was psychodynamic (family therapy training with the Menninger Foundation) formative years as a practitioner were in the late 1960's and early 1970's with AFDC families on welfare, the Veteran's Administration and the chronic mentally ill, and my practice philosophy reflects the wide-reaching exposure I have had to theories and theorists such as Satir, gestalt, transactional analysis, reality, rational-emotive, and my continuing involvement in direct practice issues.

It is my teaching philosophy that in addition to being instructed about a theory of practice students must become challenged, intellectually and emotionally, about their chosen profession. Social workers engage with people confronting highly stressful situations. Basic to carrying out this demanding work students must deal with feelings, their own and the clients; they also need knowledge of the accepted models and normative behaviors and to learn how to think guided by professional values and ethics.

To become a social worker one must study real cases emphasizing the actions of the practitioner, while at the same time knowledge is essential about the theories, available literature and emerging research. All, however, must be based upon an appreciation of the historical traditions and mores of the profession—what it is that distinguishes us from other helping professions. I write in a style that is easy to read. Revised with input from my graduate practice classes over these past years, I have worked hard to present live and exciting material, while offering more than the merely anecdotal.

Interviews with highly experienced social workers employed in almost as many different settings provide the case studies. Moreover, in addition to discussing their practice, these social workers intimately talk about themselves as they describe their motivations for entering the field and consider their client interactions. Responding to a series of general questions and through analysis of audio or video tapes or process recordings, they provide the substance for students to learn about the craft of social work—why a question or statement is chosen, how to enact a particular role, what is done to achieve a specific client outcome.

Beginning with an introductory chapter social work practice is defined and discussed within the context of professional practice including the nature and attributes of professional occupations, and a comparison of social work to other professions. Briefly reviewing the primary methods of social work, social casework or practice with individuals is defined as the method which this book covers.

Providing the philosophical base of the profession and establishing the context which shapes professional behavior, social work mission, person and environment perspective, and values and ethics are presented in chapters two and three. Each of the following five chapters examines one of the practice components—relationship, assessment, communication, self-awareness/use of self and intervention. Beginning with historical traditions, definitions are developed, followed by case material which illustrates social workers enacting the component. Relevant literature is used to ground the decision-making and behaviors into the accepted fields of knowledge. Issues of diversity are addressed through the case material and each chapter ends with Notes to the student social worker. Presented more informally than the text, these notes provide suggestions and specific advice about writing reports and interaction with the field instructor.

New concepts are introduced. Clarity is provided to the person and environment perspective through its presentation as multi-faceted including attention to communities, agency service delivery and societal policies. Relationship is defined as a belief-bonding; the social work assessment considered the social worker's case theory and self-awareness/use of self is offered as practitioner observation. Nevertheless, these novel perspectives are based upon and emerge from our profession's history and unique mission. Those long time practitioners and teachers will find all the components of practice solidly grounded in social work traditions, while old and new teachers will find case material and practice principles to help students learn what it is to be a social worker in direct practice with individuals.

The anticipated usage of the book is as the central text in first or second year undergraduate or graduate social work practice classes.

ACKNOWLEDGMENTS

As a reflection of my professional career, which itself has significantly shaped my values and outlook on life, this book has been a major undertaking. With no model I felt was available, I drew heavily on my own experiences as well as those of friends, colleagues, former and current students and teachers, and of course, clients.

To start, I cite the social workers interviewed for the case studies—

much of the dialogue is theirs, though identifying information has been modified such that no client and social worker can be matched to each other. Information has been shifted between cases and social workers, and specific variables such as race, ethnicity and gender have all been altered. Where employment changes have been made, the position where the casework occurred is indicated. While not all of the case material obtained in the interviews has been included, each social worker gave willingly of their time and talked lovingly of their work. I thank you all for sharing your expertise and your inspiration. Some material from several outstanding students is also included; I know they are already making significant contributions to the profession. Also in this list are social workers who have reviewed the material in various stages and discussed their work with me.

Cleopatra Anderson, MSS
Social Worker
Department of Health and Human
  Services
Philadelphia, PA

Jean Beamen, MSW
Clinical Social Worker
Colmery O'Neill Veteran's
  Administration Hospital
Topeka, KS

Pam Bekir, PhD., MSW
Director, Family Services
Veteran's Administration Hospital
Philadelphia, PA

Pam Bushnell, MSS
Crozier Chester Medical Center
Chester, PA

Deborah Devaney, MSS
Child Inc.
Wilmington, DE

Elaine Frank, MSW, BCD
Medical College of Pennsylvania
Infant Psychiatry
Philadelphia, PA

Gail Gardner, MSW
Director, Substance Abuse Services
Colmery O'Neill Veteran's
  Administration Hospital
Topeka, KS

Peter Gariti, PhD., MSW
University of Pennsylvania
Treatment Research Center
Philadelphia, PA

Terisita Gonzalez, MSS
Private Practice, Psychiatric
  Services
Bryn Mawr, PA

Daniel Harkness, PhD., MSW
Bert Nash Mental Health Center
Lawrence, KS

Lesley Sharp Haushalter, MSS
Easter Seals Society
Levittown, PA

Harriet Hensley, MSW
Consultant
Carbondale, IL

Diane Hirschberg, MSW
Social Worker
University of Kansas Medical
  Center
Kansas City, KS

Lilly Ann Hoge, MSS
Sexual Abuse Center
Swarthmore, PA

Bobbi Iversen, PhD., MSS
Family Services of Chester County
West Chester, PA

Carol M. Jolly, MSW
Clinical Social Worker
Menninger Foundation
Topeka, KS

Annette Kahn, MSW, BCD
Cinical Social Worker and
    Supervisor
Bert Nash Mental Health Center
Lawrence, KS

Lynn Long, MSS
Private Practice
Chester Springs, PA

Megan McGraw, MSS, MLSP
State of Delaware Social Worker
Juvenile Probation
Wilmington, DE

Virginia McIntosh, MSW
Private Practice
Bala Cynwyd, PA

Judy Nehr, MSW
Supervisor
Colmery O'Neill Veteran's
    Administration Hospital
Topeka, KS

Coleen Olevich, MSS
Drenk Mental Health Center
Mt. Holly, NJ

Barbara Schroeder, MSS
Crozer Chester Family Services
Upland, PA

Sarah Stewart, MSS
Hospice
Wilmington, DE

Barbara K. Titus, MSS
Hospice
Wilmington, DE

Norma Van Dyke, MSW
Clinical Social Worker
Child Psychiatry Center
Philadelphia, PA

Kurt Walser, MSW
Director of Professional Services
Family Services of Chester County
Chester, PA

Diana Weintraub, MSW
Executive Director, Way Out
East Meadow, New York

Written for students, this book has been influenced in important ways by those in my classes over these past years. Special mention is made of my practice class, Social Work 111 and 112, fall 1989–spring 1990.

Bryn Mawr College has not only provided a supportive environment. In my junior research leave I commenced the writing which I completed during the recent sabbatical I was awarded. Peg McConnell's commitment and hard work helped transfer the material into clean and readable copy. I have also been honored to receive support under the Alexandra Grange Mawkins Fund.

Brooks/Cole has been a wonderful publisher. From sending flowers at the start of our work together, to the birthday cards and holiday greetings, they have been warm and encouraging. Claire Verduin combines just the right balance of advice with respect for the author's own decision-making. I feel privileged to publish under Clairemont Press. The competence of Joan Marsh and Merrill Peterson was critically important in the final stages of production.

For their thorough reading of the manuscript and insightful suggestions, I want to thank the reviewers: Edith Freeman, University of Kansas;

Morley Glicken, California State University at San Bernardino; Bart Grossman, University of California at Berkeley; David Hardcastle, University of Maryland-Baltimore; Reva Fine Holtzman, Hunter College. A special thank you to Morley Glicken for his careful reading of the final manuscript. Dr. Miriam Birdwhistell, Dr. Ray Birdwhistell, and Diana Weintraub, MSW, provided thoughtful perceptions.

Dr. Jill Pierce provided invaluable editorial assistance early in this project when the writings were often mere ramblings. She helped me structure my sentences to have greater clarity; her help and friendship has been most appreciated.

My son, Graham, whose college application process caused an interruption in the writing, has always been a source of joy and inspiration for me, as have my parents, Ben and Gloria Bisman.

David Hardcastle first suggested that I write this book and without his never wavering support, and intellectual rigor in thinking about this most complex profession of social work, I would have neither started nor completed this project.

Most of my professional work has been in the name of Brownstein. I have returned to my maiden name of Bisman.

Cynthia Bisman (Brownstein)

SOCIAL WORK PRACTICE

CHAPTER ℘ ONE

If any man ask, why it is so necessary to do good? I must say, it
sounds not like the question of a good man.

—*Cotton Mather*

INTRODUCTION:
THE DOMAIN OF SOCIAL WORK

*"I wanted to work with individuals to help them lead better lives, and I wanted
to make this a better world to live in. I was led to social work, where I can do
both."*

*"I always knew I would work with people problems. Even when I was a kid, I had
a strong intuitive sense about others. My social work training taught me how to use
and channel that intuition."*

*"I practice social work because I want to change things. Ever since I can
remember, inequality and poverty have bothered me."*

In this book we examine the art and science of social work practice. We
admire the creative and intuitive, the artistic part of the social work process,
but we also respect it as an organized system with intellectual rigor. Targeted for social work practice classes, the theory of social work practice
developed in these pages provides a framework for how to think about
social casework practice and how to understand the relationship of *what* is
done to *why* it is done. In exploring a specific activity, we consider the social
worker's decision-making process and the relationship of outcomes to client
needs.

The basic components of social work practice are presented as *relationship, assessment, communication, practitioner observation*, and *intervention*. Definitions of these components are developed through studies of interactions
between social workers and clients. As a source of inspiration, the case
material captures the passion and lure of practicing social work in the
turbulence of the real world. Personal descriptions and background information on each of the social workers reveals complex people struggling
with their challenging and often formidable pursuits.

1

To provide a developmental perspective of the social work profession, we view each practice component historically. Healthy growth and development of the profession are partly a function of familiarity with the wisdom and thinking of those who have preceded us. We need to know about our profession's evolving mission and value base and about early definitions of professional concepts. With this solid historical grounding, those entering the profession can responsibly shape new directions and weigh and evaluate emerging theories.

Becoming a social worker is a process of socialization into the social work profession. More than just learning about practice components, this process includes developing one's identity as a social worker, enacting social work values, and pursuing the social work mission. This introductory chapter provides a context within which to understand social work as a profession by defining social casework and reviewing its historical development, considering the field of social work, presenting the professional mission of social work, acknowledging the essential relationship between social work practice and social policy, and raising the complex issues of prediction in social work. We stress the importance of addressing client-worker differences and introduce the peculiar challenges facing the student social worker. A preview of the rest of the book concludes the chapter. Let's examine first the need for practice theory and explore a framework for a theory of social work practice.

THEORY ABOUT PRACTICE

Theory is the set of related propositions that explain and/or predict phenomena, providing a structure to organize and interpret variables (Dubin, 1978; Reynolds, 1971). While scientists can test their theories in a laboratory, most professionals do not work under such controlled conditions; they practice instead in the chaos of the real world as providers of services. A *practice theory* explains and interprets the professional's behavior and serves to guide and control action as a test of practice. Theory is informed and shaped by the real world of practice.

Generally, the principles that relate the knowledge and technology of professionals' interaction with clients are not well developed. Otherwise well-trained medical students are often not taught "bedside manners," how to communicate and how to relate with patients. Lawyers, likewise, may have highly developed analytical skills but may not know how to prepare a client psychologically or emotionally for a trial. Social workers especially need to know how to translate knowledge about human development into understanding a client's behavior. It is this "people-processing" part of professional practice, translating the professional's knowledge into change for the client, that practice theory addresses.

Moreover, the effectiveness of professional practice is partly a function of the client's providing relevant information to the professional and of the client's following the professional's advice. If the doctor cannot get accurate information from the patient, the medical diagnosis will be faulty; the diagnosis will also be useless if the patient does not follow the doctor's orders. A good court case cannot be built unless the lawyer has necessary information from the client, yet the lawyer's knowledge of the law will not alone help the client be a good witness in the courtroom; the lawyer has to be able to prepare the client to be a witness. These problems are located in the art, not the science, of the medical and legal professions. An excellent source for a full discussion of professions and professional socialization is Blankenship (1977).

The art of practice has been addressed by the social work profession in its educational programs by means of practice classes. Knowledge covered in those classes, however, is often based on the practice fields, such as health or mental health, or on *general* approaches, such as the problem-solving model. A theory that explains what social workers do and that can serve to guide social work practice—a practice theory—should be the content and context of social work practice classes. Practice theory can serve to rationalize the art of social work in ways that specific interventive models cannot. Practitioners need theory to understand and explain the situations in their work.

Social Work Practice Theory

This book presents a theory to explain social work practice. The components of this practice theory are relationship, assessment, communication, practitioner observation, and intervention. Tacitly accepted as the basic elements of social work, they have been part of the traditional lore of the social work profession. Here, however, they are presented as a theory of practice. We will examine each of these components of practice historically, conceptualize them, then operationalize and elaborate them through case material. After examining them separately as discrete entities, we will then look at these basic components of practice theory as interactive elements constituting a whole.

Bertha Reynolds, considered one of the important teachers in the social work profession, recognized the need for practice theory in her writings of almost fifty years ago: "The security of having at least a core of theory common to all of social work, and of seeing it in a dynamic way, so that change can be welcomed instead of feared as new data come, is one of the greatest needs of social work in our time" (1942, p. 8). Yet this type of conceptual base to the profession has not been available.

Practice theory provides a structure through which to organize and interpret the unity of the social work practice elements. Here it must be noted that a theory of practice is not the same as a theory of a specific intervention. A theory of intervention presents propositions addressing strategies for specific client problems or populations. Practice theory, in contrast, cuts across the range of individual interventive theories. It provides a context, and a foundation, for the interventive approaches. Theories of intervention that develop a single approach, such as cognitive therapy, or that focus on one field of practice, such as practice with the elderly, are important in responding to changing problems in society. These theories can help practitioners remain current with the latest advances in knowledge and technology. Practice classes and books cannot encompass all the things social workers do and all the interventions they employ. These activities change over time in response to newly emerging problems and theories. AIDS was not a problem in the 1970s, and structural family therapy was not in existence in the 1960s. Such diversity and change will continually create new practice environments and previously unknown specialties.

The social work practice theory presented in this book was inductively developed through analyses of what experienced social workers did in their work with real clients. The research model used was grounded theory, developed by Glaser and Strauss (1967). *Grounded theory* is an inductive approach in which theory is developed from data and experience. The data used in developing the practice theory consist of the social workers and their cases and the social work literature. Experienced social workers were intensively interviewed about their cases, including analyses of process recordings or audio or video tapes. An exhaustive search was also conducted of the social work practice literature, identifying the shared components of practice. This research approach will be further discussed in Appendix 2 (Lincoln and Guba, 1985; Yin, 1987; Schon, 1983).

Social work practice theory allows us to address the following questions: What are the primary components of practice? How should we think about practice? Are there models of effective practice? How do we execute practice? How do practitioners and others evaluate practice? How do we distinguish good practice from bad practice? What principles cut across specific interventive theories?

THE FIELD OF SOCIAL WORK

Social workers provide help to people with problems in living their lives, including growing up, interacting with others, being members of social institutions, marrying, divorcing, dealing with psychological and psychiatric problems, caring for the family, being abused or abusive, attending to financial and work responsibilities, abusing substances, addressing health and medical issues, and dying. Social workers also intervene with societal problems of poverty, availability of health care, crime, foster care and adoptive services, domestic violence, substance abuse, and mental health services.

Social work clients are a diverse group, representing different backgrounds and educational levels, a range of cultures, lifestyles, and socioeconomic levels. Young or old, male or female, they may be individuals, families, groups, large or small organizations, communities, social planning and policy setting agencies, public or for-profit settings.

As practiced in numerous agencies, the roles, tasks, and functions of social work vary widely. Some of the settings include hospitals, mental health centers, family service agencies, nursing homes, courts, jails, schools, hospice centers, welfare departments, child protective services, rehabilitation centers, and industry. Shaped, and in large part determined by, the settings in which they are employed, the functions performed by social workers include planning or program development, administration, staff training, group work, community development, or casework and therapeutic services with individuals and families.

Social workers usually perform several roles at the same time, such as therapist, advocate, agency employee, collaborator, team member, program planner, community resource developer, and supervisee. They also perform multiple tasks, including direct services for clients, planning and goal setting, completing paperwork, consultation, coordination with other resources, evaluating the practice, meeting with supervisors, and collaborating with both intra- and interagency staff.

Reflecting this diversity, social work schools and programs offer specializations in casework, group work, community organization, administration and management, policy planning, and program development.

What appears as a haphazard, almost incongruous mix of agency settings, tasks, functions, and roles is tied together by the social work purpose of improving social functioning. While social workers may have different specializations and skills, use a range of methods and techniques, work in dissimilar settings, and see a variety of clients and problems, they share a desire to improve the fit between the needs of individuals and resources of society.

Just as the high ideals of equality and human rights form the foundation of American society, the profession of social work is based on a visionary mission to assure a just balance between a society's resources and the individual. Yet a glaring contrast continues between ideals and reality. Though economic equality is necessary for political and social equality, the income gap is widening in our society between the poorest and the wealthiest, resulting in what William Julius Wilson refers to as the "ghetto underclass" (Wilson, 1987). Increasing urbanization, specialization, and use of technology has been accompanied by family breakups and breakdowns, phobias, depressions, suicides, child abuse, sexual abuse, crime, drug abuse, mental illness, homelessness, and inadequate health care.

Addressing all these problems, social workers are "do-gooders" for people, not for abstract ideals. They do good as they help people live more effectively in society. Catching those who have fallen through the cracks and preventing others from doing likewise, social workers not only respond to problems, but also plan for the provision of better services. Choosing to work toward the alleviation of poverty and the empowerment of the oppressed, social workers are concerned with injustice and the distribution of resources within society. In this pursuit their efforts are directed toward both *individual change* and *social reform.*

SOCIAL CASEWORK

Throughout the history of the profession, social casework has been the most prevalent form of social work practice, currently accounting for almost 60 percent of the social workers practicing with a Master of Social Work degree (Hardcastle, 1987). There are many specializations, methods, and forms of social work, and this book is not advocating casework over other forms such as management, advocacy, or planning. As the case examples in each chapter demonstrate, an effective social worker must be able to use many forms of social work and draw on a range of methods and theories. A social worker whose primary function is to provide casework services to an individual must also address the quality of services provided by the agency, advocate for the client, and negotiate with community resources and services. The caseworker, nevertheless, is different from the administrator and community developer. The emphasis of the work is different, the function of the position is different, different outcomes are sought, and different areas of knowledge and skill are used.

Social casework is distinguished by its focus on *helping individuals* to improve their social functioning. This emphasis on individuals was first acknowledged by Mary Richmond in her classic *What Is Social Casework?* (1922), in which she defined casework as "those processes which develop personality through adjustments consciously effected, individual by individual, between men and their social environment" (pp. 98–99). Richmond was concerned with how individuals lived as social beings in their society. She saw the social environment as the context in which the individual's problems arise but asserted that the caseworker's function should be to place "direct action upon the mind" to help the individual to change (p. 101). An ongoing issue of social casework is the extent of attention and concern that the environment, as distinct from the individual, should receive from the casework practitioner. In later years, Richmond shifted her definition to place greater emphasis on society. In *The Long View* (1930), she defines social casework as "the art of doing different things for and with different people by cooperating with them to achieve at one and the same time their own and society's betterment" (p. 374).

Gordon Hamilton underscored the need to focus on both individuals and society:

> Society is inseparable from the individuals who compose it . . . one must infer that self-awareness, or finding oneself, and being able to relate oneself to society are two ends of the same process. . . . The

casework idea . . . may be utilized whenever people have impaired capacity to organize the ordinary affairs of life or lack satisfaction in their ordinary social relationships. The idea that we are concerned with social reality and social adjustment is fundamental (1940, pp. 28–29)

Caseworkers have always viewed relationship as central to their practice. Virginia Robinson focused on the primacy of relationship in *A Changing Psychology in Social Casework:* "only in this field of the individual's reaction patterns and in the possibilities of therapeutic change in these patterns through relationships can there be any possibility of a legitimate professional casework field" (1930, p. 185).

These early definitions, expanded and refined, have continued to influence contemporary social work literature. In her *Social Casework: A Problem-Solving Process,* Helen Harris Perlman defines casework as "a process [which] . . . consists of a series of problem-solving operations carried on within a meaningful relationship. The end of this process is contained in its means: to so influence the client-person that he develops effectiveness in coping with his problem and/or to so influence the problem as to resolve it or vitiate its effects" (1957, p. 5).

Florence Hollis's psychosocial approach evolved out of Gordon Hamilton's holistic conceptions about practice. "Psychosocial casework," Hollis explains, "is characterized by its direct concern for the 'well-being' of the individual. . . . This emphasis upon the innate worth of the individual is an extremely important, fundamental characteristic of casework. It is the ingredient that makes it possible to establish the relationship of trust that is so essential for effective treatment" (1981, p. 25).

The common thread in these definitions, from the early 1900s work of Mary Richmond to the 1980s version of Florence Hollis, is emphasis on the individual, recognition of casework as a process, and primacy of the relationship between the caseworker and the client. A good source for a more thorough review and discussion of social work theories is Roberts and Nee (1970).

As the preferred designation, the term *social casework* was used by the early founders of the profession and became the traditional name for the arm of social work practice directed toward practice with individuals. While individual change was the specialty of social casework, the "social world" remained the focus of the practice—environment, in other words, was viewed as central to understanding the client's problem and planning the intervention. In the 1980s, social work practice with individuals, families, and small groups came to be called *clinical social work.* With a strong emphasis placed on intrapsychic factors, the client's environment received less attention and clinical social workers came to be viewed as practicing psychotherapists.

With continual debate to set the parameters of clinical social work, the Board of Directors of the National Association of Social Workers (NASW), the professional organization for social workers, adopted the following definition:

> Clinical social work shares with all social work practice the goal of enhancement and maintenance of psychosocial functioning of individuals, families and small groups. Clinical social work practice is the professional application of social work theory and methods to the treatment and prevention of psychosocial dysfunction, disability or impairment, including emotional and mental disorders. It is based on knowledge of one or more theories of human development within a psychosocial context.
>
> The perspective of person-in-situation is central to clinical social work practice. Clinical social work includes interventions directed to interpersonal interactions, intrapsychic dynamics, and life-support and management issues.
>
> Clinical social work services consist of assessment; diagnosis; treatment, including psychotherapy and counseling; client-centered advocacy; consultation; and evaluation. The process of clinical social work is undertaken within the objectives of social work and the principles and values contained in the NASW Codes of Ethics. (1991)

The concepts in this definition are basically congruent with the practice of social work presented in these pages. While this book focuses on the specifics of practice interactions with individuals the paradigm of practice incorporates individuals within their environment. To explore the process of individually based practice, we will introduce new concepts, including case theory and practitioner observation.

The mission of social work—the improvement of social functioning—is further discussed later in this chapter. The following definition of social casework with individuals is demonstrated in this book as

 The process of social workers creating change with individual persons to improve social functioning. With the use of the helping relationship, based on the case theory of the social work assessment, and with the self-awareness and use of self in practitioner observation, social workers utilize a variety of communication techniques and methods to implement and evaluate interventions. The focus for change is always the person and the environment, to help clients live better in their society. Conducted within the context of the agency, practice addresses issues of service provision and follows professional ethics and values.

The helping relationship is presented in Chapter 4, and case theory is a concept this book introduces in Chapter 5. Methodology is discussed in Chapters 6 and 8. Practitioner observation, another concept introduced by this book, is covered in Chapter 7.

HISTORICAL BASE OF THE PROFESSION

The social casework emphasis on changing individuals emanates from Children's Aid and the Charity Organization Societies (COS), the forerunner of the Family Service Associations. Upheavals after the U.S. Civil War, including increases in manufacturing, production, and the immigrant population, made it necessary to provide relief operations with greater structure. Up to that time, social welfare programs were based on the English Poor Laws of 1601, which placed responsibility directly on families. Dependent children were apprenticed, and the incapacitated were placed in institutions. In 1877, the first COS in the United States was established in Buffalo by Stephen Humphreys Gurteen, assistant minister of St. Paul's Church, along with T. Guilford Smith, a parishioner and businessman (Lewis, 1977).

According to the nineteenth-century view, destitution was a result of personal failure, which could be reduced through moral insight. Through the technique of "friendly visiting," the treatment staff of wealthy volunteers were to befriend the needy and uplift and guide them out of poverty. Paid employees of the COS were the agents, who dispensed the relief and handled registration to avoid duplication of services.

By the turn of the twentieth century, there was a shortage of volunteers and those available were wholly inadequate to address the increasing numbers of poor. It was also becoming evident that the problems of the poor had less to do with moral failure and were more related to the social and economic upheavals of the time. Mary Richmond, a COS leader, advocated that advanced education and salary increases be given to those employed in "the profession of applied philanthropy" (1897, p. 186).

In 1905, noting the relationship between illness and the social conditions of poverty, Dr. Richard C. Cabot introduced medical social work at Massachusetts General Hospital. As a medical doctor, he hoped that hospital social services would influence the development of preventive medicine. Many of those early medical social workers were trained nurses who had to decide whether their identification should be with the newly forming social work profession or with nursing. The social work emphasis on the social environment and the opportunity not to be subordinate to physicians resolved their dilemma in favor of social work (Lubove, 1965).

At about this time, school administrators and teachers were becoming concerned with the child's environment. In 1905, four settlements joined forces in sponsoring visiting teachers for three school districts. These visitors were to meet children in their natural environments, which was thought to be the "logical place to detect symptoms of future inefficiency, whether they be departures from the mental, social, or physical standards" (Hodge, 1917, p. 225). Finally, psychiatrists employed in mental institutions became interested in the home environment of the mentally ill. One of these physicians, Adolph Meyer, recognized the importance of social work and home visits in his vision for the development of community mental health programs (Lubove, 1965).

Expansion from the original social work settings of child welfare and charity to include medical and psychiatric hospitals and schools not only provided a broader base for social workers but also widened the scope of social institutions in which the workers were employed and from which their clients received services. This breadth in social work role and client population has continued to be both a curse and a blessing. If social work is to focus on social functioning, then it must be carried out in the array of social institutions. On the other hand, the social worker's roles and functions differ depending on the agency and client population, making it difficult to define a particular social work domain and area of expertise.

While the thrust of the profession toward individual change and direct services has evolved from the earlier charity societies, the emphasis on social reform and social action derives from the settlement house movement. Attention for these workers concentrated on the settlement of immigrants and change in social conditions. Stanton Coit returned from a visit to England's Toynbee Hall, the earliest settlement house, and founded the Neighborhood Guild in New York in 1886. By 1910, there were more than four hundred of these settlements, one of the more famous of which was Hull House, founded in Chicago by Jane Addams. Interested in social change, the settlement workers engaged in political action to address living conditions in the immediate neighborhoods—trash collections, recreation facilities, bathhouses—and to provide needed services such as daycare, literacy classes, social clubs (Davis, 1967).

Many of these settlement workers also became involved in broader social reform, including the labor movement, public welfare, and civil rights legislation. In 1909, they helped found the National Association for the Advancement of Colored People, and its first meeting was held at the Henry Street Settlement in New York. The legacies to the social work profession from the settlement houses are many, including social reform, client advocacy, group work, self-help, and community organization (Trattner, 1979). For further elaboration of the historical development of social casework, see Popple (1983), Pumphrey and Pumphrey (1961), and Leiby (1978).

In light of the varied origins of the profession, it is not surprising that contemporary social work practice is incredibly diverse, incorporating many *fields of service* (child welfare, family service, health, mental health, schools, and corrections), with changing *problem areas and populations* (women's issues, substance abuse, domestic violence, children, adolescents, and the elderly), necessitating the use of different *modalities* (individual, couples, family, group) and requiring a complex array of *theoretical models* (psychodynamic, psychosocial, crisis intervention, problem solving, systems theory, family therapy, ego psychology, cognitive theory, object relations). Divergent streams in the historical development of the social work profession demand several core areas of knowledge. Foundation courses must cover human behavior in the social environment, including normal and abnormal development, physiology and psychopharmacology as well as behavior in groups and communities. Integrated with courses on policy and organizational theory, the foundation of social work study also consists of research and principles of practice.

Social Work as a Profession

All professions have a specialized knowledge base, a code of ethics and values, a service mission, and specific practice skills. While the balance among these components differs by profession, a professional practitioner must draw on a body of accumulated knowledge and research to make inferences about how a given situation should be handled to achieve a certain outcome.

Professionals have to integrate their skills with knowledge and theory while providing their profession's mission of "service" to individuals and to society. In order to accomplish this they must be able to analyze situations within the appropriate frame of reference. First they assess, then they select from theories and concepts relevant to the situation; their judgement is critical in this process.

Interventive choices are a reflection of both the assessment and the theoretical knowledge as well as the professionals' skills. It is through the professionals' acquisition and implementation of relevant skills that they create change. These skills are the specific abilities professionals employ to execute the elements of their practice. For lawyers, the basic elements of practice are research and abstraction from case law while relating a set of facts to case precedent. For social workers, the basic elements of practice are the development of a relationship, client assessment, critical observation and analysis of practice decisions, communication, and intervention. All professions have different specializations and different skills relevant to those specializations.

The Mission of Social Work

Professionals have a mission of service to the society. The service mission of social work is to improve social functioning, help individuals navigate through their society, and help society provide resources to its citizens. There is, however, no clear-cut definition of social functioning, nor is there a specific model that each individual can use to function in society. Models of social functioning are shaped by culture and values and are difficult to define without a context. Some cultures may view striking children as child abuse, whereas others may regard it as the childrearing norm. Patterns in care of the elderly, alcohol consumption, and family relations are determined by culture and are unique to each society. Interpreting appropriate social functioning within the cultural context is thus an important part of social work.

Nevertheless, the lack of clear parameters about what constitutes high level social functioning makes the work of social workers highly complex. To help people improve their social functioning, social work must be concerned with the interface of persons with their environments.

Social workers' efforts are designed to help individuals change themselves and their environments. Though the emphasis will vary, both individuals and their environments are considered together to improve social functioning. The environments may include individuals' immediate social contacts, family supports, local neighborhoods, institutions such as schools and hospitals, community agencies and resources, federal and local planning and programming, and policy making. Analysis of the relevant environment for each client offers the interface for social work practice.

In the ways they think and in the kinds of help offered to clients, social workers are always addressing both person and environment. This breadth of perspective makes up the discipline. Social workers engage with individuals to help them better negotiate their environments and intervene with environments to better serve the needs of individuals. Other professionals may address similar issues and concerns and may use the same areas of knowledge. The focus on social functioning, on helping people in their social milieu, however, is unique to social work.

Practice and Policy

Social work is defined by the society in which it is practiced. Just as policy is shaped by practice, practice is strongly tied to and bound by policy. Social policy is the social context that provides the goals for social development and the parameters for social control. Like social policies, social work practice is shaped by current values and mores, cultural traditions, religious beliefs, and scientific and technological knowledge. Thus, social work practice is always in flux, never static. Social work practiced in the time of Mary Richmond had different concerns than social work today. During that period the normative role for women was as wife and mother. Abortion was not an option, it was back alley and illegal; divorce was not common. A social worker in practice today, however, would not be able to avoid dealing with issues related to women's economic independence, abortion, divorce, and the complications resulting from the extraordinary increases in options for both women and men. Social, legal, economic, and medical developments in a society profoundly affect the practice of social work.

Child abuse offers another example of the strong ties between policy and practice. Views about the worth and care of children have changed drastically over time. With the rise of the middle class, the wages of children were not so necessary and attitudes toward child labor changed. Changes in mores and values followed, and it became much more the responsibility of society rather than family to assure children a protected environment. Thus, early legislation controlled and limited the nature and extent of child labor.

It was not until the mid 1970s, however, that the government stepped into what had heretofore been the exclusive sphere of the family by providing funding addressing the problem of child abuse.

Judith Nelson provides a fascinating portrayal of the developmental process of child abuse legislation, in which a small, private-sector charity concern evolved into a major public social welfare issue (Nelson, 1984). Child abuse has now become one of the predominant problems for social workers who address abuse in all economic and social classes and in all racial, ethnic and religious groups. The issues raised in practice will continue to influence funding decisions and policy planning for child abuse programs, while policy decisions impact on the availability and quality of direct services.

Prediction in Social Work

Social work practice cannot be reduced to an easy set of rules. We are learning from choas theory (Gleick, 1988) that order is evident in seemingly random events, but no single event can be predicted. Social work practice shows patterns and generalizations can be drawn, but exact prescriptions about how to respond to a specific client are not possible without the risk of committing a deductive or inductive fallacy.

The *deductive fallacy* applies generalizations about groups of persons to individuals. For example, a social worker may be seeing a Black teenager from an inner city neighborhood. While the statistics indicate heavy drug use and gang violence for this population and community, the data are not necessarily true for this worker's client. Because he is a black teenager from the ghetto does not make him a drug addict or violent. To assume that this client is "like these other inner city adolescents" is to commit a deductive fallacy. In contrast, generalizing from experiences with individual clients to other persons is to commit an *inductive fallacy*. A client's angry response to her recent divorce does not predict that the next client experiencing divorce may respond with the same set of emotions. Every client is a special and unique individual and must not be treated as a member of a class of persons. Gathering information on each client allows for careful judgments that apply only to that client and case situation.

CLIENT-WORKER DIFFERENCES

Social workers regularly relate to people who are different from themselves in many factors including age, gender, socioeconomic class, race, educational level, religion, culture, dress, language, speech, physical appearance and capacity, personality, sexual preference, and athletic and verbal ability. Though social workers should not practice with bias and prejudice, as human beings they will have personal reactions to these differences. Shaped by background and experiences in dealing with diversity, these reactions are neither immoral or unprofessional and, often, cannot be prevented.

A male social worker, for example, will have certain reactions when meeting with a middle-aged female client. These may relate to her physical appearance and style of dress or the way she talks and presents herself. Likewise, a White female social worker will respond in her own unique way to a Vietnam veteran Black male client. Her reactions may be to the same differences just mentioned or may involve negative reactions to the Vietnam War.

Uneasy with some differences, social workers may feel neutral or comfortable with others. To avoid inappropriate bias in the practice, social workers must acknowledge their feelings and take them into account in formulating their practice. Such awareness of one's biases and reactions to diversity is a lifelong task, but social workers are also responsible for addressing issues of diversity in positive ways that facilitate helping the client.

We will explore client-worker differences and their impact on practice in all the chapters and especially in Chapter 7. Workers discuss their personal reactions and describe how they incorporate difference in their practice throughout many of the case examples. Good sources for examining the effect of diversity on practice are Pinderhughes (1989) and Logan, McRoy, and Freeman (1989).

THE STUDENT SOCIAL WORKER

Social work students face difficult challenges as they prepare to enter the profession. As well as acquiring new knowledge and skills, they are expected to be self-reflective and self-critical, open to new ideas about themselves and their interactions with others. Even while they are still in training, they have to be able to integrate these new concepts and "wear them as if they fit," because they work with clients as part of their educational process.

Most of those who choose the social work profession do so because they have some "natural" helping abilities; they care about others and want to relate in a helping way. Many of the components of practice involve the use of skills we all need throughout life, such as relating to people, making judgments about information, and communicating. Social work practice involves integrating new concepts with already existing natural abilities. During this process students often experience a sense of diminution in their natural abilities along with a loss in spontaneity and authenticity—an expected result of having to be conscious and attentive. The social worker is developing a relationship, making judgments and communicating, for a specific purpose, and initially students feel stiff and artificial.

The integration process begun during social work training is never complete. Social workers are always in formation, gaining new insights as they continually acquire novel ideas and concepts. Over time, they gain

more comfort, a greater ability to accept ambiguity, and even a sense of satisfaction at not being a "finished product."

Each of the practice component chapters, 4 through 8, contains a concluding section with Additional Notes. Presented more informally than the primary chapter text, these notes offer cautions and suggestions with advice about such matters as preparing written reports, introducing oneself to clients, and distinguishing between supervision and therapy.

PREVIEW OF CHAPTERS

Chapters 2 and 3 continue the discussion about social work as a profession. Becoming a social worker is described as a process of socialization in which those entering the profession incorporate its knowledge base with values and ethics. We concentrate first on a new perspective of the person and environment framework of social casework. This is expanded to include awareness of and attention to communities, policies, and organizational service delivery. Social work is presented from its foundation in morality— accepting a "calling to serve" and altruism.

Chapter 3 emphasizes values and the social work code of ethics, including confidentiality, duty to warn, self-determination, and informed consent. Case studies demonstrate the complex process of balancing one's adherence to the basic concepts and ethical guides of the profession while providing services to clients in great need.

Chapter 4 examines the social work relationship, the "medium" or vehicle through which the practice is executed, and defines relationship as "belief bonding," a new way of understanding social work relationship. It also covers the purposefulness and boundaries of relationship, issues of helping and power, loss, attachment, and termination.

Chapter 5 focuses on assessment, introduced in this book as the social worker's case theory. The function of case theory is understanding the client's past, from which to explain the present and on which to base future change. The methodology of assessment is addressed as a process and illustrated by examples in which social workers think through the situation confronting them and formulate an assessment. The outcome of the assessment is the assessment report, which documents the facts that have been gathered, identifies the proposed hypotheses, and articulates a problem statement.

Chapter 6 covers communication, the "technology" of practice. Communication is the transmission and exchange of thoughts, feelings, and information orally, nonverbally, and in writing. This chapter examines the general communication skills used by social workers, including giving information, sustaining the dialogue, using silence, focusing, and summarizing. The social work communication methods of exploration, validation, confrontation, and reflection are illustrated and discussed. The chapter presents communication as a concept bound by culture and context. Differences between social workers and clients are explored to understand how they impact on communication choices. Examples of written reports, including agency forms and process recordings, are provided.

Chapter 7 discusses practitioner observation, a concept introduced and developed in this book. The social worker is viewed as the "instrument" through which the practice of social work is enacted. To remain an objective investigator, to keep sharp as a measurement tool, and to avoid contaminating data with personal biases, the social worker needs to be self-reflective. Practitioner observation is the social worker observing, articulating, and critiquing the practice as it is taking place while also drawing on theoretical models and practice interventions.

Chapter 8 discusses the process of intervention and examines case studies of client contacts over time. What is unique to social work intervention is reviewed in material from the earlier chapters, including practice components, the mission of social work, and ethical issues. A sample intervention plan includes reformulating the problem statement, establishing short- and long-term case objectives, contracting, planning strategy, and selecting a mode of evaluation. In this chapter we see how intervention is guided by theories and assumptions about human behavior, the presenting problem, and the process of change.

Appendix 1 contains the preamble and summary of the principles stated in the NASW's Social Work Code of Ethics. It also discusses the research methodology for the practice components and theory in this book, with an emphasis on grounded theory and naturalistic inquiry.

Case examples presented involve school phobia, truancy, AIDS, dying, depression, substance abuse, attention deficit, grief, suicide, single parenting, marriage, divorce, domestic violence, foster care, child abuse, bulimia, delinquency, infertility, schizophrenia, disabilities, and family relations. The practice settings are family service, veterans' hospitals, psychiatric clinics, child welfare, hospices, private practice, mental health centers, schools, juvenile probation, programs for handicapped children, domestic violence shelters, employee assistance programs, and community centers. Clients include men, women, adolescents, children, the middle aged, and the elderly from diverse racial, ethnic, economic, and geographic backgrounds.

To protect the confidentiality of clients and social workers, names have been changed in all cases and no one has been presented in his or her actual employing agency or geographic locale. Identifying data have been shifted so that individuals cannot be connected to the facts about them. Social workers and clients are also presented within the context of cultural backgrounds and socioeconomic milieu to widen each case's perspective. Social work is practiced by imperfect people laboring with often troubled individuals in a harsh and unfair world. Appreciating the backgrounds and unique stories of the social workers themselves illuminates our understanding of both the art and science of social work practice.

Readers completing this book should be able to understand and appreciate the breadth and depth of social work practice. They should have acquired knowledge about the attributes of the social work helping relationship, the organizing function of the case theory, the methods and techniques used in communication, the process of practitioner observation, and the relationship of intervention strategies to interventive theories.

An important point must be emphasized as we are about to begin. The components of social work practice theory are interconnected with each other in highly complex ways. Even though each practice component may appear to be linear and separate as we discuss them, we must recognize that this is an illusion. A professional relationship cannot exist without communication. The purpose of that relationship is determined by the assessment, and is part of the plan of intervention. Furthermore, the practitioner has to assure that the practice is not influenced by worker biases through practitioner observation.

There is, then, a Gestalt to the practice—a whole that is greater than the sum of its parts. Practice components by themselves are not very meaningful, but collectively they form an impressive and even beautiful system of interlocking pieces. We must study the components of practice in order to understand the totality. Just as it takes a mixture of steel and concrete to form the Brooklyn Bridge or the Eiffel Tower, it is not the elements of these structures alone that makes them so interesting, but the combination of materials and interaction of their properties. The same goes for social work practice.

Professional work is never easy. Learning social work means taking on a challenge. Social workers have to practice with a lack of clear rules and no specific prescriptions. Often, over long periods of time, they make only small gains that are barely visible. An acknowledgment to oneself of good work done is sometimes the only reward. To practice social work requires compassion, commitment, and patience; it takes a love of people and a sense of a calling to help make things better for people and for society. It is exciting, through these chapters, to journey together exploring the practice of working on the social part of the lives of individuals.

BIBLIOGRAPHY

Addams, J. (1910). *Twenty years at Hull-House*. New York: MacMillan.

Addams, J. (1930). *The second twenty years at Hull-House*. New York: MacMillan.

Blankenship, R. (1977). *Colleagues in organization*. New York: John Wiley and Sons.

Davis, A. F. (1967). *Spearheads for reform—the social settlement and the pro-gressive movement, 1890–1914*. New York: Oxford University Press.

Dubin, R. (1978). *Theory building*. New York: Free Press.

Glaser, B., & Strauss, A. (1967). *The discovery of grounded theory: strategies for qualitative research*. New York: Aldine de Gruyter.

Gleick, J. (1988). *Chaos theory*. New York: Penguin Press.

Hamilton, G. (1940). *Social casework*. New York: Columbia University Press.

Hardcastle, D. (1987). *The Social Work Labor Force*. (J. Otis, D. Austin, A. Rubin, eds., Issues in Social Work Education, Monograph 4). Austin: University of Texas Press.

Hodge, L. H. (1917). Why a visiting teacher? In *Addresses and Proceedings of the National Education Association*.

Hollis, F., & Woods, M. (1981). *Casework: A psychosocial therapy*. New York: Random House.

Leiby, J. (1978). *A history of social welfare and social work in the United States*. New York: Columbia University Press.

Lewis, V. (1977). Charity Organization Society. In J. B. Turner (Ed.), *Encyclo-pedia of Social Work* (17th ed., pp. 96–100). New York: National Associa-tion of Social Workers.

Lincoln, Y., & Guba, E. (1985). *Naturalistic inquiry*. Beverly Hills, Calif.: Sage Press.

Logan, S., McRoy, R., & Freeman, E. (1989). *Social work practice with Black families: A cultural-specific perspective*. New York: Longman Press.

Lubove, R. (1965). *The professional altruist: The emergence of social work as a career*. Cambridge, Mass.: Harvard University Press.

Mather, C. (1710). *Bonafucuis, or essays to do good*. Reprinted in O'Connell 1855 edition, *Magnelia Chrisit Americana* [America's voluntary spirit], 1, 102.

Meyer, C. (1981). Social work purpose: Status by choice or coercion. *Social Work, 26*, 69–75.

National Association of Social Workers Register of Clinical Social Workers. 1991 Edition.

Nelson, J. (1984). *Making an issue of child abuse*. Chicago: University of Chicago Press.

Perlman, H. H. (1957). *Social casework: A problem-solving process*. Chicago: University of Chicago Press.

Pinderhughes, E. (1989). *Understanding race, ethnicity and power*. New York: Free Press.

Popple, P. (1983). Contexts of practice. In A. Rosenblatt & D. Waldfogel (Eds.), *Handbook of clinical social work* (pp. 70–96). San Francisco, Calif.: Jossey Bass.

Pumphrey, R., & Pumphrey, M. (Eds.). (1961). *The heritage of American social work*. New York: Columbia University Press.

Reynolds, B. (1942). *Learning and teaching in the practice of social work*. New York: Russell and Russell.

Reynolds, P. (1971). *A primer in theory construction*. New York: MacMillan.

Richmond, M. (1897). The need of a training school in applied philanthropy. In *Proceedings of the National Conference of Charities and Corrections*. Chicago: The Conference.

Richmond, M. (1917). *Social diagnosis*. New York: Russell Sage Foundation.

Richmond, M. (1922). *What is social casework?* New York: Russell Sage Foundation.

Richmond, M. (1930). *The long view*. New York: Russell Sage Foundation.

Roberts, R., & Nee, R. (1970). *Theories of social casework*. Chicago: University of Chicago Press.

Robinson, V. (1930). *A changing psychology in social casework*. Chapel Hill, N.C.: University of North Carolina Press.

Schon, D. (1983). *The reflective practitioner*. New York: Basic Books.

Trattner, W. I. (1979). *From poor law to welfare state: A history of social welfare in America* (2nd ed.). New York: Free Press.

Wilson, W. J. (1987). *The truly disadvantaged*. Chicago: University of Chicago Press.

Yin, R. K. (1987). *Case study research: design and methods*. Beverly Hills, Calif.: Sage Press.

CHAPTER ❧ TWO

> Expertise is not mere knowledge. It is the *practice* of knowledge, organized socially and serving as the focus for the practitioner's commitment.
>
> —*Eliot Freidson*

BECOMING A SOCIAL WORKER: MAJOR CONCEPTS OF THE PROFESSION

Education for a profession entails profound personal change as students adopt a set of traditions and take up a mode for thinking about and understanding life events. As it instills a distinctive culture, professional socialization requires us to recognize the multiple role expectations and acquire complex skills to match those expectations as well as to learn general and specific values. Dan Lortie, who has written extensively in this area, states: "The development of a professional self-conception involves a complicated chain of perceptions, skills, values and interactions" (1966, p. 99).

Before entering a profession, we engage in a continual process of socialization from birth as part of learning about and integrating the norms and culture of our families and the larger society. Socialization continues during the adult years, building on attitudes and skills developed in childhood. Limited by our biological capacities and environmental opportunities we are never completely socialized.

Social workers communicate by means of a common language and conceptualize problems by means of a specific perspective. They perform a variety of roles and draw on a range of complicated skills even as they are bound by the same code of ethics. Yet no two social workers appear the same in their practice; they do not think identically about the issues, nor do they proceed in the exact same steps in like order. Through the process of professional socialization, each social work student uniquely adapts the beliefs and mores of the social work profession to his or her own requirements. Early socialization experiences have influenced choices for professional training and, later, decisions about practice. While professional ideology reflects personal differences, it also changes the thinking and values of the profession's members.

In this and the next chapter we expand the introduction to the social work profession formulated in Chapter 1. In this chapter we will examine the major ideas and philosophical base of social work, and in Chapter 3 we will consider values and the social work code of ethics. Case studies serve to integrate the material presented in both of these foundation chapters. After these basic concepts and values have been established, we turn to the primary components of social work practice—including the helping relationship, social work assessment, communication, practitioner observation, and intervention—in the remaining chapters.

Because applying these components takes much more than a simple set of skills or new knowledge, these two chapters help lay the foundation for acculturation into the profession. Becoming a social worker requires familiarity with the profession's norms and traditions, its concepts and value orientation. Considering its philosophical basis in morality, we present the *social work profession* as a *calling* and *altruistic* as we review the difficulty in integrating its central themes of *person* and *environment*. The *person and environment framework* is expanded to include attention to *community resources, policy rules and regulations,* and the provision of services through complex *organizations*.

Case examples are a model used in all the chapters to illustrate the concepts and principles. Often capturing the anguish and joy of social work practice, comments by the social workers accompany all the case studies and are central to understanding the concepts presented throughout the text. Information about the social workers—facts about their upbringing and their cultural backgrounds—provides a fuller picture of what it means to be a social worker in practice with clients.

To understand social work as a professional discipline, we must first consider the implications of the term *profession*.

ATTRIBUTES OF A PROFESSION

To *profess* initially meant to take the vows of a religious order, to accept a calling. "Professionals profess to know better the nature of certain matters, to know better than their clients what ails them or their affairs" (Lynn, 1963, p. 2).

Several frameworks have been offered to distinguish the professions from other occupations. Some of the better known include Carr-Saunders and Wilson (1933), Greenwood (1957), Bucher and Strauss (1961), and Wilensky (1964). As an ideal, the term *profession* should be considered a model used to describe and understand certain behaviors and examine patterns on a continuum. In examining the general attributes of professional occupations, we acknowledge that no profession meets all the criteria exactly, differing, as they do, on their relative strengths in each of the areas. For example, social work ranks higher on a service commitment and lower on a systematic body of theory; medicine and law, in contrast, rank high on self-regulation.

Service Commitment

Dedicated to serving the public rather than selfish pursuits, members of a profession are *called* to their work through an inherent interest in what they will be doing rather than a desire for high salaries or status. Doctors serve to rid society of disease, while social workers serve to improve its social functioning. This desire to serve is perhaps the most distinguishing feature of professional groupings. Though this ideal is not necessarily negated by substantial material rewards for professional services, the service ethic may nevertheless be difficult to discern among some professionals, who charge high fees and do little public service work. Unlike some other professions, social work practice is primarily carried out in the public sector. Even those social workers employed in for-profit settings and in private practice address issues that pertain to the public sphere.

Systematic Body of Theory

Professional knowledge typically develops into an internally consistent system, and the skills critical to the profession emerge from and relate to that knowledge. Some nonprofessional occupations involve a higher order of skill; diamond cutting and cabinet making, for example, require more intricate methods than social work practice. The use of theory and its relationship to skill is the distinguishing feature of professional groupings.

Social work has been criticized for a lack of coherent theory and heavy reliance on knowledge from other disciplines, including sociology, psychology, medicine, and psychiatry. Its advocates argue, however, that the wide breadth of social work necessitates creative borrowing and integration of knowledge and theory from many sources.

Professional Authority

Nonprofessional occupations serve customers, who have freedom of decision about their purchases and can refund them if not satisfied. Professions, in contrast, serve clients. The client does not decide on the precise services to purchase but accedes a *monopoly of judgment* to the professional, who has a specialized competence.

In recent times the power of the professional's monopoly of judgment has begun to weaken. It is not considered unusual for clients to shop around for the best professional to decide on which services they believe are needed. Insurance companies often require second opinions on medical recommendations for surgery, and legal suits against professionals are becoming more common. Social work is considered lower in professional authority than the legal or medical profession, partly as a consequence of its broad base of knowledge and its high commitment to service.

Self Regulation

Professions have control over their training institutions by the process of accreditation, with admission to professional practice restricted by required education, practicums, certification, and licensure. Each professional group is considered the only knowledgeable source to set necessary curriculum areas and standards for entry into the profession.

With unclear distinctions for its two levels of entry into practice—the B.S.W. and the M.S.W.—the social work profession has generated confusion for itself and the public. Although autonomous practice has been associated with the M.S.W. degree, the title of social worker can be used by graduates of both undergraduate and graduate course work. In professions like medicine and law, in contrast, only graduate training bestows the title of physician or lawyer. Moreover, practical training for most professional groups follow completion of course work; social work, however, primarily follows the concurrent model, in which internship and classroom work are performed simultaneously.

Certification is administered by the social work professional organization NASW, whereas licensure is regulated by states and varies from strong social work licensure in Kansas to weak coverage in Pennsylvania. For a more complete discussion of licensure, review D. Hardcastle (1990).

Regulative Code of Ethics

Related to its service mission and body of knowledge, each professional group has a code of ethics that usually reflects the values of the larger society. Emerging from the code of ethics, a professional culture guides members' behavior and establishes its folklore, defining criteria for villains and heroes. Ethical codes must be considered, along with the laws and regulations that may supersede them. In Chapter 3 we will examine practice implications of the social work Code of Ethics (the preamble of the code and a summary of its principles is reproduced as Appendix 1).

We now focus on the profession of social work by considering first its philosophical framework. We then examine the profession's perspective of person and environment, with attention to service delivery as it is shaped by organizations and policy formulations.

PHILOSOPHICAL BASE OF SOCIAL WORK

What are the mores and culture of the social work profession? What beliefs and traditions serve to direct the work of its practitioners? The practice of a profession emerges out of its philosophy, the principles and ideals that give meaning to the work.

Considered primarily a moral and social philosophy, social work has been described as "humanitarianism in search of a method" (Cohen, 1958, p. 3). Historically lacking in scientific discipline, social work began as a moralistic endeavor performed by "friendly visitors" who sought to help individual paupers and settlement workers who attempted to reform the larger society. Leiby, who has written extensively about the profession, contends that this moral base is still the strongest foundation on which to base practice. In his view, an important contribution of the early social workers was their conception of society as more than just a political organization "because it is also an association held together by many kinds of moral expectations, common sentiments, and aspirations, caring, and sharing." The social work methods, he says, "were efforts to realize and encourage that spirit in individuals, the people around them, and the society at large" (Leiby, 1985, p. 329).

Those entering the social work profession are considered to be strongly committed to a *calling to serve* and *altruism*. Because social work is neither a high-salary nor a high-status profession, the incentive for pursuing this work is, for many, a moral commitment to address poverty and the unequal and unfair distribution of goods and services, to work toward social justice, and to empower those who are oppressed. This moral motivation includes a vision of improved potential for individuals and society, a widening of the range of possibilities, and options for an improved life.

A sense of calling is, according to Gustafson, "important for one's clients and for oneself. It can affect one's perspective on the particular needs that one seeks to meet; it can enable one to envision a contribution to a larger whole, a larger good, not only of individual clients but also of the community." For Gustafson, "a 'calling' without professionalization is bumbling, ineffective, and even dangerous. A profession without a calling, however, has no taps of moral and humane rootage to keep motivation alive" (1982, pp. 512, 514).

As well as a personal moral calling to serve a greater good, the social work profession has the norm of altruism. In this perspective, the client's needs have priority over the needs and interests of the social worker. Clients are not exploited, and services are provided only when needed. Social workers serve clients out of their desire to help, not to earn more money or power. Although it is *not* unethical for social workers to expect satisfactory wages for their services, the decision to offer services is based on the client's need for help, not the worker's need for remuneration. Strengthening the profession through higher wages and better benefits could result in more capable social workers and improved services for clients.

In the next section we present the person-and-environment perspective of social work as encompassing three dimensions—community, policies, and the organization.

The Person and Environment Perspective

Social workers must address their efforts toward *person* and *environment* issues, individuals and the things that affect their lives, clients within the context of their immediate and larger milieu. While these concepts are central to the profession, efforts to translate them into clear practice guidelines have been unsuccessful. As Timms put it, "The term environment covers an unspecifiably large range of phenomena; it refers to everything that is judged to be 'outside' the person. It includes large- and small-scale organizations, social institutions, and the culture of the whole society and its sub-groups" (1966, p. 40).

Without a clear articulation of person and environment, it has been difficult to provide succeeding generations of social workers with a framework that addresses this historic duality. Many social workers define their work in terms of one or the other—individual change or community action. Some even alter their titles to "therapist" or "community organizer." Just as doctors may perform surgery or conduct research, however, social workers engage in many roles and tasks. Whether they do therapy or community organizing, policy planning or program development, they are still social workers.

Person and environment issues are defined in these pages to include the client's surroundings, the community, the social service organization, and societal policies. While the focus in this book is on change in individuals, it is not possible to practice social work without attending to conditions in the community and to the social forces that affect the individual's adjustment. To do this, we need knowledge about the kind and quality of resources available in the client's larger community, insight into the attitudes and values of the immediate neighborhood in which the client resides, data on the organization's service delivery, and information about policies impacting on the client's life.

Providing adequate counseling for someone addicted to drugs, for example, depends on knowledge about the range of drug treatment programs in the community. Helping a recently divorced woman develop self-esteem and establish herself as an independent person requires information about employment or educational opportunities in her geographic area. In working with a 16-year-old pregnant teenager, a social worker must know her family's views about abortion and their financial capacity to help her make the best choice about the pregnancy. The social worker must also be familiar with federal and state laws regulating abortion counseling. Effective services to the elderly and persons with handicaps demands knowledge about the availability of bus and other transportation services within the immediate neighborhoods along with details about insurance rates and health care regulations.

 What has been called the dual perspective of person and environment actually has three components. Person and environment mean the consideration of individuals within context of the community and its resources, societal policies and regulations and the service delivery of the organization.

Some of the case material, both in this and other chapters, illustrates these multiple components in social work practice. A social work student providing services to families and children advocates for a satellite office to reach out to an underserved population when policy changes result in funding cutbacks in community services. A social worker's intervention with a woman abused by her husband requires knowledge about available community shelters as well as familiarity with legal regulations protecting abused spouses; at the same time, the social worker must help to plan and implement the agency's programs for this population. Information about the laws regulating abuse and neglect is an absolute prerequisite for providing services to families and children in abusive situations, and by the same token the social worker's expertise is invaluable in the formulation of new policies.

Reflecting the fact that the focus of this book is on social casework, implementing change in individuals, the social work practice in most of the case examples addresses a problem impacting on a single individual. Nevertheless, social workers apply their multiple perspective to the relationship of that specific individual problem to the client's larger environment. While social caseworkers currently engaging in practice often do not have opportunities to address major social change, they are still required to pay attention to the social conditions in which the client is residing, the laws that regulate the services, and the agency providing the services.

Person and Community

Whereas today we often substitute the term *community* for the word *environment*, the very early caseworkers considered community work basic to social work practice. In 1915 Bosanquet stated: "Case work which is not handled as an engine of social improvement is not . . . Charity Organization Society work at all" (Timms, 1966, p. 41). C. S. Loch, one of the early leaders of the charity organization societies (COS) in England, urged caseworkers to work toward "good, patient, and skilful treatment in the individual cases, with a direct, constant and unflinching effort to remove the evils that produce immoral stagnation, to purge bad areas, to remove bad conditions" (Timms, 1966, p. 41).

Yet despite this old warning, incorporating attention to the community with individual work continues to be a problematic issue in the theory and practice of social work. In 1923, Mary Richmond said to students at the New York School of Social Work:

> When social movements, social agencies, social workers, have a conception of development and advance which *includes* both the welfare of the individual and of the mass, which reconciles these two points of view and assures the permeation of each by each, then the upward climbing spiral . . . will no longer lose its balance and momentum by swinging violently from one side to the other. It will take a far wider, firmer sweep in both directions, it will cover more ground more symmetrically. In some such way as this, as I see it, social work will at last come into full possession of itself and of its rightful field of service. (1930, p. 584)

Here Richmond refers to the cycles of attention between social reform and work with individuals, and implores the profession to reconcile the two. As we saw in the historical review in Chapter 1, the profession sprung from divergent roots. The charity organization societies emphasized charity relief and individual change, whereas the settlement house movement worked toward community changes to ease the settlement of immigrants.

Contributing to the continuing lack of integration may be the ambiguity of the concepts *individual* and *community*. Yet attempts to understand these terms in combination with each other seem to result in even more confusion. Human beings are each highly unique, making prescriptive "if/then" statements about an individual risky and unproductive. At the same time, the substantial amount of theory building addressed to understanding and intervening with individuals has afforded some precision to the intrapsychic part of social work practice. Knowledge about human development and therapy is also available from two other practice disciplines, psychology and psychiatry.

The concept of community, on the other hand, has not yet been so thoroughly explored. Knowledge about community is offered by the discipline of sociology. As an academic field, not a practice profession, sociology has offered contributions that have been more theoretical and lacking in practical applications. While *community* has been defined as a neighborhood composed of relationships between its residents and institutions, the physical and relationship boundaries relevant for practice with a specific client have not yet been satisfactorily demarcated. As social work continues to develop theories about its own practice, however, it may yet attain the *full possession of itself and its rightful field of service* to which Richmond refers.

A social work method specializing in community or macro change is *community organization*. (Several good books that examine this form of practice include Fellin, 1987; Grosser, 1976; Kramer & Specht, 1983; and Warren, 1978.)

The following is a case involving Naomi, a 35-year-old social worker employed by a family service agency, who had to consider a range of community factors in her practice with Elinor, both in providing direct services and in making efforts at community change. Serving a poor and lower-middle-class population, the agency was located in a semirural area, not far from a large city.

Elinor, the client, was 25, White, with two sons aged seven months and 2 years. A high school graduate, she had never held a regular job. Living with her 18-year-old boyfriend in his parents' house, Elinor received AFDC payments of about $400 per month along with food stamps and Medicaid benefits. Repeated beatings by the boyfriend, Marv, as well as concerns about housing and her parental skills brought Elinor to the agency. Children and Youth Services had recently completed an investigation of Elinor because of a report that she was abusing her children. Though no evidence of abuse or neglect was found, Elinor was feeling under stress and wanting to make some changes in her life situation.

With ten years of practice experience, Naomi was familiar with the neighboring counties and had knowledge of services available in the community. Jewish and raised in an abusive home during an era when there were few options for women (no entry in the job market, divorce frowned on), Naomi was very sensitive to the need for supportive services. Though her own parents never separated, Naomi remembered her fears as a child of what would happen to herself and her two brothers should their mother follow through on threats to divorce.

Aware of the many issues relevant for Elinor, Naomi was considering several goals with which to begin treatment. As she stated:

....

Knowing that merely focusing on Elinor gaining insight into her self-destructive behavior would be too limiting in my practice with her, I had to help her consider ways to change specific living circumstances. Having practiced with many clients involved in abusive relationships, one of my assumptions was that Elinor grew up in an abusive home. Yet while reviewing the past can be important in understanding the etiology of problems, I have found it far more important to provide support in altering the current living environment.

I therefore first focused with Elinor on parenting skills. When she eventually decided to leave Marv, her mother and stepfather agreed to have the children move in with them, but told Elinor that she would have to move into a homeless shelter. Family therapy was then initiated for the three of them, exploring past issues of Elinor's behavior only as they were relevant to the parents' current concerns about her cleaning up after herself, looking after the children, and contributing to household chores.

Much time was spent with Elinor and her mother on creating a home environment that would be comfortable for everyone—including a clear schedule of Elinor's duties and the kind of help she could expect from her mother. At the same time, I referred Elinor to parenting support groups in the local area, provided information and reading material on child development, and began to talk with her about a possible career path.

On one occasion I provided transportation for Elinor to acquire information about affordable housing so that she could begin planning for a home with her children. On another I played the role of advocate in calling the police when Marv and his family were in the parking lot of the agency at the time of Elinor's appointment.

....

Naomi took the community dimension of her practice into account as she worked with Elinor on finding a place to live; getting along with others, including her parents and children; and becoming more financially secure and independent. Her attempts to understand Elinor were based on considering the forces at work in this client's life. Even when searching for Elinor's housing, Naomi viewed the neighborhood in terms of safety; availability of resources, including shopping and medical care; and ease of transportation. Instead of a narrow clinical role that focused heavily on intrapsychic issues and increased understanding, Naomi also functioned broadly as an advocate in helping Elinor hook up with other resources in the community and acted as an educator in broadening Elinor's understanding of her children's needs.

Clients who come to social workers frequently present with the wide array of problems of Elinor's situation. Yet if social workers focus *only* on increased awareness, ignoring the mass of environmental factors, they are not practicing good social work. *Influences of the past on current life decisions can be interesting to explore, but concrete help in changing current circumstances must often precede or accompany those growth-enhancing sessions.* While it is true that abuse suffered in childhood often contributes to an adult's own abusive lifestyle, from one's partner and to one's children, more than recognition of the past is needed to break this cycle. Direct help in acquiring housing, funds, and information—the environmental part of the person-environment perspective of social work practice—can be the critical factor in helping clients to change these destructive patterns.

In her role Naomi was also responsible for promoting the improvement of resources in the community to meet the needs of Elinor and other clients with similar problems. Recognizing the lack of inexpensive housing and the limited hours for the bus line serving the neighborhood to which Elinor ultimately moved, Naomi attended one of the county board meetings. With sensitive articulation of the needs she identified in her close work with Elinor (and other clients), she made a forceful argument that the county give more attention to housing and transportation. While funds were not readily available for housing, contacts were initiated with the bus company to explore the possibility of expansion in services.

Services Shaped by Policy Formulations

As a public profession, social work operates under social policy. Governing what social workers do, whom they do it with (both clients and colleagues), and how they get paid (Hardcastle, 1993), *policies* mandate the provision of services while allocating the resources necessary for funding and implementation of programs (Martin, 1990). Helping people through social policy requires identifying basic needs such as income, food, housing, safety, health care, and education. Yet the apportionment of services and subsidization of costs must be carefully planned at the same time. These determinations are usually difficult and often favor some groups over others. Because they are socially constructed (Van der Veen, 1988), policy formulations involve negotiations between competing interest groups representing conflicting needs and unequal access to resources.

Even though social workers addressing their attention to change in individuals may not be involved in direct policy decisions, they are nevertheless obligated to be informed about the laws that regulate services and to help shape policy formulations. The interventions social workers perform in their practice are shaped by social conditions and policies, and their practice experiences can be effectively utilized in turn to inform and influence those policies. Developments in education, health care, mental health, substance abuse, civil liberties, technological advances, welfare trends, employment, organizational changes, or societal violence—in any of these areas in which social workers practice, questions of policy are of critical importance in providing social work services.

Those engaged in private practice are also involved in matters of policy. Strict licensure laws that strengthen social workers' authority to make diagnoses and receive reimbursements from third-party vendors have been strongly advocated by the Clinical Social Work Societies. Knowledge of policies is integral to obtaining payments, and facts about the tax laws assist in accurate claims for deductions. Several good sources about social work practice and policy include Haynes and Mickelson (1991), Mahaffey and Hanks (1982), and Davis and Hagen (1992).

In Chapter 7, we discuss the practice of a social worker, Tania, as she confronted her own reactions to a highly complex case of child abuse. Here, though, we will consider Tania's responsibilities in matters of policy in this case. Employed with child welfare in a large urban area, Tania had had ten years of post-M.S.W. experience. Often overwhelmed by the increasing severity of problems presented to her and the rise in her overall number of cases (the National Center on Child Abuse and Neglect has reported a 66 percent caseload increase between 1980 and 1986), Tania fully recognized her obligation to be involved with policy issues.

Traditionally one of the primary domains of social work, child welfare services have been shaped by alterations in public perceptions accompanied by changes in laws and regulations. Children are no longer considered the property of their parents, and the government's responsibility to provide protection to children is acknowledged. With no universal agreement on what constitutes abuse, the 1974 Child Abuse Prevention and Treatment Act established general categories, leaving states to form their own more specific definitions. In Tania's state the statutes remained vague, yet several cases had recently gained much public attention, placing pressure on the agency for stricter supervision of families and more stringent regulations. At the same time there were funding cutbacks resulting in a hiring freeze and a backlog of reported incidents with no agency contact.

Tania commented:

....

As I see more and more adolescent girls becoming my clients as mothers abusing their young children, I know I cannot restrict my attention to only these cases. It's so sad for me—I placed some of these young mothers when they were abused as children.

Drugs are almost always part of the problem now. All that stuff about policy taught in social work school seems so much clearer. We have to somehow get into the business of prevention—including birth control, drug treatment, and better schools. These girls drop out when they're so young, and once they realize how trapped they are it's too late. The only outlets they have is to take out their anger on their little children.

With our caseloads so high, it's hard to do anything but respond to the immediate crises. Active in the local chapter of NASW, we consider means of lobbying state and federal officials for additional monies. I also volunteer through the local school board to talk with groups of students, providing encouragement for staying in school, and even offering some tutoring. Active in my church, I occasionally give talks about recognizing abusive behavior and offer alternatives to parents for the expression of angry feelings.

....

Because they are increasingly called on to give court testimony, social workers must be knowledgeable about existing regulations while also being able to draw on their expertise and knowledge to suggest necessary policy changes. Who would understand better the limitation of current policy than the people working directly with the laws? Likewise, informing the public and lobbying for the allocation of funds can be very effective when done by those providing the services. Tania could speak eloquently (as we see in Chapter 7) about the trauma for all parties involved with child abuse. Efforts need to be directed to educating for prevention as well as to increased funding and public support.

Building coalitions and gathering with other like-minded persons, lobbying, and presenting information to policy makers are all necessary to shape policy decisions and are integral to good social work practice.

Services with and through Organizations

As a public profession addressing social functioning and social responsibility, social work is dependent on public support. Carol Meyer says: "Social work . . . has served at the expressed behest of organized society through its social agencies and social services in hospitals, clinics, courts, schools, and institutions" (1970, p. 34). Providing help or "services" through an agency that was socially sponsored helped spawn the term *social service,* while *charity* and *philanthropy* became *social work* or *social welfare* around 1910.

Since social workers are concerned with the general health and illness of the community, they conduct much of their work through *organizations,* either large or small, public or private, for profit and not for profit. Even with the increase in private practice social work, accounting for about 12 percent of the 1984 NASW data base, over 80 percent of social workers are employed in human service organizations (Hardcastle and Brownstein, 1989).

While social workers and teachers have traditionally been employed in organizations, the connection with large organizational settings has risen for doctors and lawyers. This is partly a result of the increased use of technology and the need for specialization. Physicians need the resources of large hospitals; major surgery is not feasible without the teamwork of the anesthetist, nurse, and other medical personnel, and the cost of the equipment could not be absorbed by individual physicians. Law firms employ large numbers of support staff that help prepare the lawyers with case law and precedent relevant to their current cases. The problem for all these professionals now is "finding a place in an organization system . . . to be free to do professional work" (Blankenship, 1977, p. 24). Hughes, who has written extensively about organizations, has stated: "As the professions become more organized, business organizations become more professionalized" (1963, p. 11).

The purpose of organizations is to coordinate resources. Advances in technology and increasing social complexity and disarray have obliged large and small organizations to network with each other as they provide for the social environment of the community. Previously simple matters like payment for services now often involve reimbursement through third-party vendors. Health care is increasingly being managed through large health maintenance organizations, while follow-up from inpatient psychiatric care requires intensive work with community treatment facilities and family members.

Even social workers engaged in private practice have to understand and work with organizations. An individual receiving therapy may become depressed or suicidal and in need of the services of inpatient treatment provided through the organization of a psychiatric hospital. Family therapy may uncover a child facing abuse, and the weight of the state may be needed for removal from the home and placement in foster care, a process that requires work with the organization responsible for child welfare services. It would be difficult for social workers to provide services to adolescents without coordinating their services with the school and other organizations involved in their clients' lives.

One of the most important factors in successful social work practice is the social worker's ability to navigate through and impact on the workings of an organization. The employment setting determines the nature and function of the social work practice and the roles and tasks performed by the social worker. Teamwork, collaboration with professionals, and coordination with other resources are all features of working within an organizational context.

While the social worker and client come together for the client to receive help around a set of problems, the social work services are shaped by both the function of the agency and the guidelines of the profession. Assuring that the domain of the profession and the service delivery of the organization are coordinated with each other in addressing the client's problem is the social worker's responsibility. Several authors specifically address issues of practice within the organization including Weissman, Epstein, and Savage (1983), Neugeboren (1985), Dane and Simon (1991), Lieberman (1982), and Jansson and Simmons (1986).

Working as both a member of a professional occupation and an employee of an organization, the social worker may, at times, feel conflicted or have divided loyalties. Alvin Gouldner, in the mid-1950s, posed three variables relevant to studying the professional in the organization—loyalty to the organization, commitment to professional skills, and reference group organizations (1957). Later he developed the notion of two latent identities: cosmopolitan and local. For Gouldner, those professionals with *cosmopolitan* identities are low on loyalty to the organization, high on commitment to specialized role skills, and likely to use outer reference group orientation. *Locals*, on the other hand, are high on loyalty to the employing organization, low on commitment to specialized role skills, and likely to use inner reference group orientation. Locals are more dependent on positive reinforcement from the organization and, according to Abbott, "will tend to conform readily to organizational demands" while cosmopolitans "will tend to seek opportunities for satisfaction without conforming to organizational demands" (1965, p. 11).

Blau and Scott (1962), following Gouldner's work, conducted a study of caseworkers in a welfare department. They confirmed the hypothesis that there was an inverse relationship between the professional commitment of the workers and organizational loyalty. The number of social work conferences attended by the workers and their level of involvement in welfare activities were used as validation for the extent of professional versus bureaucratic orientation. Billingsley (1964), interested in the patterns of orientation toward conflicting expectations, studied caseworkers in a private setting and identified four subsystems requiring attention by the workers—the social work profession, the agency, the clients, and the community.

Still relevant today, these studies underscore the multiple responsibilities of social workers, which include adhering to professional guidelines and following organizational rules while also being responsive to clients' needs and addressing society's problems. Awareness of these many demands must be translated into an active balancing of what may be conflicting loyalties. Identifying one's perspective as either local or cosmopolitan allows for increased awareness and rational decision making in enacting these different orientations. Membership in professional groups and participation in educational workshops that represent a broad range of professional issues can offer information and support to help manage the many claims on loyalty.

Examples in Chapter 3 present social workers Gail, Linda, and Cara confronting the complexity of being an employee in an organization while providing social work services to clients. Responsible for attending to their organization's responsiveness to client needs and to its overall quality of service delivery, social workers often find it necessary to work toward change within the organization itself. John Wax compares the process of organizational change to the casework processes of "study, diagnosis, and treatment, although the nomenclature may be somewhat different. These are (1) identification of the problem or opportunity and definition of the objective or goal of change, (2) detailed analysis of the current equilibrium of the social system or subsystem for which change is proposed, and (3) exercise of influence or power calculated to attain the objective or goal" (1968, p. 62).

Change with individuals cannot occur outside the context of the communities in which the clients reside, the policies that mandate services, and the organizations through which the services are delivered. Yet because of the dual loyalties social workers experience in their roles as employee and social worker, they often perceive organizational change as tricky. Even though the steps for effective intervention at the organizational level are, as Wax states, very similar to the process of individual change, social workers often either neglect this aspect of their work or short-circuit some of the steps.

As we explore in case material throughout this book, many of the practice components of intervention with individuals also apply to organizational change—building relationships with agency staff; establishing an assessment of the present mission and function of the agency while understanding the history and policies that mandate its services; utilizing communication methods and skills; developing self-awareness; and forging realistic goals, including a strategy of intervention.

In the following case we briefly examine an effort at organizational change. Holly, a second-year student placed in a county family service agency, became concerned about her agency's lack of outreach services. Drawn to social work because of its attention to social reform and community action, Holly was willing to challenge and confront even those in authority. Not overly worried about pleasing others (the bane of many social workers), Holly took very seriously her role as client advocate. Though its mission was to serve several townships, the agency was only reaching the White middle-class residents in nearby communities. The poor, both Hispanic and Black, comprised less than 5 percent of the agency's caseload while totaling 35 percent of the geographic area.

Holly decided to approach the agency director with her concerns:

HOLLY: I'm glad that you could see me today. In the weeks I have been here, I have noticed we don't do a very good job of reaching the minority populations. I think the problem is that some of them just can't get to the agency—they don't drive and we aren't on a bus line convenient for them.

DIRECTOR: *(Sitting stiffly and taking a deep breath)* Holly, you have only been here a short time and evidently don't know that we have tried a variety of methods to reach out to these populations.

HOLLY: I was thinking we should establish a satellite office that would be easier for the Black and Hispanic families to get to.

DIRECTOR: *(With a hint of anger)* Holly, we have tried on several occasions to develop satellite offices. There were just too many problems, which would be even worse now with our tight financial situation.

HOLLY: Well, it seems to me that we have an obligation to reach these populations regardless of the costs.

DIRECTOR: *(Very firmly)* I have many obligations. Some are to my staff around their safety. In the past, the workers staffing those outreach facilities complained of being fearful going to and from work. If anything, since that time, crime has increased in those neighborhoods. Also, I am obligated to the board of trustees to maintain a fiscally sound agency.

HOLLY: Since this is so important, I want to do some further checking about the feasibility. In our classes we learn about the importance of services reaching the range of populations mandated. I'd like to get back to you.

DIRECTOR: Sure, you can schedule another appointment in a few weeks.

While it was generally assertive, Holly's approach was ineffectual and she could easily have been turned down flat. Learning that facilitating change in the organization was not all that different from client change in *needing more than moral arguments*, Holly can turn to her field instructor, class readings, and colleagues for guidance to strengthen her position.

Two of Wax's three steps listed earlier—detailed study of the agency and a strategy for intervention—were neglected by Holly. Though she had identified the nature of the problem, she failed to analyze the equilibrium of her agency, out of which she could have calculated a strategy to achieve her objective. Constructing an assessment, including gathering information by researching the situation and developing a historical perspective, are central to the assessment process, whether working toward change with an individual or with an organization.

What Holly also did not possess was information about recent policy changes that resulted in heavy cuts in agency funding. Holly needed to engage the agency director in a relationship so that the director could see that Holly had the competence to bring about change that would benefit the organization. She could have further strengthened her position by talking with agency staff to learn if others shared her views, by obtaining information about the agency's past outreach efforts, by thinking together with them about an effective strategy for approaching the agency director and, perhaps, by considering ways to generate additional monies.

As we next discuss, collaboration with other staff, teamwork, and coordination of resources are all essential components in providing effective services through the organization.

Collaboration with Staff

To help their clients, social workers spend a good deal of time communicating with other professionals and agency staff. *Collaboration* here means coordinating treatment or working jointly with others from the same or different agencies. Taking many forms, collaboration may involve a school social worker who plans with one of the teachers how to help a child improve poor classroom performance, or a clinical social worker with a family service agency who joins forces with other neighborhood agencies to offer a community program on substance abuse.

Though it is necessary for effective practice, the process of building collaborative relationships is not always smooth or easy. Bennis, Benne, and Chin point to the use of conflict and bargaining in building collaboration: "Collaboration is always an achievement, not a gift. It is usually attained through open and grueling confrontation of differences, through conflicts faced and resolved, through limited areas of collaboration growing into larger areas of collaboration as fuller trust develops" (1969, p. 152).

Participation in collaborative activities may result in the conflicting demands and loyalties discussed earlier. Consider, for example, an inpatient social worker with a state hospital collaborating with the outpatient unit to develop community group homes. Working toward early discharge of patients into the community, inpatient staff may feel threatened by a potential loss of their jobs. At the same time, while the social worker is advocating for adequate medication checkups, the outpatient staff may not recognize the importance of such follow-up care. Whether a social worker is collaborating with other social workers or with persons from different disciplines, clarity of goals and priorities is essential. At the same time, the social worker must maintain attention to the needs of the clients, the problems in the larger society, the mission of the employing agency, and professional guidelines.

The Social Worker as Member of a Team

Usually referring to staff within one agency, the operational unit of service in many agencies is the *team*. In some agencies, the team meets only for intake purposes or for general administrative needs; in others, it is responsible for client treatment planning.

Siporin likens teamwork to the "committees of paid charity workers, volunteers, and friendly visitors who once provided direct services in the charity organization societies, settlement houses, and public welfare agencies" (1975, p. 186). While the ideal concept of the team focuses on equality among members and the unique expertise of each, reality is often quite different. As Blau and Scott point out, status hierarchies are a natural component in all group situations, even when there are no status differences (1962, pp. 121–123). Yet these differences are present in most human service teams, which often consist of social workers along with psychologists, nurses and nursing aides, psychiatrists, and other medical doctors. Likewise, as Compton and Galaway suggest, issues of power and authority must be addressed by all team members (1989).

Conditions for teamwork suggested by Kane include a common team purpose and distinct roles for team members (1982). Clarity of task can help the team maintain a focus on goals and objectives, a problem-solving orientation, with each member having something valuable to contribute regardless of status. Strength and comfort with the social work role allow for communication with authority. Social workers' unique expertise involves the extensive information presented in the social assessment, the dual perspective of individuals within context of the social environment, and their knowledge about the complex relationship of social policies and service delivery.

This broad range of knowledge and skills often provides social workers with excellent preparation for leadership roles in teamwork. Sometimes functioning as the covert leaders or in other situations emerging naturally as the acknowledged people to facilitate meetings and assure decision making, social workers can be instrumental in providing focus and direction to the work of the team while providing emotional support to team members in follow-through on planned activities.

Coordination with Other Resources

Social workers often deal with clients who have a multitude of problems, and several agencies work with the client at the same time. Through coordination the social worker helps to integrate services, performing a pivotal role in clarifying the function of each agency, helping prevent duplication of services, and keeping focus on the identified problems.

Both the settlement houses and the charity organization societies were concerned with coordination, including documentation of services and the development of efficiency in interagency cooperation. While the COS were pushing for a rational and scientific approach to relief, wanting to avoid duplication of aid, the settlement house workers were busy organizing community development projects involving many different agencies and community groups.

Case management is a function and role that addresses the dual concerns of coordination of services and cost effectiveness. A process that is intended to ensure that clients of human services systems receive the care and opportunities to which they are entitled, case management should result in services that are appropriate to client needs but are not wasteful of funds. A resurgence of interest in this important social work role has been addressed in the literature by Rothman (1991), O'Conner (1988), and Roberts-DeGennaro (1987).

SUMMARY

In this chapter we have examined the major concepts in the social work profession. Altruistic and accepting a calling to serve, social workers attend to both the troubles of individuals and societal problems. Primarily performed in the public sector, social work addresses civic problems by the means of social institutions and through policies affecting communal life. Regardless of the specific employing agency or role performed, social workers are concerned with social functioning—individuals within the context of the larger society.

Compared with other professions, social work ranks high in commitment to service and low in systematic theory and professional authority. The discipline is criticized by some for borrowing knowledge from other disciplines, while others are convinced that the strength of social work flows from its uniquely broad perspective.

The social work framework of person and environment encompasses three components—community action, knowledge of policies, and delivery of professional services through organizational settings. Case examples illustrate the central importance to the profession of this three-pronged framework. The thrust of the chapter is that social work cannot be practiced without attention to individuals within the context of the environment.

At times, conflicts will arise between professional guidelines and organizational regulations as social workers make decisions that are best for their clients while they collaborate with other staff, work as team members, and coordinate with other resources.

Facing several roles, some of which are frequently conflicting, social workers cannot hope for harmony in their work. An ability to tolerate ambiguity while simultaneously meeting multiple role expectations is needed for the good practice of social work. As they attend to the individual troubles of their clients, social workers must continually address the service delivery of their employing organization while also impacting on the community and policy, the public aspect of the clients' lives.

Now that we have considered social work as a profession with a review of its major concepts and mode of service delivery, we turn to the values and ethics that guide the practice of these ideas. Case studies present the major themes of this and the next chapter.

BIBLIOGRAPHY

Abbott, M. (1965). Intervening variables in organizational behavior. *Educational Administrative Quarterly*, Winter, 1–13.

Becker, H. S., Greer, B., Hughes, E. C., & Strauss, A. (1961). *Boys in white: Student culture in medical school*. Chicago: University of Chicago Press.

Bennis, W., Benne, K., & Chin, R. (1969). *The planning of change*. (2nd ed.) New York: Holt, Rinehart and Winston.

Billingsley, A. (1964). Bureaucratic and professional orientation patterns in social casework. *Social Service Review, 82*, 400–407.

Blankenship, R. (1977). *Colleagues in organization*. New York: John Wiley & Sons.

Blau, P., & Scott, R. (1962). *Formal organizations*. San Francisco: Chandler.

Brown, E. (1936). *Social work as a profession*. New York: Russell Sage.

Bucher, R., & Strauss, A. (1961). Professions in process. *American Journal of Sociology, 66*, 325–334.

Carr-Saunders, A. M., & Wilson, P. A. (1933). *The professions*. Oxford: Clarendon Press.

Child Abuse Prevention and Treatment Act. PL 93-247, 88 Stat. 4, 1974.

Clark, D. (1985). Emerging paradigms in organizational theory and research. In Y. Lincoln (Ed.), *Organizational theory and inquiry*, 43–78. Beverly Hills, Calif.: Sage Press.

Cohen, M., March, J., & Olsen, J. (1972). A garbage can model of organizational choice. *Administrative Science Quarterly, 17*: 1, 1–25.

Cohen, N. (1958). *Social work in the American tradition*. New York: Dryden Press.

Compton, B., & Galaway, B. (1979, 1989). *Social work processes.* Homewood, Ill.: Dorsey Press.

Corwin, R. (1961). The professional employee: a study of conflict in nursing roles. *American Journal of Sociology, 66,* 604-615.

Crozier, M. (1977). Power and uncertainty. In R. Blankenship (Ed.), *Colleagues in organization,* 337–359. New York: John Wiley & Sons.

Dane, B., & Simon, B. (1991). Resident guests: Social workers in host settings. *Social Work, 36:* 3, 208–213.

Davis, L., & Hagen, J. (1992). The problem of wife abuse: The interrelationship of social policy and social work practice. *Social Work, 37:* 1, 15–20.

Etzioni, A. (1975). *A comparative analysis of complex organizations.* New York: Free Press.

Feldman, Y. (1963). Understanding ego involvement in casework training. In H. Parad and R. Miller (Eds.), *Ego-oriented casework,* 292–306. New York: Family Service Association of America.

Fellin, P. (1987). *The community and the social worker.* Itasca, Ill.: Peacock.

Freidson, E. (1970). Dominant professions, bureaucracy, and client services. In W. Rosengren & M. Lefton (Eds.), *Organizations and clients: Essays in the sociology of service,* 71–92. Columbus, Ohio: Merrill.

Fuchs, V. (1968). *The service economy.* New York: National Bureau of Economics Research.

Gouldner, A. (1957). Cosmopolitans and locals: Toward an analysis of latent social roles I. *Administrative Science Quarterly, 1,* 281–306.

Gouldner, A. (1958). Cosmopolitans and locals: Toward an analysis of latent social roles II. *Administrative Science Quarterly, 2,* 444–480.

Greenwood, E. (1957). Attributes of a profession. *Social Work, 2,* 44–55.

Gross, N., Mason, W. S., & McEachorn, R. W. (1957). *Explorations in role analysis.* New York: John Wiley & Sons.

Grosser, C. (1976). *New directions in community organization.* New York: Praeger Press.

Gustafson, J. (1982). Professions as 'callings.' *Social Service Review.* December, 501–514.

Hage, J. (1965). An axiomatic theory of organizations. *Administrative Science Quarterly, 10,* 289–320.

Hall, R. (1968). Professionalization and bureaucratization. *American Sociological Review, 33,* 92–104.

Hamilton, G. (1946). *Social casework.* New York: Columbia University Press.

Hardcastle, D. A. (1990). Legal regulation of social work. In *Encyclopedia of social work,* 203–217. Silver Springs, Md.: NASW, (18th ed.)

Hardcastle, D. A. (1993). Personal communication. Discussions about policy with Professor Hardcastle helped inform this section. University of Maryland, School of Social Work and Community Planning.

Hardcastle, D. A., & Brownstein, C. (1989). Private practitioners: profile and motivations for independent practice. *Journal of Independent Social Work,* 4: 1, 7–18.

Haynes, K., & Mickelson, J. (1991). *Affecting change.* New York: Longman.

Hepworth, D., & Larsen, J. (1986). *Direct social work practice.* New York: Dorsey Press.

Hollis, F., & Woods, M. (1981). *Casework: A psychosocial approach.* New York: Random House.

Hughes, E. (1963). Professions. In K. Lynn (Ed.), *The professions in America,* 1–14. Boston: Houghton-Mifflin.

Jansson, B., & Simmons, J. (1986). The survival of social work units in host organizations. *Social Work, 31,* 339–343.

Kane, R. (1982). Teams: Thoughts for the bleachers. *Health and Social Work, 7:* 1, 2–4.

Kramer, R., & Specht, H. (1983). *Readings in community organization practice.* Englewood Cliffs, N.J.: Prentice-Hall.

Leiby, J. (1984). Charity organization reconsidered. *Social Service Review, December,* 523–538.

Leiby, J. (1985). Moral foundations of social welfare and social work: A historical view. *Social Work, 30:* 4, 323–330.

Lewis, H. (1982). *The intellectual base of social work practice.* New York: Haworth Press.

Lieberman, F. (1982). The triangle: The worker, the client, the agency. *Clinical Social Work Journal,* 77–90.

Lipsky, M. (1980). *Street level bureaucracy.* New York: Russell Sage.

Lortie, D. (1966). Professional socialization. In H. Vollmer & D. Mills (Eds.), *Professionalization,* 98–101. Englewood Cliffs, N.J.: Prentice-Hall.

Lynn, K. (1963). *The professions in America.* Boston: Houghton-Mifflin.

Mahaffey, M., & Hanks, J. (Eds.) (1982). *Practical politics.* Silver Springs, Md.: NASW.

March, J., & Simon, H. (1958). *Organizations.* New York: John Wiley & Sons.

Martin, G. (1990). *Social policy in the welfare state.* Englewood Cliffs, N.J.: Prentice-Hall.

Meyer, C. (1970). *Social work practice: A response to the urban crisis.* New York: Free Press.

National Center on Child Abuse and Neglect. (1988). *Study of national incidence and prevalence of child abuse and neglect.* DHHS #105-85-1702. Washington, D.C.: U.S. Government Printing Office.

Neugeboren, B. (1985). *Organization, policy, and practice in the human services.* New York: Longman.

O'Conner, G. (1988). Case management: system and practice. *Social Casework, February,* 97–106.

Parsons, T. (1954). *Essays in sociological theory.* New York: The Free Press of Glencoe.

Reynolds, B. (1942, 1970). *Learning and teaching in the practice of social work.* New York: Russell and Russell.

Richmond, M. (1899). *Friendly visiting among the poor.* New York: Macmillan.

Richmond, M. (1922). *What is social casework? An introductory description.* New York: Russell Sage.

Richmond, M. (1930). *The long view.* New York: Russell Sage.

Roberts-DeGennaro, M. (1987). Developing case management as a practice model. *Social Casework, October,* 466–470.

Robinson, V. (1936). *Supervision in social casework.* Chapel Hill, N.C.: University of North Carolina.

Rothman, J. (1991). A model of case management: toward empirically based practice. *Social Work, 36,* 520–528.

Selznick, P. (1948). Foundations of the theory of organizations. *American Sociological Review, 13,* 25–35.

Siporin, M. (1975). *Introduction to social work practice.* New York: Macmillan.

Timms, N. (1966). *Social casework: Principles and practice.* London: Latimer, Trend & Co.

Turner, R. H. (1956). Role taking, role standpoint and reference group behavior. *American Journal of Sociology, 61,* 316–328.

Van der Veen, R. (1988). Social justice by social policy. Paper presented at International Conference on Social Justice and Societal Problems, Leiden.

Warren, R. (1978). *The community in America.* Chicago: Rand MacNally.

Wax, J. (1968). Developing social work power in a medical organization. *Social Work, 5,* 62–71.

Weber, M. (1947). *The theory of social and economic organizations.* Glencoe, NY: Free Press.

Weick, K. (1969). *The social psychology of organizing.* Reading, Mass: Addison-Wesley.

Weick, K. (1976). Educational organizations as loosely coupled systems. *Administrative Science Quarterly, 21,* 1–19.

Weissman, H., Epstein, I., & Savage, A. (1983). *Agency-based social work.* Philadelphia: Temple University Press.

Wildavsky, A. (1980). *Speaking truth to power.* Boston: Little, Brown.

Wilensky, H. (1964). The professionalization of everyone? *American Journal of Sociology, 70,* 137–155.

CHAPTER ❧ THREE

We must know how to work with others, and we must know how to work with the forces that make for progress; friendly visiting . . . is . . . working with the democratic spirit of the age to forward the advance of the plain and common people into a better and larger life.

—Mary Richmond, 1899

PROFESSIONAL VALUES AND SOCIAL WORK ETHICAL CODE

Values are "those enduring beliefs we hold about what is to be preferred as good and right in our conduct and in our existence as human beings" (Lewis, 1982, p. 12). As they refer to likes and dislikes, values provide the basis for distinctions between good and bad. Pumphrey (1959) proposes that the ultimate and abstract values include democracy, justice, equality, peace, social progress, self-determination, and self-realization.

Searching for a common base of the social work profession, Harriet Bartlett addresses values in practice: "Values . . . refer to what is regarded as good and desirable. These are qualitative judgements; they are not empirically demonstrable. They are invested with emotion and represent a purpose or goal toward which the social worker's action will be directed" (1970, p. 63). Values become institutionalized through the adoption of social *norms*, behavior accepted as good and desirable. Social work is basically a "normative discipline, it deals with moral values and social norms, with conduct that is socially good, obligatory, and normal, or that is bad, offensive, and deviant" (Siporin, 1975, p. 64).

The normative nature of social work practice means that it *cannot* be value free. Upholding specific belief systems and value orientations, social workers are employed by agencies reflecting certain value positions and they intervene with clients who have their own beliefs, values, and traditions. Moreover, ethical and cultural issues are the essence of the social work enterprise—social workers and clients cannot talk together without considering values and beliefs of right and wrong. A value-laden profession, social work is concerned with questions of moral behavior by individuals and society.

There is a distinction, critical for practice, between values and knowledge. William Gordon explains that values refer not only to what we prefer, but also to some measure of the extent of that preference—"that is, the price in effort, money or sacrifice individuals will pay to achieve their preference." Knowledge, on the other hand, denotes the picture of the world "as it is . . . derived from the most rigorous interpretation they are capable of giving to the most objective sense data that are capable to obtain" (Gordon, 1965, p. 33).

Gordon quite rightly emphasizes that "the first minimum step is the separation of what social work prefers or wants for people from what social work knows about people" (1965, p. 34); the oughts, in other words, must be separate from the knows. The value-free scientific paradigm does not match the value-permeated character of social work. Because values so dominate the concerns of the profession, social workers must identify and keep separate what they would like for clients from the facts and knowledge they have acquired, while also forging distinctions between their own values and the client's preferences.

Completing the foundations of the social work profession, this chapter examines *values* and the *social work Code of Ethics* (reproduced in Appendix 1). Relating to the major concepts presented in Chapter 2, *issues of ethical behavior* are discussed, focusing on the primary social work ethical principles of *confidentiality, duty to warn, self-determination,* and *informed consent.* It presents case studies that illustrate the *interplay of these ethical principles with the perspective of person and environment as it includes attention to community, matters of policy, and the service delivery of the employing organization.*

SOCIAL WORK ETHICS

Values are usually general and abstract, whereas *ethics* are the rules of conduct that direct behavior consistent with values. Values "are concerned with what is good and desirable . . . ethics deal with what is right and correct" (Loewenberg and Dolgoff, 1982, p. 9). As we indicated earlier, one of the distinguishing features of a professional group is self-regulation based on its ethical principles and values. Reflected in its code of ethics, the profession's beliefs and traditions provide a guide to the correct course of action. For social workers, practice with clients must be enacted in accordance with the principles outlined in the social work Code of Ethics.

Along with the ethical code, Kutchins considers social workers to be bound by a fiduciary relationship with their clients. For him, "fiduciary relationships emanate from the trust that clients must place in professionals. Because professionals have knowledge and use techniques that require special expertise, clients must trust workers to act in their best interest" (Kutchins, 1991, p. 106). Attention to both legal obligations and ethical principles is fundamental in practice decisions.

Two of the ethical principles, confidentiality and self-determination, have long been discussed in the social work literature. We now address these principles and also consider the corresponding constraints of duty to warn and informed consent.

Confidentiality

Confidentiality has consistently remained a central principle in the guiding ethics of the social work profession. Its basic tenets are these: the social worker is responsible for the information obtained from client contacts, the knowledge obtained must be used for professional purposes, and the privacy of clients must be protected. Communications between clients and social workers are made in the confidence and trust that they will not be disclosed. As a fundamental part of the formation of belief bonding in the professional relationship, clients should know that the worker will not misuse confidences to hurt or betray them. Similar ethical codes bind other professional relationships, including ones with lawyers, doctors, and ministers.

In the first book written about social work practice, Mary Richmond discussed social workers' concerns about maintaining the privacy of their information about clients. At that time, workers were reluctant to share information about their clients with the Confidential Exchange, an agency established, despite its name, to avoid duplication of services (Richmond, 1917, pp. 303–316). Since the days of Mary Richmond, the concept of confidentiality has become even more complex. A thorough discussion is offered by Suanna Wilson in *Confidentiality in Social Work* (1978), where she distinguishes between confidentiality as a moral code and the legal protection of privileged communication. The fiduciary duty of confidentiality was established in *MacDonald v. Clinger*, where the court ruled that a patient could sue a psychiatrist who divulged personal information to the patient's wife learned during therapy (*MacDonald v. Clinger*, 1982).

Social workers may be bound by confidentiality in their code of ethics and limited by case law not to share information with others. Legally, however, they may be required to provide such information in certain court and other situations, as stated in the *Washington University Law Quarterly*: "The duty to keep matters confidential is governed by ethics. The right to disclose them is governed by law" (1965, p. 363). Not all states have privileged communication statutes, and they may offer only narrow protection for the privilege. Social workers are responsible for knowing and clarifying with their agencies the nature of the state regulations to which they are bound. Knowing about the privacy of notes and logs is necessary for responsible advice to the client about the confidentiality of sessions.

The Federal Privacy Act of 1974 sets standards that an agency must secure a client's written consent before releasing details about that client to another person or agency. In addition to duplication of services, which was an issue in the days of Mary Richmond, there are many other reasons for agencies to share information with each other. These might include securing additional services for the client, conducting research and evaluation studies on client services, and improving the provision of services.

Just as we have found that there is a complex interaction between the competencies of social work practice, the ethical principles are also intricately bound together in ways that result in confusion and conflicts. In some cases, confidentiality is superseded by a duty to warn.

Duty to Warn or Protect

Several legal cases have established the precedent that when the client threatens harmful or criminal acts, the "duty to warn" supersedes the protection of a "privileged communication." In one such case, *Tarasoff v. Regents of the University of California,* the clinician warned the police that his patient was threatening to kill a young woman. After being questioned and released, the patient committed the murder and the murdered woman's parents sued the clinician's employer. The California Supreme Court ruled that the potential victim herself should have been warned.

Many situations may arise during social work that demand duty to warn over confidentiality. Domestic violence, child and sexual abuse, and abuse of the elderly are just some situations in which the social worker may need to take steps to inform or protect victims of abuse, present or potential. Another situation is when clients refuse to disclose the presence of AIDS to their sexual partner. The danger of AIDS infection is not as imminent as physical abuse, making it even more confusing for social workers to decide which ethic has priority, the duty to protect or client confidentiality.

While some sources providing ethical guidelines are cited later in this chapter (also see Dean and Rhodes, 1992), social workers must inquire about practices and regulations of their employing agency and obtain knowledge about the laws in the state where they practice. Being clear with clients about the limits on their privileged communication is fundamental to social work practice and is related to the following concepts of the client's right to self-determination and informed consent.

Self-Determination

Self-determination has long been viewed as central to social work, but practitioners have continued to struggle with incorporating this ambiguous concept into their practice with clients. The definition offered in the *Random House Dictionary,* "freedom to live as one chooses, or to act or decide without consulting another or others," implies a self-mastery or autonomy over one's actions (1967, p. 1293). Charles Levy (1983) discusses self-determination as a right and a social work value and responsibility. As a right, it is the cornerstone of democratic societies and is the basis for other rights and privileges, such as confidentiality and privacy. As a social work ethic, it is directly related to the "supreme value" of the social work profession, the *innate dignity and value of the individual* (Biestek and Gehrig, 1978).

Yet it quickly becomes evident to those actively engaged in practice that there is a basic paradox in honoring this "supreme value" while also executing the profession's mission. The function of social work is to improve social functioning, and we have defined social casework as *social workers creating change with individuals.* With the thrust of social work to create change in the larger society and in the lives of people, how does the social worker reconcile the social work ethic of honoring clients' rights to make their own choices and still function at the same time as a change agent? To create change is to take a stand, to work actively at making something different than what it was. Yet self-determination means that behavior must stem from a person's own wishes and choices.

Moreover, many of the clients seen by social workers have basic needs for food, shelter, employment, clothing, medical care, and safety from physical harm. A necessary condition to make responsible life choices is the availability of resources to meet life's basic needs. Is self-determination possible while the distribution of resources remains unfair and inadequate for so many?

Social workers must struggle anew with the meaning of this concept each time they relate to a client's situation. As with most of social work practice, there are no pat methods prescribing the right behaviors. Respect for the client as an individual with free will and the inherent right to self-determination is a given. At the same time, social workers must work toward client change, so there *is* an inherent manipulation in the social work endeavor. Social workers are presented as experts, professing to know better than the client certain matters. *Balancing the act of offering expert help with respect for a client's autonomy remains a challenge for every practicing social worker.* As Freedberg put it: "Social workers need to recognize the political, ideological, and practice tensions inherent in self-determination to guide clients to true self-determination" (1989, p. 33). And this goal may be, as Helen Harris Perlman states, illusory: "Self-determination is nine-tenths illusion, one-tenth reality . . . but as . . . one of the 'grand illusions' basic to human development and human dignity and human freedom I am committed to supporting it" (1965, p. 410).

Informed Consent

To have self-determination, clients need to be able to provide informed consent. Though this concept has recently appeared in the social work literature, it originated in health care and medicine as the basis for recovery of damages in injury claims. As early as 1914, Justice Cardoza ruled that:

"Every human being . . . has a right to determine what shall be done with his own body" (*Schloendorff v. Society of New York Hospital,* p. 93).

Passage of the Federal Privacy Act of 1974 has defined informed consent as the "knowing consent of an individual or his legally authorized representative, so situated so as to be able to exercise free power of choice without undue inducement of any element of force, fraud, deceit, duress, or other form of constraint or coercion" (*Federal Register,* 1975, p. 579). This act mandates that: (1) there must be an absence of coercion and undue influence, (2) the client possesses capacity to provide consent, (3) consent is limited to specific procedures, (4) the forms of consent are valid, (5) rights to withdraw or refuse consent are retained by the client, and (6) adequate information is available to the client in reaching the decision (Rozowsky, 1977).

Clients have a legal right to be advised about the decisions and methods that relate to their treatment, including access to their records. Agencies must secure written consent from clients prior to releasing information to other persons or agencies, and they must maintain records of the disclosure. Guidelines must be followed for securing client information and policies must be established for the handling of records and maintaining confidentiality.

Just like other ethical guidelines, informed consent is not as simple and direct in practice as it is in theory. Clients may not always be capable of making informed judgments. Applebaum and Roth (1982) state that practitioners must consider clients' abilities to make choices, comprehend the facts, rationally manage information, and appreciate their situation. Incompetence should *not* be considered a given for any particular population group. Clients with lesser capacity for competence, such as minors, some of those diagnosed with mental illness and retardation, and certain medical conditions, should still be assessed for competence. When a client is assessed as incompetent, the legally authorized representative will need to be involved.

Honoring the principle of informed consent involves advising clients of one's status and experience. The position of student or intern, for example, should be identified early in the relationship. As well as being honest and in accord with the profession's ethical code, this early discussion can free students from undue guilty feelings at semester break or at the termination of the placement.

Informed consent forms the basis for self-determination. Treating clients as autonomous individuals requires those clients to be informed and knowledgeable. Social workers should be prepared to inform their clients of the nature and course of any planned treatment.

PRACTICE CONFLICTS AND DILEMMAS

The strong personal nature of the issues addressed by social workers often involves them in situations filled with conflict. Considering ethical issues during the assessment process, believes Lewis (1982), will help social workers decide whether what can be done should be done.

Frederick Reamer (1983) has written extensively about ethics and values in social work, applying his framework directly to practice issues in work with clients and agencies. Grouping categories of ethical dilemmas that relate to the field of social work practice, he poses the following areas for ethical conflicts: direct service (such as offering services or terminating services against the client's wishes); social welfare policy and programs (advocating for equitable allocation of scarce resources); and among colleagues (the social worker's responsibility to report incompetence of peers or supervisors).

Guidelines based on Reamer's moral priorities for social workers can help clarify the social worker's thinking and options. Although the usefulness of such guidelines is limited because they can never be inclusive enough to cover the breadth of all social work practice, we present them here as a starting point for thinking about issues of ethical practice.

(1) The basics such as life, food, shelter, have priority of protection. (2) These basics, moreover, take precedence over another individual's right to freedom. (3) An individual's right to freedom, however, takes precedence over his or her right to basic well-being, provided a rational and informed choice is being made. (4) One is obligated to obey laws and rules to which one has voluntarily agreed. (5) An individual's rights to well-being override rules and regulations.

Basically, Reamer is stating that one can't be self-determining at the expense of another's life or property. Yet, if someone wants to be homeless or go on a food fast, they have the right to do so as long as they are not adjudicated incompetent or irrational. Finally, he suggests that accepting employment with an organization obligates the social worker to follow its regulations unless they are harmful to the well-being of others. The following case studies explain and illustrate the use of Reamer's guidelines while also highlighting the major concepts and Code of Ethics that inform social work practice. As we will see, integrating the philosophical and ethical principles of the profession is a task that poses significant challenges to those who engage in the practice of social work.

In these practice situations, social workers discuss their management of the agency's service delivery while attending to social policies and conditions within the community in their provision of direct services to clients in great need. These case presentations of real social workers and clients are not simplistic; they portray, rather, the extraordinary complexity we face in practicing social work. Through them we begin to see why prescriptions for practice are not helpful and can even be destructive. Two of the cases illustrate practice with potentially suicidal clients in which the social workers each proceed in very different ways.

The first case considers the dilemma facing a social worker who questions the regulations of her agency. Staci, a first-year M.S.W. student placed with Juvenile Probation, was having trouble following the rules through which the agency operates. Her client, Raul, was 16 at the time he was sentenced to an indefinite period of probation. Having run away with his girlfriend, he was charged with unauthorized use of a motor vehicle (the car belonged to his girlfriend's mother) and ordered to pay restitution for damages to the car. Living with grandparents because of an absent father still residing in Mexico and a poor relationship with his mother and step-father, Raul was also flunking most of his school courses.

With little prior social work experience, Staci was initially struck by the contrast between the strict rules of the Probation Office and the messy lives of the juveniles under its jurisdiction. Working intensely with Raul and his family, in the space of several weeks she made four home visits, conducted individual and family sessions, and visited the school to help them contract with Raul for regular school attendance. Only one month into this heavy pace of work, Raul was suspended from school and ran away again. As Staci explains:

....

I felt in a terrible quandary. Division of Youth Rehabilitative Services procedure states that I file a warrant for Raul's arrest with charges of probation violation. Knowing that he was distraught over further upsetting his grandparents with this new suspension, I couldn't see how charging a confused 16-year-old with another crime was going to help him. He needed counseling and an alternative to traditional school, not incarceration!

The only comfort for me was that having Raul arrested would get him off the streets and, hopefully, out of danger. Yet filing that warrant was the single most difficult thing I did while at that setting.

....

The obligations to follow agency rules and regulations go along with one's employment or placement with that organization. Though it is the responsibility of social workers to raise questions about procedures, they also must, as Reamer indicates in his fourth guideline, obey laws to which they have voluntarily agreed. It would be a rare social worker indeed who has not had doubts or reservations about the workings of social service settings. Yet joining an agency means one is accepting some of its basic premises. As compelling as Staci's reluctance to file the warrant was her obligation to follow through with it. Should this requirement of the position continue to disturb her regularly, a change in employment is probably a good idea. Fortunately for Staci and Raul, he turned himself in. She was able to get him the services he needed and successfully made a case to the judge that incarceration was not necessary.

In the next case example, Gail, a first-year student, struggles with the ethical principles of *confidentiality* and *duty to warn* while she also balances her *loyalty to colleagues with her role as change agent and addresses resources and policies in the larger community.*

Completing her first-year field placement at a private nonprofit organization addressing the problem of domestic violence, Gail spent the majority of her time with the men's program, which provided on-call 24-hour crisis intervention counseling as well as individual and group counseling. The number of male perpetrators referred for services to this setting had more than tripled during the 1980s, with most of the men ordered by the courts to participate. Gail, whose previous work experience was as a kindergarten teacher, day-care administrator, and counselor for female victims of domestic violence, was uneasy about accepting this placement. Nearing 40 and White, she was physically attractive and felt uncomfortable about working closely with men who had histories of violence against women. Facilitating a group session for male batterers with her male supervisor helped alleviate some of her own safety concerns. The group, which could change each week, usually consisted of from five to ten males, two thirds of whom had attended previous sessions.

This was the first session for Mr. Z, a 37-year-old White male referred by Child Protective Services. He listed his residence as homeless and his occupation as disabled and had been separated from his wife for three months. Mrs. Z received AFDC and lived with her daughter, age 13, and her son, 10.

	Mr. Z:	My wife makes me angry.
*1	Gail:	What did your wife do that made you so angry?
	Mr. Z:	I caught her in bed with my friend.
	Gail:	I'm sure that was difficult for you.
*2	Mr. Z:	It sure was. Now she says I beat the kids so I can get back at her.
*3	Mr. L:	As another member of this group, well, did you beat the kids?
*4	Mr. Z:	Hell no, I didn't beat the kids. She's just pissed because I caught her in bed.

Gail comments about her feelings and observations during this exchange.

....

*At his first statement, *1, I was concerned by the quickness and strength of both his manner and content and wanted more information. He seemed to feel pain and a sense of justification, and I felt genuine empathy for his experience. By *2*

I began to perceive him as glib, that he was trying to sway the group's impression. Relief accompanied the other member's comment, *3, and I sensed he was experiencing the same concern I had for the children.

By *4 Mr. Z seemed to be enjoying the attention of the group and at the same time was becoming more agitated by the questioning. At the end of the meeting he sat silently. His body, however, was very rigid, shoulders quite tense, jaw firmly set, fingers drumming the table. There was a coldness in his eyes and a pulsing in his upper jaw. I felt very uneasy.

At first I was trying to establish a rapport with Mr. Z, but pretty quickly became concerned that information was missing from his accounting of the situation. Worried about the safety of the children, and unable to figure out what Mr. Z was trying to do, I questioned his honesty.

....

Prior to their participation in the group, Gail and her co-leader discussed the *ethic of confidentiality* with the men along with the social worker's *duty to warn.* They were told that what was said in the group was held in confidence, that each of the members and the social worker were bound not to divulge information learned in the group. Should, however, the social worker determine someone to be in danger from a group member, the duty to warn that person (or persons) would supersede the confidentiality. Promptly after the session, Gail discussed with her supervisor her acute sense of urgency to contact Mrs. Z. They reviewed what Mr. Z had shared and tried to determine whether Mrs. Z and the children were potentially in danger. Though he did not threaten to harm them, Mr. Z's manner of conveying the information was unsettling to Gail. Mr. Z was a new client, and the agency did not have much background information on the family. They decided that Gail would telephone Mrs. Z and get more information from her.

Gail introduced herself on the phone and asked if Mrs. Z would talk with her about her experience with Mr. Z's violence. In this way, Gail did not violate confidentiality. The referral from Child Protective Services indicated that Mrs. Z had filed a complaint of violent behavior, so Gail was not sharing with Mrs. Z any confidential information. Gail learned from Mrs. Z that Mr. Z had severely abused her and the children for over ten years and that he was currently under a restraining order to stay away from them. She had been in shelters several times.

In this case, Gail did not have to "warn" Mrs. Z, who was well aware of her husband's violent behavior and was already attempting to protect herself. At the next group session, in keeping with her fiduciary relationship with Mr. Z, Gail was prepared to inform him that she had phoned his wife. Mr. Z, however, did not attend, and Gail later learned that he had been arrested for violating the restraining order.

Gail discussed her placement with the men's program:

....

I had ambivalent feelings about having this as my first-year placement. I knew a lot about kids and women and very little about men, especially men who act violently. Feminist friends of mine were very critical and told me I was betraying women if I worked with these men. Some of the women who work in domestic violence hate men and I think they perpetuate the lack of communication and the victim role for the women who need these services.

I decided to take the placement because I thought it would offer me new perspectives. I wanted better understanding of those who do violence to others. Even the terms "batterer" and "victim" were beginning to bother me. Labeling these persons and placing them in their respective roles did not seem to offer a resolution or a means of improving their relationship skills.

My field instructor thoroughly reviewed with me my obligations about confidentiality and duty to warn because violent behavior is a factor for all of the male group participants. I understand that my clients must be able to trust that what they share in the group will not be divulged. At first I was more identified with the women and felt very concerned about protecting them. After a few months I have begun to also feel protective about the men. Many of them have experienced horrible abuse as children. I have seen some of them cry as they talk about hitting their wives and kids, that they really don't want to behave in this way. I can see now that treating them with respect, with a belief that they have certain rights, is integral to their being autonomous individuals.

....

Adherence to the profession's values and ethical guidelines often poses challenges for social workers because of the value-laden nature of the work. Not faced with easy right or wrong choices, they can experience a mixture of feelings and confusion of thought. Gail, while feeling uncomfortable about Mr. Z, especially after learning about the abuse of his wife, was also trying to form a helping relationship with him. While disliking his use of violence, she was opposed to condemning Mr. Z, wanting to treat him with respect and protect his rights and freedoms.

Besides the values conflicts, Gail strove to assure appropriate service delivery by her employing organization. Recognizing her responsibility to do more than provide direct services to individual clients, she knew also to address the provision of services by her setting. The antimale attitude of some of the female workers could affect, directly and indirectly, the kind and quality of services offered in this domestic violence program. Indirectly, programs for men might not be offered, or educational and outreach activities could be biased, alienating the male population from coming in for the services. Directly, the therapy offered to the women could be inappropriate and even destructive if they were handed a party line that was biased against men. Unless Gail was willing to consider her organization as an integral aspect of her practice with clients, the services might be narrow, ineffective, and harmful.

Gail commented about her dilemma in *balancing her role as change agent with her sense of loyalty to her colleagues,* many of whom were her friends.

....

Though Mr. Z did not elicit much compassion from me, many of the men had sad stories of their own involving abuse of them as children, lack of schooling, and minimal job opportunities. After several months at the center I began to relate with them, seeing domestic violence as more complicated than a strong and bad male hurting the weak and good female. As I went through this transition, I had to figure out how to handle with some integrity my role as social worker with my role as friend and colleague.

It became clear to me that the biased attitude of my female co-workers was negatively affecting some of our female clients. They were feeling pressured to not only leave their husbands, but also to feel bitterness and hatred. It also seemed to me that our "harsh" image was preventing some women from seeking our services.

After struggling over this, discussing it in practice class and with other social work students, I decided I had to directly confront the issue. At a team meeting I raised my concerns, trying very hard to not blame any particular person. I tried to frame the problem as one we all shared—how can we provide the best services to all the people in need? I was honest and direct without being accusatory or overly emotional.

This was the least I could do. I was asking my clients to be strong, to stand up to their spouses and change years of behavior. I could certainly stand and work towards shaping workers' attitudes and help them see the impact of those attitudes on the agency's service provision. Some of the workers tried to make this a personal battle between me and them, but I didn't engage in that. We had differences, but I still would relate to them and expect that they relate to me.

....

Over a period of several months, changes in the agency became evident. More referrals were coming in from a wider array of community settings. One of the neighborhood high schools asked the agency to offer a special assembly on domestic violence and more clients were continuing with services beyond one or two sessions.

Though Gail's specific role was to *provide direct services to the men, and* sometimes to *their families,* she had also to *stay abreast of the social conditions and policies of the larger community.* This knowledge of the community involved being familiar with the kinds and quality of resources for these families—the number of shelters, low-cost housing, police back-up and support, emergency and legal services, employment and job training, and transportation. Aware that policy decisions determine the availability of shelter facilities and other needed resources, Gail asked to participate in the United Way review of the agency to advocate for allocation of additional funding. She also had to understand the rules concerning removing abusive spouses from the home and providing ongoing protection to those abused.

The community environment of each specific family was also relevant— the attitudes toward violence, the acceptability of women's self-assertion, the employment picture (so that self-sufficiency for the women was a realistic possibility), and the availability of public transportation and day-care facilities.

As Gail commented:

....

At first I was really naive about this work. When requesting my first-year placement, I was quite sure I wanted to do therapy with individuals and families. Thinking that meant sitting with someone in an office and talking to them about their problems, of course, I now see that the problems my clients face are very complicated, necessitating home visits, going to the child's school, or helping them connect with area employers. Accompanying one of my clients on her first job interview, I helped her look through the classified ads and role-played with her for the interview. She was 42 years old and had never held down a job. To be helpful with my individual clients, I had to learn a lot about the community.

It was also necessary to look beyond the immediate problems of my clients. More attention to the problem of domestic violence, through media coverage and women's greater activism, has resulted in policy changes and increased services.

....

Like the social workers presented in Chapter 2, Naomi and Holly, as well as Tania and Staci in this chapter, Gail found that her social work practice directed her attention simultaneously to many systems. While her involvement began because of an individual problem—Mr. Z was homeless and without his family because he beat his wife—she could not intervene with Mr. Z without also talking with his wife and addressing the service delivery of the agency and consequent outreach into the community. Moreover, she could not restrict her perspective to only the Z family but had to explore the availability of funding and services to families with domestic violence. Illustrating the multiple perspectives of social work, *person* issues cannot be successfully resolved without considering the *environment*, including the service organization, the community, and matters of policy.

At the same time, the ethical principles of confidentiality and duty to warn can easily seem to conflict with each other. Careful attention to the intent of the ethical guidelines, to federal and state laws, and to the policies of the agency can offer direction for the practice.

The next case focuses on *self-determination and duty to protect* while also examining the social worker's *attention to the organization and matters of policy.* Linda, a white second-year M.S.W. student placed at a large Veterans Administration hospital in outpatient psychiatry, had been seeing her client Dale on a weekly basis for three months. Dale was White and 32 years old, with a long history of inpatient and outpatient treatment, including homicidal and suicidal attempts. Employed as a licensed practical nurse at a local hospital, she led a socially isolated life and was engaged to be married in one month to John, who worked on a small family farm.

LINDA: Well, how have things been going this week?

DALE: *(Long pause)* I've been spending more time sleeping.

LINDA: Have you still been able to work? Tell me more about the sleeping.

DALE: Well, I get myself to work, and do all right when I'm at the hospital. But when I'm home, I mostly sleep.

LINDA: What has John noticed and has he had anything to say about your sleeping?

DALE: Well he's very busy on the farm now. And with my working night shift, he hasn't really noticed that anything is different.

LINDA: What does the increase in sleeping mean to you?

DALE: That I'm getting depressed.

LINDA: Are there other indications of you being depressed?

DALE: *(A very long pause)* Well, I've been feeling like hurting myself.

LINDA: What do you mean, specifically?

DALE: I've taken home one of the surgical knives from the hospital. It's very sharp and I have considered using it to cut my
wrists.

LINDA: I am glad that you are telling me about this. You have talked with me that at various times in your life you have had these feelings. What do you think is going on with you that you are considering killing yourself at this time?

DALE: I'm not sure. *(Showing her wrists)* I have hurt myself in the past.

LINDA: Yes, I know. How bad are these feelings?

DALE: Oh, I don't like feeling like this, but I can handle it.

*1   LINDA: Do you need to come into the hospital as an inpatient?

DALE: No, I don't want to become an inpatient. I have had this worse in the past.

LINDA: If you do not want to enter the hospital for a few days, I'm going to ask you to make an agreement with me which will involve several things. I want you to make a contract with me that you will not try to kill or harm yourself, and that if you have those feelings you will call me, or someone on duty on the ward. I also would like you to call Dr. Strauss to discuss whether you need an increase in your medication.

DALE: *(Long silence)* I can agree to those things. I was thinking about taking more medicine, but I don't like the side effects—my mouth gets so dry feeling and it upsets my stomach.

LINDA: I know that there are unpleasant reactions to more medicine, but I do think you need to consult with Dr. Strauss. Now today is Wednesday, I'd like to schedule an extra appointment for Friday, and would like you to bring in that surgical knife, or return it to where you took it from? What does that sound like to you?

DALE: Yes, I can come in on Friday. It will be good to see you before the weekend. Why do you want me to bring the knife in?

LINDA: It would symbolize your agreement to this contract, and I would feel more comfortable.

DALE: *(Long silence)* O.K. I'll bring the knife in on Friday.

LINDA: Now let's talk some about your next two days. What will you be doing with your time between now and Friday?

Immediately after this session, Linda went to find her supervisor. Early in her practice with Dale, the topic of suicide had come up. Linda's initial reaction was fear and she wanted Dale rehospitalized for her own protection. With the help of the other members of her team, her field instructor, and her practice class, Linda became familiar with the concept of *self-determination*. She began to realize that Dale had struggled for many years to reach her current level of independence. She was living by herself in her own apartment, was employed in a responsible position, and was now committing herself to a marital relationship. These behaviors warranted her being treated with respect as a competent adult individual. Infantilizing Dale by telling her she needed inpatient treatment could work to undo much of the progress made over these years. Linda's approach—asking Dale whether she needed to be hospitalized (*1)—both acknowledged the seriousness of her current situation but at the same time did not take control of Dale's life away from her.

On Friday Linda and Dale had the following exchange:

LINDA: I want to thank you for bringing the knife in. Tell me about your past two days.

DALE: Well I worked both nights, and then, as we talked about on Wednesday, I scheduled myself for some errands in the afternoons. I set several alarms and radios around the house so I would be sure to get up. I managed all right and didn't need to call anyone.

LINDA: What about your medication?

DALE: I didn't call Dr. Strauss, I decided I didn't need to do that right now. The wedding is coming up in a few weeks and I don't want to be increasing my dosage.

LINDA: What is your thinking about that?

DALE: Well, taking more medicine would mean I'm getting sick again, and I don't want to think that.

LINDA: I see. You know, I have trouble with my stomach, and there are various times I need to take medication to help me. I'm not always sure why it starts up at a particular time, but I do know that when it does I need the help of the medicine. It's usually time-limited. So please consider getting that help if you need it now. You know, this has got to be a very stressful time for you. Getting married, making that kind of commitment to someone, and facing that big wedding with your relatives coming and staying for a few days.
Do you still want to go through with your plans?

DALE: I was just thinking that the other night. *(With hesitancy)* Maybe I'm not ready for all of this just yet.

LINDA: You know, there are other ways to get out of getting married than getting crazy and needing to go back in the hospital or killing yourself.

DALE: *(Chuckles and then laughs)* I know. I love John and I want to go on with my life, have children, have a family. I'm probably as ready as I'll ever be.

LINDA: *(Smiles and laughs)* Probably so.

Throughout the interaction one can see that Linda treats Dale with respect and honesty. Linda commented:

....

It was hard for me to not try to control the situation for Dale. I wanted to make her safe in the hospital, yet of course, I knew that being an inpatient was not a full life. Dale had already had many years of that and was now opting for the real world, which involved dealing with tough decision making.

This was also one of my early cases as an M.S.W. student. I knew it was important for me to learn to not have people emotionally dependent on me, or I would have a very hard time being effective at this work and probably wouldn't last very long because my own emotional state would begin to crumble.

I began to realize that the ethic of self-determination was fundamental to the practice of social work. This business was about loving people enough to let them make their own choices, to educate them and coach them so they could handle their freedom of choice with responsibility and competence.

I did talk with Dr. Strauss, the medical head of the team. He agreed that Dale needed to call him if she wanted to discuss a change in medication.

....

Linda's established relationship with Dale had built a foundation of trust, the belief bonding we will discuss in Chapter 4. They already had an understanding together, reflected in the smooth flow of their communication. They were able to discuss Dale's thoughts of suicide and they reached a consensus on a reasonable course of action.

Practicing in a large organizational setting that employed many different professions, Linda had to work at *establishing her identity as a social worker,* distinguishing her role from those of the psychologist and psychiatrist, the occupational therapist, and the nurse clinician. She also had to establish identity via the V.A. hospital and the social work profession—was she primarily a civil servant with allegiance to the Veterans Administration, or was she primarily a social worker with her referent group orientations to other social workers?

With many years of perspective, Linda looks back to her first few months as an M.S.W. student and then as a beginning employee:

....

It was easier at first to clarify what social work was not and much harder to determine what it was. The nurse seemed very involved in handling medication, maintaining client records and supervising the nursing aides. The occupational therapist conducted activities and exercises with the patients. The psychologist and psychiatrist both did therapy; the psychologist was called on for testing of patients, and the psychiatrist stressed diagnostic categories and prescribed the medication.

After the first few months I began to see that the other staff turned to me for family background history and information about the patient's current social situation. I was the one who brought in an historical perspective on earlier social functioning—education, employment background, inter-personal relationships—and provided an update on current functioning—living arrangements, job and finances, social contacts.

My first job was at the V.A. and it wasn't until I had been an employee for about a year that I realized I had two roles at the hospital—I was a member of the Department of Social Work and an employee of the V.A. hospital, a federal civil servant. I suppose I became more identified with the social work profession—I joined NASW, attended local, state and national social work conferences, and read social work journals. I think working in a multidisciplinary setting was good for me—I had to sort through how my professional role and expertise were distinct from the other professional occupations. I also developed more respect for my own profession. I saw myself as a social worker providing services to clients, and the V.A. was the vehicle through which to do that. When I worked on inpatient units, the hospital environment was truly the patient's community, and I worked very hard at making that community a positive one for the patients.

....

Linda has touched on many of the important issues discussed in the literature about role theory and professionals in organizations. The expectations of others for Linda's role as a social worker helped her clarify the expectations she had for herself. Using Gouldner's typology introduced in Chapter 2, Linda would be considered a cosmopolitan. Relying on outer referent groups, she was highly committed to the development of her professional social work skills and did not define her work by her V.A. employment but rather saw the employment as a means of accomplishing her mission of service to her clients. She had a professional rather than a bureaucratic orientation.

Just like Gail, Linda had to address ongoing matters in the *organization* and issues of policy to function as a responsible social worker. At the time of her placement, inpatient services were favored over outpatient, which were barely developed. Hospitalizations of several years duration were not unusual, with little attention to follow-up services if the person were finally to get discharged.

Working with the staff psychiatrist and unit psychologist, Linda advocated for better resource allocation to outpatient services. Arguing for frequent and regular meetings with discharged patients and their families, she helped her building gradually develop a model outpatient program that resulted in fewer readmissions. Because staff could rely on a strong outpatient unit, hospital stays also became shorter, with less disruption in the lives of the patients.

Yet with the movement away from long-term psychiatric care in the 1980s and the closing of many institutional facilities, inpatient care became difficult to provide even for those patients in need of such services. In the following case we explore another problem resulting from changes in mental health policies, and examines *self-determination* and *duty to protect* along with *confidentiality* and *informed consent.*

Cara, a first-year M.S.W. student, was an African American in her late twenties who used a wheelchair because of a serious car accident some years ago. Having made some major life decisions after recovering from the accident, Cara was committed to working with people suffering from mental disabilities. Designated as one of the county's screening centers, the hospital-based Psychiatric Emergency Program where Cara was placed had some walk-in clients, but the majority were referred by police, jails, schools, families, and the hospital's emergency room. Cara covered a late afternoon and evening shift.

On arriving one Friday afternoon (emergencies do seem to occur on Friday afternoons—and the more alone and busy one is, the greater the emergency), she was informed that an adolescent female, Lenora, was brought in by her mother and they were waiting for an emergency evaluation. As is often the case with emergencies, Cara had no preliminary information. Through initial questioning, she learned that Lenora was 17 years old and currently lived with her 19-year-old brother, 43-year-old mother and 50-year-old stepfather in a small three-bedroom house located in a working-class neighborhood. The mother did office work and the stepfather was employed as a laborer.

Because Lenora was close to 18, the legal age for adulthood, Cara explained that she would meet alone first with Lenora and then with her mother, and they would then all three meet together. In Cara's agency it was customary practice to provide summaries of these initial client interviews. In the following summary Cara obtained information and described her interaction with Lenora during the first part of the interview:

....

Lenora informed me that she quit the school band, where she was drum major, and also the lead in the class play, because she felt she was not doing well in her classwork and wanted more time to study. She also stated she felt the kids in the band and the play did not like her anymore because she was bossy. She concurred with their view.

She continued that she hated high school and wanted to quit and go into the service. When I told her that she would need a high school diploma to be accepted, she appeared genuinely disappointed, as if she had never considered this.

She stated that she was stupid and ugly, that everyone in school thought so also, from teachers to classmates. She had no friends anymore, no current boyfriend, and only had one in the past. That relationship lasted eleven months and ended two years ago. She was not interested in having another relationship.

She shared that she had no problems getting along with her mother, but felt that her mother did not really understand her. She got along okay with her brother, although he was hardly ever home. Her stepfather was an ornament and never talked. She had little interaction with him, and did not sense any tension between him and her mother.

When I asked about her natural father I learned that he died when she was thirteen. Her parents had already been separated. He had come for visits with her and her brother, which she felt were regular and went okay. She was able to say that she missed him.

She reported a hospitalization following an overdose on aspirin four years before. She was hospitalized on a mental health unit for two days. She went for counseling for one month, and her mother was involved in that.

....

The exchange between Cara and Lenora then focused on Lenora's present situation:

....

Lenora sat on a couch directly in front of me, her arms braced to her side, one leg tucked under her, the other leg shaking with her foot on the floor. She was neat in appearance, dressed in jeans, sweater and high school jacket with her band letter on it. Her speech pattern was short and quick and her voice was somewhat high. She appeared a bit defiant. She had mixed racial heritage, appearing to be part White, part African American and part Hispanic.

I was already almost frantic as it became clear that Lenora was probably not in good shape and hospitalization would most likely be warranted. I found myself thinking about which of the psychiatrists were on duty, as I would need to consult with one of them. I tried to stay focused on Lenora.

....

Armed with this information Cara now proceeded with what the agency refers to as the mental status exam. Since this setting primarily addresses crisis situations, often potentially suicidal clients, they have established a routine set of questions—the mental status exam that Cara completes with Lenora. There were a series of questions she had to ask to determine the suicidal risk of the client.

CARA: I am now going to ask you some questions and I need you to be honest with me.

LENORA: Okay.

CARA: Have you been feeling anxious?

LENORA: No.

CARA: Have you been feeling depressed, a lack of energy and a lack of interest in things and people?

LENORA: Yes.

CARA: Are you feeling suicidal?

LENORA: Yes.

CARA: Have you thought about how you would do it?

LENORA: Yes.

CARA: How would you do it?

LENORA: Well, I first thought about taking an overdose, but I tried that a couple of years ago and it didn't work. Then I thought about hanging myself, but no. I thought about jumping off the roof of our house, but it is only one story high. I then thought of jumping off of an overpass over the highway in front of a tractor-trailer. I am sure that would work.

CARA: Do you plan on doing this?

LENORA: Yes, I cannot see any reason not to.

CARA: How have you been sleeping?

LENORA: I'm not sleeping. I lay there most of the night. I may fall asleep but it is not for very long.

CARA: What is going on in your mind when you are not sleeping?

LENORA: I think about a lot of things. How stupid and ugly I am. How nobody likes me at school. Tests I have coming up. It just goes on and on. Then I look at the clock and it is ten minutes later.

CARA: How long has this been going on?

LENORA: For about a month.

CARA: How about your appetite?

LENORA: I don't have one. I hardly ever eat, but that doesn't bother me because I have to lose weight.

CARA: Have you lost weight?

LENORA: Yes, about 13 pounds.

CARA: For how long have you not had an appetite?

LENORA: About a month.

CARA: How has your concentration been?

LENORA: Poor.

CARA: What do you enjoy doing?

LENORA: Nothing, really nothing anymore.

CARA: Have you been hearing any voices? Like somebody is talk-
          ing in the room, but nobody is there, or does the TV or
          radio have any special messages for you?

LENORA: No.

CARA: Is there anything strange going on? Something that you
          can't figure out?

LENORA: No.

CARA: Do you use any drugs or alcohol?

LENORA: No.

CARA: Is there anything else you might want to tell me or think I
          should know?

LENORA: No.

CARA: I want to let you know that I am very concerned about
          what you said about wanting to kill yourself. I am going to
          consult with the psychiatrist and other staff. Should we de-
          termine that you should be hospitalized, would you agree
          to sign yourself in?

LENORA: No, it is not normal to be in the hospital.

CARA: It's also not normal to be suicidal . . . it is dangerous.
          (Long pause) Would you be agreeable to taking some
          medication to help you with how you are feeling?

LENORA: No, it is not normal to take medication.

CARA: Okay. I am now going to talk to your mother. Is there any-
          thing that you told me that you would not want me to tell
          her?

LENORA: No.

Cara was determining Lenora's risk for suicide and finding out whether
or not she was actively psychotic. Unlike the previous exchange between
Linda and Dale, the professional relationship here had not yet been established. Cara was not asking open-ended questions (discussed in Chapter
6), she was looking for affirmative or negative responses so that she could
quickly assess this client's suicide risk. By the end of this time, Cara was
seriously considering that Lenora was at risk and in need of hospitalization.
The following exchange took place between Cara and Lenora's mother:

CARA: Please tell me how it is you brought Lenora in today.

MRS S: Well, she has talked about feeling depressed, about jumping
          off a bridge, saying she is stupid and ugly and nobody likes

her. She quit the band and the school play. She gave away her saxophone, saying she never wanted to play it again and this is something she used to take a lot of pride in.

CARA: Mrs. S, I'm very concerned about your daughter. She is talking about suicide and has a specific plan. I am going to consult with one of our psychiatrists about hospitalization for her.

MRS. S: Well that is why I brought her here, to get help.

CARA: At this point, she is refusing hospitalization and medication.

MRS. S. She is the type to not even take an aspirin.

CARA: Has anyone else in the family committed suicide?

MRS. S: No, her father was mentally unstable, but he would never go for help. He was verbally abusive. The holidays have always been a rough time for my daughter, so when she became quiet around Christmas I wasn't too concerned. But it has just gone on.

CARA: What is it about the holidays for her?

MRS. S: When she was 10, her father left us on Christmas morning. He woke the kids up at 2:00 A.M. so they could watch him leave. That's how he was.

CARA: Was your daughter ever sexually molested?

MRS. S: No, their father was verbally abusive. He was always telling her that she was stupid and ugly.

CARA: I notice that your daughter's complexion and features are different from your own. What was her father's race?

MRS. S: Partly African American and partly Hispanic. My current husband is White.

CARA: How do they relate together?

MRS. S: Well, he is strange. Nobody really relates to him. He comes home from work and sits in front of the T.V. and that's about it.

CARA: Thank you for sharing all this information in such a short time. It's helpful to know some of this in making our decision about hospitalization. Her situation is serious. If you took her home, would you be able to watch her 24 hours a day?

MRS. S: No, I work, no one is home during the day.

CARA: What we are dealing with is that at her age, you signing her in will not be enough. If she continues to refuse to sign herself in, we are talking about commitment against her will. What are your feelings about this?

MRS. S: I don't know what to say. I brought her here to get help.

CARA: I am going to consult now with other staff and the psychiatrist, who will need to sign the commitment if Lenora doesn't change her mind. Would you please join with your daughter now in the other room, and do try to talk with her about her options. It would be best if she signs herself in.

Cara shared her observations about this exchange:

....

Mrs. S came into the room humming, with a smile on her face and a cheerful hello. She sat on the couch next to me, leaning on the arm. She sat there smiling, waiting for me to start. I began to feel even more frantic. Her affect seemed so inappropriate to the situation. Wondering if she was uncomfortable with my being in a wheelchair, I realized I was angry at this woman and knew that this would not be useful in getting information from her. Also, we needed her help in getting the right help for Lenora. By the end of my questioning she appeared more serious and I began to feel less angry with her.

....

Cara was experiencing great anxiety. Her assessment was that Lenora was in need of hospitalization based on the following factors—Lenora had a specific plan for killing herself, she had had trouble eating and sleeping for over a month, she had isolated herself from former friends and activities. Cara now needed to proceed quickly within the organization to determine support for a commitment should Lenora and her mother not cooperate in a voluntary commitment. As Cara states:

....

I then went scurrying around to talk with two co-workers to be sure I didn't miss anything or forget to ask something. They were busy with their own cases. My field instructor was out with another case. I presented the information to the psychiatrist, Dr. W. She was busy on another commitment and asked me to briefly summarize the information. After a few comments from me, Dr. W. stated that Lenora could not be allowed to leave, and I was to offer her the opportunity to sign in or be committed against her will. I asked her if she would be willing to meet with Lenora, and she said only if I couldn't talk her into signing herself in. I called the unit and they had a female bed. I then alerted security, told them what was happening, so that if she attempted to elope, they could stop her.

....

In this situation, Lenora was clearly not able to be as self-determining as Dale in the previous example. Lenora was younger and more of a suicidal risk. One might also say, however, that she would not have shared that information with Cara if she did not want help—that she would not have talked about her suicide plans unless she wanted someone to take control and stop her. Framed this way, Lenora was self-determining. This stance, however, probably avoids the social worker's responsibility to make a decision about what the client needs at an urgent point in time. There are occasions where *the duty to protect life supersedes the ethical principle of self-determination*. As stated earlier, the principle has priority over the basics of life and prosperity providing that the client is not irrational. The ultimate dilemma, though, is the question of whether clients can be considered rational if they are actively suicidal.

Policy changes regarding involuntary commitment proceedings have made it extremely difficult to commit a person for mental health treatment against that person's wishes. In most states commitment laws favor individual rights, placing a three-day limit on commitment unless a panel of psychiatrists deem the individual an active danger to himself or others (this panel ruling is tough to obtain). So without an individual's agreement to seek help by commitment to inpatient care, family and professional staff are limited in their power to secure treatment. Fortunately in this situation, Lenora responded to the social worker's pressure and ultimately agreed to sign herself in.

The other interesting dilemma here concerns the ethical principles of *confidentiality* and *informed consent*. Because Lenora was a minor and a significant part of her life environment was her high school, Cara knew that for successful treatment the school needed to be involved. At the same time, Cara believed that Lenora did not want the school system to know that she needed hospitalization. Though Cara felt tempted to call the school for additional background information, she decided to wait and discuss this issue with Lenora. In building belief bonding, Cara hoped to gain Lenora's trust and permission to talk with school officials. And Cara remembered how important it was in her own hospitalization that staff discuss directly with her any plans to consult with other resources.

Again, because of the severity of Lenora's symptoms, Cara could consult with the school without technically violating the confidentiality ethic. Yet allowing herself to be guided by the spirit of the principle demonstrated her trust and respect for the client. Just as in Linda's dilemma in the previous case situation, Cara's choices were not clear-cut and she needed to consider the various options and possible consequences very carefully. When a client's life is not in jeopardy, it is best to follow the confidentiality guideline and obtain the client's permission before communicating with others about the client's situation. In this case, Lenora's mother also needed to be involved in decisions on notifying the school about Lenora's pending absence.

The principle of informed consent also posed challenges for Cara in this case. As we discussed earlier, the Federal Privacy Act of 1974 mandates that clients be advised about methods to be used in their treatment. While Cara was confident that Lenora needed hospitalization, she was also aware that *cure might not follow treatment.* Should Lenora be diagnosed with depression, several effective drugs were available, but they brought the risk of undesirable side effects. Advising Lenora and her mother about the poor success rates for the treatment of mental illness would not instill confidence and might jeopardize the commitment.

Though she was uneasy that it might make them change their minds about hospitalization, Cara did inform Lenora and her mother that Lenora needed the immediate protection afforded by the hospital. At the same time she acknowledged that more information was needed before a long term prognosis could be discussed and information obtained over the next days to develop the diagnosis would help in understanding Lenora's condition and provide direction for future treatment and prognosis.

Summary

All professions integrate practice skills with the theoretical knowledge and values on which the profession is based. Ethical codes emerge from values and concepts, and practice behaviors are a manifestation of these more general principles.

Serving to regulate the profession, ethical codes inform and restrain the decisions and behaviors of social workers. Focusing on the major ethical guides to social work practice, we have inquired into the dimensions of confidentiality, duty to warn, self-determination, and informed consent and have considered a set of priorities for value decisions provided by Reamer.

The inherent complexities in the practice of social work were illustrated in the case histories in which social workers Staci, Gail, Linda, and Cara struggled to integrate the concepts of the profession discussed in Chapter 2 with its ethical code. The enduring impact of policy is evident as many of the ethical guides have been modified through changes in policies and regulations. At the same time, problems appearing in practice are used to influence policy decisions. Successful social work interventions require knowledge about individual clients within the context of their larger community and environment, attention to the service delivery of the social service agency, and relevant policies and legislation as well as adherence to the values and ethics that guide professional social work practice.

The identity and subject matter of the social work profession are expressed in its major concepts and ethical code. Those ingredients that serve to make social work unique—its purpose and overall mission and the principles that guide the behaviors of its practitioners—provide the foundation on which to build the specific components of social work practice. Discussion of these components begins with the next chapter, which examines the professional relationship.

BIBLIOGRAPHY

Albers, D., & Morris, R. (1990). Conceptual problems in studying social workers' management of confidentiality. *Social Work, 35:* 4, 361–362.

Applebaum, P. S., & Roth, L. H. (1982). Competency to consent to research. *Archives of General Psychiatry, 39,* 951–958.

Bartlett, H. (1970). *The common base of social work practice.* New York: National Association of Social Workers.

Biestek, E. P., & Gehrig, C. C. (1978). *Client self-determination in social work: A fifty-year history.* Chicago: Loyola University Press.

Cohen, N. (1958). *Social work.* New York: Dryden.

Compton, B., & Galaway, B. (1979, 1989). *Social work processes.* Homewood, Ill.: Dorsey Press.

Curtis, P., & Lutkus, A. (1985). Client confidentiality in police social work settings. *Social Work, 30:* 4, 355–360.

Dean, R., & Rhodes, M. (1992). Ethical-Clinical tensions in clinical practice. *Social Work, 37:* 2, 128–134.

Federal Privacy Act of 1974. Public Law 93-579, enacted December 31, 1974 and effective September 27, 1975. *Federal Register,* Part V–VI (October 8, 1975).

Freedberg, S. (1989). Self-determination: Historical perspectives and effects on social work practice. *Social Work, 34:* 1, 33–38.

Gordon, W. (1965). Knowledge and value: Their distinction and relationship in clarifying social work practice. *Social Work, 10:* 3, 32–39.

Kopels, S., & Kagle, J. (1993). Do social workers have a duty to warn? *Social Service Review, 67:* 1, 101–126.

Kutchins, H. (1991). The fiduciary relationship: the legal basis for social workers' responsibility to clients. *Social Work, 36:* 2, 106–113.

Lewis, H. (1982). *The intellectual base of social work practice.* New York: Haworth Press.

Levy, C. (1983). Client self-determination. In A. Rosenblatt & D. Waldfogel (Eds.), *Handbook of clinical social work,* 904–919. San Francisco: Jossey Bass.

Lindenthal, J. J., Joran, T. J., Lentz, J. D., & Thomas, C. S. (1988). Social workers' management of confidentiality. *Social Work, 33,* 157–158.

Loewenberg, F., & Dolgoff, R. (1982). *Ethical decisions for social work practice.* Itasca, Ill.: Peacock.

MacDonald v. Clinger, N.Y.S.2d.801 (App. Div 1982).

Meyer, C. (1970). *Social work practice: A response to the urban crisis*. New York: Free Press.

Note. (1965). The social worker–client relationship and privileged communications. *Washington University Law Quarterly*, 362–395.

Perlman, H. H. (1965). Self-determination: Reality or illusion? *Social Service Review, 39:* 4, 410–421.

Pumphrey, M. (1959). *The teaching of values and ethics in social work education,* 40–49. New York: Council on Social Work Education.

Random House Dictionary. (1967). New York: Random House.

Reamer, F. (1983). Ethical dilemmas in social work practice. *Social Work, 28:* 1, 31–36.

Reamer, F. (1987). AIDS, social work and the duty to protect. *Social Work, 36:* 1, 56–60.

Richmond, M. (1899). *Friendly visiting among the poor*. New York: Macmillan.

Richmond, M. (1917). *Social diagnosis*. New York: Russell Sage.

Rozowsky, F. A. (1984). *Consent to treatment: A practical guide*. Boston: Little, Brown.

Schloendorff v. Society of New York Hospital, 105 N.E. 92 (1914).

Schwartz, G. (1989). Confidentiality revisited. *Social Work, 34:* 3, 223–226.

Siporin, M. (1975). *Introduction to social work practice*. New York: Macmillan.

Tarasoff v. Regents of University of California, 13 Cal3d. 177 (Sup. Ct. 1976).

Timms, N. (1964). *Social casework: Principles and practice*. London: Routledge & Kegan Paul.

Watkins, S. A. (1989). Confidentiality and privileged communications: Legal dilemma for family therapists. *Social Work, 34:* 2, 133–136.

Wilson, S. (1978). *Confidentiality in social work*. New York: Free Press.

CHAPTER ✢ FOUR

Human services . . . are to meet human needs in ways that deepen and fulfill the sense of social caring and responsibility between fellow human beings.

—*Helen Harris Perlman, 1979*

RELATIONSHIP:
THE BELIEF BONDING

"I use every opportunity to build the relationship. There needs to be the sense of a successful connection for both the worker and the client."

"I look for the little windows where I can say, 'Hi, I'm here, do you want to play together. . . . My client was like a kid in a grown-up suit. I tried to let her smell me a little."

"I see myself as a midwife of self. People have a sense of—this is me, that they may be only vaguely aware of. I help them gradually identify this self-hood and be empowered so that they can trust and use it."

"A client shared with me that what made the difference for her was that I'm just 'there.' I believed in her and gave her hope that she could get through the rough times, that she could do it."

These social workers are talking about the professional social work relationship they develop with their clients. The connection of a relationship provides astonishing power and extreme vulnerability, a sense of affinity or of alienation and hostility. Participating in a relationship invites exposure to the range of human emotions, including feelings of joy, fear, sexuality, anger, and sadness.

The practice of social work is initiated by this often volatile event, the meeting of one human being with another, a social worker and a client. Before any assessment or specific intervention has begun, a rapport must be developed that provides the means of interacting, talking, caring, communicating, and working together. Relationship can be understood as the *medium* or *vehicle* of practice. When a social worker and client engage in human contact with each other, they create a process through which the social work practice is generated.

The sharing that occurs in a relationship has a curative effect. The simple act of talking with another person is sometimes enough to create insights. Just being able to express one's troubles and problems to another person can feel good and can initiate intimacy and openness to other ideas and experiences. The business of social work is to have people "tell their stories," and relationship is the means by which the client's narration can begin.

Humbling and ennobling for social workers and clients alike, the social work relationship unfolds the layers of indomitable strength of spirit while exposing the vulnerability of the human body and mind. The extraordinary human capacity to feel and think and soar beyond the mundane is bounded by defenselessness in the face of disasters, both natural and self-inflicted. While control over life events is often elusive, the social work relationship can offer true comfort and support, a firm foundation for a person to build validation as a worthwhile human being.

Many issues impact on the helping relationship. Clients may feel powerless and exposed. Social workers can foster dependency out of misplaced notions about "taking care of" clients rather than "caring about" them. Uses of language and authority often place barriers between social workers and clients. One of the best complete treatments of these themes is *Things that Matter: Influences on Helping Relationships* (Rubenstein & Bloch, 1982).

In this chapter, we examine the social work relationship as an element of professional social work practice and consider it in contrast to other relationships. We also review the historical treatment of the social work relationship in the literature.

Social work relationship is defined and illustrated as a *process of belief bonding that has purpose and is unique*. Following the model used throughout this book, case material in which social workers discuss themselves and their practice is integrated with development of the principles. Case analyses explain the establishment of the social work relationship with *issues of difference* highlighted by the social workers. As part of the chapter conclusion, Additional Notes offers advice and suggestions specific to the student role, including general issues of authority and helping, identifying oneself as a student, getting started, client-worker differences, loss, and termination.

Throughout this chapter it is important to view social work practice as interactive and dynamic, as discussed in Chapter 1. The components of practice theory, like those of all theories, are interrelated. This chapter's focus on relationship as a concept makes it seem to be a discrete entity. The social worker–client relationship, however, does not take place in a vacuum. It is intricately linked with all the other elements in the complex process of practicing social work.

RELATIONSHIP IN THE SOCIAL WORK LITERATURE

The early and influential definitions of social casework reviewed in Chapter 1 all presented the social work relationship as a central concept in the practice of social work. Relationship was the first identified, and has been the most discussed, component of social work practice. This strong historical connection between social work and relationship can be understood by considering the origins of the profession.

Social work began with the model of the "friendly visitor" who gave alms to the poor and helped in the settlement of immigrants. Lacking theories to guide them in their work, these early helpers provided aid as they met and established a relationship with those in need. Referring to this relationship between the friendly visitor and the family being helped, Mary Richmond was the earliest writer to observe that there was more to the charity work than direct aid: "Friendly visiting means intimate and continuous knowledge of and sympathy with a poor family's joys, sorrows, opinions, feelings, and entire outlook upon life" (1899, p. 80).

In her acknowledgment of relationship as an integral part of the social work practice, Richmond laid the foundation of social work as a profession. In 1917, she published *Social Diagnosis*, the first attempt to formulate in a book the methods and techniques of social casework. Based on cases from children's agencies and medical and family settings, the book developed casework as a discipline that studies people and their problems. Richmond suggested that the relationship functioned as "mind over mind" and was influential in helping clients further their own best interests (1922, p. 102).

As described in Chapter 1, Richmond was important in the development of the charity organization societies (COS) active during the late 1800s and early 1900s. The goal of these societies was to make almsgiving scientific, and they pushed for "not alms but a friend" to provide "expert personal services." This way of viewing charity help also served to acknowledge the importance of relationship. The contact with the friendly visitor was seen as a significant aspect of the help along with financial aid.

Social work came to be taught in a university program in the early 1900s, when Walter Wilcox of Cornell University pushed for the linking of universities and the charity organization societies to strengthen the theoretical and scientific base of charity work. The COS were to serve as sociological laboratories in the belief that the theoretical input from the universities joined with practice from the field would provide a more efficient and scientific approach to the elimination of poverty. Even now, however, issues of integrating practice and theory and the question of whether social work practice is more science or more art have still not been resolved.

Another continuing tension in the profession, especially among academics, arises out of attempts to identify common social work skills and unify social work as a single calling. By the 1920s, concern about lack of unity in the social work profession prompted the formation of the Milford Conference, named after a meeting in Milford, Pennsylvania, of executives and board members from national social work organizations. The conference attempted to identify universal social work skills and provide some cohesion to the profession of social work, which did not seem to have a clear focus. One Milford Conference report stressed the importance of relationship: "The flesh and blood is in the dynamic relationship between the social caseworker and the client, child or foster parent; the interplay of personalities through which the individual is assisted to desire and achieve the fullest possible development of his personality" (*Social Casework—Generic and Specific*, 1929, p. 29).

Other conference papers during this period continued to address the social work relationship, acknowledging the importance of relationship to treatment: "the success of any except a fool-proof plan (and of such, how many are there?) may be made or marred by the relationship between client and visitor, and . . . more and more in the medium of the interplay the plans for the family evolve" (Clow, 1925, p. 272). Milford Conference reports also recognized the importance of the worker's contribution to the relationship. "The interplay of her [the caseworker's] personality and her clients forms the medium of her work and sets in operation the casework process of disintegrating the present situation for the purpose of reintegrating it on a new and better level" (Dexter, 1926, pp. 436–442).

This theme continues to be sounded in later writers. Helen Harris Perlman, for example, states that relationship is "an essential accompanying condition, because it is the nourisher and mover of the human being's wish and will to use the resources provided and the powers within himself to fulfill his personal and social well-being" (Perlman, 1979, p. 11). Kasius also emphasizes the importance of the relationship to social work practice: "Using function, structure and time the primary instrument of the helping process is the professional relationship between the helping person [caseworker] and the client" (1950, p. 28).

Attachment in Relationship

In the 1930s and 1940s, Freudian theory strongly influenced the field of social casework. An early work in this area is *Transference in Casework* (Sterba, Lyndon, & Katz, 1949). The book's title reflects the fact that transference and countertransference became important concepts in the practice of social work during this time. Freud developed the term *transference* to identify repetitive relational patterns exhibited by his patients. He determined these to be the result of an unconscious transfer of early experiences to later objects, including their analysts. Accordingly, patients may respond to the analyst as they would respond to a parent figure. Conversely, *countertransference* is the process in which the analyst relates to the patient as to an earlier figure in his or her own life. In other words, transference refers to the patient's patterns, countertransference to the therapist's patterns.

According to psychoanalytic theory, the analyst employs the transference to help patients gradually break down their defenses. Patients relate to the analyst as they would to a parent figure as preparation for exploring the deep layers of their unconscious. In order to work effectively with their patients' transference, analysts themselves must work through their own countertransference in their own analytic training.

These concepts, though central to psychoanalysis, are not as useful in the practice of social work. It is true that social workers often have to help clients address early experiences in their lives. The thrust of social work, however, is not on revealing layers of the unconscious. Rather, the past is examined so that the client can better understand the present in order to change the future.

A more useful theoretical framework for social work is derived from the concepts of *case theory* and *practitioner observation*. The case theory is the worker's explanation of the client's behaviors and is developed during the assessment. If relational patterns appear to be part of the client's problem, the worker can include hypotheses in the case theory to explain these patterns. In practitioner observation, the worker examines his or her own social work practice for signs of overidentification with a particular client or of confusing clients with figures from his or her own past. These concepts are much broader than transference and countertransference and fit better with the social work purpose, which is to improve social functioning. Case theory will be discussed in great detail in Chapter 5, and practitioner observation will be examined in Chapter 7.

SOCIAL WORK RELATIONSHIP DEFINED

The benefits obtained through the helping relationship accrue from the formation of human bonding and are maximized with a clear sense of purpose and direction. The social work relationship is defined in this book as

 A belief bonding formed between the social worker and client, through which the client develops self-worth and trust in the competence of the social worker and establishes belief that the social worker can help initiate change in the client's circumstances. The social work relationship has as its purpose to achieve specific ends determined by the social worker's case theory of the assessment.

Each relationship is unique, structured by boundaries and reflecting the function of the social work agency. Allowing for the enactment of the social work practice, relationship is the medium for social worker and client to connect together in an intimate journey and can be accompanied by sharing of feelings and the development of affection and intimacy. Changing over

time, the social work relationship is targeted to helping the client create change of self and of circumstances.

Often, clients who see social workers have not been effective in meeting their basic life needs of being accepted, receiving love and intimacy, and experiencing respect. They have either had very little exposure to close and meaningful interactions or have had unpleasant or even harmful relations with others. A caring relationship, one that gives a message of "I am interested in you, I accept you, you are important," is in and of itself a significant contribution of social work practice.

Just as an old motto in medical practice—"comfort always, cure rarely" —is returning to the fore, care as cure acknowledges the critical importance of the caring relationship to social work practice. Despite the high technology of modern medical practice, studies have related positive attitudes and a belief in healing to the successful treatment of illness. Links are being examined between emotional states and the ability of the immune system to fight disease. A 1990 study conducted at Stanford University found that women with breast cancer participating in support groups lived an average of eighteen months longer than predicted by their medical regimes. Accordingly, physicians are now being urged to address both the psychological and physical realms with their patients and are admonished that failure to recognize emotional distress neglects half the treatment (Simon and VonKorff, 1991).

While social workers have long recognized the inherent value of the helping relationship, they have also tended to be critical of its lack of scientific rigor and researchability. Although the techniques available to social workers are vulnerable to criticism for being "soft"—they cannot be tested in laboratory experiments—this does not mean that these methods lack meaning or power. Delegitimized by the push to quantification, relationship must be accorded its rightful claim in the social work process. The early work on empathy by Rogers (1951) and recent studies on the therapeutic alliance by Luborsky (1993) support renewed attention to the richness and significance of relationship.

Relationship as Belief Bonding

Gordon Hamilton was one of the first to discuss the social work relationship as a bonding: "All human relationships imply a bond, but in any treatment relationship there is a strong affective bond. . . . Treatment starts . . . only when mutual confidence is established, only when the client accepts your interest in him and conversely feels an interest in you. . . . If, and only if, some sort of rapport is established, he becomes your client" (1940, pp. 189–190).

Relationship is presented in these pages as a belief bonding (Hardcastle, 1988). The worker *and* the client each need to believe that the worker has something applicable for the client, that the worker is competent, and that the client is worthwhile and has the capacities to change the presented situation. Polansky and Kounin concur that "important in the . . . relationship is the client's trust in the worker's competence and . . . trust in the worker's good will" (1956, p. 239). Forming the crux of most professional relationships, this bonding is a necessary, though not sufficient, condition for the accomplishment of the client's goals and objectives.

To use an analogy, successful teachers generally bond with their students. The teacher and the students share a belief that the teacher knows the material and can teach it. Likewise, the teacher and students also believe that the students are educable and that they can learn the material being taught. Being liked by students is insufficient and may be only minimally necessary to being a good teacher; likewise, having knowledge about the material is necessary, though not sufficient, to teach successfully.

What is necessary and sufficient is the bonding between teacher and students (the shared belief that the teacher is knowledgeable and that the student is educable and has the capacity to grasp the material), combined with the teacher's knowledge of the material and mastery in the technology of teaching it, along with the students' capacities to learn the material. A successful bonding, is partly dependent on the teacher's creation of an environment conducive to learning and presentation of the material in such a way that students learn.

Similarly, in social work practice, the successful social worker develops a bonding with clients in which both social worker and client believe that the worker is competent, can practice social work, and has knowledge about the problems presented by the client. Additionally, each believes that the client is worthwhile and has the capacity to change. Whether or not the client likes the social worker is not at issue and may be important only to the extent that it initially allows for the formation of the bonding. Moreover, the social worker must not only be regarded as an expert but must actually possess the expertise—have the knowledge and be able to get whatever other information is deemed necessary to help this client. The social worker must have knowledge about the problem being presented by the client, but this in itself is not a sufficient condition for the practice to be effective.

Necessary *and* sufficient conditions include the social worker's knowledgeability accompanied by abilities to utilize and implement that knowledge in an environment conducive to client change. In other words, the practice must be structured and the material presented in such a way that the client can use it. Knowledge of social work practice components— including assessment, communication methods and skills, practitioner observation, and planning and implementation of the intervention—impact on the success of the practice. The client must have more than a belief in the social worker's and his or her own capacities. For a successful outcome, the client must also possess the abilities and resources necessary to achieve the goals and objectives.

The social worker has the responsibility of establishing belief bonding with clients. The three main components of belief bonding are: belief in the social worker's competence, belief in the client's capacity to incorporate a change in the situation, and belief in the client's worthiness.

Belief in the Worker's Competence

A central part of belief bonding is communicating to clients the social worker's own sense of self-confidence in his or her ability to help the client. Both social workers *and* clients need to believe that the worker is capable of helping. Though the social worker may not feel like an authority in every situation, the worker's presence should convey a strong and positive message to the client of *I can help you.*

This does not mean that the social worker has a "cure" for the client or answers to all the client's questions. Ready solutions to the complex problems clients present are not easily available, but social workers do need to trust in their own ability to practice their vocation and clients need to share in this trust. We have all met with professionals who are not comfortable in their role. They have to use their title, the trappings of their office, or facial expressions and mannerisms to impress us with their authority. Behaving this way renders the social worker an authority in image only. The professional who can relate to clients as one human being to another, who is comfortable with the role, who feels expert without feeling superior, is the one who instills confidence in the client.

Approaching their clients with a strong sense of self-esteem, social workers should expect respect and recognition for their knowledge and expertise. Presenting oneself as a model of a good social worker—as one who knows how to conduct this business—is an essential ingredient of the social work practice.

Belief in the Client's Capacity to Incorporate Change

Besides believing in the social worker's professional competence, workers *and* clients also need to have a belief in the client's capacity to change. Just as patients diagnosed with cancer are told that their belief in the cancer treatment can positively influence their ability to survive the disease, clients receiving social work services need to feel empowered that their situation can be improved. The social worker's message here is: *You can do something about yourself and your situation. I believe in your capacity to incorporate change.*

One must not, however, expect clients to have a clear sense of the nature of their problem. Though they may be hurting and aware that something is "not right," they may not know what they want changed. That is, in fact, why they are coming to see the social worker! It is the social worker's task to cultivate a sense that things can be different, that the client is capable of creating change in personal behaviors or perceptions or in external events.

There are also occasions where it is necessary for the social worker to initiate the change. This might involve developing linkages with community and other resources or clarifying options. Though the social worker must convey the belief that the client can maneuver through the change on his or her own, sometimes the vision and generation of new possibilities may need to be the social worker's contribution.

Belief in the Client's Worthiness

Social workers *and* clients must also have a belief in the client's worth as a person. The relationship furthers in clients a sense of self-esteem, including the conviction *I deserve to be helped, I merit change and improvement in my situation*. The social worker's task is to convey respect and interest in the client with such messages as *You are an important person, I respect you, I am committed to you*.

Most relationships do not incorporate "unconditional acceptance," in which participants are loved and accepted just for being themselves. Early in life, from the time babies begin to smile and respond to their environment, the message is clear that only certain behaviors will be recognized and rewarded. The social work relationship, however, *is* an unconditional acceptance, a determined commitment by the social worker to the client. Some clients have engaged in destructive and abusive acts, either to themselves or to others. Yet the social worker has to separate individual actions from the person who commits them. While social workers can be critical of what a client has or has not done, they must never be disdainful of the client as a human being.

Like the larger population, all social workers are not nurturing, nor do they all possess especially good social skills. Furthermore, they will not have personal experience with all the problems their clients bring to them. Whether social workers exude warmth and an ease at meeting people or are more reserved and perhaps distant is not relevant, however, just as personal familiarity with client problems is not pertinent to the provision of expert help. What is important is that social workers convey attention and respect, express their compassion for and interest in the client, and are willing to acquire the knowledge necessary to help with the client's problem. From the time of Plato, we haven't expected judges to learn about evil from their own experience, nor have we wanted physicians to suffer the ailments they treat. Knowledge is the guide, not personal experience. The crucial factor in the social work relationship is letting the clients know that the social worker is interested in them, wants to learn more about them, and can help them.

The social work Code of Ethics includes an admonishment that social workers must not exploit relationships with clients and must "serve clients with devotion, loyalty, determination, and the maximum application of professional skill and competence" (1990, p. 4).

Relationship is the formation of a belief bonding between the social worker and the client through which the client develops self-worth and trust in the competence of the social worker and establishes belief that the social worker can help initiate change in the client's circumstances.

In the following case history we examine how a social worker, Jim, developed belief bonding with a client. But first, as we will for all the social workers presented in these chapters, we must learn about Jim's own beliefs and about the factors that shaped him as a social worker, including physical attributes. These personal traits help present the social workers as real people and assist us in appreciating the remarkable diversity among social work practitioners.

Jim was a 47-year-old White social worker who had been practicing social work for over twenty years. Born during World War II, he grew up on a farm along the German border. Issues of war and peace, Jim believed, were influential in his development. Forces of discord and harmony and the alleviation of human suffering continued to hold his attention as he practiced with clients. Jim comments: "My schooling in Switzerland helped me to develop a comprehensive view of people, to think about the human condition, and to feel responsible for doing something to improve it. My practice is influenced by my spiritual life—what is a human being, who am I, why am I here—these are my private questions. They influence in the broadest sense how I look at people."

Jim was confident that he could use his experiences to facilitate clients' engagement in a spiritual journey of exploration—to discover their place in the world. Of small build, Jim captured his audience with an attentive gaze, serious manner, and interesting accent.

Employed at a family service agency, he commented about his work: "I like that I work in an agency. Our clients are treated equally, and my own livelihood is not dependent on whether each client can pay. Though I would like to see social workers be paid more, my existence is minimally guaranteed. Every person I see, I feel privileged to be part of that person's life, and to help that person understand life and move on with less conflict and more clarity."

The client, John, was White, had been employed as a laborer since leaving high school at the age of 17, and currently earned a salary in the upper teens. His first wife left him with their daughter, and his relationship with his girlfriend, Jan (he and his daughter lived in the girlfriend's house), was not satisfactory. He was soft spoken and in his mid-twenties. This was his second session with Jim.

> JIM: It doesn't sound like your relationship with Jan is going well. I would like to see you both together. Do you think that she would come in with you?

JOHN: *(Hesitatingly)* I don't know. I don't even know how to put it to her. I have a hard time wording things.

*1 JIM: You have been articulate and clear when we talk together. You are capable of clear communication. I understand that you have difficulty in communicating clearly with Jan. We will work on changing that.

JOHN: Well, if she comes in with me, I don't want us to sit here and get mad at each other. When she gets mad, I get mad.

*2 JIM: What's wrong with you getting mad? I can handle you both being mad at each other. Just leave it up to me. I will be doing the conducting.

JOHN: *(Smiles)* She thinks I have an "attitude," that I am the one who needs help. I do get angry with her.

*3 JIM: Well, you do have problems in that relationship. In other areas of your life you are not having problems. You are a good father—many fathers would not do all that you do. You take your daughter to school, to the babysitter, you feed her, buy her things, take her to see her grandparents, talk to the school about how she is doing—you are a very involved father. I don't take these things for granted. You are a hard worker, you pay your bills.

JOHN: I have stress at the job, but I don't get angry there.

*4 JIM: Sure, you are pleased with how you handle things there. Look, this is what I see. You come in here, you want to improve things. Some guys would say, "I'm not going to talk to any counselor." I see that you think about things, you think about the past and how you can change mistakes. I see you as a thoughtful guy and capable of changing your situation with Jan.

JOHN: She has said that if we separate we can still see each other. She has the same confusions that I have.

JIM: You have been together for three years. A lot of it has been good. It is worthwhile to look at it and see what you can do. You need to give her the chance to come in and talk with you about what is happening.

JOHN: I don't know whether she is willing to come in here. How do I put this to her?

JIM: You can say to her that you would like her to come with you, that you would like to understand her better. Your relationship is not as good as it once was, and you want to see if you can improve it.

Let us now discuss how Jim formed the belief bonding with John. The exchange given here was the third time that Jim and John met together. At *1 and *4, the worker demonstrated *belief in the client's competence and ability to change* the way he related to Jan. Jim affirmed John's abilities directly by telling him he was capable and acknowledged the strengths that John had demonstrated in his other relationships.

At *3, Jim developed *belief in the client's worthiness*. He identifies the areas of strength in the client's life. Jim treated John as a valued person and pointed out the good qualities John tended to dismiss in himself.

Jim discussed his relationship with John:

....

My belief in others is authentic. I believe that they can master and overcome their issues. I am what I am, the clients are who they are—now where do we want to go?

John has a serious problem with trust. His self-image has been challenged. He was raised by a very critical father. He married at a young age, put a lot into that relationship, and, one day, found her in their bed with another man. That really shook him up.

Shortly after this experience with his wife, John met his current girlfriend, Jan. He is now feeling that she is distancing from him. He is getting another message that he is not okay. His sense of self is shaky. He wonders what is wrong with him that he cannot keep a woman. He questions whether he can love, and whether others can love him.

I can help John with his sense of self-esteem and his self-confidence. I believe in John, and I convey that belief to him. I see it as my responsibility to help John believe in his own capacities and to trust his worthiness as a person. John has had custody of his daughter since his divorce. He does well as a father, he is a sincere, though frightened guy, who doesn't feel very competent. A General Education Development (GED) and some career planning might also be down the road in my work with him.

....

The social worker also presents himself as *a competent helper*. At *2 Jim told the client that he could handle seeing the client and girlfriend together, that he, the worker, would be in charge. At *4 he was forthright about sizing up the situation, letting the client know directly what he saw and thought about what the client described. This assertiveness let the client know that he, the social worker, had command of the situation.

Jim commented on his belief in his own competence:

....

I have dealt with my own difficult questions and struggles in life. I feel comfortable that I don't have all the answers, knowing that answers are not what is needed to do this work. Bringing a sense of my own self as a person, I have strength and courage to help people ask questions and embark on a journey of finding themselves. Seeing myself as a midwife of self, I am like a guide.

....

Jim also addressed his approach to *difference:*

....

I got into social work later in life, having started out in business and then traveling extensively through the Mideast and became interested in family therapy after moving to the United States. Being a foreigner, I was constantly reminded of my difference—my clients sounded different from me and we didn't share the same cultural backgrounds. Having tried different religions and exposed myself to different cultures I am now settled on a spiritual outlook that works for me. It's very clear, however, that my answers don't work for my clients—they need to find their answers in response to their own questions.

I believe my clients experience me as accepting of them, of who they are, and the dreams they have for themselves. There is something deeper than sharing a common cultural or spiritual heritage, and that is—one human being interacting with another—it is at that level that I try to relate with my clients.

....

Relationship is the formation of a belief bonding between the social worker and the client, through which the client develops self-worth and trust in the competence of the social worker and establishes belief that the social worker can help initiate change in the client's circumstances.

In the next case history, the social worker, Felicia, demonstrated the formation of belief bonding with an 11-year-old boy, George, who was just placed in emergency foster care. Felicia knew very little about George other than that he was White, this was his first contact with the child welfare system, and his teacher at school reported possible abuse. While Jim met with John for the third time and planned for at least ten weeks of sessions, Felicia came together with George out of a crisis situation and might only meet with him for one other session. Whether there is a single contact or sessions over several years, in its development of trust and confidence belief bonding is still central to the effectiveness of the practice.

In her mid-forties and White, Felicia practiced in child welfare since the completion of her M.S.W. eighteen years before. As a supervisor with a county department of human resources, she directed the initial course of treatment on new cases and assigned the social worker who would continue with the case. Felicia grew up in a small town in the Midwest where houses were large, land was ample, and lots of other kids were always around for play. She remembered one of the boys in the group often showed up with bangs and bruises. Though it was not unusual for boys to be rowdy and get into lots of scrapes, something about this boy had made Felicia uneasy. Feeling that he was hurt, she had wanted to help him but never knew what to do or whether even to talk with anyone about her worries.

Child abuse, during Felicia's youth, was not yet recognized as a problem. What happened between parents and their children was considered private business. Moreover, some of what today is accepted as child abuse was in those years considered strong parental supervision. Though as an adult Felicia still got that old discomfort from some of the cases handled by her agency, she believed she now knew what to do. Though the nature of her work could make her feel uncomfortable, she felt sustained by her conviction that what she did was important and necessary.

Felicia was of somewhat stocky build and average height. Even though she worked in child welfare, a traditional and highly bureaucratic setting, in her personal life she was rather nontraditional. Never having married, she had many friends, both gays and straights, liked living in an urban area, and was a devotee of avant-garde art.

On her first meeting with George, Felicia greeted him in the home of the foster family on the day after his placement.

*1 FELICIA: Hello, George, I'd like to tell you who I am. My name is Felicia Carter and I work with the county. I've come to talk with you and to give you information about what's happening in your life now and to the people you care about.

*2   Do you have any questions about who I am?

    GEORGE: No, not really. But I'm feeling confused about what's happening.

*3 FELICIA: I can understand that. Right now you are staying with a family who specializes in having children live with them who can't be with their own families. It's my understanding—tell me if I'm wrong—that your teacher got alarmed when you got to school yesterday as she noticed some bruises on your arm. She sent you to the nurse who found bruises on other parts of your body. Next thing you probably knew, you were being taken to this foster family.

*4   Is that about right?

    GEORGE: Yeah, just about.

*5 FELICIA: Let me explain why this is happening. The government has concern for the safety of children; in fact, until you are 18, the County Welfare Department is responsible to help you if you are in an unsafe home environment. After our office received the call from your school nurse, one of our workers visited your house and found your Mom to be pretty drunk.

GEORGE: Well, she drinks pretty often.

*6 FELICIA: In light of the bruises and her being drunk, we had serious concerns for your safety. This is a legal situation— we had to bring this information before a judge—and she gave us the authority to temporarily place you with this foster family.

*7   Any questions about what I have said so far?

GEORGE: Well I don't do things right, I do things and don't think, then my Mom gets angry with me. Did someone stay with her last night?

*8 FELICIA: We are going to be talking with you, and with your Mom, about how you and she got along. It sounds like you are thinking that you caused your Mom to hit you. We have serious concerns about your bruises and want to see if we can make things different and better for both of you. For today, however, I want to get more information from you and consider some possible plans. How did things go for you last night at the Millers?

GEORGE: Well, pretty good. It felt like a hotel—it was nice, not really like home.

*9 FELICIA: What would you like to have happen now?

GEORGE: (Long pause) It might be nice if I could live with my Dad.

Unlike Jim in the previous example, George did not willingly come to see the social worker but was legally required to receive Felicia's help. In working with nonvoluntary clients, or clients who have not directly asked for social work services, it is particularly important that social workers clarify their role and legal obligations to the client. Felicia provided George with this information and in doing so helped establish her belief bonding with him.

At *1, *3 and *5, Felicia put herself forward as a *competent helper*. Confident as the authority, she demonstrated experience and knowledge in the matters confronting George. Informing him about who she was, her role, and how she came to be seeing him, her manner was one that conveyed comfort with herself and with what she was doing, even though the circumstances themselves were not always comforting.

Very evident in this exchange was Felicia's respect for George as a *worthwhile person*. Throughout her conversation with him she directly asked him (*2, *4, *7) whether he had any questions of her. Though George was only 11, she let him know that it was important to her that he understand

and follow her presentation of information. At *6 she specifically stated that there were concerns for him and his safety.

While at *8 Felicia commented that they would be working on *change* for both his mother and him, in asking George, at *9, what he would like to happen next, she indicated that he had some say over the future—that he was an active part of the change process. She, or other workers, would have to obtain more information from George and do some checking about his father as they considered future options.

Felicia commented on the *differences* between George and herself:

....

Being of the same race, we are both White, seems to be the only thing that is not different about George and myself. I am female, grew up in the rural Midwest, and am of a totally different generation. George is male, from a poverty-ridden urban city in the Northeast, and easily young enough to be my son. I let George know that I can help him, not based on our similarities or differences, but based on my knowledge about his problem and that I care about and want to help him make things different in his life.

....

Relationship Has Purpose and Is Unique

Like other relationships, the social work relationship is a complex, unique, and idiosyncratic interaction. Yet it is different from other relationships in that it is intentional. The social worker plans and crafts the relationship needed to help a given client in a given situation.

Within the social work relationship the worker and the client come together with different roles and functions. Whereas mutuality may be a component in other relationships, in the social work relationship the mutuality lies in determining and pursuing the client's journey. The social worker is "at work," assessing and communicating to determine who the client is, what the client's situation is, and how the client can benefit from social work help. Clients, however, are not passive recipients of a particular treatment or cure. The subject matter is clients' navigation of their biological, psychological, and social environments, and they actively provide the information that helps define the problem. Clients are central to the work of bringing about change.

The relationship, just as the other elements of practice, is unique to each worker and client and changes over time. Chapter 5 will present the social worker's understanding of the case as the case theory, which continually modifies the case objectives. In responding to the case theory and case objectives, the relationship shifts. Alterations in the client and the client's situation, and in the social worker's experience and knowledge also occasion change in the social work relationship. Responding to crisis situations, the relationship may, in fact, differ somewhat in each session. For example, a relationship focusing on specific goals of job training may have to diverge temporarily if the client has been evicted from her home.

 The social work relationship has as its purpose to achieve specific ends determined by the social worker's case theory of the assessment. Each relationship is unique, structured by boundaries and reflecting the function of the social work agency. Changing over time it is targeted to create change.

These elements of relationships as purposeful and unique are defined and discussed by social workers in individual case histories. We again include *issues of difference* in the case presentations and provide descriptions about the social workers along with their interests and cultural backgrounds.

Alleviating the client's presenting problem in social functioning forms the basis on which the worker-client relationship is established. Because the practice is targeted to the concerns that have brought the social worker and the client together, often its objectives are unclear at the outset. The relationship is used to help identify those objectives, attain them, and plan for new goals and objectives.

The purpose of social work practice, however, is *not* solely to have a relationship with a client. *Relationship is not an end in itself.* Nevertheless, elements of relationship may be included in goals for a client, such as learning to trust or the development of intimacy. At times, the social work relationship can serve as a model for the client in acquiring those skills. If these are the goals, however, the client will need to learn how to get these needs met with people other than the social worker. While relationship itself is not a sufficient goal, it is often a contributing factor in the helping process.

Negotiated as a planned interaction, the relationship is the adhesive that holds the practice together in the process of change. The relationship reflects the different stages and levels of treatment enacted between the social worker and the client. Goals are often modified and sometimes entirely new directions are plotted, casting the relationship into a new form and purpose.

Relationship Is Shaped by the Assessment

Assessment of the client and the client's situation determines the purpose of the relationship. As the social worker's case theory, *assessment* is the stated understanding of the client and the client's problem. Based on that conception, the social worker makes decisions about client needs and goals and gears the relationship to fulfill them.

The worker-client relationship is continually formed and shaped by the assessment.

Not relating to the client as just one person to another, the social worker is responsible for shaping the relationship based on professional judgment about the client's specific relationship needs. This assessment includes clarification about the client's experiences with relationships, knowledge about recent relationships, and information about past relationship successes and failures. These considerations are then used to determine the kind of relationship with the most potential for helping the client to change.

One client may be in need of nurturing and closeness, another may need a more distant and cool relationship. Some may need a mixture of both at different points within the same meeting. In making these determinations, the social worker takes into account the nature and duration of the presenting problem, the client's history and current functioning, the objectives for the practice, and other factors that will be discussed in Chapter 5.

Boundaries Structure the Relationship

Each relationship is distinguished by its boundaries, which are the form or pattern of interaction between client and worker. Boundaries provide the shape to each relationship and are visible through verbal and nonverbal cues, including such factors as use of titles, vocabulary, intensity of emotion, voice tone, seating, and body movement. Frequency and location of sessions also help set boundaries. Organizing the amount and flow of contact between social worker and client, boundaries structure the foundation of the relationship.

Social workers may opt for fluid boundaries with some clients, providing ample opportunity for interaction within and outside scheduled sessions. With others, they may decide on more rigid boundaries, constraining the interaction. For some clients, calls between sessions and adding sessions may be appropriate, while social workers may insist on restricting contact with other clients to regularly specified times. There also may be differences in form of address (formal or informal) and the amount of material allowed for discussion that doesn't relate directly to the specified ends.

Based on the case theory, the social worker decides on the boundaries that will be most useful to a specific client. If the client experiences difficulty in maintaining a self-identity and becomes unduly dependent on others, the relationship may be used to model separateness. Maintenance of formal and rigid lines within the social work relationship can teach a client to manage closeness appropriately while retaining autonomy. Clients who are not voluntarily seeing the social worker and are angry may benefit at first from a more formal relationship that respects their wish for distance. Involuntary clients may include abusive parents, delinquent adolescents, nursing home patients, and persons committed to state institutions. Cues communicated by the client can inform the social worker's decisions about boundaries. This subject will be covered in Chapter 6.

The Agency Impacts on the Relationship

The worker-client relationship formed is also determined by the employing agency. In an agency that focuses on direct services, such as the Salvation Army or the Red Cross, the relationship will be structured to meet the objectives of providing direct aid. In a family service agency, in contrast, the relationship will reflect the expectations and responsibilities of talking with the client and enhancing insight to create change. Emerging from and congruent with the worker's function, the relationship reflects the purpose and mission of the agency.

In other subtle ways, the setting of the practice can have an impact on the relationship. Workers in a private practice situation need to negotiate fees, and in their discussions with clients they must balance the worth of their time with the ability of clients to pay. Here direct confrontation that the client is paying for a service occurs in the relationship. In large bureaucratic settings, fees may not be discussed by social workers, but they usually have many more forms and reports to complete and will consequently need to spend time during sessions acquiring the necessary information.

Agencies also have their own milieu or climate, often with unwritten codes about acceptable behaviors with clients. Friendly, more informal contacts are encouraged by some agencies, with workers and clients on a first-name basis and coffee available in the waiting room. On the other end of the spectrum are highly formalized settings with little opportunity for interaction outside established roles.

Each Relationship Is Unique to This Worker and This Client and Changes over Time

One of the social worker's major tasks is to determine the nature of the relationship each client requires at a given point in time. Social work relationships are structured to the needs and situation of the client, and each client is unique. At the outset of the relationship, the worker begins to formulate judgments about the type of relationship needed with the client. Perpetually modified by new information and changes in the client, the assessment continues to influence variations in the ongoing relationship. At later stages in the practice, the relationship may appear very different than it was initially. Assessment by the social worker and the idiosyncratic interaction of a given worker with a given client result in a specific and unique worker-client relationship at different points in time.

We see a purposeful and unique relationship demonstrated between Betty, the social worker, and her client, Sam. Sam initiated treatment with Betty eight years before, when he first came out as a homosexual at the age of 38. At that time, he needed help in telling his wife and family of his homosexuality and in dealing with his subsequent divorce and ongoing relationship with his children. Sam saw Betty on and off for treatment over the years, as needed. He started seeing her regularly for the past year, when he learned that one of the former lovers of his long-term partner, Bill, had become ill with AIDS. Then Sam himself was diagnosed as HIV positive. A high school graduate with computer training, Sam was White and held a good position with a large company, earning in the mid-$30,000 range.

Betty, Black and in her mid-forties, practiced social work with the Veterans Administration, five years at the B.S.W. level and another fourteen years as an M.S.W. With a range of varied positions, including acute and long-term psychiatry, outpatient mental health, alcohol and drug abuse, independent living and physical disabilities, Betty brought a deep appreciation of people and their difficulties to the relationship.

Comfortable with herself as a person and as a social worker, Betty exuded strength and vitality. She had a great laugh and a wide and inviting smile. Betty was divorced and remarried, living with her husband and their blended family of seven children, ages 4 through 17. She presented as capable of handling anything.

	SAM:	I am so angry with everyone. I don't want to go to support group. I can't stand it. I just want to die.
*1	BETTY:	What happened that is making you so angry?
	SAM:	I wanted to talk in group about the fact that I am dying and how scared I am—it's bullshit that some of us will be carriers. They told me to think positively, that my negativism would kill me. Then Bill called to tell me that his T cell count was in normal range. I hung up on him. The S.O.B. gave me this virus and he is still well and I am getting sick. I gave him everything, including my life, and then he rejected me. Well fuck them, fuck him. (*Tears . . . silence . . . sobbing*) Am I going crazy?
*2	BETTY:	No, but it sure might be tempting to go crazy so you wouldn't have to feel.
*3	SAM:	I see your eyes are teary. This hurts you, doesn't it?
*4	BETTY:	I do hurt to see you in so much pain. I don't understand why these things have happened to you, it is unfair!
	SAM:	I am sorry for hurting you.
	BETTY:	Why are you sorry about that?
	SAM:	If I make you unhappy, you won't want to work with me, and I need you. Maybe I want to push you away. I don't know. (*More tears*)
*5	BETTY:	Why would you want to push me away?
	SAM:	(*Angrily*) I don't want anyone to feel bad.

*6   Betty: Are you saying you don't want anyone to care?

Sam: Yes, I don't want anything to count. I don't want to need anybody because I'm afraid they won't be there when I'm sick and ugly. Maybe I am just testing you to see if you can hang in there if I'm not nice.

*7   Betty: Gee, I'm sort of insulted that you would see me as a fair weather friend, that I'm only around for the good times, that I can't handle the bad times, that I can't be sad, that you need to protect me from these things.

Sam: (*Long pause . . . softly*) I never thought about it like that. I'd be real upset if someone thought that of me. I think I don't want to care about anything or anybody—so I won't mind dying—but I don't think I can shut it all out—that's not who I am.

The end Betty was working toward was helping the client live his life with AIDS as independently as possible. Without creating undue dependency or excessive sentimentality, she acknowledged the feelings. At *1 and *2 Betty gave Sam an opportunity to talk about what he was feeling. First, *1, she commented directly on his anger and asked him to talk about it. Sam immediately responded by identifying what was happening to him. At *2 Betty continued to address the client's anger. Using Sam's own words of "going crazy," she focused on the difficulty of acknowledging and dealing with feelings. The thrust was not on Betty's feelings but on how best to help Sam manage *his* feelings. Helping clients with their issues is the purpose of the relationship.

Betty's *assessment shaped her relationship* with Sam. The interaction was influenced by her understanding of him and his situation. Based on her assessment that Sam needed permission to acknowledge and accept his own sadness about having AIDS, Betty responded to his question, *3, with an acknowledgment of her own sadness, *4. Direct and confrontive, *5–*7, Betty pushed Sam to continue relating to her with trust and closeness. Not mired in the sadness, she simply affirmed her commitment to him.

Betty's decision not to be overly nurturing with Sam was grounded by her assessment. She directed the relationship to foster Sam's independence and autonomy. This was their objective, the current purpose of the practice.

Boundaries between Betty and Sam could be described as loose. Betty preferred to work with clients in an easy and relaxed style, even to the point of shoes off and feet up on the desk. Yet she recognized that decisions had to be made about the boundaries of each client relationship:

. . . .

If I'm working with a client who needs a lot of boundaries, I have to work at keeping my shoes on—literally! There are clients who need 'professional' distance. They need me to be a nonperson, to only reflect what is going on with them. This kind of client is uncomfortable with small talk or any social tone to our talking together. They don't want to know much about Betty, the person, they just want to deal with Betty, the social worker. Then there are other clients who wouldn't see you, if that's how you were. Sam is this latter client.

. . . .

Betty's *employing agency* was a Veterans Administration hospital where Sam was seen through an outpatient clinic. In this setting the role of the social worker involved meeting with Sam as frequently as needed. Since Sam had some service-connected disability, fees were not an issue. With great flexibility in the role, Betty could spend her time with clients talking or teaching them life skills, like shopping. Because of the many forms to be completed, Betty had to be sure to obtain the information necessary to keep files current. In her private practice Betty kept very few forms, yet there she continually faced the issue of fees. As we have emphasized, each setting will place its own constraints on the social worker/client relationship.

This *relationship is unique* to Betty and Sam. Even if we agree with the approach Betty took, each and every one of us would have a relationship with Sam different from this one. Relationship is a product of each of the parties' interacting together. An infinite array of factors shape the relationship, including personality attributes, cultural backgrounds, values, knowledge, and experience. A specific worker-client relationship cannot be predetermined or duplicated.

Though it may be hard to appreciate the warmth and bonding between Betty and Sam without observing them in their interaction, we can learn from Betty her deliberations in developing this particular relationship. While recognizing the spontaneity and intuition relevant to the establishment of relationship, practitioners are accountable to provide an articulation of the relationship they have with their clients, including a rationale for the different roles and functions they perform.

The purpose of the relationship between Betty and Sam *changed over the years.* As Betty put it:

. . . .

When I initially met Sam, he was in need of my help in making some major lifestyle decisions. He had a good relationship with his wife but was feeling increasingly uncomfortable about his bisexuality and was considering becoming homosexual. At the beginning, my purpose was to help him sort out the different issues he was confronting, "coming out of the closet," getting a divorce, es-

tablishing a different relationship with his children, renewing contact with his father, who he hadn't seen in years.

I had to do some pushing to see where the edges of things were for him. At the beginning, I used the relationship to help find the sore spots, where things were slippery, and where intact. The relationship helps me do the assessment, the figuring out what is going on. Then the assessment helps me better decide what kind of relationship to continue to have with the client.

The assessment, now, is different than what he came in with and the relationship is different. Initially, he was starting his life over, making new relationships and establishing a different lifestyle. My relationship at the beginning was focused on building his trust in me, that I would be able to help him. The purpose of the relationship, at that point, was educational, sharing information with him about what other clients I had worked with experienced as they came out.

We then moved toward his independence with his new life, the relationship provided help, as he needed, with decision making. The purpose of the relationship became focused on helping him trust in himself again, to rely on his own resources. I functioned something in the role of a consultant, someone he could turn to for expert information.

Now, of course, there is a lot of comfort and security in the relationship. There is also a lot of sadness. The purpose now is to help him live his life to the fullest with AIDS. In the exchange you can see that I encourage him to bounce any of his feelings off of me. I am pretty confrontive with him, I talk straight and direct with him, I always have. My role now is probably more like a coach, guiding him in dealing with his dying.

....

Betty was also very comfortable in establishing the *belief bonding* discussed earlier in the chapter. She recognized her expertise and knew that she could help clients to change while actively conveying her respect for them—a self-confidence acquired over nineteen years of practice. As Betty discussed herself as a social work expert, she compared her practice to driving a car:

....

I learned to drive on a standard transmission, and I had to think constantly about the different things to do. I would wonder how anyone could drive smoothly and turn on the radio and smoke a cigarette all at the same time. At the beginning of my practice I would get very tired. I was trying to have all the answers, to resolve all these awful problems clients brought in. I began to realize that I had to focus on myself and my practice, not focus solely on the client. By focusing on myself as a practitioner, I could think about the help I needed to better help *the client. I was able to begin to see myself as the expert, without being expert about all the specifics of the client's problems.*

....

As a skilled social worker, Betty ably addressed issues of *differences* between herself and clients. Most of her clients were White, as were most of her professional colleagues. She commented about the role of race in her practice:

....

Occasionally I will notice a client reacting to the color of my skin—just a flinch or quick movement of the eye. I used to get angry, now I just ride it out. I know I'm good at what I do, once we get moving along in our work the fact that I am Black and the client is White becomes irrelevant. We deal with so much difference here—difference of money and social class, difference of physical and mental abilities—our work is about dealing with difference!

....

Determined in her pursuit of specific objectives, Betty established relationships that were both purposeful and evolving. Modifications in the assessment prompted by changes in Sam and in her own skills effected adjustments in the relationship.

The social work relationship has as its purpose to achieve specific ends determined by the social worker's case theory of the assessment. Each relationship is unique, structured by boundaries and reflecting the function of the social work agency. Changing over time it is targeted to create change.

In the next case history we examine another social work relationship for its sense of purpose and unique character. Joan was working with a patient who was also gay and had a history of chronic mental illness. The setting, a private psychiatric facility, offered inpatient and outpatient treatment. Practicing social work for twenty years, Joan spent the last fifteen doing individual and group psychotherapy, including sexual functioning and eating disorders. White and Catholic, she dressed with great flair, sewed many of her own clothes, and traveled widely. Twice married and divorced, Joan recently renovated an old house and threw herself into decorating.

Her client, Barry, 38 years old, was Jewish and had been seeing Joan for the past three years. Initially an inpatient, he had been living in his own apartment for the past eighteen months and received both group and individual outpatient services. In and out of psychiatric treatment for a total of eleven years, Barry had a long history of suicide attempts with some delusions, depression, and substance abuse. His last job was seven years before, when he was employed with a book publisher in stock maintenance. Since that time he lived on social security disability payments along with some assistance from his parents.

*1   JOAN: It sounds like you are feeling very manicky, is that so?

     BARRY: Yes. I took a large dose of my medicine last night and still couldn't sleep. I couldn't close my eyes a wink. Gosh, here I am falling apart again. *(Pause)* Both you and my doctor will be gone at the same time for the next two weeks. I've just had two friends die of AIDS. My mother is paralyzed.

*2   JOAN: This is a hard time for you now. You're dealing with several losses all at once.

     BARRY: I'm not paranoid, but I am aware of that tape machine.

*3   JOAN: Me, too. Would you like me to move it out of your vision?

     BARRY: No, it's okay. Well, Gary has not corresponded with me for several weeks now. I'm thinking of contacting him.

*4   JOAN: There is so much going on for you now. This is probably a decision better left for after I get back from vacation when we have time to discuss it more fully.

     BARRY: I agree. I know that I'm dealing with a lot of loss. I've recently had two friends die of AIDS, my mother is probably dying, I seem to have lost the relationship with Gary and you and Dr. Barton will be gone. These last two are temporary, but they are still losses.

        I did something the other day, I called that woman, Lea, to have dinner. I told her I couldn't pay her way and we agreed dutch treat would be fine. I feel good about calling her.

        I went to the young men's rap group the other night and that felt good.

        I want to read you this note I wrote. The other day I was at the Partial Treatment Center, and saw this young guy, a good-looking kid. I had seen him before. He made a point of coming over to sit by me. We introduced ourselves, he's from San Diego, I love that, I'm fascinated by California. He was recently in Children's Hospital.

*5   JOAN: Are you presenting this letter for my opinion?

     BARRY: Yes. "I met you yesterday. I've been trying to expand my circle of friends, my therapist and coordinator think this will be good for me. I realize there is an age difference, you are 17, I am 38, but that won't bother me if it won't bother you. You also need to know that I am gay, so if we are seen together people might think you are gay, too. Though I do find you attractive, I am proposing only a platonic relationship."

*6 JOAN: Well, if you were to sit and think about this letter, what would be your thoughts? *(Pause)* You identified in the letter the pros in making this contact, what do you think might be some of the negatives?

BARRY: Well, he could share this letter with others and reject me, that could be embarrassing.

*7 JOAN: Can you think of any other negatives?

BARRY: Well, he is very young. I'm old enough to be his father. On the other hand, I'm pretty immature myself.

*8 JOAN: Yes. This young man is in the process of maturing and he is a minor.

BARRY: I hadn't thought of that.

*9 JOAN: You were honest in sharing a lot about yourself, including that you were attracted to him. That can be scary for him. With him, you were not only wanting a friend, weren't you also attracted to him and considering him as a lover possibility?

BARRY: No, not really. *(Pause, laughter)* Yes, you're right. I think I shouldn't mail the letter. Is that what you think?

*10 JOAN: I think he could get very anxious getting a letter like that from you. Think of yourself at that age, how would you have felt?

BARRY: Of course, especially from someone old enough to be his father.

*11 JOAN: You are also currently in a manicky stage, and as you know, when you're feeling like this it is not a good time for you to make decisions.

BARRY: There is a name in the gay culture for someone like me, chicken queen, going after young chickens. I do feel, though, that I have a lot to offer a younger person.

*12 JOAN: You know, we have talked together about your loneliness and pain both when you are in and out of relationships. Could your attraction to young males have something to do about where you are in your life right now?

BARRY: You know, in the rap session the other night I asked that we have as a topic for discussion "the problem of growing older in a subculture that caters to youth and beauty." In the gay culture, over 29 you're nothing unless you have money.

*13 JOAN: For some time you have been talking in here about commitment, about intimacy.

BARRY: I've had so many one-night stands. I've really wanted one special relationship. *(Pause)* How many people do you do therapy with?

*14 JOAN: How is it you're asking me that now?

BARRY: I wonder how you decided to tape me?

*15 JOAN: *(Pause)* I chose you because I thought you would be comfortable with the taping, and as well I'm comfortable with you and my work with you. You're an interesting person. *(Pause)* I also think that the ways you and I have learned to talk together about some important and difficult issues may be useful in teaching others who also do this kind of work. I will be reviewing this tape with someone who is writing a book to teach people how to practice social work.

BARRY: It's a crazy time now. I just can't stand these guys I know dying of AIDS. It seems like everyone I know is dying of AIDS.

*16 JOAN: Except you. You haven't contracted the AIDS virus.

BARRY: My getting crazy saved my life. If I hadn't gotten psychotic and tried to kill myself, and then spent two years in the hospital here, I probably would have gotten sick with AIDS also. Next time I want to show you some more things from my scrapbook. I've only shown these things to two other people.

JOAN: You've piqued my curiosity. I'll see them when I get back.

The ends Joan is working toward with Barry were different than Betty's goals for Sam. Sam had always functioned independently and Betty wanted to continue to enable him as an autonomous, self-governing person. Barry, however, had had difficulty with independent functioning since his early adult years. Joan's work with Barry focused on helping him control his impulsive behavior. Basic to this end was making distinctions between feelings and behavior—one is not responsible for one's feelings, responsibility comes only with behavior and the decisions made in responding to and addressing the feelings. Joan, therefore, encouraged Barry to recognize and accept his feelings while working with him on controlling his actions. Asking Barry, at *1, whether he was feeling "manicky" brought the identification of feelings easily out into the open. Joan then presented, at *2, the feelings as a normal reaction to issues in his life, while at *4 she made the point that a decision could be postponed—a specific reaction did not need to follow immediately the recognition of feelings.

Here again understanding the problem shapes the type of relationship established with the client. Disagreeing with the initial diagnosis of "ego-dystonic homosexuality," which labeled the client's homosexuality as the primary problem, Joan believed the client's difficulties were exacerbated by the world's intolerance of his homosexuality. As she states:

....

I don't believe he needs help in coming to terms with his homosexuality, he has already accepted that. Afraid of intense relationships with women and intimate relationships in general, my sense is that he is an anxious and self-critical person who handicaps himself with homosexuality as his excuse.

....

This *assessment of Barry shaped Joan's relationship* with him. She used the relationship for him to experience her as accepting and respectful of him as a person. Homosexuality was not at issue in the relationship; the thrust was that he gain in feelings of self-respect and be less critical of himself. Clarifying, at *5, his purpose in reading the letter to her, she treated Barry with respect and a belief that he could think through the consequences of his options, *6 and *7. When she felt he was still missing a piece, she did offer him further information to consider, *8, expecting that he be responsible for his decision making. Done in a caring and constructive way, the relationship reinforced self-confidence, conveying the worker's belief that the client could approach decision making as a responsible adult individual.

While the *boundaries between Joan and Barry* were not as loose in conversational tone as those between Betty and Sam, one of their twice weekly sessions was held over lunch. With a protective, caretaking stance adopted by Joan, they accepted a parent-to-child relationship between them. Confronting Barry, at *9, with her push for him to be more honest about his intentions, Joan took the role of a strong parental figure when she told him he was not currently capable of making a good decision, *11.

Joan explained—

....

I see Barry twice a week. He currently can't be trusted to handle his mood swings responsibly. This frequency affords less urgency to each contact. He was initially not comfortable with the two hours per week, but I felt it was essential, at least to get him out of his apartment. I offered him an option for one of the hours to have lunch together, on the grounds. I've not done this with any of my other clients, but it's definitely worked well with Barry. It has given him another level of connectedness to me and an opportunity to have a relationship with closeness without also having sex and abandonment.

I function as a caring, strong parent figure for him. I posture myself differently for each client. Even the physical arrangements in the room are different with Barry. He chooses to sit in the chair closest to my desk making it necessary that I turn my chair around to face him.

. . . .

Joan's *employing agency,* a private psychiatric hospital and training facility, specialized in long-term treatment. Although he was managing living on his own, Barry was considered by both himself and Joan to be a chronic patient who would continue to need intensive support over an indefinite period of time. Knowledge about Barry across many years of treatment afforded Joan not only extensive background information but also ample opportunity to follow up with touchy subjects in future sessions.

Her confrontation, at *10, pushed Barry to consider his own responses if he received such a letter, and her comments, at *12 and *13, nicely forge an association between previous work they did on loneliness and his current feelings. While, at *16, she could only introduce a potentially explosive issue—the AIDS virus—she knew she could pick up on it further during a later session.

Though fees were expensive at this facility, the patient's visits were covered under insurance payments. Such coverage is not the norm, making such intensive, supportive services impossible for most people. The atmosphere was pleasant, the physical surroundings were lush, and there were warm, positive work relationships between the different professional disciplines. Confident that other staff will be available to Barry while she was on vacation enabled Joan to leave comfortably for a few weeks and not feel guilt or worry.

Barry's diagnosis changed over the years, with new social workers and through shifts in the understanding of psychiatric disorders. Joan viewed diagnosis as reflective of the agency philosophy:

. . . .

Still heavily psychoanalytic, homosexuality is viewed by many at the setting as a perversion. As I see it, throughout history a proportion of the population has been gay. Recent literature supports a genetic explanation for homosexuality, which I believe is a much better one than early childrearing.

This client asked to have me as his worker and in our first session told me he had heard I was liberal and tough. We clarified that this meant I was not judgmental of his sexual orientation—in fact my belief is that people should have the most satisfactory sex lives they can—and that I didn't put up with bullshit in sessions—I expected clients to behave responsibly. We laughed together and have had a good working relationship over these years.

In this setting we heavily rely on the DSM-III-R [Diagnostic and Statistical Manual] for diagnostic categories, which we also use for billing purposes. When I became the social worker with Barry, we changed the diagnosis from "Major Depression" to "Bipolar Disorder," continued with the "Alco-

hol and Other Mixed Substance Abuse," dropped the "Ego-dystonic Homosexuality" and kept the "Borderline Personality Disorder."

....

Unique to Joan and Barry, their relationship remained special to both of them. As evident in Joan's last remark, they began their relationship with an open and direct discussion about his homosexuality and her therapeutic style. Just as it did with Betty and Sam, the purpose of their relationship changed over the years. Initially Barry was an inpatient and their work was to stabilize him and reduce the suicidal risk. Since he began living in his own apartment, they worked toward maintaining his independence. Over future months they would probably move toward some attempt at minimal employment. Joan commented on her interaction with Barry presented earlier:

....

In getting ready to leave for vacation, I was trying to get everything in order. Already geared to being more directive because of my anxiety, Barry brings out the letter to the 17 year old. This touches a chord for me—coming on sexually to an adolescent. Having been abused myself as a youngster, physically by both parents, sexually by a neighbor, I know I have to watch that my own issues don't get in the way of my work with clients. Recognizing that, with Barry I believe a more aggressive stance on safe sex is the best approach. One of the primary areas of our work together has been his impulsive behavior, and when he impulsively acts out sexually I see it as my responsibility to help him consider consequences. Shortly after he moved into his own apartment, we discussed safe sex and I taught him where to go to buy condoms—I have a responsibility to this guy and to the world we live in.

....

Their comfort together is also apparent in the discussion about the audio taping. Early in the session, Joan validated Barry's discomfort with the tape machine by concurring that she too was aware of it and asked if he'd like it moved, *3. After clarifying, *14, that he was questioning her decision to tape him, she further clarified what the taping means:

....

It's always interesting to me how clients deal with audio- or videotaping sessions. Most of the time they accept these as routine parts of the treatment. Though I've worked with Barry for several years, I had never taped any sessions with him and I think he was curious. I was pleased that he felt comfortable enough with our relationship to pursue the matter with me.

....

Joan further elaborates about her own background and development as a social worker as *different* from her clients:

....

I've learned to separate my personal views from my work with my clients. Though I wouldn't myself get an abortion, that is my choice and not necessarily the right one for everyone. Though I was reared as a Catholic, I don't believe the world works that way. Being Catholic is my ethnic piece, like being White and Irish.

In my background, women are strong and men are weak. I have to be careful that I don't bring that expectation into my work with couples and families. I was the overachieving and overresponsible oldest child, so I watch out for the sibling position of my clients so that I don't get competitive with them. I used to try hard to not work with abusers because of my childhood, but I can handle that now.

That's what I love about this work—it's an endless challenge—my own growth and change often parallels what goes on with my clients. Relating to such different and interesting people, and getting paid for it, I consider myself lucky to have the capacities to do this stuff.

....

ADDITIONAL NOTES

In this concluding section we look at issues related specifically to the student role and the social work relationship, offering some cautions and suggestions.

Assuming the Role of the Expert Authority

Beginning social workers often struggle to feel comfortable with the authority of the social work position. Some of this difficulty is a result of confusion about the foundation of expertise. Lack of prior experience with the kinds of issues presented may prompt students to anguish over their ability to help. Proficiency, however, does not lie in familiarity with all the problems of clients, but rather in executing the skills covered in this book, in integrating the knowledge from the classroom with the experience of the practicum, and in engaging in continual professional development.

You will not have answers to resolve your clients' problems. You are not trained in living life; you are only expert on helping others and cannot serve as a model for living. Social work practice is a process of enabling clients to develop answers to live *their* lives, and it requires its practitioners to engage in a perpetual process of learning with peers, supervisors, and clients. Field instructors can be an important source of support, so try to gain comfort in reaching out to them for help.

Identifying Oneself as a Student

Because you are placed in your practicum for a specified period of time, the practicum will end before some clients have completed treatment, terminating the relationship. Acknowledging your student role at the beginning of the relationship results in a smoother and less traumatic termination for both yourself and clients. You will feel less guilt about leaving the client and the setting when there has been honest discussion about your student status. If the facts are presented clearly and not apologetically, clients will usually not be unduly concerned about working with a student. You can mention smaller caseloads, intense supervision, and concurrent classwork as some of the advantages of having a student worker.

Helping

While providing "help" to another is the essence of the social work relationship, this concept has different meanings for different people. One person will react to a cry for help by running away; another will rush over to see what to do. Each of these persons may feel vulnerable, even afraid; they just handle their feelings differently. You will also confront a range of personal responses when faced with needy and hurting clients. Even experienced social workers may initially react to a gritty life story by wanting to get out of the room. Being a social worker does not mean one never has negative reactions to what clients present, or that one is always comfortable in the role.

Beginning social workers especially are expected to experience anxiety resulting from fears of not being able to help and lack of knowledge about what to do with hurting clients. Under such circumstances, it is important to guard against becoming overly authoritative or emotional as a defense against the fear and discomfort you may be feeling.

In offering help to so many types of people suffering such a vast array of problems, recognize the judgments you make about clients and their situations. Clients who are physically disabled can still think and respond to the world. Those who are mentally ill can still engage in conversation, can listen and understand. The term TABs, temporarily able bodied, is a useful phrase to keep in mind when practicing social work; it refers to those people who are not now disabled. At any time, anyone can become incapacitated and be unable to carry out simple physical and mental functions. Everybody alive has social problems, and some are more handicapping than others. The social worker is not automatically in a "one-up" position by being the helper.

Getting Started

There are different ways to direct initial contacts with clients. In many agencies social workers meet clients in a main waiting room and make small talk in first greeting clients and walking together to their office. While some social workers feel it is respectful to greet clients in the waiting room by both their first and last names, others avoid last names to protect confidentiality.

They might talk about the weather or might ask whether the client had trouble finding the office. Some social workers try to respond to the client's comments—appearance of the agency, trouble parking their car, and so on. Diane, who works with young children and their parents, will usually make remarks about the child. She explains, "The younger the baby, the more important it is for me to form a connection with the parent. I try to say something positive about the baby, how cute, how nicely dressed, that type of thing."

Differences in introductions range from a title such as Dr. if they have a Ph.D., or Mr., Ms., Mrs., with first and last name. With no right or wrong etiquette, means of addressing each other depends on the worker's comfort, the kind of agency, and the specific client. Mark, who has both an M.S.W. and a Ph.D., makes a specific decision about how to introduce himself based on prior information he may have about the client: "I was meeting with a young client, who I knew had trouble dealing with authority. I decided to introduce myself by saying, 'I'm Mark.' I thought I might diffuse some of the client's possible reactiveness by not using my title."

Ellen Baron comments: "How I address clients and myself differs with each client. I see an elderly Hispanic man who is very respectful of me, always waits until I sit down before he will sit. I am aware of his cultural background, where respect for a woman gets conveyed in certain ways. I am Ms. Baron with him."

A good rule of thumb is to refer to the client in the same way you refer to yourself. If you are using the client's first name, introduce yourself with your first name. In the initial sessions, ground rules get set about how each person will be addressed, seating arrangements, length of time for the session, and other such basics. Attention to these factors is important, with ongoing consideration about whether to continue in the same manner as the relationship proceeds.

In an initial contact each person tends to size up the other; there is a "reactive" quality that occurs almost instantaneously when people interact with each other. Just like other people, social workers respond out of an intuitive sense of what will be necessary to relate to this other person. Yet you must be able to act on your intuitions with deliberation and planning. Chapter 7 covers in more detail the use of your personal reactions to fit the needs of the client.

Integrating your thinking and knowledge with intuition and natural abilities becomes easier with more experience. At the start of the professional relationship, you will rely heavily on initial spontaneous reactions while trying at the same time to access the contributions of theory and experience to what the client may need. Because you are responsible for establishing the professional helping relationship and for shaping it to meet the needs of the client, you determine what this client needs from you so that the helping process may begin.

Betty commented about her relationship with Sam: "When I initially met

Sam, I reacted to him very positively. I sensed that he was honest and upfront. He was motivated for things to be better, had access to his feelings, and could tolerate his own discomfort. I knew that with him I could function like I'm most comfortable, my shoes off, relaxed." While she acknowledged these reactions, at the same time Betty was thinking through what practice experience and theoretical knowledge she had about Sam's situation. She had to consider all these factors as she established the relationship with Sam.

Client-Worker Differences

As discussed in Chapter 1, social workers regularly relate to people who are different from themselves. These differences involve age, gender, socio-economic class, race, educational level, culture, dress, language, speech, physical appearance, personality, sexual preference, athletic and verbal ability, and many others.

All differences are a dynamic in the social work relationship. Though social workers are trained not to be biased and prejudiced in their work, they are still human, and on meeting a client they will be aware of differences and similarities. These reactions are shaped by their cultural background and previous experiences with diversity. A Black female worker will have certain reactions when she meets a White male client—reactions to his maleness, to his skin color, and perhaps to his height, to the way he talks, and so on. A female Hispanic worker will respond in her own unique way to an elderly male client. Her reactions may be to the same differences just mentioned or may involve her concern about a male's needing help from a female because this is discordant with the cultural image of the Hispanic male.

The effect of differences on the practice is partly a function of the social worker's skill in developing the case theory from the assessment and in engaging in practitioner observation to articulate personal reactions. The case theory, covered in Chapter 5, includes the information about the client's problem and as such focuses the relationship on the client's needs. Practitioner observation, discussed in Chapter 7 as the social worker's self-surveillance and critique, prevents biases from contaminating the relationship. Addressing differences in the relationship is part of the excitement and challenge of social work practice. Discussion by social workers about differences between themselves and their clients is included in most of the case examples covered in these chapters.

Different feelings about each of your clients will reflect a greater or lesser degree of affinity and affection—you may like or dislike the client, or just feel neutral. While these emotions cannot be controlled, you must be able to adopt an analytical stance so that your personal feelings do not control your behaviors with clients.

Loss and Termination

Loss is part of life. One cannot live without experiencing loss—loss of capacities in aging or through an accident or illness, loss of friends and relatives through death or geographic separation, loss of pets by death or disappearance, loss of familiar patterns and habits through deliberate change (like quitting smoking) or through growth into another life stage or developmental phase. Loss is part of living, growing, and changing. It may be as intangible as the ending of one's youthful idealism or as concrete as the breaking of a favorite vase.

Entering the role of student social worker is often experienced as a loss. Most students begin social work programs in their thirties and forties. Having had well-established roles in other occupations, they usually perceive returning to being a mere student as a loss in status.

Since social work addresses people in their social context, loss is also one of the recurring themes in the social work relationship. A useful book in examining loss and helping workers address loss in their practice is *A Time to Grieve*, by Bertha Simos. When defining loss as "being deprived of or being without something one has had and valued and includes the experiences of separation" (1979, p. 1), Simos encourages social workers to be attentive to themes of loss in their practice. Loss is to be considered on a continuum from simple losses, such as a favorite book, to major losses, such as death. Both the simple and severe can bring disruption and a deprivation of security.

Be alert to issues of loss experienced by your clients. Although they are not always evident when the client presents the initial problem, past losses may still be affecting the client's current functioning. An interesting example of this continuing impact was a client who came in to see Mara, a social worker at a mental health center. The client, Carol, brought in her two sons, ages 13 and 9, and presented the problem as her 13-year-old's soiling of his pants. Formally called encopresis or fecal incontinence, this condition afflicts from 1 to 2 percent of children over the age of 4. For Carol's son the problem had started within the past month, with no prior history of this difficulty.

Mara completed a social history, obtaining information about the functioning of Carol and the two boys. She learned that both boys had friends and were doing fine in school. Carol, on the other hand, appeared very anxious, talking rapidly without finishing her sentences. Mara also observed that Carol had dark circles under her eyes and she reported having trouble sleeping. In response to Mara's request, Carol described what her life had been like over the past few months. Carol became teary and reported that her husband had died within the past year, suddenly, from a car accident.

Mara began to hypothesize that Carol was the person who might be in need of treatment, that perhaps she was dealing with unresolved grief from her husband's death. She asked Carol to commit herself to three to five visits for an assessment while also referring Carol and her son to their family physician for an evaluation of the fecal incontinence. As discussed fully in Chapter 5, it is essential to evaluate the biological component of presenting problems. Often incontinence has a physiological basis which can be effectively treated with medication. Encopresis is usually related to constipation and problems with the colon.

Fortunately, in this case, the pediatric examination did not uncover any problems with the rectum or colon. Once Carol entered treatment with Mara, her son's soiling disappeared in the next two weeks. Perhaps he was acting out his mother's unresolved grief. The important point is that he wasn't placed in the position of therapy patient without a physical examination while, at the same time, the mother's situation was explored.

Mara's initial hypothesis of the mother's unresolved grief was validated in her ongoing assessment. Carol had not yet completed her grieving over her husband's death and also had many other losses to address—her loss of being a wife, her loss of having someone with whom to share parenting, and so on. Sensitivity to the issues of loss enabled Mara to help the client identify the real nature of her difficulties so that the 13-year-old did not mistakenly become the patient.

The social work relationship itself must be considered when addressing the topic of loss. Often meaningful and close for both clients and social workers, when it is time to terminate the relationship, feelings aroused by that loss need to be acknowledged and "worked through" by both social workers and clients. A complex mix of feelings are usually experienced by clients when they confront the termination of the relationship with the social worker. These may include excitement at being ready to terminate, fear of not having someone to rely on, and sadness at the loss of the relationship with this person.

Also responding with a range of feelings, social workers may feel happy that the work has been completed, relief that they will no longer have to see the client, or sadness and even guilt if they were not effective. While you are responsible to help clients with their feelings, peers and supervisors are available for helping you process and gain support for your emotions. Moreover, the relationship with your field instructor may become one of the more significant experiences of your social work education. Because this relationship often serves as a model for relating not only to clients but also to colleagues, you will probably have feelings of loss connected to the termination of the field instruction as well.

One positive approach in worker-client termination is to use the last few sessions as a review of the help offered to the client. An examination of accomplishments in your work together and the client's plans and objectives for the future offer an excellent opportunity to receive feedback about the kinds of things the client found useful and suggestions for changes in your approach.

Creativity is required when you meet with clients for the final session. In some cases, an exchange of pictures may be appropriate; in others some small means of celebration is suitable, such as sharing some food. Plan together with clients how to spend the final meeting.

These suggestions assume that there is some ability to control the ending of the social work relationship. This work, however, is not always so tidy. It helps to remember that while the termination is sometimes planned and mutually agreeable to the social worker and the client, there will be times when clients terminate suddenly or before there is agreement that the goals have been achieved. Such abrupt endings may feel uncomfortable, and you may need to process your feelings with field instructors and colleagues.

SUMMARY

Relationship has been presented as one of the historically central components of social work practice. In the early 1900s, Mary Richmond first discussed social workers as friendly visitors, and Gordon Hamilton introduced the importance of bonding in the 1940s.

With heightened interest in the scientific process, relationship came to be considered a "soft" concept and was increasingly ignored by many of the social work texts. Now that relationship is included in training programs for other helping professionals such as psychiatrists and psychologists and is receiving expanded attention in medical schools, social work must not abandon, but rather restake its rightful claim to, this important, hard-to-quantify concept.

In this chapter relationship is defined as

A belief bonding formed between the social worker and client, through which the client develops self-worth and trust in the competence of the social worker and establishes belief that the social worker can help initiate change in the client's circumstances. The social work relationship has as its purpose to achieve specific ends determined by the social worker's case theory of the assessment.

Each relationship is unique, structured by boundaries and reflecting the function of the social work agency. Allowing for the enactment of the social work practice, relationship is the medium for social worker and client to connect together in an intimate journey and can be accompanied by sharing of feelings and the development of affection and intimacy. Changing over time, the social work relationship is targeted to helping the client create change of self and of circumstances.

Often challenged personally, professionals engaged in helping relationships frequently obtain help and support from peers, colleagues, and supervisors. Field instructors can serve as a significant source of advice and assistance for students.

For some social workers and clients, relationship is the real substance of social work practice. Living in this world is often a painful and lonely experience. The social work relationship provides a means of connection and support. Long after other parts of the social work practice have been forgotten and the initial problems have been resolved, the relationship itself can remain a treasured memory.

BIBLIOGRAPHY

Clow, L. (1925). The art of helping through the interview. *Proceedings of the National Conference of Social Work.* Chicago: University of Chicago Press.

Dexter, E. (1926). The social caseworker's attitudes and problems as they affect her work. *Proceedings of the National Conference of Social Work—1926.* Chicago: University of Chicago Press.

Hamilton, G. (1940). *Social case work.* New York: Columbia University Press.

Hardcastle, D. (1988). Personal communication. Concept of belief bonding contributed by Professor Hardcastle in discussion about this book. University of Maryland, School of Social Work and Community Planning.

Kasius, C. (1950). *A comparison of diagnostic and functional casework concepts.* New York: Family Service Association of America.

Luborsky, L. (1993). The role of the therapeutic alliance in psycotherapy. *Journal of Consulting Psychology, 61:* 4, 561–573.

Perlman, H. H. (1965). Self-determination: Reality or illusion? *Social Service Review, 39:* 4, 410–421.

Perlman, H. H. (1979). *Relationship—The heart of helping people.* Chicago: University of Chicago Press.

Polansky, N., & Kounin, J. (1956). Client reactions to initial interviews: A field study. *Human Relations, 9:* 237–264.

Richmond, M. (1899). *Friendly visiting among the poor.* New York: Macmillan.

Richmond, M. (1917). *Social diagnosis.* New York: Russell Sage.

Richmond, M. (1922). *What is social casework.* New York: Russell Sage.

Rogers, C. R. (1951). *Client-centered therapy.* Cambridge, MA: Riverside Press.

Rubenstein, H., & Bloch, M. (1982). *Things that matter: Influences on helping relationships.* New York: Macmillan.

Simon, G., & VonKorff, M. (1991). *American Journal of Psychiatry, 148:* 1.

Simos, B. (1979). *A time to grieve.* New York: Family Service Association of America.

Social Casework—Generic and Specific. (1929). New York: American Association of Social Workers.

Sterba, R., Lyndon, B., & Katz, A. (1949). *Transference in casework.* New York: Family Service Association of America.

CHAPTER ❦ FIVE

Actualities seem to float in a wider sea of possibilities from out of which they were chosen; and somewhere . . . such possibilities exist, and form part of the truth.

—William James

ASSESSMENT: THE CASE THEORY

As the meaning the social worker has attached to the client's discourse, assessment provides the basis for the social work practice. It establishes the "why" of the client that directs the "why" and "how" of the practice. There are many explanations for actual events, and they form only part of total reality. The social work assessment draws a deliberately circumscribed picture of clients and their life events. Taken from a specific set of perspectives, the assessment offers one way of understanding the client.

The function of the assessment phase of practice is the same for all professional practitioners. The social worker gathers information on the presented phenomena and organizes it into a framework for understanding in order to plan an intervention. Professionals have to conceptualize, and respond to, clients' problem situations. Medical doctors construct diagnoses based on patients' physiological symptoms; teachers develop learning and teaching plans based on students' learning needs. In the same way, social workers formulate assessments based on clients' social functioning within their social situation. Though social workers consider psychological and physiological functioning as these factors relate to and impact on social functioning, their area of expertise is social functioning, and this is accordingly the focus of their assessment.

This "commitment to a diagnostic process" is, according to Drucker, considered part of the established rules for successful management in any profession: "Medical educators say their greatest problem is the brilliant young physician who has a good eye. He has to learn not to depend on that alone but to go through the patient process of making a diagnosis; otherwise, he kills people. An executive, too, has to learn not to depend on

insight and knowledge of people but on a mundane, boring, and con-
scientious step-by-step process" (1990, pp. 145–146).

Forming a direct link with the intervention and shaping the other practice components, assessment is the most critical component of social work
practice. If the assessment is faulty, the intervention may be appropriate to
the assessment but inappropriate to the client. Assessment determines the
kind of relationship to form with a client and which communication skills to
use; hence it determines the intervention itself. The accuracy of the intervention is a function of the accuracy of the assessment.

A medical doctor plans treatment based on a diagnosis of the patient's
condition. An inaccurate diagnosis will result in deficient treatment. Surgery
on a heart valve may be a beautiful piece of technical medical practice, but if
the patient's problem was in the kidney and not the heart, the treatment can
be hurtful, even deadly for the patient. In social work, if the assessment is
wrong, even the best practice will not relate to the client's needs; it will be
wrong practice and the client won't be helped. An assessment that a client is
experiencing unresolved grief from her divorce can produce a topnotch
intervention for treating grief after divorce. If, however, the client actually
has fear of success syndrome, is afraid of being autonomous, and has
ambivalence about her new independence, the intervention will be ineffective and could even be harmful.

In this chapter we define assessment and illustrate how interpretation
and comprehension of client information progress by using actual case
histories. Our concern here is primarily with the social worker, not the
client. Unlike many other approaches to assessment, our foremost goal is
not to diagnose the clients but to demonstrate the process of assessing. In
this framework our understanding of clients develops from our observation
of the social workers.

Assessment is presented as *an information gathering and organizing process that evolves from the specific to the general to the individualized. Formulated
through distinctions among facts, observations, and judgments,* examples demonstrate the assessment, *providing a theoretical linking of the client's past with the
present and future,* and *organizing the approach to each case situation.* Issues of
difference are addressed in each of the cases. Additional Notes concludes
the chapter with suggestions and guidelines for writing an assessment
report.

Let us first consider social work assessment historically through a review of the literature.

ASSESSMENT IN THE SOCIAL WORK LITERATURE

Assessment was the social work profession's first attempt to provide itself
with scientific respectability. Abraham Flexner, who had been a critic of the
medical profession, was asked by the National Conference of Charities and

Corrections to study and analyze social work as a profession. His report derided social work because it lacked a distinctive professional method (Flexner, 1915).

Mary Richmond responded to these criticisms by offering "social diagnosis," or assessment, as the profession's method. Richmond wrote: "The primary purpose of the writer, in attempting an examination of the initial process of social casework, is to make some advance toward a professional standard" (1917, p. 26). Assessment thus became the first defined component of social work practice. "Social diagnosis is the attempt to arrive at as exact a definition as possible of the social situation and personality of a given client. The gathering of evidence, or investigation, begins the process, the critical examination and comparison of evidence follows, and last come its interpretation and the definition of the social difficulty" (Richmond, 1917, p. 62).

Richmond's "evidence" was the facts on which the social worker's inference about a client was made. In her efforts to supply professional credibility, she established a lengthy and detailed method of obtaining this social evidence. Much of her 1917 book *Social Diagnosis* is devoted to the first interview with the client and the gathering of evidence from outside sources, such as relatives, medical sources, schools, employers, neighbors, documents, and other social service agencies. Variations in the method were possible depending on the type of clients, including families, the immigrant family, the neglected child, the unmarried mother, the blind, the homeless man, and the insane. It was important for Richmond that the history-taking process be very thorough: "Social evidence, like that sought by the scientist or historian, includes all items which, however trifling or apparently irrelevant when regarded as isolated facts, may, when taken together, throw light upon the question at issue; namely as regards social work, the question what course of procedure will place this client in his right relation to society?" (1917, p. 39).

Social Diagnosis was a major contribution to the professionalization of social work. In the same year this book was published, the name of the National Conference of Charities and Corrections was changed to the National Conference of Social Work to reflect more accurately its orientation toward social work. As the first formal attempt to systematize the diagnostic phase of social work practice, *Social Diagnosis* remains an important document in understanding the historical development of social work.

Building on the tradition of Mary Richmond and influenced by the economic turmoil of the 1920s and 1930s, the psychosocial approach represented a further evolution of Richmond's diagnostic school. Sensitive to criticisms that the concept of social diagnosis implied a medical or disease model of practice, Gordon Hamilton (1941) renamed it *psychosocial study*, emphasizing the person-in-environment and systems perspective of social workers. Florence Hollis, in her development of the psychosocial approach, stressed that the purpose of the diagnostic assessment was to develop *differentiation,* the basis for treating each client as a separate individual. She explained that in the psychosocial study the social worker "must learn what the client sees as his problem, what he thinks can be done about it, what he himself has tried to do about it, and what he sees as having brought about his present difficulty" (Hollis, 1970, p. 46).

The *problem-solving model* developed by Helen Harris Perlman in the 1950s was, as its name implies, a problem-oriented approach to practice. Viewed as a "by-product" of the problem-solving process, diagnosis was correspondingly diminished in importance. In this model the social worker's primary responsibility was to frame a clear problem statement which then directed the diagnosis and intervention (Perlman, 1957). Reflecting an emphasis in the 1980s on the organic basis of disorders, the psychosocial study became known as the *bio-psycho-social report.* Although physiological factors are considered in the social work assessment, the social worker's understanding of the client's social functioning is the main focus of what is currently called the *assessment report.*

Through all of these theories the actual details of the assessment process remained vague, and in the 1980s some practice authors began to treat the assessment as a series of specific steps and behaviors. One such example is *Direct Social Work Practice,* by Hepworth and Larsen (1986), in which assessment is presented as a lengthy list of questions to be covered by the worker. Influenced by the behavioral school of psychology and the problem-solving model, this approach tries to reduce assessment to a standard questionnaire.

In 1980, the third edition of the *Diagnostic and Statistical Manual of Mental Disorders* was published and became extensively used in mental health programs. Further revised in 1987, it is known as the *DSM-III-R,* and its increasing popularity is partially explained by insurance payers' need for an assigned diagnosis. Moreover, the ease of classification provided by the *DSM-III-R* has facilitated efforts at research. The ability to group clinical data and findings is attractive to advocates of the evaluation of practice and documentation of social work service effectiveness.

The concept and practice of assessment still has its limitations. The emphasis in Richmond's time of including all data, even the "trifling and apparently irrelevant," tended to generate too much information. Social workers spent inordinate amounts of time asking in-depth questions about all areas in a person's life. Lacking a focus to their information gathering, the social workers became lost in the data and produced an array of possible problems, none of which might be the critical one for the client. With no constraints to the kind of evidence to be gathered, social workers came to be seen by many as intruding in areas of clients' private lives where they didn't belong.

At the same time, the series of questions outlined in the recent prescriptive approaches to assessment are not adequate in themselves. As part of an intellectual process, the information gathered must be categorized and prioritized; judgments must be made about the meaning and relevance of what has been learned. Assessment is both more than obtaining answers to a set of questions and less than an entire history of a client's life. To be useful to both the social worker and the client, it can be neither as global as Mary Richmond recommended nor as narrowly task oriented as some of the more recent approaches require.

Meyer, who is critical of contemporary trends exemplified by the *DSM-III-R* and other pre-packaged scales, comments: "While classification is important, it also is extremely complex in fields like social work and mental health, because the human condition does not lend itself easily to discrete analysis, where one is able to select particular units or variables that describe complex bio-psycho-social phenomena in reliable ways" (1993, p. 94). Other criticisms directed at social workers' reliance on this type of psychodiagnosis have been advanced by Hutchins and Kirk, 1987; Abbott, 1988; Ikver and Sze, 1987.

Despite the idealism of social work theories, practice is not conducted in a world of absolute truths. Only rarely do clear problem statements direct the course of practice. The nature of the problem usually evolves while the practice is well underway, and, as some of the case examples in this chapter demonstrate, the problem statement changes over the course of the practice. Gregory Bateson expresses this phenomenon: "Sometimes—often in science and always in art—one does not know what the problems were until after they have been solved" (1972, p. 271).

Social workers, in effect, embark on a journey with their clients to determine the nature of the problem. That journey is itself helpful to the client, and together the social worker and client decide on what areas are needing help. As Richmond was seeking understanding of the factors that created the client's problems, she acknowledged that this was a difficult search: "In social diagnosis, the kinds of evidence available, being largely testimonial in character, can of course never show a probative value equal to that of facts in the exact sciences." She believed, though, that what "is possible for us is to obtain proof that amounts to a reasonable certainty" (Richmond, 1917, p. 55).

The search for causes can be a neverending quest. Knowledge of all the underlying reasons for the client's current life is not as important as being able to explain and describe the client's situation *as it relates to what the client is bringing in for help.* Together, the social worker and the client formulate an understanding, a picture about the client's past as it relates to the present circumstances, in order to change the future. *The social worker's role is to help, not just to know!* Relying on clients' perceptions, recollections, and feelings, which change over time and with new circumstances, social workers do not create a whole play; they merely shape one small section of one particular scene. Practice is directed toward helping clients change one aspect of their lives, not to start all over from day 1. As a slice of life at a specific point in time, the assessment is intended to determine the nature of the client's current problem situation.

For Richmond, assessment included both what the social worker does and what the social worker produces. Siporin, writing almost sixty years later, offers a thoughtful and comprehensive definition in which he says: "Assessment is both a process and a product of understanding" (1975, p. 219).

This dual meaning assigned to assessment has continued to plague the profession and has contributed to a fuzziness about the term. In this book the *process* of the assessment is the social worker's understanding and defining of the problem situation to formulate the case theory. The *product* of this process, an assessment report, consists of the problem statement including the case theory with history of the problem. An example of an assessment report is offered in Additional Notes.

Social Work Assessment Defined

In this book the assessment is defined as

The generation of a set of hypotheses forming the construction of a case theory that explains clients within the context of their circumstances. It is an information-gathering and -organizing process that evolves from the specific to the general to the individualized. Distinctions are made among facts, observations, and judgments, and attention is paid to issues of difference. Through a theoretical linking of the client's past with the present and future, a map is developed that organizes the social work practice by shaping the relationship and communication and determining the intervention. Literature and research inform and are used to validate the hypotheses.

We have emphasized that the domain of social work practice includes persons and their environments. Reflecting this multiple focus, the assessment considers clients within their circumstances. In the first case study of this chapter the assessment encompasses the client within the environment of her engagement and marriage, and in the second example the client is understood within context of her family. The environment of the school system features prominently in the final case study.

Whereas the relationship dimension of social work practice might be seen as an interaction experienced by both the social worker and the client, the assessment is a one-sided conceptual experience. The social worker begins with thoughts and hunches. Purposive and goal directed, the assessment develops a picture about the client's past and current situation in order to help the client change the future.

The social worker generates hypotheses that offer a means for understanding clients and implementing appropriate change. These hypotheses comprise the case theory. As discussed in Chapter 1, theory is the explanation and prediction of events. Practitioners use a variety of theories to influence the situations they confront. The *case theory*, in contrast, is constructed *by* the social worker to explain events in the client's life that are relevant to the problem situation. Providing a framework for a plan of intervention to change the client's future, the case theory elucidates the client's current situation within the context of past events while creating a means for changing subsequent events. The social worker routinely tests and retests hypotheses to develop a case theory that explains what is happening with this client at the present time.

The *process* of theory construction results in the *product* of an assessment report, usually called a psychosocial report, social history, or bio-psychosocial assessment. Providing a written account of significant aspects of the client's life relevant to the client's problem situation, the report also documents the social worker's thinking about and understanding of the client. In the articulation of a *problem statement*, the worker takes a stand, proferring an argument for this particular understanding of the case—that is, for the case theory.

The assessment report includes theories about human behavior or human development. Often there are several such theories that have informed and guided the social worker's process of understanding this particular client and the client's environment. A psychoanalytic framework may have been utilized to interpret the client's history, a developmental theory employed to understand the client's current behavior, and a systems perspective drawn on to view the client within the context of the environment. Shaped by their training and current employment, social workers have their own frames of reference that influence the kinds of theories they use with each case. The function of the employing agency and its own treatment orientation, as well as the supervisor's perspective, also determine the theories that are utilized. The process of theory selection is covered in the case examples in this chapter and in Chapters 7 and 8.

The important point here is that these theories are not the same as the social worker's case theory. Offering means to understand broad classes of people, they are conceptual models about how people think or feel or act. Whether they are specific, indicating definite stages of development, or more general and philosophical, these theories are *nomothetic*—that is, they apply to groups of persons. The social work case theory, in contrast, is *idiographic*—it applies to only one person. By definition, if the case theory fits this individual case, it will totally fit no other client situation.

Because it is constantly being outdated by changing events in the client's life and new information, the assessment must be periodically modified. In the first case example we will look at, the client, Dale, is initially diagnosed with chronic schizophrenia; she is actively hallucinating and talks of suicide. Over the year covered in the sessions, the changes in Dale's behavior are so considerable that this assessment is no longer relevant. Interim summaries are necessary that update the information and the worker's assessment.

Since schizophrenia is considered to be incurable, Dale's change in behavior raises provocative questions: Was the diagnosis of schizophrenia inaccurate in the first place? Can schizophrenia still be present even if it is not visible? Is the disorder perhaps correctable? Though they are not the focus of our current discussion, these questions point to the lack of clear answers and the need for addressing this work with an open and inquiring mind and a tolerance for ambiguity.

Social workers must also stay abreast of the professional literature. Never a straightforward process, the choice of a theoretical model is complicated by a lack of consensus in the literature. In fact, valid pros and cons are frequently directed toward theories and treatment models. Moreover, advances in technology and research provide constantly changing possibilities for comprehending clients' problems and subsequent treatment. A brief review of our changing knowledge of depression graphically illustrates this point.

In offering an explanation of depression, Freud posited that "melancholia is in some way related to an unconscious loss of a love-object . . . [and since] . . . through identification, the shadow of the object fell upon the ego . . . the loss of the object became transformed into a loss in the ego" (1917, pp. 170–171). This process of "sadistic" self-hate, Freud believed, could be reversed with the psychoanalytic method, a process of intensive analysis of the patient's dreams and unconscious desires.

While psychotherapy continued to be the preferred treatment for depression through the 1950s, pharmacology and electroconvulsive or shock therapy were available for the more difficult cases. Psychotropic medications were not yet widely available, and shock treatments were considered "superior to any of the present day drugs. The effect is rapid, eight ECT's generally eliminating the depression" (Wolberg, 1967, p. 1001). Shock treatment was the only available technology to help control the behavior of severely depressed patients, although its administration produced a different set of problems, including loss of all emotions and possible paralysis.

Despite Wolberg's optimism about shock therapy, patients with depression were considered resistant to treatment, exhibiting "a facade of conventionality and sociability which . . . served as a defense against true intimacy . . . with strong underlying feelings of dependency, hostility, envy, and competition" (Volkmar, Bacon, Shakir & Pfefferbaum, 1983, p. 159). Depression was still viewed as an unconscious process, linked in etiology to the individual's psychosexual development.

With later breakthroughs in pharmacology, however, the drug lithium combined with group therapy became the treatment of choice in the early 1980s, whereas Prozac became the wonder drug of the late 1980s and early 1990s. The apparent quick relief of depression with the use of Prozac convinced even some of the diehard believers in psychoanalysis of a neurobiological basis to depression.

This change in our conception of depression as an unconscious process of ego splitting to a theory of chemical imbalance has shifted the preferred choice of treatment to drugs, with psychotherapy as a possible accompaniment, which constitutes a distinct reversal from thirty years before. What our perceptions and treatment of depression will be thirty years from now cannot be forecast with any precision. New technologies in treatment will challenge current theories of etiology, which in turn will produce new treatment choices. Treatment options alter understanding of the etiology of disorders and in turn shape further treatment.

Labeling is another continuing issue in executing the assessment. While criticism can be leveled at categorizing individuals, it is nevertheless an essential component in accountable treatment. Decisions about the type of problem confronting the client determine the theories utilized to understand and change the situation. As we cautioned in Chapter 1, social workers must guard against fallacious thinking and circular reasoning. In the three case examples presented in this chapter, clients are diagnosed with schizophrenia, depression, and attention deficit hyperactivity disorder. Rather than dehumanizing the clients, shaping the practice through an understanding of these diagnostic categories allowed for compassionate and individually oriented treatment.

The social work process is strikingly dynamic, with constant movement back and forth between all the components of practice—from assessment to intervention to relationship and communication, and then back to assessment. To demonstrate the comprehensiveness of the assessment process, we will examine three cases that apply the principles stated in our definition. Information about each client is followed by the social workers' own analysis of their process of formulating the assessment. Though we are working toward an understanding of the client, the case studies focus on the social worker's process, from initial thoughts to generating hypotheses into constructing the case theory. As before, we also provide details about the social workers' personal lives to present them as real people actively struggling with their challenges.

 Assessment is an information-gathering and organizing process that evolves from the specific to the general to the individualized. Distinctions are made among facts, observations, and judgments, and attention is paid to issues of difference.

Although it is more conceptual, assessment shares with relationship the difficulty in being quantified. Scales and measurement tools can provide needed data about clients. Decisions about which of these devices to use, however, are often based on hunches. The data provided then get used to help develop more formalized hypotheses. Standardized tests assist in formulating the case theory, but decisions to use specific scales reflect the social worker's judgment. It is that *judgment,* the decision-making process inherent in social work assessment, including the social worker's hunches, that we want to examine. We "look inside" the questions and responses of the social workers in our cases to figure out why they say what they do and where they want to go next. The third case study, which pays greater attention to information gathering outside the context of the social worker and the client, deals with specific measurement tools.

Meeting a client for the first time, the social worker experiences a wild rush of thoughts and feelings. Acknowledging and being aware of one's spontaneous reactions, and articulating them, allow practitioners to make use of these pertinent and usually significant early intuitions.

A generalized way to view separate events begins to form that adds to these first insights and draws on theories about human behavior and the social environment, on one's training and education, and on prior experiences. This occurs shortly after (or sometimes, for experienced workers, along with) the first spontaneous reactions. Balancing and integrating generalizations with reactions produce a picture of the client. By grappling with this mix of thoughts and feelings, the social worker molds the disparate and sometimes contradictory data into the main groups or categories of the assessment. The social worker then examines the resulting generalizations and shapes them into a unique configuration of the client. Shifting from specific to general to individualized, this assessment will fit no other client, though it may have similarities to assessments of many other clients.

The simultaneous demands of thinking, talking, and relating means that the social worker must juggle many demands at once. Building awareness of the decision-making process as it goes on inside oneself allows for a continual monitoring and adjustment of one's progress in understanding the client. Along with this heightened attention to process comes an increased possibility for accurate and relevant hypotheses.

Making distinctions among facts, observations, and judgments is basic to this endeavor. Facts are the details of what is going on, the events that are actually happening—specifics about employment, health, eating and sleeping patterns, living arrangements, family relationships, social supports, ethnicity, class, and cultural background. *Observations* include the range of cues the social worker perceives while interacting with the client. Often these cues are nonverbal and arise from the client's affect, manner of dress, tone of voice, body posture. Observations of the social worker's own feelings and reactions, such as feeling fidgety, sad, angry, confused, are also important to consider. Judgments are the hypotheses the social worker is developing, the emerging conclusions about the client within the context of the circumstances.

As we will see in the case studies, social workers can formulate an accurate and relevant understanding of the problem only when they keep the facts, observations, and judgments separate and distinct. When a patient presents to a doctor with back and chest pains, for example, the physician needs to obtain information about the frequency, duration, and intensity of the pains and get a medical history that will help explain the etiology and current onset of the difficulty. Usually a general physical examination will be undertaken to provide information about the patient's overall physiological condition. Obtaining *facts* from the patient, the physician directly observes the patient and begins to form some *hypotheses* to explain the back pain. These hypotheses are weighed in relation to additional facts and further observations. Forming the foundation for the medical diagnosis, this process produces an explanation of the patient's pains and a proposed plan of treatment to alleviate them.

Likewise, when a client presents to a social worker with a symptom such as frequent loss of employment, the social worker obtains information about the frequency and length of past jobs and about the consequences of the current unemployment for the client. The social worker, who requires knowledge about the client's employment history within the context of that person's social and emotional functioning, asks questions to obtain facts about the client's current living arrangements and available social and financial supports to get a picture of the client's current functioning in the environment. At the same time, the social worker observes the client's nonverbal cues in reporting the information as well as the interaction between the client and family members. Additionally, the social worker is making observations about his or her own feelings about the client and about the information presented. Tentative hypotheses formulated by the social worker, validated and modified by further facts and observations, will produce a case theory to explain *one specific* client's loss of jobs and a plan of intervention to help the client achieve a more stable employment record. There are many possible explanations for the client's employment problems, including psychological reasons (he has personality problems), emotional issues (he is depressed), and sociological factors (the economy is bad and jobs are hard to get). Clarification of the facts, observations, and judgments builds an explanation that fits this client's situation.

Because social workers practice with clients who come from different cultural backgrounds, races and religions, and economic and social classes, attention to issues of difference is also requisite for accurate assessments. A complex process of thinking and feeling, the assessment is easily vulnerable to the social worker's biases and personal preferences. While Chapter 7 has been devoted to this component, we also examine it in these next case examples.

Our first case begins with a very brief summary of the client's basic identifying information and her circumstances—employment, treatment history, family contact, and presenting problem. Information on the client is presented factually; no judgments are made on the client or her situation. As a rule, basic information about the client should be neither qualified nor explained. (Full discussion about the presentation of information is covered in Additional Notes.)

....

Dale is a 32-year-old female who has had inpatient and outpatient treatment at a Veterans Administration hospital for a period of seven years. She has been seen for delusions, trouble with sleeping and eating, homicidal and suicidal attempts. She was raised in a rural community in one of the Rocky Mountain states where she lived, with her parents and elder sister until the age of 18. She has maintained contact and feels support by her family. They do not now live in the same geographic area. After high school, Dale was in the WACs for several years. She then received LPN training and worked as a nurse until her first hospitalization at the age of 25. At the point of the following intervention, she is employed as an LPN at a metropolitan hospital, has been receiving outpatient treatment at the VA hospital for three years, and with this social worker for one month. The client resides alone in an apartment and has almost no friends. She is considering getting married in about four months. The current situation is that the client has been feeling increasingly anxious, has had further trouble sleeping, and is experiencing suicidal urges.

....

Let us now examine an exchange between the social worker, Linda, and the client, Dale, and explore the way in which the assessment moved from specific to general to individualized as Linda gathered and organized the information and began to form judgments that integrated the facts and observations. The emphasis here is on the process of understanding this client. We join the social worker in the complex journey of formulating a means of understanding what is going on with the client and determining how she can be of help.

During the following interaction, the client, Dale, sat very erect, an almost stony look on her face. She spoke in a flat tone of voice, the only sign of movement was her heavy puffing on cigarettes.

*1 DALE: Right now I think you are angry with me.

   LINDA: How am I showing you that I'm angry with you?

   DALE: I just don't know. *(pause)* It's not anything specific that any-body does. It's different things. *(long pause)* You're far away today. I see you very far away.

   LINDA: What do you mean I am far away?

   DALE: I'm not sure. People get that way sometimes for me. All I can see is this big space *(motioning a circle with her hands)* and you're in the center and you're very small.

*2 LINDA: I'm not angry with you. *(hesitating)* Are you angry with me?

   DALE: No, I don't get angry.

   LINDA: Is that a problem for you?

   DALE: What?

LINDA: That you don't get angry.

DALE: No, I don't think so. I don't think you're supposed to get angry. *(long pause)* I used to get angry a lot, but I don't anymore.

LINDA: How did you get angry before?

DALE: I'd yell, slam doors, do stuff like that.

LINDA: You don't slam doors anymore? What do you do?

DALE: Now, I stay pretty much to myself. I get mad at myself for getting angry. I'm not supposed to do that, so I don't do it.

LINDA: You don't allow yourself to express anger. You feel it by being upset with yourself, by being angry with yourself, you're feeling it.

*3   *(pause)* Sounds like there is a connection between these feelings and when you see things at a distance.

*4   *(long pause)* What does getting angry mean to you?

DALE: Well, you're not supposed to get angry. It's committing a sin. You're supposed to control your temper.

LINDA: I understand that you think you shouldn't get angry, but I'm not clear what you mean when you say you are angry at someone.

DALE: Well, I used to . . . *(pause)* I used to hurt people when I'd get mad.

*5 LINDA: How? Hurt them how?

DALE: Oh, when I used to get mad at my sister, I'd hit her, and with my mom and dad, I'd say something I didn't want to say.

LINDA: You say the ways you've dealt with anger in the past weren't successful. You hurt people and felt sorry about it. How successful is what you do now, controlling everything inside you? What happens to you when you do this?

DALE: Well, I sometimes cut myself. *(shows the cuts on her wrists)*

Linda observed her own *specific* feeling reaction in the assessment process to be discomfort with the client's stony appearance and confusion and fear when the client accuses her of anger. Linda discussed her initial reactions:

....

Dale was one of my first cases when I was a second-year M.S.W. student. I knew some of the homicidal and suicidal history about this client and had done some reading about schizophrenia. All of my thinking left my awareness when

Dale started telling me she thought that I was angry with her (*1). She looked so odd on this day—very stiff and a faraway look in her eyes, I felt unsure about what to do. For what seemed to me a long time, but what was probably just the flash of a few seconds, I couldn't think and was aware only of my fear and anxiety.

At the same time I was aware of the need to get more information. It was important for me to know what anger meant for Dale, to have a personalized picture of her life and the manner in which she dealt with things.

....

From her setting, which worked with schizophrenia, with her supervisor's help, and through reading about this condition, Linda learned that clients who have schizophrenia may project onto the worker feelings that they have difficulty expressing. She began to think that Dale might need help in learning how to express feelings appropriately. Linda also discovered that one of the side effects of the phenothyazine drugs prescribed for Dale was dryness of the mouth, which might result in exaggerated facial movements. Linda commented about her question to Dale at *2:

....

When I ask Dale if she is the one who is angry, I am beginning to remember what I know, to start using my knowledge along with my feelings to both understand this client and say something to her during the session.

....

At this point Linda's knowledge was at a *general* level. Drawing from her reading and previous experience, she conjectured that the client might have a problem in dealing with anger. This generalization inhibited personalization of the interaction and helped Linda shift away from feeling that Dale was angry with her or from having angry feelings toward Dale. By framing what was happening more conceptually, the social worker could begin to respond as a helper, not just as an individual reacting to another person. There was movement from Linda's specific reaction of fear and discomfort, prompted by the odd way this client looked and strange way she talked, to a generalized picture of the client's trouble with anger and overall difficulty with the expression of feelings.

By *3, when Linda commented on a possible connection between the manner in which Dale handled anger and her "telescopic vision," Linda was proposing a means of explaining Dale's behavior. Questions *4 and *5 elicited more specific information from Dale, which helped Linda begin to formulate an understanding of how this client dealt with feelings of anger.

....

I can still remember my incredible relief when I realized that for me to get a handle on what might be going on with Dale, I needed more information, and that I could get it directly from her.

....

Asking her what the anger meant to her was really quite a good question. Often social workers get stuck in their initial feelings or cling to whatever theories or experiences they have had, convincing themselves that by these means they understand the client. Asking clients direct and pointed questions, however, is crucial in moving beyond the specific into the individualized. A picture emerged of the client's losing control when she was angry, first by striking others and then by hurting herself.

Possessing some of the *facts*, Linda had to *distinguish* them from her *observations* and *beginning judgments*. The *facts* included the following: Dale had several previous psychiatric episodes, receiving both inpatient and outpatient care; had not formed close relationships with others and functioned with minimal social supports; was in good physical health; worked regularly and had a solid employment record; reported a recent increase in time spent sleeping. Additionally, Dale had two previous engagements but had not come this close to actually getting married before. She was White and grew up in the rural West.

Linda noted her *observations* of Dale. With little emotion evident in her voice tone and almost no body gestures used when talking, Dale sat rather still, with a noticeable lack of affect. Though she was a neatly dressed and groomed woman, she made odd-appearing facial movements, as if she had a dry mouth.

Linda also made *observations* of herself. Noting that her voice got hoarse as she talked with Dale heightened her awareness that she was feeling afraid or anxious. At the same time that she leaned forward in her chair, as if to reach out to Dale, she was also placing her handbag on her lap. Linda was aware of feeling ambivalent, both wanting to form a relationship and help Dale while also feeling uneasy about Dale's past psychiatric history and odd looks.

In sifting through the facts, observations, and judgments, Linda needed to consider issues of *difference*. In addition to her struggle to interact with someone with a diagnosis of schizophrenia whose behavior is peculiar to her, she had to examine how issues of background and class might be shaping her understanding of the client. Linda was Jewish and grew up in a large city in the Northeast, whereas Dale was Protestant and raised in a rural community in one of the Rocky Mountain states. Both families were working class—low income, high school or lower for the educational level, and employed in manual work. Farming was Dale's family occupation over their several generations in the same area. In Linda's family the occupation was factory work: Her grandparents had emigrated from the Polish-Russian border in the early 1900s and became employed in the garment industry.

Having spent her first twenty years in the crowded Northeast, Linda grew up and went to school with people who were White, Black, Hispanic, rich and poor. Although comfortable with these differences, she had no experience with people from rural backgrounds. Very aware that the cadence of Dale's speech was much slower than what she was used to, Linda was forced to examine the new "differences" to which she was now exposed. This continued to be crucial later in the practice, when Dale married John, who spoke even more slowly and with a Southern drawl. (The impact of these cultural differences on practice interactions are covered in Chapter 6). At this point Linda clarified for herself that the difficulties lay in what Dale said, not in how she said it, and that the concerns were cross-cultural.

Linda began the process of constructing the *case theory of the assessment*. She had been forming *judgments* about the facts and observations. Linda considered that Dale had kept isolated from any close relationships while getting angry at herself when she began to have angry feelings toward others. In the area of social functioning, Dale had almost no social supports. Though Linda learned that minimal social interaction was the norm for Dale's family, she came to believe that Dale's social isolation was more than a reflection of culture. Linda theorized that when Dale cut herself off from close relationships, she did not have to deal with her angry feelings and avoided feelings of fear and vulnerability. Difficulties she encountered in handling her emotions in this way were lack of support, with no opportunity to share her feelings and gain recognition and acknowledgement from others. Linda reflected that the recent increase in Dale's symptoms of sleeping too much, increasing anxiety, and urges of suicide might be linked to the pending marriage. These hypotheses would need further validation in the ongoing work with the client.

Linda then realized that their developing relationship might be one of the closer relationships that Dale experienced. Linda speculated that if her hypotheses about Dale were confirmed, this relationship might provide a model for Dale about having close relationships and expressing feelings appropriately. In this way Linda came to regard the professional relationship as an important part of the treatment.

In this case the *specific* became *general* and then *individualized; facts, observations,* and *judgements* were identified; and *issues* of *difference* were considered. Linda sorted through her own initial uncomfortable feelings, used some of her knowledge to help her understand the client's odd behavior, and was in the process of constructing a picture of Dale.

 Assessment as the case theory is the theoretical linking of the client's past, present, and future.

The function of the assessment is to develop an understanding of the client's problem in order to help the client change. The social worker requires knowledge of the client's past to shed light on the present to create change in the future. Hypotheses generated out of the assessment process provide the means of understanding the client's current situation within the context of past events while creating options for changing subsequent events through the intervention.

Bruner, in describing the process of learning, talks about "going beyond the information given" (1964, p. 13). A Gestalt had to be formed—the creation of a whole picture from the bits and pieces. To go beyond the information, the social worker makes inferences from what the client presents. These inferences receive further refinement, or are dropped, depending on further information and continued work with the client.

The following contact between Linda and Dale took place four weeks after the previous session. The client was engaged to be married in six weeks. She had just returned from a visit with her parents.

DALE: A fog is all around me. Nothing matters, I don't feel anything.

LINDA: How do you feel about having this fog?

DALE: I don't feel anything. I never thought about it. I don't want it to go away. I feel like I'm in the center of a cloud.

LINDA: What would you feel if the cloud went away?

DALE: I don't know.

LINDA: What did you feel before it came?

DALE: Oh, kind of mad.

LINDA: What do you mean by "mad"?

DALE: I was feeling angry with my dad.

LINDA: Is having the fog your way of dealing with anger at your father?

DALE: I suppose. I just don't listen to him.

LINDA: You need some way of dealing with your dad. Seems like the best way you have come up with is feeling like you are in a cloud. When did you first start having this cloudlike feeling?

*6 DALE: Oh, I remember having this in high school. It doesn't just all of a sudden start. It has a process how it goes.

LINDA: Sounds like the fog helps you turn off your feelings?

DALE: You're way far away.

Continuing to construct the case theory, Linda framed an understanding of the problem in context. Learning, at *6, that the client had experienced visual hallucinations since high school, she inferred that Dale had difficulty, at least since that time, with forming relationships and with functioning in her environment. Information gathered by Linda, in additional talks with Dale and in reviewing the case record, validated her hypothesis that anger was a recurring problem for Dale, particularly in past family interactions. Linda theorized that anger was a metaphor that this client used to talk about her feelings in general.

Further development of Linda's theory suggests that this client's method of dealing with feelings was related to her pattern of forming social relations and to her depression and suicidal thoughts. To better understand such a client's behaviors, the social worker must examine theories about schizophrenia (Menninger, 1948), while models of social work treatment (Smalley, 1967; Hollis, 1970) offer practice approaches in working with these clients.

The nature/nurture debate has provided two perspectives through which to explain schizophrenia. Kraepelin (1896) originated the term *dementia praecox* to refer to "a tangible morbid process occurring in the brain." In this organic view heredity plays an important role in the transmission of schizophrenia. Recent technological advances have brought a resurgence of interest in the biological basis of schizophrenia, with research focusing on the brain's frontal and temporal lobes and limbic system (Taylor, 1987).

The nurture perspective, on the other hand, considers schizophrenia to be acquired behavior. Some have believed that it is the result of being raised by a "double-binding" mother who is overtly accepting but covertly rejecting (Bateson, Jackson, Haley, and Weakland, 1956), while others considered the impetus to be dysfunctional family interaction—growing up in a family composed of an "undifferentiated ego mass" (Bowen, 1960).

Though clarity is lacking about the etiology of schizophrenia, there is general agreement about prognosis. Schizophrenia is not discussed in terms of a cure but is presented as an ongoing condition that can present varying degrees of difficulty. Persons with this diagnosis have trouble forming relationships, do not effectively manage their feelings or thoughts and behaviors, and are often only marginally effective at coping with their environment. Problems with feelings of anger are considered typical. Menninger (1948) calls it "unassuageable anger," consisting of chronic or pervasive feelings of rage.

Informing and shaping the social worker's assessment, the choice of theoretical background for a specific case is influenced by the employing agency and the social worker's own frame of reference. Linda was employed at a V.A. hospital, closely affiliated with a major psychiatric center and hospital. This setting, and the social worker's educational preparation and training, drew on a psychodynamic model for understanding clients and a casework focus for treatment. Linda also relied on the worker-client relationship (Smalley, 1967) and a continual observation of herself as a practitioner, emphasizing self-awareness and use of self. Psychosocial casework supports "reality-oriented" treatment utilizing an active, reaching-out approach of reorienting the client to the present social reality rather than resolving internal psychological conflicts, and it is the recommended treatment approach with this population (Farber, 1958). Improvement of social functioning is the thrust, to enhance the client's capacities and skills of interacting with the environment. The large multidisciplinary character of Linda's employing setting also affected her ability to incorporate physiological treatment approaches into her psychodynamic framework. Availability of physicians allowed for a well-integrated balance of chemicals and casework (Gottesman and Shields, 1982).

Linda examined her own hypotheses in light of the theoretical literature. Her educational background, frame of reference, and employing agency and supervisor influenced the literature she drew from. The assessment shapes and is, in turn, shaped by, the available knowledge in the field, the individual social worker, and the mission of the agency.

Linda began alternating weeks of individual sessions with the client and couple sessions with the client and her fiancé.

DALE: I don't like it when we argue because arguing makes me think about getting angry, it is a first step of getting angry. I worry about losing control.

LINDA: How did that come across to you, John?

JOHN: I never knew that she lost control when she was angry before.

DALE: I don't think you've ever seen me angry.

LINDA: Can you define for John what you mean by "angry"?

DALE: Oh, get mad, yell and stomp around, do stuff like that.

JOHN: Now when she gets in a bad spell, she gets depressed, she sits around and doesn't do anything. Isn't that right?

DALE: (smiling) Yeah, I guess so.

Linda considered the continuing impact of Dale's past on her present behaviors and planned means to help the client function differently in the future. Utilizing material from the professional literature and incorporating the positives and negatives—the strengths or benefits accruing to the client and the limitations or problems—Linda now formulated her developing hypotheses over these many sessions into the case theory, *linking the client's present to the past and to the future:*

. . . .

Dale came in for help with feelings of depression, suicide, and anxiety. With a history of difficulty in acknowledging and dealing with her emotions, she has had minimal social contacts and support. The literature on schizophrenia provides a basis for understanding the hallucinations and problems in forming relationships (Menninger, 1948) and the utilization of medication to alleviate some of the problematic symptoms (Gottesmann and Shields, 1982).

Anger is a metaphor that Dale uses to talk about her feelings in general. For her, having feelings has meant loss of control. She has not only tried to hide her feelings from herself, she has also maintained an isolation from social contact. The benefit she has gained by this behavior has been protection from feeling vulnerable. The negative outcomes have been almost no support and continued feelings of depression and suicide. Dale is afraid of her own feelings, afraid that she will lose "control" of her behavior and hurt others or herself.

Demonstrating strengths at social functioning, Dale has held a steady and responsible job supporting herself in her own apartment. She has developed a close relationship with John, her fiancé, with a commitment to get married and have a family. While on psychotropic medication, she has been able to continue to do well on reduced dosages. Limitations include continued social isolation with some visual hallucinations and suicidal feelings. During previous times of stress, Dale has sometimes stopped taking her medication and has needed renewed inpatient treatment.

Ego psychology (Freud, 1937; Parad & Miller, 1963) and systems (Ackerman, 1958; Hartman, 1983) and communication theories (Haley, 1959; Jackson, 1957) provide approaches to understanding the client's current behaviors. Ego psychology attaches importance to gaining awareness of the client's coping capacities and the maintenance of balance. Difficulties of clients with schizophrenia in dealing with feelings and emotions are viewed as ego defenses which "may be buttressed by unreasonably strong superego prohibitions" (Nelson, 1975, p. 147).

Systems theory views the identified patient as a member of a family and community, with a focus on the individual within the context of the environment. Drawing Hartman's ecomap provides graphic evidence of Dale's social isolation. Communication theorists point to the nature of the interactive behavior between the client and family members. Consideration of the interpretation of messages conveyed and received in Dale's family point to Dale's perceptions of being disqualified—not given affirmation and encountering inconsistent messages. Dale's behavior may be seen as serving a function within her family, as "normal" for her family.

Pharmacological treatment has been considered important (by the client and the outpatient team) in Dale's improvement. Wolberg states "the first line of attack in schizophrenic breakdown is somatic therapy" (1967, p. 1005). While the dosage and type of drugs and duration of medication treatment need to be discussed, it is important not to rashly change the medication at this point in time. During these next months, many changes may be occurring in the client's life and the support provided her by the thorazine is probably needed.

The psychosocial approach suggests additional treatment possibilities. Focusing on the person in situation, this model essentially applies systems theory to casework (Hollis, 1981). Change for Dale will entail learning how to talk about and gain validation for her feelings. With the knowledge from the literature (Farber, 1958) about the importance of the casework relationship, the relationship will serve as a crucial vehicle in modeling with Dale how to process and gain support for one's feelings. Psychodynamic theory also emphasizes the value of the helping relationship. "The key to the treatment of schizophrenia lies in the ability to establish some sort of contact with the patient. Most schizophrenics . . . erect various obstacles to any interpersonal threat. The withdrawal from reality, and the archaic type of thinking and symbolism, enhance the individual's isolation from people, since there is no common means of communication. Yet beneath the surface the patient yearns . . . for a friendly and loving relationship" (Wolberg, 1967, p. 1007).

While a relationship between the worker and client will initially be the crux of treatment, it will be applied to lessen the client's fears of close relationships and provide her a model in developing relationships with others, and especially with her fiancé, John.

....

As illustrated above, the case theory succinctly records the background relevant to the client's seeking help, briefly captures the essence of the social worker's understanding of the problem, draws on the relevant theoretical literature, and highlights the plan of intervention.

Assessment provides a map that organizes the approach to each case situation.

Assessment may be conceived of as a map or blueprint that guides practice. *Cognitive mapping* is defined as "the mental process through which people come to grips with and comprehend the world around them" (Downs and Stea, 1977, p. 61). In navigating the physical world, one engages in an interactive process with the environment, deciding which pieces of information to store and developing means to order and prioritize that information. One has to organize the information in order to be able to get from "here" to "there." In social work practice, the social worker frames a cognitive map for each client, detailing the situation as it is now, envisioning the circumstances at subsequent times, and developing a plan to get from the now to the later.

The development of an accurate map depends on the worker's knowledge about what the client desires to change, the client's background, and current information. In planning a trip, the necessary knowledge includes the type of vehicle being used, the amount of fuel needed, and the driver's prior experiences with this type of vehicle and journey. Social workers need to know something about who the client is, what type of resources the client has used in navigating the social environment, what might be needed to address changes in the client's social functioning, and the client's prior background in dealing with similar experiences.

The map shapes the establishment of the relationship, the choice of communication methods and skills, and the plan of intervention. The other components of practice are encompassed under the assessment, which serves as an umbrella. As we will see in the following section, several important decisions flowed from Linda's assessment, including: (1) to have a relationship with loose boundaries (on a first-name basis; Dale has Linda's home phone number for use in emergencies), (2) to use structured communication, with confrontation, validation, exploration, silence, focusing and sustaining the dialogue (communication methods and skills covered in Chapter 6), and (3) the modality of intervention (to work with the client and her husband as a couple, focusing on their feelings and interaction).

Proceeding with our case example, Dale and John got married. At the time of the following session they were married for one month and were being seen together as a couple. Linda believed it was no longer necessary to alternate individual and couple sessions; since John had bonded sufficiently with her and with Dale, it would now be helpful for Dale to shift some of her reliance onto John.

LINDA: *(to John)* I hear you saying that you do talk when you have something to talk about, and you don't quite know what Dale means when she asks you to "just talk."
(to Dale) What does it really mean to you, what's so important about talking?

DALE: I'm with somebody, I'm not alone.

LINDA: Could John take this from now on, that when you say you say you want to talk, you're actually saying that at that moment you're feeling kind of lonely?

DALE: Yeah, I've never told John how I felt about this.

JOHN: I'll remember that.

LINDA: *(to John)* You know, you could still have a problem. If Dale says to you that she wants to talk, you might know that she may be feeling lonely, but you might still not know what to talk about.
(to Dale) I wonder if you could help. What kinds of things could you begin talking about to make it easier to get the conversation going?

DALE: I guess I could think of something I want to talk about at the time.

LINDA: Oh, you mean you will help create the conversation. That sounds good, that will help John and you be able to talk together.

By the next session the client had been married for two months. The couple had switched seats. Dale was sitting straight up in her chair, with more affect than usual showing on her face. She spoke loudly, in an agitated, angry tone of voice, and looked directly at John.

DALE: It embarrasses you, doesn't it? You told me not to smoke in front of other people, and I don't smoke in front of those certain people because it will embarrass you.

JOHN: I don't remember that.

DALE: Yes, you certainly did! You said it looks tough for a woman to smoke!

LINDA: It sounds like this has something to do with women, with what women should be doing. John, what are you thinking?

JOHN: It's not right for a woman to smoke.

DALE: John's idea of what a woman should be and my idea are two different things.
(to John) You said it would be nice if I could sew like your sister, and about my cooking you said I should make pies like your mom.

LINDA: So, what's behind this? What are you really saying when you talk about John having these models that you feel he wants you to live up to?

DALE: He doesn't accept me the way I am. He wants to change me, make me over into something else, that I'm not and can never be.

LINDA: It's kind of hard, isn't it, John? It seems like the women you knew before you got married did certain things and acted certain ways, and you now find that you want your wife to be the best of all those people. What are you feeling now?

Practice with this client continued to be organized by the social worker's case theory that this client used anger as the metaphor for talking about uneasiness with feelings and her fear of losing control. Linda facilitated Dale and John in a discussion about arguing. Anger provided the topic, the entree, through which they would begin to talk and share and get to know each other. As the basis of the plan of intervention, Linda had Dale present to her husband feelings about arguing and anger so that she could lessen her fears and form a basis for trusting herself as well as her husband. Teaching the couple new ways of interacting, Linda enabled Dale to talk about her anger in a safe environment (in the social worker's presence) so that she could learn ways of dealing with her feelings other than hurting herself and others.

Again, the literature provided guidance to direct practice with this client. Farber states: "It is important that the beginning phases of treatment be concerned primarily with the establishment of the vital patient-worker relationship. . . . The schizophrenic patient . . . needs actual direction in turning his attention toward externalities . . . it is important to consider ways in which the patient may be held to discussion of important realities" (1958, pp. 13–15). Judith Nelson agrees that the development of the relationship is one of the areas basic to effective treatment for clients diagnosed with schizophrenia. In forming the relationship, she maintains, social workers must be able to present clear and consistent messages, tolerate long periods of silence, and handle clients' ambivalence about dependency and independence: "A client may have his first real experience that negative feelings can be expressed and understood in a close relationship" (1975, p. 339).

Supported by the literature, Linda's hypothesis that her client had need of a strong, supportive relationship with Linda in the role of teacher or coach, carried over into Linda's judgment about the husband's needs. From the history taking she learned that both Dale and John had little experience at relating intimately with others; both grew up as loners, with no truly close relationships. Linda assessed that for this couple the normally difficult process of learning how to relate as a couple would be particularly tough because of their lack of experience in relating closely to anyone. Changing the modality of intervention from individual sessions to working with the client and her husband as a couple allowed Linda to teach them basic communication skills, such as ways they could share feelings, ask questions, and handle feedback. Using her strong relationship with Dale and their established pattern of communication as a model, she provided a foundation for the newly developing relationship between Dale and John.

The emphasis remained on the present social reality. Through discussing the petty and trivial details of life—feeding cats, making pies, sewing clothes, smoking cigarettes—this couple began to establish the rules in their relationship and formulate their respective roles and responsibilities. The assessment shaped the use of a strong and supportive relationship, including teaching and coaching roles for the social worker, and determined the modality of intervention to be work with the client and her husband as a couple focusing on their feelings and interaction.

The social worker continued to practice with this client and her husband for about three years. Over twelve years past the last session with the client and her husband, Linda continued to receive occasional Christmas notes. The following note was received after no correspondence for several years:

John and I and our family are well. John has a farm job this year and is going to school in the evening. He wants to be a History teacher. He is halfway there. I tried to work as a nurse, but my back said no. So I am home taking care of the family. I am a Den Mother in a Cub Scout den and I enjoy that.

Mary, our eldest, is 13½ now. A beautiful, tall, young woman. Andy, our 12 year old, is a straight 'A' student and also a gifted musician. He will be travelling to Europe this summer for a concert. Kate is next at 10. She is somewhat immature for her age and has trouble with studies. Last but not least is our Willie. He is 7 and in second grade. He has been in counseling for two years due to behavior problems. He is coming along fine.

Well that's about all now. Middle age has gotten to me. I'm 47 now. I'm glad I waited until late to get married. I am very happy with my life and family.

We do have problems like everyone else but I wouldn't change it for the world.

Though long-term contact with a former client is rare, this letter is very precious to Linda. She knows that she helped make a difference in the lives of Dale and John. When she questions her ability to practice social work and has feelings of hopelessness about her clients, she rereads this letter and can remind herself of the remarkable and unpredictable possibilities for clients who receive the help of social workers.

Linda continued to develop her social work skills and, while maintaining her direct practice with clients, moved into the role of supervisor and teacher of practice. Her work with Dale first prompted her to recognize the critical importance of the assessment process to social work practice. As she states:

. . . .

I began to realize that there were many possible theories of the case that could have directed the practice with Dale. One might have focused on her social isolation, or the schizophrenic symptoms. These alternative ways of conceptualizing Dale's situation would have resulted in different maps, and different plans of intervention.

Practicing social work can be a humbling experience. I feel so good about my work with Dale, about the change in her life course related to some of the things we worked on together. On the other hand, these other maps could also have resulted in significant changes, perhaps overlapping with the ones accomplished here.

It is clear to me that there is not one way to understand each client. Yet I must articulate my particular understanding, my case theory of a client, because it is that understanding that shapes everything else I do.

. . . .

The sessions we have examined come from one year of practice. Not always, however, does the social worker have an opportunity to practice with the client over a long period of time. In the following case we examine practice with a client that lasted only a single session.

Deborah, the worker, had twenty-six years of post–M.S.W. experience, with her primary expertise in practice with children. Employed in the infant psychiatry program at a major medical facility, she received a referral from one of the psychiatric residents who became concerned while doing a consult in pediatrics. During a routine physical check-up, he observed Trish to be "one of the most depressed-looking little girls" he had ever seen—she didn't smile, didn't seem to want contact with her mother, and lacked energy in her movements. The resident shared this with Deborah, along with the following basic information:

....

Trish Scott is a 21-month-old physically healthy female, the third of four children—an 8-year-old brother, a 6-year-old sister, and an 11-month-old brother. Her mother is 28 years old. The family is African American, they reside in a housing project and are covered by medical assistance. The mother and father have been separated for about two to three months due to abuse by the husband of the wife.

....

Assessment is an information-gathering and -organizing process that evolves from the specific to the general to the individualized. Distinctions are made among facts, observations, and judgments and attention is paid to issues of difference.

Deborah's *specific* thoughts when the resident first approached her were mixed. Labeling a child so young as depressed was worrisome to her. While she knew that he was somewhat new and inexperienced, she hoped that he wasn't overly quick to place people in diagnostic categories. On the other hand, over the six years she had been with this program she too had seen depressed-looking infants and children. Deborah comments on her immediate reactions:

....

I felt so uneasy, I don't like thinking in terms of depression for such a young toddler. This resident, however, seemed pretty capable. It's also better to consider

*the matter seriously and not overlook something problematic. I immediately
worried that the dad has been sexually abusive to Trish, and considered that the
mother might be abusive to Trish and/or to the other children. I was somewhat
concerned for the safety of the child. I knew I needed to quickly either elaborate on
these initial judgments of mine or discard them.*

....

During their first, and what turned out to be their only, contact Deborah
began with introductions. The use of surnames reflects the tone of the
interview. Though we are examining the assessment process, also note the
formation of the relationship and the communication methods and skills
used by the social worker. Deborah was establishing a belief bonding with
Mrs. Scott by presenting herself as a competent authority who believed in
Mrs. Scott's capacity to take charge of the situation. Friendly, Deborah
remained centered on establishing a professional relationship by making it
easy for Mrs. Scott to talk about the issues that had brought her into the
office.

MRS. MARSH: Hi, Mrs. Scott, I am Mrs. Marsh. I am with the Infant
              Mental Health Program. Dr. Harris here has told me
              about his meeting with you last week. *(reaching down)*
              And this must be Trish. Hello, what a cute bow you
              have on your hair. Would you both come with us?
              The playroom is around the corner and up one flight.
              We can use the elevator over here. *(continues to make
              small talk with the mother with some overtures to Trish)*
              Please come in.
              Trish, if you want to play with these toys, you can.
              The mirror over there is actually a mirror only on this
              side, there is a room on the other side. There are
              times when other doctors and social workers sit in
              there and observe what is happening in this room.
              There is no one observing us now. In the future, if
              someone is observing us, I will let you know.

              Dr. Harris has said that Trish was looking very un-
              happy and depressed last week during her visit with
              the pediatrician and that he talked to you for awhile
              and asked you to come in again to talk with him and
              meet with me.

MRS. SCOTT: Yes. I told him that it had been like that for quite a
              few weeks, probably more like a few months. It's
              been worse since her daddy left.

	Mrs. Marsh:	I'd like you to tell me what you can about her. We'll be watching her while you and I talk, and then I'll ask you questions if there are other things we're going to want to know about. We'll see if we can figure out what's wrong.
*1		Tell us how you noticed something was wrong.
	Mrs. Scott:	In the beginning I didn't notice. After I talked with you (*motioning to Dr. Harris*), I began to think. She has been very close with her dad. After he brings her back from a visit with him, she clams up.
*2	Mrs. Marsh:	Does he come and take her with him?
	Mrs. Scott:	Yes. I can tell she is happy to see him. She has been closer with him than with me. But after the visits she is cautious.
*3	Mrs. Marsh:	What do you mean by cautious? (*noticing Trish is scratching her eye*) Do you have an itch?
	Mrs. Scott:	She won't let me hold her. She'll push me away. There was a lot of conflict between us. Maybe she is remembering what went on.
*4	Mrs. Marsh:	So she knew that there was conflict between you and her dad and then her daddy goes away and is gone for long periods. It is hard to know with one so young. She may have felt angry or scared or sad. She could see her daddy wasn't around very much. Did you and her dad have conflict before?
	Mrs. Scott:	When she was very young. I don't think she would have noticed then.

(*Dr. Harris is giving Trish some coloring paper. She looks at it and leaves it.*)

*5	Mrs. Marsh:	How do you and her dad get along now?
	Mrs. Scott:	We don't talk much. He comes to pick her up and also see her brother William, who is 11 months old.
*6	Mrs. Marsh:	So he picks them both up and takes them away for a while. Do you know what he tells them?
	Mrs. Scott:	I don't know. I did bring up to him that she seems clammed up, but he didn't say anything. Her brother is happy-go-lucky, he doesn't always go for the visit.
	Dr. Harris:	Yes, he seems lively.
	Mrs. Marsh:	So he doesn't seem affected. Was your husband upset at leaving the children?
	Mrs. Scott:	Oh yes. He wanted to take her, but I wouldn't let him. He would keep her to himself, like all day play

in her room with her. I would tell him that I thought he was alienating her from the others. She didn't play with the other children, maybe she thought she wasn't supposed to. I think when her sadness came, she started daydreaming and was in her own little world. It's been only two months that we separated.

*7 MRS. MARSH: Sounds like what you are describing is a really big loss for her.

DR. HARRIS: What is it like now? When he takes her, are they together by themselves?

MRS. SCOTT: Last time I brought him William, too. He lives with his mother.

*8 MRS. MARSH: What have you said to his mother? Is she close with the children?

MRS. SCOTT: My mother is closer. But his mother has also noticed. She even mentioned to me that Trish doesn't want to play with other children and cries if they try to play with her.

*9 MRS. MARSH: What was it like before he left?

MRS. SCOTT: It was like their own world when he was home. He would read to her, she would talk to him. When he wasn't home and I'd put her outside, she would just sit there on the step.

*10 MRS. MARSH: What was the effect on her of William's birth?

MRS. SCOTT: She was already closer with her daddy. I didn't see any change.

*11 MRS. MARSH: Was her daddy home a lot?

MRS. SCOTT: Yes, in her waking hours he was home.

MRS. MARSH: What have you told her about her daddy leaving?

MRS. SCOTT: I really didn't tell her anything. I wasn't sure that she would understand. I'm surprised she is acting friendly in here, she doesn't even know you.

MRS. MARSH: *(to Dr. Harris)* Was she as close to Mom the day you all met?

DR. HARRIS: Even the way she is trying to get on the chair now, she wouldn't get near her the other day.

Throughout Deborah's ten years of experience at her setting, she had seen many families with issues of incest and abuse. Remembering that when she was a new worker these problems would not initially have occurred to her, she was aware that she now regularly considered them as possibilities. Her professional experience, the rise in the reported number of child abuse cases, and the increase of related articles in the literature all served to enhance Deborah's sensitivity to the potential of abuse. From 1980 to 1986, the reported incidence of child abuse and neglect increased by 66 percent from 9.8 to 16.3 children per 1,000 (National Center on Child Abuse and Neglect, 1988). Nationwide, there may be more than 1.5 million children who are victims of abuse each year.

Deborah knew from the literature that sexual abuse continues to be underreported and often treatment is not effective (Cohn and Daro, 1987). She was also well aware of the increase in poverty among Black families headed by single mothers. According to the 1990 Census, single mothers under the age of 24 accounted for more than 66 percent of all Black families with children, and 69 percent of these families had incomes below the poverty line (U.S. Bureau of the Census, 1990). Many of the families Deborah saw as clients were headed by single mothers, were Black, were poor, and had dealt with issues of abuse in the home.

At the same time, Deborah had to be careful not to fall prey to the deductive fallacy. Just because this family might share characteristics of abusive families did not mean that abuse was present, abuse did not necessarily accompany poverty. This is why the assessment is so important. Deborah needed to integrate general information from the literature with her own personal reactions to formulate an individualized picture of this family.

Moreover, a debate exists in the literature both about whether depression exists in childhood and about the use of drug therapy. Some argue for a biochemical component in depressed children, finding that the clinical response of children to imipramine and desnethtlimipramine is similar to that of depressed adults (Lewis and Lewis, 1981). Others are not convinced about the effectiveness of the pharmacological treatment of depression and believe more research is needed (Toolan, 1981).

Meeting clients jointly with a member of another discipline can be very helpful in sorting through these complex issues. Deborah stated:

....

I was pleased that the resident would be joining me for the interview of Trish and her Mom. It is becoming increasingly evident to me that there is often a physical basis for many of the disorders we see, and it is important that social workers not ignore that dimension. The psychiatric resident would be sensitive to the symptoms of depression, while also being respectful of my psychosocial orientation. Working in an interdisciplinary setting has greatly enhanced my skills of assessment and intervention.

....

Deborah directed her *information gathering* so that she could move beyond her *general* hypotheses about possible sexual abuse of Trish by the father or possible physical abuse by the mother. Should she continue to have concerns about abuse, she would be legally required to involve the Department of Health and Human Services.

She first gathered information about the mother and the particulars of the father's visits. At question *1 Deborah wanted to learn about the level of awareness the mother had about Trish's problem, and at *2 she obtained the facts about the visits with the dad. Following questions *3 and *4, in which Deborah clarified and summarized for the benefit of Mrs. Scott and herself, Deborah obtained data (questions *5–*7) about the relationship of Mr. Scott with his wife and the other children and about his feelings.

The *facts* Deborah knew prior to this interview included that Trish had not been showing much affect or any interest in interacting with anyone other than her father since his separation from her mother. The facts also included that the mother was only 28 years old and had the sole responsibility for four children. Finances were a problem. They lived in a housing project and relied on medical assistance.

From these questions Deborah now also knew that the father was maintaining minimal contact with most of the family except for Trish, whom he picked up at the home. Her behavior changed from happy when she saw him to cautious with her mother on her return. The mother also reported that there was long-term conflict with her husband, that he was unhappy with the separation, wanted to take Trish with him, and had been giving Trish much of his attention since her birth.

Deborah *observed* that Trish was clean and nicely dressed and during the session was smiling and making some overtures to sit on her mother's lap. Deborah's observations of her own reactions included positive feelings about the relationship between Trish and her mother. Mrs. Scott appeared to be open, willing to talk about her family situation, and attentive to what Deborah had to say. Deborah was aware that she was feeling less concerned about possible abuse of Trish.

Additionally, Deborah attended to issues of *difference* and how they might impact on her assessment. As a Black woman she was of the same race and gender as Mrs. Scott, but not of the same class. Deborah's father was a school principal, her mother was a lawyer, and she attended one of the best private schools in the area. Used to living with many physical comforts, Deborah was raised with a strong sense of doing good for others. Social work was a natural career choice for her. From the time of her early teens she was aware that she wanted to work in some capacity with children. Her second-year field placement was at a school for children with special problems. Over the twenty-six years in her vocation Deborah continued to develop her special and unique set of skills as she interacted with this increasingly vulnerable population.

While Mrs. Scott grew up in the same city, her childhood experiences and access to resources were very different than Deborah's. Raised by her maternal grandmother with her four siblings, they also lived on welfare in one of the large housing projects in another part of the city. She had very little contact with her mother and stepfather, both of whom abused alcohol, and hardly saw her natural father.

Just as Deborah had to guard against the deductive fallacy in her assessment of the presence of abuse in the home, she also needed to evaluate Mrs. Scott's parenting based on the current picture of Mrs. Scott and Trish, not on the sorry picture of Mrs. Scott's mother and father, and not on the basis of the financial resources available to this family.

The issues of difference were further complicated by the fact that the medical resident was of Asian background and was not yet experienced in working with families from this community. Unsure about the effect of his unfamiliarity with the culture on his diagnosis of depression, Deborah had to attend seriously to his diagnosis while also clarifying her own thinking.

By *7, Deborah was starting the *formulation of her case theory.* Her initial *specific* consideration of depression moved to a *generalization* that this was possibly an abusive situation, either sexual by the father or physical by the mother. As both of these early judgments were not validated by the facts and her current observations, Deborah's hypothesis, *individualized* for this client, began to switch from a troubled child due to abuse to a sad child dealing with loss of her primary relationship, which had been with the father. With questions *8–*11, Deborah broadened her perspective by asking about the role of the paternal grandmother and learning about the situation prior to the separation. She knew she wanted to learn more about Mrs. Scott's capacities to parent. Just like Linda, she moved (albeit more quickly) from the *specific* to the *general* to the *individualized.* Through her use of the literature and awareness of her own reactions, she continued to talk with Mrs. Scott, at the same time thinking of child development theories and recent research on grieving and loss.

 Assessment as the case theory is the theoretical linking of the client's past, present, and future.

As we discussed in the earlier case with Dale and John, information about the past is obtained in order to understand the present so that the future can be changed. Deborah's questioning was purposive, in her own words, in order to

. . . .

locate the problem—is it in the baby, the mother, the nature of the relationship? I needed to learn if Trish has been this way all her life, if not, what has happened? I wanted to look at her developmentally—is this child where we would expect her to be? The child is in the parent's environment, so a very important question concerns the emotional supports provided by the parents—who are their advocates and what are their problems?

....

The agency in which Deborah was employed used Mahler's developmental stages to assess their young clients. Based on Mahler, Deborah understood Trish, who was 21 months old, to be ending the rapprochement crisis, "characterized by the rapidly alternating desire to push mother away and to cling to her . . . to use mother as an extension of the self . . . a process in which is denied the painful awareness of separateness" (Mahler, Pine, and Bergman, 1975, p. 95). Typical behavior for girls during this period is that they "become more engrossed with mother in her presence, demanding greater closeness and more persistently enmeshed in the ambivalent aspects of the relationship" (Mahler et al., p. 102). Trish has not experienced these more "normal" stages of development with her mother.

Because Deborah's own theoretical background was psychoanalytic, she relied on Fraiberg for her understanding of infant development. For Fraiberg, attachment between infant and mother is fundamental to the child's normal growth and development:

> What we see in the evolution of the human bond is a language between partners . . . which becomes a highly differentiated signal system. . . . It is . . . the matrix of human language and of the human bond itself. . . . We have an extended period in infancy for the development of attachment behavior and a sequential development that leads to the establishment of human bonds. By the time a baby is eight or nine months old he demonstrates his attachment by producing all the characteristics that we identify as human love. He shows preference for his mother, he initiates games of affection with her, and he shows anxiety, distress, and even grief if a prolonged separation from her takes place. (1977, pp. 57, 56)

Though it appeared that Trish had formed a human attachment, Deborah was concerned that it was not with the mother. Because of the reported abuse by the father and his removal from the home, Trish did not have available, on a regular basis, her primary human attachment. Moreover, the deprivations experienced in the early, formative years might have permanent consequences. According to Fraiberg, "children who have been deprived of mothering, and who have formed no personal human bonds during the first two years of life, show permanent impairment of the capacity to make human attachments in later childhood, even when substitute families are provided for them. . . . The period of greatest vulnerability with respect to later development is in the period under two years of life" (1977, pp. 52–53).

Deborah continued to formulate her case theory.

MRS. MARSH:　*(to Trish)* Are you biting Mommy's finger?
(to Mrs. Scott) Does she do anything aggressive to you?

MRS. SCOTT:　She hits if I refuse something from her.

MRS. MARSH:　So she wants you, but she wants it in her own way.
(Trish is holding onto mother's lap)
(to Trish) Are you feeling closer to your mommy? You've been away from her for a few days and now you have her back. Maybe you're thinking Mommy is a pretty good person to have.

MRS. SCOTT:　I need to pay attention to her reaction the next time he brings her back. Maybe he should stay away. Maybe the visitation is not the best thing for her.

MRS. MARSH:　I'm glad you said it that way and not the other way, that she should stay away from you. It must be very hard for a little girl where the daddy was the most important person. Maybe she was having a grieving reaction.

MRS. SCOTT:　Yes, she seemed so depressed.

MRS. MARSH:　Yes, little children can be depressed. Maybe there is something she can hear about what happened. That Mommy and Daddy didn't get along, Daddy is now living with his mother, and she has you, her mother.

*12　　　　　　　Can you tell us what happened that is different now?

MRS. SCOTT:　To make her come to me more? Well, on Saturday I took her to an amusement park, and she started coming to me. Yesterday I took her to a skating rink, she didn't skate, but she was screaming like the other kids. She's not acting so different from the others. She seems a whole lot better.

MRS. MARSH:　So, you went to the park, and that was a new thing. You decided to stay closer to Mommy, Trish, and there's that big smile.

*13　　　　　　　Tell me what she was like when she was first born.

MRS. SCOTT:　She was never a very outgoing child. She would do things, like sing and march. Not wild, but she did participate in things. Then, if you tried to hug her she would say no.

*14 MRS. MARSH:　So maybe she was angry with you? Is how she is acting now different?

MRS. SCOTT: Yes, this weekend, she was like a flower. You know it's hard for a parent to be rejected. I feel loved again by her.

MRS. MARSH: Is she talking more now?

MRS. SCOTT: No, but she brings me things if she wants me to do things. She would call the other kids and talk with them. With me she would say eat, or potty, she would let me know if she needed something.

MRS. MARSH: Do you tell Mommy when you have to go potty? (*Trish smiles and goes up on mother's lap*) Here you are on Mommy's lap. She knows you are concerned about her.

*15   Have you had anything like this in your experience?

MRS. SCOTT: No, not like this.

DR. HARRIS: What was it like for you at first when your husband left?

MRS. SCOTT: I was depressed and angry. Life goes on, I started to carry on.

*16 MRS. MARSH: Had you suspected that you would end up separated?

MRS. SCOTT: Yes, I knew it was leading up to it. I tried to not let it affect my children. But they know, they can sense if something isn't right.

*17 MRS. MARSH: How have you been feeling by yourself lately and how long were you together? Was the abuse a one time thing?

MRS. SCOTT: Physical or emotional, emotional abuse is important, too.

MRS. MARSH: Both.

MRS. SCOTT: The emotional was more than the physical. He was a very emotional person, it didn't take him much to storm.

*18 MRS. MARSH: What do you think was going on from his side, why were they so close?

MRS. SCOTT: Maybe because it was his first child, if she had disagreements with the others, he would pick her up and separate them.

*19 MRS. MARSH: She didn't have to deal with it. How did he feel about your mothering?

MRS. SCOTT: This was stupid to me, he felt I didn't love her as much as I did the other children. That was his reason for taking her more. For me that was ridiculous.

*20 MRS. MARSH: How was he with the other children?

Mrs. Scott:	He wasn't violent with them. But he wasn't very close, not even with his own son. That's why I think she took it so hard, it was him and her.
Dr. Harris:	Were there any struggles between you and him about his relationship with her?
Mrs. Scott:	I got tired of arguing with him. I figured I would have to deal with it later.
Mrs. Marsh:	Are you ready to deal with it now?
Mrs. Scott:	Yes, that's why when the doctor brought it up the other day I thought, "Well, now it's time to deal with this because I noticed it myself and I want to do something about it."
Mrs. Marsh:	How has it affected your older ones?
Mrs. Scott:	My 8-year-old hasn't said anything, and my 4-year-old also, they just go out and play.

Deborah was building an understanding of Trish's behavior within the context of the larger family situation while beginning the road map, her route through which to bring about change. In her questions *12–*14, she learned about changes in Trish's behavior and her developmental progress over time. In questions *15–*17, Deborah focused on the mother and her experience of the separation. Deborah then acquired information about the mother's perceptions of the father (*18–*20). The additional information about Mr. Scott was important in formulating the case theory that Trish was in a special relationship with him and consequently was the family member to be grieving his absence from the home.

Grieving and loss became the themes in Deborah's case theory to explain Trish. Simos (1979), who presents loss as a universal and integral part of human experience, nevertheless agrees with Bowlby that permanent loss or prolonged separation from the caretaking figure during the second half of the first year to age 3 brings a grief reaction (Bowlby, 1961). According to Simos, there is some agreement among child development theorists that the normal child is capable of experiencing and expressing longing by the second part of the first year of life, called the stage of object constancy. Loss of the mother figure between 6 months and 3 or 4 years of age places the child at emotional risk.

In her case theory, just as in Linda's earlier, Deborah utilized the professional literature and tried to consider both positives and negatives as she *linked the client's present to the past and future:*

....

Trish, brought in by her mother, has been looking sad and depressed, spending time by herself and not interacting with her siblings or mother. Her father and mother separated two to three months ago. Trish had a very close, albeit, isolating, relationship with the father. Up to the point of his separation from the mother, Trish was developing normally, though lacking substantive interactions with other persons, including her siblings and mother. Child development literature points to the importance of infant-mother bonding during the early period of life (Klaus & Kennell, 1976).

The individual attention she received from the father helped her feel special, while she is now suffering with a reactive depression tied to the father leaving (Spitz, 1965). In a state of grieving, Trish is experiencing double losses—the loss of the mother figure (the father in this case) and a lack of connection with the caretaking figure (the mother).

Though this could result in serious disturbance in Trish's future (Freud & Burlingham, 1944) the situation currently does not appear too severe. With the mother's evident capacity and concern for Trish, a quick and effective intervention might be possible. The mother has self-esteem, is articulate and functions at a high social level. The approach might be—let's work on this together to strengthen what is already good. This could involve helping the mother to strengthen her own relationship with Trish and better integrate Trish with the other siblings.

Continued meetings with the mother and Trish would be good to consider, with perhaps some individual and group sessions for the mother. Individual meetings with the father might also be useful.

....

❧ *Assessment provides a map that organizes the approach to each case situation.*

Unfolding from the case theory is the guiding map that provides the route to follow for practice with a client. As Deborah stated:

....

When I met Mrs. Scott, I was struck with how "with-it" she looked. I became curious about what's going to be in this story to account for Trish's behavior, it did not seem "run-of-the-mill." She had some success in the first few days after she saw Dr. Harris and she was ready for more information. Some people come here feeling embarrassed, guilty over whether they have caused the problem. This was not the case with Mrs. Scott—this lady felt she was as important as we were. I approached my relationship with her as—Yes, I am the expert, now what can we all do to work on this together. My language and way of talking change with the client's educational level and social functioning—Mrs. Scott was intelligent and high functioning—I spoke with her candidly and saw myself in a role of educator.

....

Deborah's theory that Trish needed to have a closer relationship with her mother, and that the mother was capable and ready to provide what

Trish needed, organized her approach in the practice. Deborah recognized that Mrs. Scott's situation was not easy—Mrs. Scott was young, managing on welfare, and raising her kids in a housing project. Prior to the separation the husband had been in charge of Trish's care and earned money. Mrs Scott now had four children, no husband, and limited financial resources. Deborah let Mrs. Scott know she was supported and acknowledged the tough issues she faces.

*21 MRS. MARSH: You wonder how hard it is for her. I also wonder if a child can make a decision that it's time to perk up and get back to the other parent. I also wonder whether you think her dad might be willing to come in?

MRS. SCOTT: I don't think so. When I tell him I brought her here, I don't know what he'll say.

*22 MRS. MARSH: I wonder if you could tell him that the separation has been harder for her than you thought, and that it might be helpful if you both came in with her together.

MRS. SCOTT: See, he feels he came from a split-up family, he doesn't see it as such a big thing. But I told him they were so close together. *(Trish sits on her lap, singing)*

*23 MRS. MARSH: I wonder if you could tell her a story, explaining that Daddy is not living here anymore, Dad loves her, Mom loves her a lot, too. She will be spending more time with Mommy now, Mom will feed her and put her to sleep.

MRS. SCOTT: I'm wondering after he gets her each time, will she revert back?

*24 MRS. MARSH: I don't know, that's what we want to see, if a change is happening now for the better. That's what would be good, if he could also tell her that she will be with you more and he still loves her. I don't think you can cut off his relationship with her, but he can help encourage her to relate more to you.

DR. HARRIS: She has a lot more expression today than I saw last week the whole time. She just sat in a chair with no expression.

*25 MRS. MARSH: Well I'm glad to hear that. Now she may get angry with you. You need to tell her that little story— "You're going to stay here with me, you'll be visiting Grandma and Daddy and then you'll be coming back home with me."

(to Trish) You're going to be living with Mommy and William and your older brother and sister.

(to Mrs. Scott) I'm wondering if you'll be willing to visit us each week with her.

MRS. SCOTT: So to see if there is a change, how she is doing?

*26 MRS. MARSH: Right. The way she is sitting with you now, you both had a relationship, a connection before or she wouldn't be able to do this.

(to Trish) I think you're getting a little upset. You know you'll be staying with Mommy, and Daddy isn't in that house anymore.

(to Mrs. Marsh) He may have his own reasons for having so much trouble in sharing her. She has a little brother who she'll get to play with. She needs to learn how to get what she needs from the other people in her life. It may have been the best thing for her to grieve, though it's hard to tell what's happening at such an early age. The way it developed, he was closer to her.

MRS. SCOTT: That didn't bother me, it was the alienation from her.

MRS. MARSH: Do you have any questions?

MRS. SCOTT: No, they have been answered.

MRS. MARSH: Can we call you for an appointment?

MRS. SCOTT: Yes, I'm home.

Based on her case theory that change needed to come from the parents, in questions *21–*22 Deborah pursued the possibility of involving the father in treatment. For the rest of the session, *23–*26, Deborah offered specific advice to Mrs. Scott on strengthening her relationship with Trish. Deborah believed that the mother needed to take steps to help Trish get over her reaction to the father's absence and involve herself in a more appropriate relationship with her daughter.

Though Deborah had initially worried about a sexual relationship in the father's closeness with his young daughter, by the end of this session she no longer had this concern. The mother was comfortable that sexual abuse was not an issue (Dr. Harris had asked her about this possibility during his first visit with her). Beginning to see this as somewhat like a custody case in a middle-class family, Deborah planned to meet with Mrs. Scott and Trish for at least another two to three sessions. In her experience, the work could often be completed during this time. Though surprised that Mrs. Scott did not show up for the next appointment, Deborah hoped that she might have gotten enough out of the one session they had and was able to continue on her own.

This case demonstrates that even in practice of merely one session's duration, social workers proceed on the basis of hunches that are influenced by their own backgrounds, knowledge, experiences, and training. If they continue to articulate the hypotheses during the formulation process, they will produce more accurate and theory-supported case theories.

While in the previous cases information gathering was limited primarily to interactions with the client, in the following case the social worker makes use of measurement scales and has to coordinate treatment with the client's school and family. This example pays more attention to content, the kind of information the social worker gathers, whereas the two previous cases focused more on process, the manner in which the social workers proceeded and their thinking about what was happening. As treatment progressed in this next case, the social worker found that his initial case theory was faulty and altered it based on new information and insights.

Kevin Burton shared a suite of offices with another social worker and a psychologist, and they rented one of their offices to social workers doing private practice on a part-time basis. With a doctorate in social work and certification in family therapy, he held an adjunct faculty appointment in a school of social work, where he taught an elective course on practice with children and adolescents. Throughout most of the eighteen years since completion of his master's in social work, Kevin held teaching and consulting positions.

The case was referred to him through the school attended by a third grader, Chris, age 9. Refusing to do any work in school or any homework, Chris was failing all his subjects, was socially isolated, and caused disruptions in the classroom. Kevin also had the following basic information:

....

Chris resides with his mother (age 32), stepfather (age 35), and half siblings, a 4-year-old brother and a 2-year-old sister. Mrs. Simon works as a supermarket cashier, Mr. Simon drives a bus, and their family income totals about $35,000; they are both high school graduates. Mr. and Mrs. Simon have been married for six years. Mrs. Simon was divorced from Chris's dad six months before she remarried, and that was the last time Chris saw his natural father. Chris's problems have persisted for the past three years and have been getting worse. He doesn't listen to her or her husband and fights with his siblings.

....

 Assessment is an information-gathering and -organizing process that evolves from the specific to the general to the individualized. Distinctions are made among facts, observations, and judgments, and attention is paid to issues of difference.

Kevin's routine procedure in receiving referrals for children or adolescents was to meet first with the parents for 90 minutes, then have two individual sessions alone with the child, followed with another lengthy session with the parents. He informed parents to be prepared for discussion at that initial session about the child's developmental history. By the second meeting with parents, Kevin would have formulated his assessment, which he shared with them. Should he recommend treatment of the child, he would use part of that session to assist them in preparing the child to begin therapy.

On the basis of the initial information he had, Kevin believed that Chris's difficulties could be emotional. Attentive to the birth of the siblings four and two years before, Kevin had an early hunch that Chris had difficulty in adjusting to the newly blended family. Drawing on his extensive practice experience, however, Kevin knew he had to file away this hypothesis and be open to the unfolding of other explanations for the client's difficulties. During the phone call to set up the first appointment, the mother sounded angry and said she was getting increasingly frustrated with Chris. In beginning the initial session, Kevin's *specific* worry was whether there was still enough time to help Chris by working with him or if more drastic action—a change in schools, or at the worst, residential placement—would be necessary.

Introducing himself for the parental session as Dr. Kevin Burton, he was usually Dr. Burton to his clients. Correspondingly, he used last names in referring to the parents and first names for the children.

DR. BURTON: Hi, I'm Dr. Burton, I'm glad to meet with you after talking with you on the telephone, Mrs. Simon. *(to Mr. Simon)* I hope you were able to find the office without too much difficulty.

(After Kevin offers them a choice of seating, Mrs. Simon chooses the couch and Mr. Simon sits on one of the comfortable lounge chairs.)

As I explained on the phone, I would like to spend this time in having you teach me about Chris. I'm interested in knowing lots of things about him, including his current situation and his past. I will also want to know some things about your family life.

Perhaps we could begin with the current problem. I would like for each of you to describe what brings you to see me.

*1   Following up with other questions about the "problem," Kevin explored how it got started, how long they had been worrying about it, how they dealt with it, other help they sought, what had been successful, and what had not worked.

*2   He next obtained a thorough developmental history
          about the child from conception to the present, includ-
          ing: what happened in the child's life, developmental
          milestones (walking, talking, toilet training), and
          physical health (illnesses, appetite, sleeping patterns).

*3   School history was covered next, focusing on when
          Chris began, how he did academically, and his in-
          teractions with peers and teachers.

*4   Moving to a discussion of the family, Kevin asked
          about physical and mental illnesses in the family his-
          tory and the emotional life of the family. Linking the
          family with Chris, he asked how they dealt with his
          temper tantrums, his feelings of sadness and anger,
          and how they handled Chris between the two of
          them.

*5   Ready to wind down the interview (this is a great deal
          to fit into 90 minutes), Kevin kept a quick pace by not
          offering his own thoughts at this time, mainly phras-
          ing the questions. He made note of things he might
          want to follow up more fully the next time he saw
          them and explored strengths and positives they identi-
          fied about Chris. He asked what they liked best about
          Chris and what they would most like to change.

Kevin also provided help at this time to prepare Chris for his first visit, which would follow in a week. Showing the parents to the play room used to meet with children (equipped with books, clay, dolls, small trucks and trains, and an assortment of games) he encouraged them to tell Chris they would be taking him to a "worry doctor" who would be talking with him about his feelings.

Extensive background information was available to Kevin through his structuring of the *information gathering* around themes *1, the problem; *2, developmental history; *3, school history; *4, family history; and *5, emotional history between the family and the child presenting the problem.

Central to this stage of the assessment for Kevin was gathering informa- tion directly from the child. Anxious about meeting Chris, he prepared himself to meet with an angry child, possibly depressed and having trouble with reality. Worried about whether Chris would act out during the hour- long session, he asked the parents to be available in the outer office and advised them all that they would take between half and one hour.

*6   Dr. Burton: *(reaching out his hand and shaking hands with Chris)* I'm
                   Dr. Burton and I'm glad to meet you, Chris. I met
                   with your parents last week and they tell me they
                   have been worried about your behaviors.

CHRIS: I'm happy to meet you, too. Are you going to help me with my worries?

*7 DR. BURTON: That is what I want to do. I don't know much about you yet, so I was hoping that you would help me understand more about your worries. I want to understand you better so I can see how to help you get rid of your worries. What has been your biggest worry these past few days?

CHRIS: Do you know what happened to me a few weeks ago?

*8 DR. BURTON: I think I may know, but I'm not sure exactly what you are referring to.

CHRIS: I found out my Daddy is not my real father.

*9 DR. BURTON: Tell me more about this.

CHRIS: Well, my Daddy is signing some papers soon to be my father. He's my Dad, but not my father yet.

*10 DR. BURTON: Your parents told me that they have started adoption proceedings so that your Dad becomes your legal father. How has this been a worry for you?

CHRIS: Well, I don't understand why they didn't tell me this before.

*11 DR. BURTON: I don't know, either.

Starting with a statement, *6, that his parents were worried about him, Kevin left the door open for Chris to help structure the content of the interview. When Chris asked whether help would be available for his worries, Kevin knew that the parents had done their job in preparing Chris for the session.

Using Chris's own words of "help with his worries," Kevin tried to get more specific information about what was worrying him, *7. At *8 and *9, instead of answering for Chris, he asked Chris to elaborate on what he meant. After Chris brought up the impending adoption proceedings, Kevin, at *10, still pushed for specificity. At *11, he shared with Chris his own lack of understanding about why this was a family secret for so long.

Facts obtained from the two interviews indicate that while Chris had last seen his natural father when he was 2½ years old, he had been told by his mother that his stepfather was not his natural father only three weeks before. According to Chris's mother, her husband's mother had shared this information with Chris about a year and a half before.

Chris had always been an active child, and his mother reported having a difficult time during his early years. Traveling frequently, Chris's natural father had little interaction with him. For the past three years she received an increasing number of complaints from the school. Since she and her husband each worked different shifts, there were not many opportunities for the family to spend time together. Though she had been the person to talk with Chris's school, she had not talked much about doing this with Chris. At home, Chris spent most of his time watching television and playing at friends' houses.

Observations by Kevin include awareness of his own alarm along with relief. Not expecting Chris's sad and downcast appearance on meeting him in the outer office with the parents, he was surprised by Chris's ability to articulate and relate during the interview. Yet even while talking with Kevin, Chris barely raised his head and made no eye contact.

Confused by the parents' failure to talk with Chris about his natural father, Kevin could not understand their recent abrupt introduction of the impending adoption. He was also puzzled by the extent to which Chris seemed upset about the adoption. Knowing that Chris was aware he had a different last name from his mother and siblings, Kevin couldn't comprehend what Chris understood that to mean. While appearing to have intact thought processes and to be bright enough—he had good use of language, expressed himself clearly, and explained things in interesting ways—Chris seemed restless. Though this was not unusual for a 9-year-old, they had spent about half of the session in game playing and the balance in talking.

The parents were casually dressed. Mrs. Simon, extremely overweight, was the more active talker, though Mr. Simon did talk and appeared interested and concerned about Chris.

Always attentive to issues of *difference*, Kevin was careful not to allow premature judgments to influence his understanding. He himself had grown up poor, White, and working class in a Northeastern city, and so his family was similar to the Simons. Kevin had always felt different from his family; he liked music and art and disliked sports, unlike almost everyone he knew. When, in his twenties, he had come out as a gay man, his father had almost disowned him. Since that time Kevin had had very little contact with his family. Because many of Mr. Simon's mannerisms (and, he assumed, attitudes) reminded Kevin of his own father, he knew he had to remain very aware of these negative feelings and not rehash issues relating to his family of origin. Responding directly to Mr. Simon, and not to his own father, was essential in Kevin's understanding of Chris's relationships within his family.

Distinguishing the facts from his observations, Kevin formulated tentative *judgments* that Chris's behavior problems were a reaction against his parents and home situation. Before his mother's second marriage, Chris lived with much turmoil but did have his mother totally to himself. When Chris was three years old, his mother married his stepfather. Relying on his background in psychoanalytic theory, Kevin knew that Chris was moving from the anal to the phallic stage of development at this time (Baldwin, 1968). At the very moment Chris was experiencing growing interest in his genitals and the start of his oedipal stage, a stepfather came on the scene. With the stepfather came two young siblings who probably got much of his mother's attention. In fact, it appeared that the problems began when his brother began to walk and his mother was pregnant with his sister. Living in an increasingly frustrating situation could well have induced greater aggressive behavior in Chris (Mussen, Conger, & Kagan, 1969).

Though he was not yet ready to rely on this first judgment for his case theory, Kevin recommended to the parents that Chris have individual treatment. Acknowledging that they knew him best and therefore that he wasn't telling them anything they hadn't known, he stated that he found Chris to be bright and verbal. He assured them that their perceptions were accurate—that his behavior in the school and home did need to be changed. Accordingly, Kevin offered weekly sessions (at a discounted fee due to the low family income). His *specific* reaction of seeing a troubled and problematic boy and his negative feelings about the parents had moved to a *general* view of a capable child coping with uninvolved and, perhaps, insensitive parents.

 Assessment as the case theory is the theoretical linking of the client's past, present, and future.

Meeting with Chris on a weekly basis, Kevin first practiced on the assumptions—in his not yet fully developed case theory—that Chris's problems were primarily emotional, including aggressive feelings toward his stepfather and unresolved issues from his phallic stage of development (Freud, 1923). Kevin's psychoanalytic background formed the basis for his work.

Having reviewed early history with the parents, Kevin found nothing unusual with Chris's development. Acknowledging to himself that he needed further information from the school, he began to understand Chris as a lonely, scared, confused kid. Alternating their weekly contacts, every three weeks Kevin met with Chris's parents for an hour. Teaching them parenting skills, he also addressed their relationship with their other two children.

Admiring an extraordinary use of therapy by the parents and Chris, Kevin noted major behavior changes in the home in the space of six weeks. Chris's adoption, which was completed shortly after the start of treatment, was no longer a topic of discussion. Pleased with Chris's calmer behavior at home, the parents reported that he was much less oppositional and got along better with his siblings. More relaxed during sessions, Chris made regular eye contact and interacted positively with Kevin through symbolic play and talk.

Chris, however, was still failing many of his subjects at school! Recognizing that he must now expand his information gathering through contacts with the school, Kevin knew he also needed to develop his case theory more fully and validate the assumptions that were guiding his treatment.

Kevin was shocked during his phone call with the school psychologist to learn that a recommendation was being considered to transfer Chris to a special education school for disturbed and retarded children. Chris had continued to be a disturbance in the classroom and had recently locked himself in a closet to avoid taking a test. Referring Chris for a psychiatric evaluation, which showed nothing abnormal, Kevin arranged for a neurological workup with a pediatric neurologist. Confirming what Kevin had come to recognize, the evaluation suggested *attention deficit hyperactivity disorder* (ADHD).

While constituting the most chronic behavior disorder and the largest single source of referrals to child mental health centers (Barkley, 1981), ADHD is one of the most complex and difficult-to-diagnose disorders of childhood (Goldstein & Goldstein, 1990). To determine this condition, "mental status testing is usually divided into six categories including fundamental processes, language, memory, constructional ability, higher cortical functions and related cortical functions" (Brunquell, Russman, and Lerer, 1988), and testing results must be considered in the context of a comprehensive multidisciplinary evaluation including parent and child interviews and school evaluations along with the neurological, medical, and psychiatric examinations. Usually no single one of these examinations is conclusive; the diagnosis is made on the basis of several of them considered together.

In spite of the claim by William James that "everyone knows what attention is," the meanings of this term vary and accordingly it has been difficult to develop a clear definition of the attention deficit disorder. The common-sense understanding of ADHD includes four components: inattention and distractibility (remaining on task and focusing attention), over-arousal (excessive restlessness and intensity of emotional arousal), impulsivity (lack of thinking before acting), and difficulty with gratification (working toward long-term goals) (Goldstein & Goldstein, 1990).

Coming into increasing attention in the early 1980s, the cluster of problems we now call ADHD was first referred to as *hyperkinetic reaction* of childhood in the *Diagnostic and Statistical Manual* (DSM) of the American Psychiatric Association (APA, 1968). According to the 1988 revised *DSM-III-R*, the child must present symptoms before age 7, have experienced them for at least six months, and not meet the criteria for *pervasive developmental disorder*. Coexisting diagnoses can exist with schizophrenia, retardation, and severe emotional or behavior problems if relevant symptoms are excessive.

Like schizophrenia, ADHD is viewed as a disorder that is managed, not cured. Horn and colleagues (1984) argue for multimodal treatment, such as medication and behavior management at home and school; medication and self-control training; parent management and self-control training; and medication, self-control training, and teacher and parent behavioral management.

While medication is common to three of these four modes, serious concerns have been voiced about the use of medication for children and the accompanying side effects, including insomnia, anorexia, toxic psychosis, seizures, Tourette's syndrome, growth suppression, and drug abuse. At the same time, the benefits of medication have been extraordinary, offering, in some cases, immediate and obvious behavior changes (Conners & Wells, 1986). Ritalin, the brand name for methylphenidate, is the most common chemical substance used in the treatment of ADHD.

Armed with this new knowledge from the literature and, ultimately, confirmation from the school records that Chris tested in the average range of intelligence, Kevin believed that ADHD seemed an accurate diagnosis. Finally formulating his theory of the case, Kevin linked the client's present to the past and future:

. . . .

Brought in by his mother and stepfather due to behavior problems in the home and school, Chris initially presented concerns about not knowing that his stepfather was not his real father. An impending adoption proceeding by his stepfather seemed to initiate treatment. His mother and father divorced when he was 2½ years old, and not having much interaction even during the marriage, his natural father has made no contact with him since that time. When Chris was 3, his mother married his stepfather and they have since had two children, currently 4 and 2 years old. Coming during an important time in his development (phallic stage), Chris probably had difficulties in accepting his stepfather, sharing his mother, and grieving the abandonment by his natural father (Rochlin, 1965).

Making no eye contact during the initial session and continually looking down as he spoke, Chris may be experiencing depression (Weiss et al., 1971). At the same time, he articulated clearly his concerns about the status of his father, and genuinely asked for help and engaged in the helping relationship (Smalley, 1967).

Because Chris is oppositional in the home and having serious problems with his performance at school, plans are being considered for his transfer to a special education school.

Medical, psychiatric and intelligence testing has all been at the normal range. A neurological evaluation pointed to the consideration of ADHD, attention deficit hyperactivity disorder, with the support of various scales including The Teacher and Parent Social Skills Assessment *forms (Goldstein, 1988),* The ACCESS Placement Test *(Walker et. al., 1988), and* ACTeRS *(Ullman, Sleator, & Sprague, 1991).*

Parenting training will continue along with regular weekly sessions for Chris. Contacts will be initiated with the teachers and school counseling and guidance services. Work will be toward an integrated approach between the home, school, and family and individual therapy, and consideration will be given to the use of pharmacology as a component of the treatment.

....

Having delayed the formalization of his case theory, Kevin integrated his early and later understanding of Chris, presenting the psychodynamic and biological/social theories about ADHD that he ultimately utilized. While initially relying on psychoanalytic theory to understand Chris, for his approach to practice Kevin also drew on functional social work (Smalley, 1967) and the problem-solving approach (Perlman, 1957), with their emphasis on the helping relationship and a focus on the particular set of problems brought by the client.

Briefly summarizing the relevant background information, Kevin identified his intervention plan. Comprehensive, it emphasized contact with Chris and the parents and also included intervention with the school.

Assessment provides a map that organizes the approach to each case situation.

Delayed by the slow formulation of the case theory, the guiding map of practice with Chris was also slow in development. As Kevin stated:

....

This is in many ways a classic example of the need to follow a bio-psycho-social approach in the conception of clients and their problems. The odd circumstances of Chris's adoption and the apparent lack of parenting skills in this family seemed to point toward emotional problems. While I had some concerns in the back of my mind prompted by reports of his extremely disruptive behavior in the classroom, I told myself that at some point I would need to check into that. At the same time, psychoanalytic theory offered me what seemed a valid framework for understanding Chris, and my reliance on the use of the relationship and a focus on the presenting problem of Chris's behavior in the home came right out of my training in functional social work and the problem-solving method.

....

Kevin's initial mapping of his work with Chris determined that his intervention would include individual and family therapy, a heavy use of relationship with Chris and the parents, and work toward more structured parenting in the home. Reflected in the simultaneous strong belief bonding between Kevin and Chris and between Kevin and the parents, the relationship became very important in the initial stages of this practice.

Communication skills emphasized the social worker's use of silence, which fostered Chris's own talking and sharing while respecting his slow pace. In keeping with his hypothesis that depression was a possibility, Kevin relied on heavy use of validation and reflection as the communication methods, with attention to and acknowledgement of Chris's feelings.

Although it was effective in improving the home situation, however, this organizing approach to practice was deficient in its neglect of an important system in the life of a child—the school. Involvement with the school and knowledge about Chris's testing results were crucial for Kevin to map an appropriate and relevant intervention strategy. Asking for testing results (accompanied by signed parent release forms), Kevin was denied any access to records.

....

When I ran into trouble in obtaining information from the school, I knew I would have to start taking an advocacy role—to support and champion for Chris's rights within the school system. At first I was told that Chris had never been tested, which did not make sense—that by the third grade no standardized testing had been completed on a student. In talking with the school social worker and guidance counselor, I ultimately learned that Chris had in fact been tested when he moved to this state—in the first grade. With no recent testing, any special education placement would be in violation of state regulations.

....

Ultimately learning that testing completed when Chris was in the first grade reported an IQ on the WISC-R of 103 and a Bender score of 6–6.5, Kevin knew that a special education program was not what Chris needed; there was not a problem with his intellectual capacity. Once Kevin learned that Chris had tested in the average range for intelligence, he was able to advocate that placement in a program for learning disabled kids was wrong for Chris. Furthermore, current test results would be required for such placement.

Armed with this new knowledge, Kevin decided to intervene with the school system directly to see whether he could prevent the school transfer:

....

Fortunately, I knew the school's principal. I was easily able to reach her because of our social connection, and we first chatted for a few moments. Sharing briefly that I was working with one of their students and the parents, I told her I thought her staff was considering placement of the student because he was disruptive in the classroom. Letting her know how difficult it had been to obtain the testing results, I asked her what help she could now give me.

....

It is the responsibility of social work to intervene directly with the various systems clients are engaged with. As discussed in Chapter 2, and illustrated in many of the case studies, system change is often necessary before individual change can occur. Getting the school system to be responsive and attentive to Chris's needs would be essential for any lasting stabilization.

At the same time, it is important to recognize that intervention with systems encompasses work with individuals. Practice components of relationship building, communication methods and skills, and practitioner observation are all embodied in intervention directed toward systems change. Utilizing the range of these social work components, Kevin refurbished his map, incorporating work with the school to help them construct an environment for Chris that would elicit fewer destructive behaviors. He also added to the map a modification of the work with Chris's parents to include a consultation with the pediatric neurologist who had diagnosed the ADHD.

After the consultation, Kevin met alone with the parents, offering them an opportunity to sort out their feelings about the diagnosis and to plan subsequent treatment for Chris:

*12 KEVIN: Though we've all experienced the positive changes in Chris's behavior in the home, it was clear that we were missing something when he continued to do so badly in school. That's why I called Dr. Sands in to conduct some testing. Now that you've had a chance to hear him talk about attention deficit hyperactivity disorder, do you have any questions or things that you would like to clarify?

MRS. SIMON: Yes, there was such a dramatic change in how he acted after taking the Ritalin. I just don't know, though, about him taking a drug. It's not like he is sick or anything.

MR. SIMON: I agree with my wife. What happens if he starts taking too much of it or something? I feel like we're leading him into drug addiction.

*13 KEVIN: Yes, those concerns are very real. Chris is young to start on a drug which he may need for many years. As Dr. Sands explained, we don't know how long he will need to take the prescribed drug, Ritalin. Though Chris is not sick, there are physiological reasons why he has so much trouble sitting still and paying attention, which, as you know, puts him at a terrible disadvantage in the classroom. Perhaps if we consider the pros and cons of the Ritalin.

Drawing on the strong belief bonding established with the Simons, at *12 Kevin acknowledged with them the gap in his intervention and was respectful in exploring with them their current thinking.

Again validating and reflecting their feelings, at *13, Kevin also confronted them with Chris's problematic behavior in the classroom. Focusing with them (another of the communication skills) on the positives and negatives of medication, Kevin was working toward helping them make a decision for themselves and their son. Utilizing another of the components, practitioner observation, Kevin was careful not to impose his own preferences on the Simons. Having worked with several children who were taking Ritalin, he knew there could be dramatic improvement. This was, however, a very important decision that the parents had to make for themselves.

Including the ADHD diagnosis into the case theory also modified Kevin's approach to practice with the Simons. Structure and consistency are of primary importance for children with this diagnosis, requiring that Kevin spend some time in the session providing this information and helping the Simons plan how to incorporate these changes into their home. Advising the parents of a published resource on hyperactivity and Ritalin (*The AD Hyperactivity Workbook for Parents, Teachers and Kids*, 1988) Kevin also provided some help to the parents in how to talk about this subject with Chris.

Deciding to put Chris on the Ritalin for a trial period of three months, all three Simons and Kevin were awed by the astonishing results. Between April and June, Chris accomplished a complete turnaround in his school behavior. Receiving evaluations of "Outstanding" in the areas of *Respect for others* and *Self-discipline* that he had previously been failing, he also got "As" for *Effort*, and "As" and "Bs" in his subjects. Chris's performance was even acknowledged by the principal, who gave him a commendation.

By the summer, after about four and a half months of treatment, Kevin began to talk with Chris about reducing the frequency of sessions. What was critical for Kevin was that child and parents were able to negotiate their lives together. Believing that the therapy and Ritalin had proven enormously useful to this family, Kevin did not want to create an ongoing need for himself or the therapy.

	KEVIN:	You know how happy I am that you have been feeling better and are performing at such a high level in school.
	CHRIS:	Yes, I sure have been happy, too. It's nice not getting into trouble all the time.
*14	KEVIN:	You are doing so well that pretty soon you won't need to come here so often.
	CHRIS:	*(looking dismayed)* What do you mean?
*15	KEVIN:	Remember when you started coming here, it was because you had too many worries. Well, now your worries are much less. Perhaps after next week you can skip a week and we can continue that until summer begins. I know your parents have enrolled you in a wonderful program run through the Parks and Recreation Department. We can

> schedule a few visits then, but it would be nice to not in-
> terfere with your playing and having fun.

CHRIS: You've been the very best friend anybody could ever have.

*16 KEVIN: I'm so glad that we have been friends and that you now
can have other friends and enjoy yourself.

Beginning the process of termination, Kevin introduced, at *14, that Chris would not have to come in so frequently. Not wanting to make it harder for Chris by dwelling overly on the emotional content, Kevin recalled for them, at *15, what initially brought them together. Giving Chris permission to have fun and enjoy his life and not need the therapy, he also genuinely validated, *16, the importance to him of his relationship with Chris.

ADDITIONAL NOTES

Here we offer recommendations and instructions about writing the assessment report. Often called the *social study* or *intake report*, this product of the assessment documents in written form the assessment process at a given point in time. While most settings require these written statements on new clients after the first few sessions, the time frame and format is determined by the function and mission of each setting.

The extent of information gathering is partly dependent on the agency setting and the client's presenting problem. You may need to talk with several referral sources or other community settings involved with the client, have lengthy contact with family members, or primarily rely on the information offered by the client. Here it is absolutely essential to distinguish among facts, observations, and judgments and to clearly identify *who is presenting the information* and *whose observations you are reporting*. Usually there are many versions of an event, with each presenting some kernel of truth. Acknowledging differing views helps prevent you from taking sides and provides a fuller picture of the situation. Indicate evidence to support any hypotheses you offer and use ordinary language to present the client and situation with simplicity and clarity.

Drawing on the case situation of Dale and John, we present a model for organizing information into the written assessment report, including the basic ingredients to be covered in these first client summaries. This assessment was written one month into Linda's practice with Dale, at the point of the intervention that began the case example.

Assessment Report

Setting
Though this element is not necessary at most agencies, it is a good idea to begin with a brief description of the setting, providing information about the

size of the facility, the types of services, auspices, and accessibility to its population.

....

The setting is an outpatient psychiatry department of a 600-bed publicly funded Veterans Administration hospital. Providing both long- and short-term medical care to veterans, this multidisciplinary setting offers the services of social work, psychiatry, nursing, psychology, occupational therapy, physical therapy, and vocational rehabilitation. Partial day treatment is also available. The setting is accessible by public transportation. Patients from out of the immediate area coming for consultations which take longer than one day can easily locate temporary living arrangements.

....

Identifying Information
The identifying information is a feature of most assessment reports and should include only the bare facts (a popular show in the early days of television was *Dragnet*, where the investigating police officer would say "Just the facts, Ma'am," and that injunction applies here). A mistake that novice report writers frequently make in this section is including their own thinking and assumptions, diagnostic categories, or value judgments. Primarily, only basic demographic information should be covered here including client's age, gender, race, ethnicity, education, income and employment status, household members and living arrangements.

....

Dale M. is a 32-year-old female who is employed as an LPN at a nearby metropolitan hospital, earning a salary of about $20,000. She is White, a high school graduate with one year of college, and LPN training. She was a member of the WACs for several years following high school, according her eligibility as a veteran. She currently resides by herself in an apartment.

....

Reason for Referral
How the current worker became active on this case is covered here, including who referred the client, when, and why. For example, if a school refers a student for family therapy, the basis for referral should be presented in this section.

....

Dale M. was transferred to this worker due to the previous social worker's change to another unit in the hospital. A transfer summary was received two weeks prior to the first meeting with Dale M., recommending a continuation of supportive casework services and medicine maintenance.

....

Presenting Problem

Details about the problem may be communicated by several sources, necessitating presentation of the different views. Again in the case of a school referral, usually when an adolescent is referred from the school to a family service agency, the parents and teenager are involved in the social work treatment and each have their own perceptions about the problem. A good approach to organizing this information is to structure paragraphs for each explanation of the presenting problem, being sure to identify whose view it is.

Include here the statement of the problem, its duration and significance to the client. While clients are not always clear about what they want from the worker, it is possible to begin a formulation of what the client is expecting from both the worker and the agency.

....

Dale M. presented herself as recently having trouble with sleeping/wanting to sleep too much, and eating/not wanting to eat. She explained that she was planning to get married in five months, that she had been engaged before but had always broken off the relationship. Sharing that she had received inpatient treatment for several years because she sometimes felt like hurting herself or others, she has been thinking about stopping her medication because of her concern that it might be harmful to any children she might have in the future. Dale was not clear about what she wanted from the worker except that the previous social worker had arranged for her to continue visits to the outpatient department.

....

Client's Description and Functioning

In this very broad category, more in-depth detail is provided about the client. You can begin to include your own observations as well as information reported from the client and from records. Information may also be gathered from clients, family members, other involved community settings, and additional sources. Subcategories are very useful and should be used to describe what is distinctive to this client's life experience. These might include a physical description of the client; current family situation; current social, medical, and economic functioning. Again it is important to clarify whether statements are based on your own observations or on reports and who is responsible for the information. You can emphasize salient factors through your use of specific headings that reflect your client's situation and can follow up on some areas in the section on history.

....

CURRENT SOCIAL SITUATION

Dale M. currently resides by herself in a small apartment located not far from where she is employed. She reports having no close friends and that she interacts only minimally with her co-workers. She talks each day with her fiancé, whom she has known for almost two years, and they see each other two or three times a week. They are planning to marry in about five months.

Her parents and sister live in another state, several hundred miles away. They have remained her closest contacts and she speaks with them by telephone a few times a month.

Dale is not presently involved with any religious activity nor is she a participant in any other community groups.

EMPLOYMENT

Dale has been employed as an LPN at a local hospital, where she is currently on the surgical unit. She has been with this hospital for two and a half years, having started work with them about one year after her discharge as an inpatient.

She reports that she likes her work and has received regular raises and positive evaluations by her supervisor.

HEALTH

Dale indicates her health is good and that she has had no major illnesses. Her physical complaints center around side effects of the medication she is taking. Experiencing dryness of the mouth and some stiffness in her movements, she is worried about long-term effects of the medication and (as her wedding approaches) potential harm to any children she might have.

Medical records support that Dale has been physically healthy. She is somewhat overweight and a moderate smoker.

PHYSICAL DESCRIPTION

Dale M. is about 5'5" and of stocky build. She presents herself appropriately for her sessions, dressing in a neat and casual manner. She shows little range in her display of emotions, speaks mainly in a monotone and walks and carries herself rather stiffly.

....

Relevant History

Similar to the category *Description and Functioning,* in presenting your client's history you need to make some decisions about which information to present and how much detail to provide. The type and duration of the problem considered in conjunction with the age and current functioning of the client will help determine your portrayal of historical information. While the trend has been away from early history, there may be situations where a detailed account of the past will be very important. Again, you can use subheadings to represent salient factors.

....

Extensive records are available on this client due to her long history of services from the V.A. Information relevant to Dale's current situation will be briefly summarized here, including a short review of her psychiatric treatment, social functioning and employment. These areas were chosen because it would be useful to have a synopsis of her psychiatric treatment and a focus on any discernible patterns in her social relationships and employment.

PSYCHIATRIC HISTORY

According to Dale and her records, she first became aware of difficulties with her feelings and trouble with her vision when she was in high school. She would sometimes feel like hurting her sister and would have bursts of temper. During stressful occasions people would suddenly appear small when she looked at them. Not happening too frequently, however, after graduation from high school Dale joined the WACs.

Dale doesn't remember much about what precipitated her first psychiatric hospitalization. According to hospital records, after about a year her ability to function became increasingly impaired. She didn't show up for work and appeared disheveled and confused. On the advice of their family physician her family brought her in for a psychiatric consultation.

Over the following four years Dale had several discharges to outpatient status and spent a total of two and a half years as an inpatient in a V.A facility near her family. She was given a diagnosis of "schizophrenia, chronic, un-differentiated type." After what appeared to be a homicidal gesture toward one of her team leaders, she was transferred to this V.A. hospital, several hundred miles from her home and family. A new combination of medication was tried along with group therapy. Good progress was made and Dale has been receiv-ing outpatient treatment for the past three years. This includes brief monthly visits with the outpatient psychiatrist for medication monitoring and week-ly visits with the outpatient social worker for casework services. On several stressful occasions Dale needed brief inpatient stays and a rebalancing of her medication.

SOCIAL FUNCTIONING AND EMPLOYMENT

Dale describes herself as a loner. Never having developed close relationships with friends in school, she spent lots of time reading and "thinking about things." She looked up to her older sister, who seemed to have an easier time of making friends.

Upon high school graduation, Dale explains, she found herself with no real plans. Though she was a decent student, college did not feel right to her. She decided to join the WACs and after completion of her army duty she returned to live near her family, received her LPN training, took some college courses, and began employment as a licensed nurse in a nursing home.

Demonstrating strong skills of adapting to a new community, after discharge to outpatient status Dale found herself an apartment and a good job. She reports feeling good with her life here and never made plans to move closer to her sister and parents.

....

Assessment

The crux of your report, the assessment, is where you develop your case theory generating your *own* hypotheses to explain the client. It is here that you state the views you have formulated. Depending on the amount of time you have spent with the client, your assessment will vary in its clarity and depth of understanding. Again, feel free to use further subheadings. Subsections of *Impressions* or *Thoughts* can be a good place to set down your current thinking, which can later be further clarified and validated.

Present a balanced view of the client, addressing both strengths and limitations of the client's capacities and the consequences of the problem on the client's life, including benefits and adversities. Should you be in a setting where specific diagnostic measures are used, such as versions of the *DSM* or other scales, those results may be presented here.

This is also where you discuss the theories you have used to understand the client. After you have presented your ideas, provide theoretical models of treatment, such as problem solving or psychosocial, and frameworks for understanding the particular population or problem area represented by your client, such as substance abuse or domestic violence. You are integrating theoretical principles with your case, not merely summarizing readings of interest to you.

The case theory formulated for Dale is comprehensive. Offering a succinct introduction to the client's presenting problem, an explanation of what is happening with the client at this point in time, the relevance of theoretical frameworks, and a basis for the treatment plan, it provides the reader with a clear picture of this client and her situation. Because discussion of the literature is provided earlier in the case example, especially in the sections covering the case theory as linking the past to the future and as a guiding map of the practice, the following presentation of the literature is brief.

....

Case Theory

Dale came in for help with feelings of depression, suicide, and anxiety. She has had a history of difficulty in acknowledging and dealing with her emotions, and has had minimal social contacts and support. The literature on schizophrenia provides a basis for understanding the hallucinations and problems in forming relationships (Menninger, 1948,) and the utilization of medication to alleviate some of the problematic symptoms (Gottesman and Shields, 1982).

Anger is a metaphor that Dale uses to talk about her feelings in general. For her, having feelings has meant loss of control. She has not only tried to hide her feelings from herself, she has also maintained an isolation from social contact. The benefit she has gained by this behavior has been protection from feeling vulnerable. The negative outcomes have been almost no support and continued feelings of depression and suicide. Dale is afraid of her own feelings, afraid that she will lose "control" of her behavior and hurt others or herself.

Demonstrating strengths at social functioning, Dale has held a steady and responsible job supporting herself in her own apartment. She has developed a close relationship with John, her fiancé, with a commitment to get married and have a family. While on psychotropic medication, she has been able to continue to do well on reduced dosages. Limitations include continued social isolation with some visual hallucinations and suicidal feelings. During previous times of stress, Dale has sometimes stopped taking her medication, and has needed renewed inpatient treatment.

Ego psychology (Freud, 1937; Parad & Miller, 1963) and systems (Ackerman, 1958; Hartman, 1983) and communication theories (Haley, 1959; Jackson, 1957) provide approaches to understanding the client's current behaviors. Ego psychology attaches importance to gaining awareness of the client's coping capacities and the maintenance of balance. Difficulties of schizophrenic clients in dealing with feelings and emotions are viewed as ego defenses which "may be buttressed by unreasonably strong superego prohibitions" (Nelson, 1975, 147).

Systems theory views the identified patient as a member of a family and community, with a focus on the individual within context of the environment. Drawing Hartman's ecomap provides graphic evidence of Dale's social isolation. Communication theorists point to the nature of the interactive behavior between the client and family members. Consideration of the interpretation of messages conveyed and received in Dale's family point to Dale's perceptions of being disqualified—of not being affirmed and being given inconsistent messages.

Dale's behavior may be seen as serving a function within her family, as "normal" for her family.

Pharmacological treatment has been considered important (by the client and the outpatient team) in Dale's improvement. Wolberg states "the first line of attack in schizophrenic breakdown is somatic therapy" (1967, p. 1005). While the dosage and type of drugs and duration of medication treatment need to be discussed, it is important not to rashly change the medication at this point in time. During these next months, many changes may be occurring in the client's life and the support provided her by the thorazine is probably needed.

The psychosocial approach suggests additional treatment possibilities. Focusing on the person in situation, this model essentially applies systems theory to casework (Hollis & Woods, 1981). Change for Dale will entail learning how to talk about and gain validation for her feelings. With the knowledge from the literature (Farber, 1958) about the importance of the casework relationship, the relationship will serve as a crucial vehicle in modeling with Dale how to process and gain support for one's feelings. Psychodynamic theory also emphasizes the value of the helping relationship. "The key to the treatment of schizophrenia lies in the ability to establish some sort of contact with the patient. Most schizophrenics . . . erect various obstacles to any interpersonal threat. The withdrawal from reality, and the archaic type of thinking and symbolism, enhance the individual's isolation from people, since there is no common means of communication. Yet beneath the surface the patient yearns . . . for a friendly and loving relationship" (Wolberg, 1967, p. 1007). While a relationship between the worker and client will initially be the crux of treatment, it will be applied to lessen the client's fears of close relationships and provide her a model in developing relationships with others, and especially with her fiancé, John.

DIAGNOSIS

At a psychiatric facility, clinical diagnoses are given to all patients. Dale was diagnosed on her first hospitalization as having "schizophrenia, chronic undifferentiated type." This diagnosis has not changed through her seven years of treatment.

IMPRESSIONS

Dale strikes me as a most likable and interesting woman. She has articulated her hallucinations with clarity and has approached her sessions with energy and commitment. My fears of her (she can appear strange and intimidating), and my feelings of inadequacy (can I offer her anything?) are gradually decreasing. A firm bonding in our relationship seems to be forming and we both believe that she can achieve greater human intimacy and fulfillment in the future.

. . . .

Treatment Plan

Though the strength of your treatment plan is partly a function of the amount of time you have spent with the client, it is important that you offer some specificity of areas for intervention and the goals you have each begun to identify. A nicely developed case theory will lead you right into treatment goals and a plan of intervention. Try to be precise about what it is you want to do that will result in the desired change, including the behaviors for which you and the client will be responsible. Treatment models from the literature may also be included here.

....

Weekly sessions will be held with the client, alternating individual meetings with conjoint sessions between the client and her fiancé to assist them in one of the primary goals, which is that they learn to relate to each other in a positive and supportive way. This will be accomplished by enabling them to talk with each other about their daily activities. Since they are not familiar with sharing their feelings, permission and structure will be provided to discuss intimate matters.

Gradually sessions will move toward primarily conjoint, with possible elimination of the individual sessions. Accompanying this change will be a shift in the treatment, away from Dale's psychotic symptoms to an emphasis on supportive and positive interactions between Dale and John.

An additional goal is that Dale address her feelings directly. Anger and displeasure with others will be presented as ordinary components of life. Encouragement will be offered to both John and Dale to disagree with each other and to state their views honestly.

Reality therapy, with its assumption that there is no mental illness and its emphasis on accepting responsibility for one's behavior (Glasser, 1965) provides useful approaches to practice with Dale. Focusing on the present, not the past, exploration of what Dale is doing, not why she is doing it, are the methods for Dale learning to confront issues more candidly and with less trauma.

While we have committed to weekly sessions, we have also contracted for Dale to call as needed. I have agreed to be available for extra sessions, or for telephone calls. Dale is also to inform me, or contact the treatment team, of any suicidal feelings.

....

Prognosis

In a prognosis section, which is not always included in these reports, you conjecture about the likelihood of satisfactory completion of treatment, considering the factors impacting on the success and/or failure of your work with this client. You may also incorporate this discussion under *Impressions* subsection in the Assessment section. Try to address any concerns you may raise.

....

Prognosis for Dale is fairly good. She appears committed to changing, as demonstrated through her regular attendance at sessions and her active sharing of her feelings and thoughts. She routinely asks questions of the worker, and appears to have established a relationship where she experiences mutual trust and respect. This is evidenced through her talking about herself and her family background.

On the down side—Dale has a long history of psychiatric difficulties and very little experience with close relationships. No modeling of intimacy is available to her. The changes she is now sustaining may prove to be too tumultuous.

In consideration of this, I plan to not rush the client and to provide support and permission for Dale to take her time. I will "check in" with her routinely about how she is doing, and whether changes are moving at the right pace for her.

....

Other Reports
Just as the format of the assessment report varies according to the agency function, other means of written documentation will also reflect the type of setting and the social worker's role. *Interim summaries*, brief reports that capture changes from the last documentation, are critical to accountable treatment. At a minimum of every three months, written summaries should incorporate changes in the client's circumstances, in the worker's treatment plan, and in the reformulation of the case theory and treatment goals. If client practice is limited to three months or less, such changes should be reflected in *termination* or *transfer summaries*.

SUMMARY

The case theory has been introduced as a concept that incorporates the social worker's hypotheses about a specific client and the client's social functioning. Explaining events in the client's life relevant to the presented problem, the case theory forms the basis for the plan of intervention.

The most critical component of social work practice, the assessment is the foundation for the other social work components; it is the "why" of the practice. The adequacy of the intervention is a function of the adequacy of the assessment. As a *process* of theory construction, assessment results in the *product* of an assessment report. Including a range of explanatory theories that describe human behavior and human development, the written document must include the social worker's own understanding and explanation of the case.

Assessment was defined in this chapter as

 The generation of a set of hypotheses forming the construction of a case theory that explains clients within context of their circumstances. It is an information-gathering and -organizing process that evolves from the specific to the general to the individualized. Distinctions are made among facts, observations, and judgments, and attention is paid to issues of difference. Through a theoretical linking of the client's past with the present and future, a map is developed that organizes the practice by shaping the relationship and communication and determining the intervention. Literature and research inform and are used to validate the hypotheses.

Traditionally, social workers have been fascinated with historical information leading to a diagnosis and an understanding of the client's past. This chapter has demonstrated that knowledge of the past is important only in order to help the client change. A beautiful statement by Carl Jung emphasizes this point:

> A person is only half understood when one knows how everything in him came about. Only a dead man can be explained in terms of the past, a living one must be otherwise explained. Life is not made up of yesterdays only, nor is it understood and explained by reducing today to yesterday. Life has also a tomorrow, and today is only understood if we are able to add the indications of tomorrow to our knowledge of what was yesterday. (Jung, 1928)

The social work assessment offers only limited, albeit very critical information about the client. A road is chosen, though many others are available. The chosen road exposes some vistas and hides others. While the road may dead end or detour, the journey eventually ends but is not complete. A total understanding of the client is never achieved. Practice is implemented and terminated based on a select set of issues facing a client at a specific point in time.

Assessment is the intellectual challenge of social work practice. Developing the case theory requires the best of the social worker's ability to problem-solve with ambiguous and confusing information. The social worker thinks and formulates judgments while simultaneously relating and communicating with the client. It is during assessment that social workers can feel the sense of pride that comes from solving a difficult jigsaw puzzle. Even though some critical pieces may be missing, the form and illusion of the whole can be appreciated. Lacking a picture of the total person, social workers can perceive the client as intact—with a past, present, and, hopefully, a better future.

BIBLIOGRAPHY

Abbott, A. (1988). *The system of professions: An essay on the division of expert labor.* Chicago: University of Chicago Press.

Ackerman, N. (1958). *The psychodynamics of family life.* New York: Basic Books.

The Ad Hyperactivity Workbook for Parents, Teachers and Kids. (1988). Plantation, Fla.: Impact Publishers.

American Psychiatric Association. *Diagnostic and statistical manual of mental disorders* (1980, 3rd ed.; 1987, rev.). Washington, D.C.: APA.

Baldwin, A. (1968). *Theories of child development.* New York: John Wiley & Sons.

Bardhill, R. (1975). A series of teaching tapes on assessment with children. Available from Walter Reed Army Medical Center, Washington, D.C.

Barkley, R. A. (1981). *Hyperactive children: A handbook for diagnosis and treatment.* New York: Guilford Press.

Bateson, G. (1972). *Steps to an ecology of mind.* New York: Ballantine Books.

Bateson, G., Jackson, D., Haley, J., & Weakland, J. (1956). Toward a theory of schizophrenia. *Behavioral Science, I:* 4, 251–264.

Bonkowski, S., & Yanos, J. (1992). Infant mental health: An expanding field for social work. *Social Work, 37* (March), 144–149.

Bowen, M. (1960). A family concept of schizophrenia. In D. Jackson (Ed.), *The etiology of schizophrenia,* 346–372. New York: Basic Books.

Bowlby, J. (1961). Processes of mourning. *International Journal of Psychoanalysis, 42,* 317–340.

Bruner, J. S. (1964). The course of cognitive growth. *American Psychologist, 19.* 1–15.

Brunquell, P., Russman, B. S., & Lerer, T. (1988, September). *The mental status examination by pediatric neurologists in children with learning problems.* Presentation at the seventeenth national meeting of the Child Neurology Society, Halifax: Canada.

Cohn, A. H., & Daro, D. (1987). Is treatment too late? What ten years of evaluative research tell us. *Child Abuse and Neglect, 11,* 433–442.

Compton, B., & Galaway, B. (1986). *Social work processes.* Homewood, Ill.: Dorsey Press.

Conners, C. K., & Wells, K. C. (1986). *Hyperkinetic children: A neuropsychosocial approach.* Beverly Hills, Calif.: Sage.

Downs, R., & Stea, D. (1977). *Maps in minds.* New York: Harper & Row.

Drucker, P. (1990). *Managing the nonprofit organization: Policies and practices.* New York: Harper/Collins.

Farber, L. (1958). Casework treatment of ambulatory schizophrenics. *Social Casework, 39,* (January) 9–17.

Flexner, A. (1915). Is social work a profession? In *Proceedings of the national conference of charities and corrections.* Chicago: The Conference.

Fraiberg, S. (1977). *Every child's birthright: In defense of mothering.* New York: Basic Books.

Freud, A. (1937). *The ego and the mechanisms of defense.* Trans. C. Baines. London: Hogarth.

Freud, A., & Burlingham, D. (1944). *Infants without families.* New York: International Universities Press.

Freud, S. (1917). Mourning and melancholia. First published in *Zeitschrift,* Bd. IV; reprinted in Sammlung, Vierte Folge; *General Psychological Theory,* 170–171. New York: Collier Books, 1963.

Freud, S. (1923). *The ego and the id.* London: Hogarth Press.

Glasser, W. (1965). *Reality therapy.* New York: Harper & Row.

Goldstein, E. (1979). Mothers of psychiatric patients revisited: An ecological perspective. In C. Germain (Ed.), *Social work practice: People and environments,* 150–173. New York: Columbia University Press.

Goldstein, S. (1988). *Social Skills Assessment Questionnaire.* Salt Lake City, Ut.: Neurology, Learning and Behavior Center.

Goldstein, S., & Goldstein, M. (1990). *Managing attention disorders in children: A guide for practitioners.* New York: John Wiley & Sons.

Gottesman, J. J., & Shields, J. (1982). *Schizophrenia and genetics.* New York: Academic Press.

Haley, J. (1959). The family of the schizophrenic: A model system. *The Journal of Nervous and Mental Disease, 129,* 357–374.

Hamilton, G. (1941). The underlying philosophy of social casework. *NCSW Proceedings.*

Hartman, A. (1978). Diagrammatic assessment of family relationships. *Social Casework, 59:* 8, 465–476.

Hartman, A. (1983). *Family-centered social work practice.* New York: Free Press.

Hepworth, D., & Larsen, J. (1986). *Direct social work practice.* Homewood, Ill.: Dorsey Press.

Hollis, F. (1970). The psychosocial approach to the practice of casework. In

R. Roberts and R. Nee (Eds.), *Theories of social casework*, 33–76. Chicago: University of Chicago Press.

Hollis, F., & Woods, M. (1981). *Casework: A psychosocial therapy*. New York: Random House.

Horn, W. F., Ialongo, N., Popovich, S., & Peradotto, D. (1984). *An evaluation of the multi-method treatment approach with hyperactive children*. Paper presented at the meeting of the American Psychological Association, Toronto, Canada.

Hutchins, H., & Kirk, S. (1987). DSM-III and social work malpractice. *Social Work, 32:* 3, 205–211.

Ikver, B., & Sze, W. (1987). Social work and the psychiatric nosology of schizophrenia. *Social Casework, 68,* 131–139.

Jackson, D. D. (1957). The question of family homeostasis. *Psychoanalytic Quarterly, 31,* 79–90.

James, W. (1892). *Psychology*. New York: Holt.

Jung, C. (1928). *Contributions to analytical psychology*. New York: Harcourt, Brace.

Klaus, M. H., & Kennell, J. H. (1976). *Maternal-infant bonding (The impact of early separation or loss on family development)*. St. Louis: C. V. Mosby.

Kraepelin, E. (1896). *Psychiatrie*. 5th ed. Leipzig: Barth.

Lewis, M., & Lewis, D. (1981). Depression in childhood: A biopsychosocial perspective. *American Journal of Psychotherapy, 35,* 356–367.

Mahler, M. S., Pine, F., & Bergman, A. (1975). *The psychological birth of the infant*. New York: Basic Books.

Menninger, K. (1948). The diagnosis and treatment of schizophrenia. *Bulletin of the Menninger Clinic, 12:* 3, 96–106.

Meyer, C. (1993). *Assessment in social work practice*. New York: Columbia University Press.

Mussen, P., Conger, J., & Kagan, J. (1969). *Child development and personality*. New York: Harper & Row.

National Center on Child Abuse and Neglect. (1988). Study findings. *Study of National Incidence and Prevalence of Child Abuse and Neglect*. OHDS report, contract 105-85-1702 Washington, D.C.: U.S. Government Printing Office.

Nelson, J. (1975). Treatment issues in schizophrenia. *Social Casework, 56* (March), 145–153.

Parad, H., & Miller, R. (Eds.) (1963). *Ego-oriented casework: problems and perspectives*. New York: Family Service Association of America.

Patros, P., & Shamoo, T. (1989). *Depression and suicide in children and adolescents*. Boston: Allyn & Bacon.

Perlman, H. H. (1957). *Social casework: A problem-solving process*. Chicago: University of Chicago Press.

Richmond, M. (1917). *Social diagnosis*. New York: Russell Sage Foundation.

Rochlin, G. (1965). *Griefs and discontents: The forces of change*. Boston: Little, Brown.

Simos, B. (1979). *A time to grieve: Loss as a universal experience*. New York: Family Service Association.

Siporin, M. (1975). *Introduction to social work practice*. New York: Macmillan.

Smalley, R. (1967). *Theory for social work practice*. New York: Columbia University Press.

Spitz, R. (1965). *The first year of life*. New York: International Universities Press.

Taylor, E. (1987). The biological basis of schizophrenia. *Social Work, 32:* 2, 115–121.

Toolan, J. (1981). Depression and suicide in children: An overview. *American Journal of Psychotherapy, 35*, 311–322.

Towle, C. (1954). *The learner in education for the professions*. Chicago: University of Chicago Press.

Ullman, R., Sleator, E., & Sprague, R. (1991). *ACTeRS Profile*. Champaign, Ill: MetriTech.

U.S. Bureau of the Census. (1990). General social and economic characteristics, U.S. Summary. *1990 Census of the Population*. Washington, D.C.: U.S. Government Printing Office.

Volkmar, F., Bacon, S., Shakir, S., & Pfefferbaum, A. (1983). Group therapy in the management of manic-depressive illness. In F. Turner (Ed.), *Differential diagnosis and treatment in social work*, pp. 169–167. New York: Free Press.

Walker, H. M., Todis, B., Holmes, D., & Horton, G. (1988). *The Walker Social Skills Curriculum: The ACCESS Program*. Austin, Tex: Pro-Ed.

Weiss, G., Minde, K., Werry, J .S., Douglas, V. I., & Nemeth, E. (1971). Studies on the hyperactive child: VII Five-year follow-up. *Archives of General Psychiatry, 24*, 409–414.

Wolberg, L. (1967). *The technique of psychotherapy*. New York: Grune & Stratton.

CHAPTER ❦ SIX

Reason and heart will give you words.

—Homer

COMMUNICATION:
THE METHODS AND SKILLS

Interactions between people, how information is conveyed and received, the meanings attached to things said and heard have long been of interest to philosophers and have been the themes of great literature. Communication maintains the existence of human life as we know it today. Reproduction, through which the human race is continued, cannot take place without some means of communication. With advancing industrialization, even the basic needs of food and water are met indirectly, through interaction between one person and another.

Likewise, social work practice cannot exist without communication, which includes both the specific conversations between social workers and clients and the written reports through which the practice is documented. Social work communication is also the process through which the assessment information is gathered, the relationship is enacted, and the intervention is carried out. Far more than an exchange of words, however, communication encompasses all the behaviors, which are sometimes subtle, exhibited between workers and clients along with the meanings these behaviors convey to the recipient.

The formal study of communication did not begin until the middle of the twentieth century, when advances in psychology, sociology, and anthropology after the late 1940s allowed for this examination and analysis of human interaction. Ray Birdwhistell was one of the first anthropologists to study human communication, offering the significant contribution that communication encompasses not just words but body movements. In *Kinesics and Context*, he discusses the intricacies of the concept of communication and points to its central position in the maintenance of the human species. Birdwhistell defines communication as "a complex and sustaining system through which various members of the society interrelate with more or less efficiency and facility. . . . [It is, in fact] . . . that system of coadaptation by which society is sustained, and, which in turn, makes human life possible" (1973, p. 14). For Birdwhistell, communication is a Gestalt that lies beyond the simple verbal meaning of the message.

In this chapter we again examine practice interactions. While the social workers explain their use of the communication methods (*exploration, reflection, validation, confrontation*) and skills (*giving information, sustaining the dialogue, using silence, focusing, summarizing*), they also discuss their communication choices for each client. Further elaboration is offered on nonverbal cues and the impact of cultural *difference* on communication. Additional Notes, finally, discusses *forms of written communication*, with suggestions for maintaining agency documents and other means of communication with supervisors and peers. Also included is an example of a process recording, one of the traditional means of communication between student social workers and their field instructors.

COMMUNICATION IN THE SOCIAL WORK LITERATURE

Communication is not discussed as a separate component in the first social work texts because it had not yet been introduced as a concept in the late 1800s and early 1900s. During the early days of the profession's development, people like Mary Richmond, Gordon Hamilton, and Bertha Reynolds were concerned with defining the domain of social work and with clarifying the primary practice components—assessment and the casework relationship.

Interviewing, now central to the concept of communication, was, at that time, considered part of the assessment process. Bertha Reynolds, in her discussion of assessment, says of interviewing: "The art of listening may be stressed, and that of feeling with a person in order to get what he is trying to say with the language of gesture and tone as well as with words" (1942, p. 165). Hamilton sees interviewing as central to the social case method: "In social work, interviewing, together with observation, must be relied upon to provide our most significant case data. . . . The interview *can* motivate, *can* teach, *can* secure information, *can* help people bring out things that are bothering them. The interview is one of the best ways of getting a chance to observe behavior" (1951, pp. 89, 93).

Much of what is currently encompassed in discussions of communication, if not included as elements of the assessment, was considered to be part of the casework relationship, as in a Family Service Association publication: "The relationship is the sum total of all that happens between participants—all the words exchanged, the feelings, attitudes, actions, and thoughts expressed; everything, in fact, that the worker and client do whether open and overt or devious and hidden" (Lyndon, 1948, p. 16).

Major advances in the sciences occurred during the 1960s and 1970s, with technological breakthroughs in space travel, applications of nuclear energy, and molecular research. Behaviorism heavily influenced the social sciences and social work. Demonstrating direct relationships between objects was emphasized; clear-cut cause-and-effect experiments were the vogue, focusing efforts on the standardization of professional practice. "Helping" and "human relations" became big industries, causing expansion of counseling and guidance programs. Terms like *helpers* and *helpees* were popular, and what was unique to the different professions became blurred.

Psychologists and human service professionals appropriated the domain of communication from the philosophers, sociologists, and anthropologists. Diverging from learning about the process of individuals interacting with each other and the meanings they attach to those interactions, the study of communication emphasized behavioral components. *How* was replaced by *what*. Communication came to be viewed as a set of behaviors that, if identified, could make more systematic the interaction between individuals.

Search for specificity in helping others *is* important. As we have seen, the practice of social work is often difficult, vague, and ambiguous. Nevertheless, overly standardizing the helping process can result in helping that is ineffective or harmful (unfortunately, the same negative results are also achievable from nonstandaridized practice). The extraordinary uniqueness of human behavior brings futility to current endeavors that attempt to apply rigid prescriptions to the helping process. As Birdwhistell has said: "The term 'interaction' is the significant concept here. The order of phenomena we are tracing, analyzing, and describing cannot be reduced to the familiar action-reaction formula" (1973, p. 12).

While recognizing that social work practice is more than the mechanical utilization of communication techniques, much can be learned from studying the rich range of theories exploring human interaction. Watzlawick, Weakland, and Fisch (1974) present a fascinating approach to the use of communication in helping people change, and the works of Bateson (1972) and Bandler and Grinder (1975, 1976) continue to challenge and stimulate in their exploration of levels in communication and examination of metacommunication or the messages about the communication. Prepackaged scales and procedures offer training in the development of helping skills such as warmth, genuineness, and congruence; an example is the accurate empathy manuals of Truaxx and Carkhuff (1967). Shulman (1979) and Kadushin (1972) are social workers who have focused on the development of communication skills.

COMMUNICATION IN SOCIAL WORK DEFINED

Communication is defined in this book as

 A purposeful set of activities focused on altering the problem situation pre-sented by the client. As the process that allows for the information gathering of the assessment and the enactment of the relationship and intervention, communication is the primary technology of the social work practice. Con-sisting of the transmission and exchange of thoughts, feelings, and informa-tion, communication occurs through verbal and nonverbal means and in writing. Transactions are between social workers and clients, social workers and colleagues and peers, social workers and other related persons. The methods—exploration, reflection, validation, confrontation—and the skills— to give information, to sustain the dialogue, to use silence, to focus, to summarize—are shaped by the social worker's understanding of the client and of the presenting problem.

Weaving a complex fabric with the other elements of social work prac-tice, communication is shaped by the relationship while the assessment directs what is communicated. How the social worker and client get along together has an impact on the specific things they say to each other. At the same time, the social worker's understanding of the situation affects the words and attitudes exchanged. In turn, the communication behaviors shape the worker-client relationship and influence what information is obtained for the assessment.

Communication is specific and unique to this client, situation, and social worker. The manner is which each addresses the other; the choice of words, gestures, seating arrangements, body posture, particular phrases and ex-pressions are all idiosyncratic to each worker-client dyad and what brings them together. Every interaction will have its own "feel," its own climate or atmosphere.

Birdwhistell has reported that over two-thirds of what is communicated between people is manifested in nonverbal exchanges that are beyond our conscious awareness. Voice tone, vocabulary, speech pattern, body posture, eye contact, and gesturing all send subtle and important messages to the client about the relationship, about the social worker's understanding of the client and the problem, and about the kinds of goals being considered for the intervention.

Comprised of a complex set of phenomena, communication is sent and received simultaneously on many levels. The content of what is said may not be congruent with the context or voice tone and body posture. Hidden messages are often transmitted based on the past history of a rela-tionship or on unspoken expectations for the future. Confusion and mis-communication are probably more common than clear and functional interaction.

Shaped by cultural backgrounds as well as individual preferences, the communication cues may reflect the mores of a particular ethnic group. Through her writings about families and ethnicity, McGoldrick has enhanced understanding about the cultural basis of communication styles. Denying the notion of a melting pot, she believes "there is increasing evidence that ethnic values and identification are retained for many generations after immigration and play a significant role in family life and personal development throughout the life cycle" (1989, p. 70).

Demonstrated in a variety of behaviors and mannerisms, these identifications may become an integral aspect of one's style of personal interaction. For example, avoiding eye contact is frequently considered a sign of discomfort or avoidance in Western culture. In many Native American cultures, however, direct eye contact may be viewed as impolite, and talking with a stranger will tend to be slow, with more initial testing and pauses (McGoldrick, Pearce, & Giordano, 1982, p. 59). Resisting the temptation to fill in the silences or talk fast to cover one's own discomfort will be easier for the practitioner who can consider and respect the client within context of Native American cultural traditions.

Likewise, a Jewish person's articulate verbal behavior may not signify a high level of understanding or agreement with the social worker, but simply reflect a cultural emphasis on verbal skills and self-expression (McGoldrick, Pearce, & Giordano, 1982, p. 372). The expressive intensity of someone of Italian descent who engages in many body gestures may equally seem violent and out of control to a social worker with a British background, who is more comfortable with self-containment (pp. 353, 459).

Yet caution is necessary about stereotyping. All Italians don't necessarily gesture and Jews are not always articulate. While considering cultural influences on verbal and nonverbal cues can help social workers better understand their clients, attention to the uniqueness of each individual is, as always, a basic requirement. Good sources on social work practice with cultural diversity are Pinderhughes, 1989, and Logan, McRoy, Freeman, 1989.

Central to much of social work practice are the following communication methods and skills, which provide the means to talk with and hear from the client. We offer definitions along with examples and discussion by the social workers, and we include commentary about watching for nonverbal cues and the influence of ethnic differences.

Methods and Skills of Communication

Communication methods and skills are important components in effective social work practice. They are, however, tools to help the client, not ends in themselves. They should be considered the ingredients of social work, not the totality. It is the social worker's conception of the client and how to help that is critical. Communication is the transmission of that conception, a response to what is needed. Decisions are made continuously about which of the communication methods and skills to use, based on judgments about what will be most effective in the helping.

Social workers conduct their work through communicating. They require information from clients and it is imparted to them. For social workers to help, clients have to talk about themselves and the situation that brings them to the social worker. The clients' talking, in turn, is shaped by the questions and statements expressed by the social workers. For clients to change themselves and their situations, they need to receive knowledge from the social worker.

The four primary methods of social work communication are *exploration*, *reflection*, *validation*, and *confrontation*. Later in this chapter these methods are discussed and illustrated in specific social worker–client practice interactions. First, however, we will review general skills that are basic to the utilization of these methods.

The General Skills: To Give Information, to Sustain the Dialogue, to Use Silence, to Focus, and to Summarize

Ordinarily, interactions between social workers and clients are considered from the perspective of the social workers' questions. Just as social workers need information from the client, however, clients will also have questions for the social worker. These may relate to such issues as the process of helping, professional experience and background, or the client's situation. Social workers both acquire and share information. *Sharing information is the social worker's provision of knowledge to the client directly, clearly, and honestly.*

This is not to say that social workers should always provide answers to the questions clients have. Providing information about professional experience and supervisory backup is appropriate and relates to issues of informed consent, discussed in Chapter 3 on professional ethics. Clients, however, may start out asking for instructions or advice about solving their problems. Here the social worker would not want to offer facile advice or false hope, but should respond that more time is necessary to formulate an assessment, out of which some of those answers may be found.

If the client asks about something the social worker does not know or does not want to talk about, that must be said in a simple and straightforward manner. Some clients, for example, like to ask personal questions. Depending on their nature and the reason for the client's seeking help, it can be acceptable either to answer these questions or to refocus onto the client.

As well as acquiring and sharing information, social workers are responsible *for sustaining the dialogue* during the practice session. Clients vary in their ability to continue talking. Some do it easily and can share freely about their situation, while others are uncomfortable and may have a great deal of difficulty discussing personal issues. *Sustaining the dialogue is the social worker's continuing the flow of the interview through asking and answering questions and making statements to the client.*

Related to the belief bonding and purposefulness of the social work relationship discussed in Chapter 4, the social worker wants to present as the competent expert. Helping clients narrate their story is what social workers do when they sustain the dialogue. There are also times where the worker must *use silence* as the most effective means to obtain information and maintain the session. After asking questions or making statements, a pause is often necessary, sometimes for longer than feels comfortable, to allow the client to comment. Silences can often be a powerful encouragement for clients to share information or to ask questions when they are confused.

As well as affording clients (and workers) an opportunity to think through a puzzling issue, an important point can be emphasized through silences: *By the use of silence social workers keep to a minimum the amount of talking they are doing during sessions and encourage thinking and talking by the client.* Good guideline questions for social workers to monitor their use of silences are:

Am I talking too much here?
Am I rushing in to fill uncomfortable moments?
Am I making the pace too fast for this client to get into their own thoughts?

Usually, what feels like several minutes of silence during a worker-client interaction is really only a few seconds.

As social workers and clients are talking together about what is relevant to the client's problem, they are working toward a *focus*. In presenting their situation, clients often bring in a lot of information, not all of which is germane to the help they want. It is important to recognize that the client is not necessarily knowledgeable about the parameters of the problem. Often things feel "not right," but the client is not savvy about what is not right— and neither is the social worker. It is the social worker's function to help target what is "not right." This is done by *focusing,* which is *the social worker's helping the client "attend to" and "zero in" on the most important and relevant pieces of the client's situation. Focusing involves centering on and highlighting the most essential or significant facts. Focusing allows for a narrowing of considerable information into what is relevant for the situation.*

Since so much is happening for the social worker at the same time— listening, sorting out what is being heard, assessing what it all means, and responding to and asking questions of the client—focusing is the means to stay on track. Engaging in a self-dialogue that raises a range of concerns is often useful. Such questions might include:

Do I understand the main point here?
What is the most critical issue?

Do I have enough information to support what I think is the crux of the matter?

I'm feeling confused. I wonder if we have gotten off the track?

Compton and Galaway, in their book about generalist practice, say this about focusing: "Focusing is helpful in that it can be used to emphasize a feeling or idea from a vast array of verbalization and to reduce confusion, diffusion, and vagueness. Thus the worker assists the system in focusing on assumptions, ways of thinking, notions, or feelings" (1979, p. 370).

Just as important as the spotlighting obtained by focusing is the synopsis achieved by summarizing. *To summarize is the social worker's review with the client of what has been covered. This "pulling together" can center on the current session or may be a more general update on the work completed.* Summarizing is not only helpful as a review of the practice thus far, it can also provide the thrust for future work and help consolidate the goals that have been accomplished.

Helpful to both client and worker, summarizing can slow down the process. Stopping every so often to "check in" with the client serves to keep everyone on track. Comments such as: "I'd like to review with you what we have been talking about," or "The things we have covered so far are . . ." offer the opportunity to determine whether they have each understood the same thing.

The Methods: Exploration, Reflection, Validation, Confrontation

The specific methods that social workers use in communication are exploration, reflection, validation, and confrontation. These methods are defined and illustrated as social workers discuss their choice of method for each client interaction.

Just as the elements of social work practice are interconnected with each other, the various methods of communication are intricately bound together. A social worker does not simply finish one method and then start using another, but rather might use an exploring statement followed by a validating comment, perhaps followed by another exploration. Furthermore, these methods are not always easy to recognize: exploration may appear to be confrontation and reflection may sound like validation. *The context determines the purpose.* Nor are they mutually exclusive; a single statement may include both confrontation and validation. We separate these methods for the purposes of definition and illustration even though all the statements in a practice example do not necessarily make use of just one method.

Exploration   In Chapter 5 we viewed the social worker as an explorer embarking on a journey with the client to provide clarity and understanding about the nature and scope of the client's situation. Seeking the details of the problem situation, the social worker probes the personal attributes and qualities of the client.

Exploration is statements and behaviors by the social worker that further the client providing information. Knowledge is enhanced about the client and the client's situation with the disclosures elicited from the social worker's questions. Exploration provides details about the characteristics and scope of what is happening with the client. Especially important in the initial sessions, when data are gathered to learn about the client and the client's problem, exploration continues to be valuable through the later phases of practice as the social worker encourages the client to elaborate and expand on what has already been said.

In *The Skills of Helping Individuals and Groups,* Shulman discusses the skills of elaboration: "The elaborating skills are important . . . since they help clients tell their own story. The focus of the worker's questions and comments is on helping the client to elaborate and clarify specific concerns" (1979, p. 47). Another term Shulman uses to explain exploration is "reaching for" (1979, p. 55). The social worker encourages the client to share more thoughts, feelings, perceptions, and information.

By asking questions and making statements, social workers engage in the process of exploration with their clients. Asking questions, or interviewing, is probably the most basic means of obtaining information. A comprehensive treatment of interviewing in social work has been provided by Kadushin. In *The Social Work Interview,* he discusses the means of obtaining information:

> Questions may be classified in terms of a number of dimensions. One is the amount of freedom or restriction the question offers. . . . The open question . . . gives the interviewee the responsibility, and opportunity, of selecting his answer from a larger number of possible responses. The interviewee has the opportunity of revealing his own subjective frame of reference and of selecting those elements in the situation which he regards as of greatest concern. Open-ended . . . questions also communicate clearly that the interviewee has considerable responsibility for, and freedom in, participating in the interview and determining interview content and direction. (1972, pp. 149–150)

Questions and statements are called "open ended" when they *cannot* be answered with a simple yes or no. These types of questions are usually effective in facilitating clients to share information. For example, the questions "Are you sad?" or "Why did you do that?" can be answered with a simple "no" or "I don't know." On the other hand, open questions such as, "What has that situation been like for you?" or "How have you been feeling?" have the potential for eliciting more extensive information.

We first met the social worker Mara and her client Carol in Chapter 4 during our discussion of loss. We now examine Mara's use of exploration.

Mara, who worked at a mental health center, had seen Carol, who was 44 years old, for several months. Defining herself as a radical feminist, Mara was a recent emigré from Israel, where she worked primarily with women's groups and advocated for women's issues. Acknowledging these personal and political positions, Mara was alert for cues from her clients about their comfort with a feminist orientation. Believing that women needed to take a more activist and assertive stance for themselves, she worked hard at "reading" her clients—to follow the social work ethic of respecting where the client is while also expanding clients' life choices. Of the Jewish faith, she was used to displays of emotion. Raising the voice was a regular occurrence for her when conversing with others along with hand movements to emphasize particular points.

Carol was employed by a county welfare department, where she checked income verification records. With an income in the low $20,000 range, she was raising two sons, 13 and 9; two daughters in their twenties did not reside in the home. Her husband died ten months before in a car accident. In Carol's background (her ancestors moved to the United States from Britain in the late 1700s), sentiments were not easily expressed. Taught to "not wear her emotions on her sleeve," Carol was not always aware that she had feelings, and when they were too powerful to hide she had little ability to articulate them.

*1   MARA: *(enthusiastically)* So, tell me about your day today. *(looking directly at Carol)*

    CAROL: I'm at my wit's end. *(said with no evident emotion and looking down at the floor)*

*2   MARA: *(still energetic)* Tell me about what's been happening.

    CAROL: Work has gotten me upset. I can't explain how I'm feeling now. *(again, no emotion and avoiding eye contact)*

*3   MARA: Just take a minute and think about how you are feeling. *(silence)* Now, describe to me what you are feeling. *(authoritatively and looking directly at Carol)*

    CAROL: *(more of a complaining tone than anger)* I'm so mad about work. I went to the director to find out whether this new guy is actually going to be my supervisor. I told her I just can't understand how that can happen. *(tone of real displeasure)* He is at the exact same level as me and has only been here a short time.
                            (long silence)
        (slowly) I'm really feeling frustrated, I got in this unit to help out a friend who is now gone. *(pause)* I don't even want to be in this unit. *(making more direct eye contact)*

*4   MARA: What options do you have? *(said in a straightforward way)*

CAROL: *(pensive)* Well, he should have to take a supervisor's test, which I can also take. He would have to score higher. But *(now looking directly at Mara)* it doesn't always work this way.

*5 MARA: *(with some hint of indignation)* What would you like to do about this?

CAROL: *(with a little bit of conviction)* I think I'd like to take the test and see if I can get the supervisor position.

*6 MARA: What else have you considered?

CAROL: I've thought of asking to be transferred to another unit. *(pause)* I just don't think they'll do that for me.

*7 MARA: How come?

Each of Mara's statements and questions helped the client to elaborate and provide further information. At *1 and *2, she started the session with simple, open statements to Carol to talk about her day and what was happening with her. Picking up on what Carol said about not being able to explain her feelings, *3, Mara "reached for" her to say more by telling her to take a breath in order to relax and think. Then, using silence, Mara followed with a direct statement for Carol to describe her feelings. After the next long silence, where Mara continued to look directly at Carol, it would have been difficult for Carol not to elaborate further. Mara's communications elicited information from Carol about anger with her job.

Continuing with exploring, *4, *5, *6, Mara asked questions about the job options Carol considered for herself and what she wanted to do about them. At *7, a simple "how come" provided a good opening for Carol to talk further about her job situation.

Mara commented about her use of exploration with Carol:

. . . .

I think people will tell you what you need to know. My method is to let them tell me by making it easy for them to talk. Carol is not used to talking about herself; in fact, she thinks talking about her problems is being self-indulgent. And feelings are something she was taught not to acknowledge. So it usually takes a few initial statements by me to help Carol elaborate on what is happening with her. Exploring comments by me, in a way, gives Carol permission to further examine what is going on with her. She is not used to doing that, on her own.

The exploration helps both Carol and me to begin to identify the areas of concern. Though one might think that exploring is done primarily in early sessions, I find I am exploring throughout my work with a client. In most every session I spend some time exploring, helping the client elaborate further on something she has said, or something I have thought about over the week.

I use exploring when I need more information about something, and/or when I think the client will find it useful to get into a subject area more deeply.

....

Mara also took nonverbal cues into account to further her understanding of Carol and to direct treatment planning. Following her style of communication over these two months, Carol did not show emotion in her tone of voice or in her body movements. Noting that Carol sat still, looking somewhat uncomfortable with herself and her body, Mara modeled matching the nonverbal with the verbal. While accomplishing some small gains toward the end of this session, Mara acknowledged that Carol was just developing awareness of her lack of assertiveness and that movement toward a more feminist stance would not happen in the near future (and might not occur at all for this client). More basic right now was helping Carol to recognize and acknowledge that she had feelings and that she had the right to assert her own needs. Mara would need to remain aware that she and Carol had very different orientations to handling emotions. While Carol might never wave her arms in excitement or wildly fluctuate her voice tone, the objective was to gain greater and easier access to herself as a whole individual, with ability to acknowledge and articulate her feelings.

Reflection   Throughout the interaction, the social worker is thinking about and analyzing the information presented by the client. At various times, it is necessary to review with the client the thoughts and hypotheses being considered. ***Reflection is sharing with the client the social worker's speculations and pondering them together with the client. Involving feedback, paraphrasing, reframing and interpretation, reflection provides an opportunity for the social worker to check out and further shape the hypotheses.*** Reflection allows for greater depth of understanding for both social worker and client, resulting in insight, behavior change, or a reworking of the hypotheses.

Reflecting statements indicate that the client is being heard, that a shaping and organizing of the client's information is taking place, and that the social worker's questions are not merely a random fishing for information. They demonstrate to the client that the social worker is interested in the client and has been paying attention. Reflecting statements often involve feeding back specific phrases and words used by the client. Compton and Galaway call this *paraphrasing:* "This means that the worker restates the basic message in similar, but usually fewer, words—both as a test of the worker's understanding but also in order that the system might hear its own productions. . . . The worker . . . must remain very close to what is being expressed, simplifying to make clear, and synthesizing what the content, feelings, thinkings, or behavior mean to the worker" (1979, p. 370).

Kadushin says about reflection: "The reflective comment indicates that one is ready and willing to hear more about a particular topic" (1972, p. 143). Shulman talks about the importance of "tuning in": "Some of the most important client communications are not spoken directly. By tuning in, the worker may be able to hear the client's indirect cues and then respond directly" (1979, p. 15). Reflection statements demonstrate that the social worker has "tuned in" to the client's chief concerns. Reflection may also involve reframing, in which the client statement is rephrased in a different and usually more positive light. The term *reframing* was first introduced by family therapists, who used the technique to help family members see behavior as creative and healthy instead of "dysfunctional" and "bad."

Hollis distinguishes between dynamic and developmental or historical reflection:

> When we consider dynamic factors with the client, we are simply extending the process of intrareflection, using procedures—comments, questions, occasionally explanations—the content and timing of which is designed to help the individual to pursue further some of the intrapsychic reasons for his or her feelings, attitudes, and ways of acting, to understand the influence of one personality characteristic upon another—in other words, the ways in which thoughts and emotions work. . . . There are other times, however, when the client can be helped greatly in understanding unhealthy and unprofitable ways of acting by coming to understand some of their historical sources. (1981, pp. 147, 155)

For Hollis, both types of reflection promote greater understanding. The difference is whether the focus is on the individual's own personality characteristics or on factors that influenced the individual's development.

Interpretation was a concept frequently discussed in the early social work literature and may be included in the process of reflection. Aptekar offers a useful definition of interpretation:

> Interpretation must be thought of as a part of a dynamic process in which both worker and client play a part. . . . The client is moving when he reaches the worker. He uses the worker so that he may move further. The worker's task is to assist him in moving, if possible, along constructive lines. Interpretation . . . is devoted to this end . . .
>
> Insight sometimes follows movement. However, insight is not one of the goals of the caseworker who interprets to facilitate movement. One stimulates movement by bringing something new into the picture to which the client can react. The worker's insight into the nature of the client's difficulty can be used for this purpose. . . . The worker presents his own insight as something to which the client will inevitably react in one way or another. Reaction involves movement. (1941, pp. 115, 114)

A good example of reflecting statements is presented in the following session as we observe the impact of reflection on client change. We have already met the social worker, Linda, and her client, Dale, in Chapters 2 and 5. In the following session, Dale and her fiancé John were now married and had been meeting jointly for several months. One of their goals was to learn how to communicate better with each other. As we learned earlier, both grew up as loners, did not have much experience in having close relationships, and exhibited discomfort in talking together with Linda. John made very little eye contact, slouched in the chair, and appeared very distracted by furnishings in the room, particularly when the sessions were videotaped.

With very different cultural backgrounds—Linda was Jewish from a large city in the Northeast and Dale and John were both Protestant from rural farming backgrounds—Linda had to guard against stereotyping her clients. Used to people who were easy, even glib, talkers, Linda was taken aback by John's slow, drawling cadence. Yet she could not assume they were unable to access their emotions. Expectations for improved communication were as realistic for Dale and John as for more verbal clients:

*1 DALE: *(turning in her chair to look directly at John)* It embarrasses you, doesn't it, you tell me not to smoke in front of other people, and I don't smoke in front of those certain people because it will embarrass you! *(said very firmly)*

   JOHN: *(squirming in chair and looking down)* I don't remember that.

*2 LINDA: *(looking directly at John, with an eye on Dale's reactions)* John, in light of some things we've talked about before, I wonder if this has something to do with how you feel about women, your thoughts about what women should be doing. *(said thoughtfully and questioningly)*

   JOHN: *(looking down, much squirming)* Um-hum, It's not the place for a woman to smoke.

*3 DALE: *(firmly, looking directly at Linda)* John's idea of what a woman should be and my idea are two different things! And he wants me to do all these things in addition to my job. *(gesturing with hands)* He said it would be nice for me to sew like his sister, and cook pies like his mother. I don't like to sew, and I have my own way of making pies! *(very emphatic)*

*4 LINDA: *(looking first at Dale, then John, then both of them)* I hear you saying that you're upset about John having these models that you feel he wants you to live up to. What are you really saying?

*5 DALE: *(quickly, and said with conviction)* He doesn't accept me the way that I am. He wants to change me, make me over into something else, that I'm not and that I never can be. *(glancing over at John)*

*6   LINDA: *(said with a sense of compassion and looking directly at John)* It's kind of hard, isn't it? John, it seems like the women you've come in contact with before you got married did certain things, or acted certain ways. It sounds like you want your wife to be the best of all those people.

JOHN: *(looks up with a slight smile)*

At *2 Linda, pulling on information gained in past sessions with the couple, reflected that the husband's complaints about the wife's smoking suggested his views about women. As the issue of smoking was mentioned frequently, Linda tried to think about what larger issue was behind the smoking, what was significant about the smoking for both Dale and John. Hypothesizing that smoking had become a metaphor about John's image of women, she related that to his expectations for his wife. It became an issue for Dale in terms of her sense of identity, acceptance by John, and self-esteem (which she acknowledged in *5). Though staying with the specifics the clients raised—the smoking—Linda's intervention brought the discussion to a deeper and more meaningful level.

At *4, even though "I hear you saying" is considered social work jargon, it is a good way to introduce a reflective statement. This comment by Linda reflected her hypothesis of what lay behind Dale's concern with John's "bugging her" about the smoking.

Change in Dale was evident in her use of confrontive, assertive, and direct statements (*3, *5) and her nonverbal cues. It is striking to compare these statements with those of Dale in Chapter 5. At that time, an earlier phase of the practice, Dale's remarks were very brief and curt three- or four-word sentences. In the excerpt just given, in contrast, Dale's responses to John's expectations of her were the most assertive Dale had uttered in the year of treatment. Moreover, in contrast to her usual very stiff and rigid body movements and lack of affect in her voice, Dale used gestures and allowed her anger and conviction to show in her tone of voice. Following *2, Dale forcefully, and with no trace of guilt or apology, shared her feelings of not being accepted by John, which brought even greater intimacy to the session.

Linda's use of reflection demonstrated to this couple that she "tuned in" to them, had been listening and thinking about what they were saying to her and had been organizing into a picture the data they discussed. The reflective statements used with Dale and John resulted in a more direct and honest expression by Dale about her feelings. Behavior change was demonstrated not only by the words Dale used, but also through her nonverbal cues of body language and voice tone. Though the details might focus on smoking, there were important underlying issues that Linda helped to identify through reflection.

Linda commented on her use of reflection in this exchange:

....

I had come to know Dale and John and became very aware during this session that some big changes were happening. John indicated in a variety of ways— through his squirming and playing with the microphone cord—that he was not comfortable. It was also clear that Dale—by her body posture and voice tone— was ready to confront John and share some of her feelings directly with him. This was new behavior for her and I wanted to support her in that change. Through reflection I was able to let each of them know that I was "with them" while also encouraging growth in their interaction.

And as always, I was struck with the incredible capacity of people to stretch beyond their boundaries. Both through cultural background and psychiatric disorder, Dale has had minimal experience in openly discussing her feelings with those close to her. When offered the opportunity, however, she was able to respond with honesty and forthrightness.

....

While awareness of cultural differences was important for Linda in understanding Dale and John, she also had to move beyond any deterministic view in developing goals for client change. Just because Dale and John had little experience in discussing their feelings did not mean they were incapable or unwilling to learn.

Validation   As we discussed in Chapter 4, the development of a belief bonding is central to social work practice. ***Validation is the enactment of trust and confidence, establishing belief by the worker in the client's worth as a person. Validation is acceptance and empowerment of the client. It is "staying with" what the client is expressing. Validation provides support and respect for the client.*** Social workers may validate by responding to something the client has reported, picking up on words the client has used, or by commenting on expressed or unexpressed feelings or on nonverbal cues. Validating statements may be very specific to what has happened in the session, such as, "I see that you are sad about this." Validation may also be a generalized statement about the client's experiences, such as, "I know you have been feeling angry about the events we have discussed."

Virginia Satir, one of the very early social workers to focus on practice with families, considers validation a basic need: "All messages, when viewed at their highest abstraction level can be characterized as 'Validate me' messages. These are frequently interpreted as 'Agree with me,' 'Be on my side,' 'Validate me by sympathizing with me,' or, 'Validate me by showing me you value me and my ideas' " (Satir, 1983, p. 103).

Being supportive is basic to social work practice. In fact, some workers may say it is the single most effective help they can offer. To support is to nurture, to provide an underpinning or to buttresss. Naturally, social workers want to support their clients, but this support is not a carte blanche. There are occasions when the actions of the clients do not warrant support.

Making distinctions between individuals and their behavior is a necessary component of the helping process. Social workers often work with clients who have behaved badly. Some clients may have engaged in delinquent or even criminal acts. Negative reactions to clients' behavior are not unusual. Critical to effective practice, however, is the ability to separate judgment about clients' actions from their worth as individuals. Alan Keith Lucas comments in his book on helping: "It is extremely difficult for human beings to get away from the idea that to care about a person in trouble is not to condone what he has done. . . . It is very easy to reject those who have let one down especially where this has been accompanied with anger, blame, or ingratitude" (1972, p. 87).

Earlier in this chapter we analyzed an exchange between Mara and her client, Carol, focusing on Mara's use of exploration statements. In the subsequent exchange given here, Mara validated Carol and had just asked her to explain why she did not think she would be allowed to transfer to another unit.

	CAROL:	Sometime back, I asked to get into the nursing home unit, but nothing has come of it. (turning half away from Mara) It's going to be boring for me to go into this anymore. (quietly and with no pleasure in her voice)
*1	MARA:	How come you think I'll find this boring?
	CAROL:	The government got after our county for not checking whether accurate payments have been made. There could be fraud.
*2	MARA:	I want us to stay with this. Where does this assumption come from that I find this boring? Do you want to know if I find this boring?
	CAROL:	(sitting up and paying attention to what Mara has just asked her) Yes, I think people find this boring.
*3	MARA:	I don't think this is boring. I know the work is important, and that it needs to be done or your department will have trouble with funding. I know it is tedious for the person who has to do it because it has to be very precise. The other part of this that is not boring by any stretch of the imagination is this position you are in with this job. A guy who does not understand what is going on gets to take the information you have so carefully prepared and goes to court with it; he has the fun! This same guy may get to be your supervisor and will be able to tell you what to do.

CAROL: *(sitting straight up, her voice expressing real indignation)* Right, right! I can't stand the injustice of it.

*4   MARA: I understand why you are feeling such stress. This is hard to put up with day after day.

Mara discussed her reasons for picking up on the client's use of the word "boring" (her intervention at *1):

....

I knew that for Carol self-esteem was a major issue. She has really been struggling with some unfair treatment at her job, yet she doesn't feel justified in ventilating about it. She sounded almost apologetic about bringing up the topic and I know she thinks that all the things she is struggling with are not worth my time. My question about how come she thinks I find talk about her work boring was to bring out in the open her discounting of herself, and for me to offer support and respect for what she does.

....

At *2, Mara's statement that she wanted to stay with the topic was an affirmation of Carol, conveying her belief that what Carol was talking about was important and warranted further attention. Mara commented:

....

One of the issues that has come up in the work with Carol is that she operates on many assumptions that she doesn't check out. I wanted to deliberately call to her attention that she had made an assumption about my feelings concerning her employment. She assumed that I was bored by hearing about her job, but she had never checked out that assumption with me.

....

Showing respect for Carol's work, at *3, Mara specifically discussed the work situation and empowered Carol through affirming the importance of her work. A generalized statement, *4, then acknowledged the feelings that Carol was experiencing.

Mara remarked:

....

Carol does not easily ask for herself. She believes she should be doing things for others and should have no needs of her own. She dismisses any of her own needs or desires. Validation is a critical part of my work with Carol. My belief in Carol's worth as a person will gradually enhance her belief in her own worth.

....

Toward the end of this session, Carol's body language showed a definite change, with the expression of real and appropriate emotion and a total alteration of body stance. Mara's observations of these cues helped her evaluate the effectiveness of her validation comments with Carol.

Confrontation   While being supportive may be considered a central component of social work practice, at first glance the use of confrontation may not seem equally germane. Yet the ability to assist clients in facing their problems directly is basic to helping them.

At times, clients may have difficulty talking. They may have trouble acknowledging particular feelings or may be reluctant to discuss certain experiences. Some topics may be deliberately avoided or may even exist beyond their awareness. In the process of confrontation, social workers help clients talk openly and honestly even when they are uneasy, or unaware, or directly resistant. Confrontation may involve pushing, prompting, and actively encouraging clients to face the uncomfortable and to make changes in their behavior.

Individuals see the world through a particular mindset, a unique and usually idiosyncratic lens. A person's view of the world allows in some details and filters out others—and what gets filtered out is often more significant than what gets included. Clients sometimes have a narrow and biased view of their situation, and they may distort the reasons that they are in a given situation. Confrontation involves challenging clients with statements and interpretations which help broaden their perspective and understanding. It may also involve giving advice or an opinion that conflicts with the client's views.

Confrontation means that social workers take a forceful stand on issues. *Confrontation is directing the client's attention to discrepancies in what has been said or to discrepancies between what is said and nonverbal cues and expressions. Confrontation educates, informs, and challenges clients to develop new and different ways to behave.*

If the social worker assesses that the client feels angry but the client denies any angry feelings, the technique of confrontation may be used: "If I were in that situation I would be feeling angry" or "In my experience other people in similar situations have had angry reactions, but that might not be your reaction."

Kadushin says about confrontation:

The worker strives to be consistently useful rather than consistently popular. This might require, on occasion, the use of confrontation in which the interviewer presents the interviewee with contradictions between his words and his behavior; it might require the use of authority, for example, to protect a child from abuse; it might require an unequivocal statement of the expectation the worker has that the client will implement whatever responsibilities he agreed he would accept. (1972, p. 43)

Most people who enter social work want to "do good" and may perceive confrontation as negative. Yet Reid and Shyne (1969) reported in their study that the most frequent change-oriented technique used by caseworkers, after exploration, was confrontation.

To confront is to treat clients with respect. During confrontation, the social worker makes the assumption that the client is a responsible individual, capable of direct and honest dialogue. Just as with the other techniques, confrontation can result in movement, insight, and behavior change. When used effectively, where social workers are comfortable and effective in their use of the technique, confrontation can be received by clients as supportive, loving, and helpful.

In this exchange, occurring during the same session in which we reviewed Mara's use of exploration and validation, we examine how she used confrontation.

	CAROL:	*(pause, long sigh)* My daughter's baby is being moved into the transitional unit. He's doing a lot better. *(long sigh)* Everyone is now asking me about a baby shower. I thought, please, I just got over a wedding, an operation, the baby being sick! My sister-in-law is interested in this, I'm sure they'll help me.
*1	MARA:	Is there somebody who can help you by being the one to organize it? You could help them.
	CAROL:	There is no one. My sister-in-law just gave her daughter a shower.
*2	MARA:	Does this sound to you like anything we've talked about before?
	CAROL:	*(long silence—appearing somewhat limp in her chair and with little expressed interest)* No, like what?
*3	MARA:	One of the patterns in the way you do things, the ways you deal with people's demands.
	CAROL:	*(looking sad, taking time to respond, hoarse voice, then said slowly)* Yeah, you mean I just go ahead and do it.
*4	MARA:	Yes. You are very attentive to other people's needs— someone says something needs to be done and you agree to do it. I don't see you giving yourself the time to ask if you really need to do it, or if somebody else can do it, or maybe it doesn't need to be done, or to just say no. You're so willing to care for other people, and I'm concerned because I don't see much of that care for yourself.

CAROL: *(long pause, clears throat)* I guess you're right. I think the more I'm busy, I don't have time to sit around and think of anything.

*5 MARA: What would happen if you did sit and think about things?

CAROL: *(said pretty quickly and directly)* Then I might sit there and feel sorry for myself.

*6 MARA: Now there is one person to do what two people used to do. It's just been over a year since your husband died. You also have a 40-hour-a-week job, which has been frustrating you, and two kids to take care of, and a daughter who's just had a Caesarian operation, a new grandchild who's been in intensive care. How do you mean to tell me you're feeling sorry for yourself?

CAROL: *(now sitting up, looking directly at Mara and very engaged in the dialogue)* I don't even know why I feel like that. It's always been like that. I don't know why I feel that I don't need anything. I just don't want to put anybody out.

*7 MARA: Maybe it's time to change that.

CAROL: I guess. It's hard to change.

*8 MARA: Yes, it's hard to change. It's also hard on you to keep going this way. You do so much for other people, its okay for you to ask that they do something for you. Also, you seem to have punitive ideas about what I think about you, like I think your job is boring. You assume there is negative stuff coming toward you, that you don't check out, and that I don't feel. I think it's important that as we go along you check things out with me.

CAROL: *(pause)* I've been so busy running around with everything. I was thinking about whether you think I need to come here every week. What about every two weeks?

*9 MARA: I don't think it's a good idea.

CAROL: Don't you think I'm doing any better?

*10 MARA: Yes, I think you're doing better. How come it is that the first thing you think of cutting out is something that is for yourself?

CAROL: It's the easiest thing to do. I never looked at it that way.

*11 MARA: It seems to me that you're still feeling depressed, angry about things on the job, and trying to sort out feelings about your dead husband. It's okay if something has to change in your schedule, but not if it's for yourself.

Mara discussed her intervention.

....

Perhaps my comment, at *1, seemed surprising. I asked Carol about the possibility of assisting someone in arranging a shower for the daughter, instead of her being the one in charge. Having decided not to commiserate with Carol being overburdened, I felt it was time to frame things differently, to provide an alternative perspective with new options for her, rather than Carol continually being called on to run and do everything.

....

Mara asked Carol if what she was doing sounded to her like something they had discussed before (*2). This type of comment is a useful technique to determine whether the client is aware of, or remembers, previous discussion of a particular behavior pattern. Mara had to prompt Carol to confront the manner in which she responds to the demands of others (*3).

Educating Carol on how to say no (*4), Mara challenged her to consider a new and different way of thinking and responding when asked to do things. Mara commented:

....

Carol was touched when I confronted her with the difference in care and attention she lavishes on others and the kind of care she gives to herself. She was visibly moved, she got a sad look on her face, and had to take some time before responding. When she did speak, her voice was hoarse.

I knew that it was hard for Carol to take time for herself. Often, when people keep so busy the way Carol does, they are trying to avoid uncomfortable feelings like sadness or anger. I did not think that Carol was aware of trying to avoid any feelings. A lot has always been expected of her; even as a child her parents looked to her for strength. I felt it was time for me to question her about what would happen if she took time to sit and think, time for herself.

....

It is evident that Mara was on target because Carol quickly and directly responded to her confrontation (*5) that she would sit around and feel sorry for herself. Challenging Carol's "feeling sorry" as a distorted view of her situation (*6) and noting the change in Carol's demeanor, Mara reviewed the very tough responsibilities she had to carry and confronted Carol that she really had been overburdened.

With further confrontation at *7 and *8, Mara pushed for specific behavior change. She asked that Carol check out her assumptions and question more directly. Immediately responding, Carol suggested that she cut back on the frequency of her sessions. This is not an unusual proposal by a client. At *9 and *10, Mara presented her opinion that she did not consider it a good idea for Carol to cut back on sessions and confronted Carol on her willingness to give up something that was important for her. Mara was forceful, *11, as she described Carol's progress and advised against a change in the treatment schedule at this time.

Mara discussed her approach with Carol:

....

My thrust in this session was Carol's compulsive caretaking. She seemingly grew up with this pattern. Her parents still rely on her a great deal. It appears that in her third marriage, which had lasted for over thirteen years, she felt loved and accepted and was able to rely on her husband. It was the calmest and most satisfying period of her life. With his sudden death, almost a year ago, she became depressed, and has returned to her frenetic "busy-body" manner. In confronting her, I am wanting her to both feel support from me and to consider alternatives to the ways she deals with others. I use confrontation to state directly to Carol where I see her getting into trouble and to push directly for behavior change.

....

We have defined and examined the principle communication methods— *exploration, reflection, validation, confrontation*—through the use of case material with some discussion about the impact of *cultural differencs.* Not to be used as rigid prescriptions for practice, these methods offer explanations for specific messages conveyed to achieve specific client goals and objectives. The final section of this chapter includes suggestions about written communications, scheduling, and other types of formal communication.

ADDITIONAL NOTES

Accountable to an employing agency, perhaps required to complete insurance forms, and sometimes called on to make referrals or appear in court, you will be responsible to communicate professionally through written documentation, including agency records and other recording. As determined by the needs and functions of each agency, information is reported about the client and the nature of the work through agency records, intake reports, interim summaries, and transfer or termination summaries. As is traditional to the profession, you will also engage in some means of continuing professional development through presentation of your work in less formal structures, such as process recordings or logs.

Agency Records

A range of social work forms are maintained that are specific to each setting. These may include brief sheets with only identifying information or lengthy reports requiring extensive detail. Some agencies have highly standardized means of recording and transmitting data, while others allow a more informal format with greater discretion left to the staff. Hospitals, for example, usually require daily entries of progress notes, while family service centers do less frequent reporting, relying on periodic written summaries. With the increase in insurance payments, it has become the norm in most agencies to maintain forms necessary to receive reimbursement.

Intake Reports

Most settings have some means of reporting on initial client contacts. The *psychosocial report,* which was covered in Chapter 5, is the contribution of the social work profession to the early information-gathering stage. Though it varies in format, this report is a means for providing information about the client's functioning within his or her environmment while also considering the client's past history. The psychosocial report offers an understanding of your clients within the context of their circumstances.

Interim Summaries

Continual changes in the client's situation are reflected in periodic written reports called *interim summaries.* Though not necessarily required by all settings, reports updating client information at the minimum of every three months help maintain accurate agency records while encouraging regular review of goal achievement. Depending on the function and record-keeping demands of the agency, these summaries may consist of just a few paragraphs reviewing what has happened since the last report.

Transfer or Termination Summaries

Necessitated by the time-limited nature of social work practice, *transfer* and *termination summaries* reflect the work accomplished. Usually generated when the social worker is leaving the agency, the transfer summary succinctly introduces the client to the new social worker. Although other records are available, the transfer summary provides an opportunity for the old worker to "talk" to the new worker about the facts relevant to this client. Important to include here are your thoughts and suggestions for ongoing treatment. Useful in sharing past experiences with this client, this report should preferably be an informal narrative.

Whereas transfers usually result when the social worker is making a job change, terminations most often reflect the client's movements. As discussed in Chapter 4, the termination of the practice may reflect either achievement of the stated goals or an unplanned and unwarranted cessation of the treatment. Records should be brought up to date with a thorough review of the practice in the termination summary, which is similar to the psychosocial report. It is a good idea to include sections addressing your current assessment, impressions, and prognosis. Since the client may return in the future, perhaps after you have left the agency, a thorough report is recommended. Goals, both accomplished and unmet, and recommendations for future areas of work should also be included.

Process Recording

Long a fixture of social work education, the *process recording* is a means through which students examine and analyze their work with clients. Before the advent of audio- and videotapes, the process recording was the only tool available for field and practice class teachers to review the practice behaviors of students. Though there have been pleas for greater structure to the process recording (Dwyer and Urbanowski, 1965), its format has remained basically unaltered. Beginning with a brief introductory paragraph stating the number of sessions previously held with the client, relevant details, and identifying information—sex, age, race and ethnicity, employment status and income, education, living arrangements, and houshould members—the thrust of the recording is the dialogue that took place between you and the client.

The format of the process recording is two vertical columns. The actual dialogue is recorded in the lefthand column, and the social worker's observations, feelings, and perceptions of the client's feelings are presented in the righthand column. The intent is to examine the relationship between statements and feelings, considering both verbal and nonverbal cues. In composing the righthand column, you must reflect back on the words said and feelings experienced during the dialogue, attending to how feelings impacted on things stated by both yourself and the client. The increase in self-awareness that this exercise promotes can enhance your capacity to regulate the words you use, preventing undue influence of your personal feelings on the interaction. Contemplation about the client's feelings can result in greater understanding of the issues presented and provide areas for further follow-up in subsequent interviews.

The two columns of dialogue and feelings in the process recording are followed by two or three paragraphs of analysis in which you offer observations about possible connections between feelings and statements. Almost as important as the actual dialogue is your capacity to draw the linkages and understand the relationships between what you feel and what you say.

Although it is typically employed as the basis of supervision, you may make use of this instrument throughout your professional career. The process recording offers a means to review comments made to clients in which you consider what was said while contemplating feelings and perceptions during the interview. Shortened from the lengthy and detailed reporting of the entire interview, 5-minute sections can provide ample material for examination of a session.

The following is a process recording made by a first-year M.S.W. student covering the initial 5 minutes of a client interview. Particularly powerful is the analysis in which she has been able to recognize limitations in her interaction. The worker, Joyce, is in her early thirties with two children, ages 3 and 5. Having experienced some bouts with panic attacks, she found social work treatment highly beneficial to her and decided to pursue a social work career. After she was placed in a hospice program, her field instructor had been focusing on how to practice with clients with sad feelings, how to acknowledge and accept feelings without being maudlin.

IDENTIFYING INFORMATION

This was my first contact with Mr. L, a White, 45-year-old son of a Hospice patient, whose family I've been asked to follow for several months. The father died of cancer several months before at the age of 75. Mr. L has two older brothers and a twin sister who live in the area. Owning a restaurant, he completed two years of college and has an income of about $60,000. He lives in a pleasant home with his wife and two children under the age of 10. He was not his father's primary caregiver and was not present at the death event.

	STATEMENTS	JOYCE'S OBSERVATIONS AND FEELINGS, PERCEPTIONS OF CLIENT'S FEELINGS
	JOYCE: Mr. L?	
	MR. L: Yes.	
*1	JOYCE: My name is Joyce Green. I'm a member of the Hospice bereavement team, but actually, I'm a graduate student in social work doing an internship at the Hospice. I noticed you were getting our correspondence and am now making a follow-up visit. We usually check in several times in the first year of bereavement to see how people are doing.	I feel like I'm imposing on this man. He didn't ask me to call and probably has no interest in telling all of this to a stranger. How do I tell him I'm a student—I'm not even an expert on this stuff.
	MR. L: It's funny that you should come today. I've really been missing him this day.	He sounded sad and warm and tender, all at the same time.
	JOYCE: That's what your wife said.	I feel like he's ready to share—can I handle this?

MR. L: I was outside working on the house and that's when he would usually come around and spend time with me; we'd go out to eat for breakfast or lunch. I don't usually feel this way, but today it's hit me. It's sad.

He sounds like a little boy missing his daddy. I want to make it all better.

JOYCE: And I guess it's hard to predict when that's going to happen. It's such a pretty day outside, too.

The stupidity of commenting on the weather struck me as soon as I said it. Clichés!!!

MR. L: It really is. He was in construction and used to get into all the technical stuff, ask me what I was doing, that sort of thing.

It sounds as if it's painful for him to talk about all the relationships he lost when he lost his father.

JOYCE: Well, it hasn't even been a year yet for you. We call people several times in the first year because many people who have lost someone still need contact with Hospice during that first year.

I hope I'm sounding warm, caring, open, and CALM! I'm trying to lean forward and look compassionate.

MR. L: The one good thing that has come out of all this, if there can be a good thing, is that I've learned to enjoy the loved ones I still have even more, and to ignore the bullshit, the little stuff that drives you crazy. I've learned to tell people how I feel . . .

I think he's feeling that he has to be philosophical about this, that he somehow owes it to me to teach me something. He's shifting in his chair and crossing his arms.

JOYCE: Because that moment might not come around again. And I guess you have to steel yourself for the next pretty Sunday.

I hate it when I interrupt. I'm feeling so uneasy, like I need to go and call my own dad.

MR. L: Yeah.

JOYCE: You really seem to have your priorities straight about all of this, to be handling it so well in spite of the sad days like today. I haven't lost either of my parents yet, but wonder how I will cope.

I feel like I have to share something, too. He could just as easily have been one of our friends. I like him and I feel myself equalizing all of this.

MR. L: My wife hasn't lost hers, either, and I try to tell her that it's important to put up with the little stuff with the people you love because it really doesn't matter. I can't say enough good things about Hospice. My mother died a horrible death eleven years ago from a disease no one knew how to deal with. Hospice was starting about then and they called us to see how we felt about all that was going on. It was so much better for my dad. He came out to see the house on Monday, came into my restaurant on Tuesday, got sick that night and died on Friday.

I get the feeling that someone at home drives him crazy and he's made a conscious decision to ignore it. He sounds glad to have had a chance to do it differently with his dad. Sad, but matter of fact.

JOYCE: I guess we can't ask for more than that.

I'm feeling so helpless. Nothing I say will alleviate the pain.

MR. L: No, we can't. I had hoped to finish the addition before he died, that was my goal, but I didn't make it. But when I do finish it later this fall, we're going to have a big party and dedicate it to him.

He sounded resigned about not meeting his goal, but really pleased by the prospect of the party.

JOYCE: I hope you can call me, or Caro, the bereavement coordinator, if you want to talk some more. We have a support group about to begin, but you sound like a busy man.

This could be me. I feel genuine concern and warmth. I hope he hears that. I start packing up my stuff.

MR. L: *(laughs)* And what is your name again?

This makes me feel needed, even though he probably won't ever call.

JOYCE: Joyce Green.

MR. L: I have a restaurant and catering business and I'd really like to do something for Hospice in terms of the food for a fundraiser.

I admire him for the way he is channeling his grief.

JOYCE: That's so nice of you. I'll pass your name along to the volunteer coordinator. I'm sure she'd love to have your help. Good luck with the house.

MR. L: Thanks, bye.

ANALYSIS

I erred on the side of caution because I felt that I might be perceived as being nosy, a meddling social worker. And, I was offering services that hadn't been specifically contracted for.

I could have asked more, followed up on his leads about his mother and his failure to "reach his goal" if I'd been able to let go of my notions about what's socially correct and flow with the Hospice process, which includes genuine involvement with the family's grief. I also focused too much in my mind on the fact that I had no answers for this man and I guess I believed that was what he wanted from me. I should have realized that he simply needed to tell me about *his* grief. I know I'm not supposed to have the definitive word on grief, but it was hard to relax, slow down, and let him take a few more steps towards his own understanding of it all.

Somehow, being the facilitator of a helpful conversation didn't feel like enough to me, and yet at other times I was too hesitant to ask the right questions, mostly because I initiated the whole thing and I wasn't sure of his feelings about talking to someone from Hospice.

As well as providing a specific piece of practice that can be reviewed during a supervision conference, the act of writing the process recording led to Joyce's own astute observations about her interactions. Insecurities about her abilities to be a helper, to address issues of death and dying, about social work as a helping profession are all reflected in her statements. Pleased by Joyce's analytic abilities, her field instructor could encourage Joyce to continue considering alternatives to what she said. Based on the self-awareness evidenced in the Feelings column, the field instructor could facilitate further discussion about effective practice with loss and pursue ways to enhance, rather than cut off, clients when they talk about their feelings. Also alerted, *1, to Joyce's discomfort with the role of student social worker, they could talk about potential contributions to her clients and the agency and help her feel more confident in the role of helper.

Because Joyce demonstrated that she understood the relationship of her sadness and fear of death with her comments about the weather to Mr. L, her field instructor and practice class teacher both considered this an excellent process recording. It is important to remember that though the process recording can be used to evaluate the effectiveness of practice, its real value is to examine your abilities to attend to both verbal and nonverbal cues and to draw linkages between feelings and statements.

Logs

Used as a diary about one's practice behaviors, *logs* are a running narrative about thoughts, feelings, and observations. Lacking the practice dialogue of the process recording, the log emphasizes your personal contemplations. Entries may be made after every client interview.

SUMMARY

Communication is a more recent component of social work practice, and issues pertaining to communication were initially subsumed under the relationship or assessment components of social work. Not studied formally until the mid 1900s, the investigation of interactions between people was spurred on by the related fields of psychology, sociology and anthropology.

Communication was defined in this chapter as

 A purposeful set of activities, focused on altering the problem situation presented by the client. As the process that allows for the information gathering of the assessment and the enactment of the relationship and intervention, communication is the primary technology of the social work practice. Consisting of the transmission and exchange of thoughts, feelings, and information, communication occurs through verbal and nonverbal means and in writing. Transactions are between social workers and clients, social workers and colleagues and peers, social workers and other related persons. The methods—exploration, reflection, validation, confrontation—and the skills— to give information, to sustain the dialogue, to use silence, to focus, and to summarize—are shaped by the social worker's understanding of the client and of the presenting problem.

Acknowledging tendencies among social workers and others in the helping professions to establish prescriptions for practice behaviors, we have examined various methods and skills of communication to establish clarity and provide meaning for the things social workers and clients say to each other. They are not presented, however, as rules or standards. As Birdwhistell put it:

> A Human Being is not a black box with one orifice for emitting a chunk of stuff called communication and another for receiving it. And, at the same time, communication is not simply the sum of the bits of information which pass between two people in a given period of time. (1973, p. 3)

Much of what is communicated between social workers and clients is shaped by nonverbal cues and is influenced by cultural backgrounds and experiences. While it can be helpful to have knowledge about the impact of ethnicity on communication styles, it is equally important not to stereotype clients. Just like the other social work components, communication is a complex process, utilized by the social worker to help the client create change.

BIBLIOGRAPHY

Aptekar, H. (1941). *Basic concepts in social case work*. Chapel Hill, N.C.: University of North Carolina Press.

Bandler, R., and Grinder, J. (1975 and 1976). *The structure of magic, I and II*. Palo Alto, Calif.: Behavior and Science Books.

Bateson, G. (1972). *Steps to an ecology of mind*. New York: Ballantine Books.

Beulter, L., Johnson, D., Neville, C., Jr, & Workman, S. N. (1970). Accurate empathy and the A-B dichotomy. *Journal of Abnormal Psychology*, 82, 273–277.

Birdwhistell, R. (1973). *Kinesics and context*. Great Britain: Penguin Press.

Chinsky, J. M., & Rappaport, J. (1970). Brief critique of the meaning and reliability of "Accurate Empathy" ratings. *Psychological Bulletin*, 73, 379–382.

Compton, B., & Galaway, B. (1979). *Social work processes*. Homewood, Ill.: Dorsey Press.

Dwyer, M., & Urbanowski, M. (1965). Student process recording: A plea for structure. *Social Casework* (May), 283–285.

Hamilton, G. (1951). *Theory and practice of social casework*. 2nd ed. New York: Columbia University Press.

Hepworth, D., & Larsen, J. (1982 and 1986). *Direct social work practice*. Homewood, Ill.: Dorsey Press.

Hollis, F., & Woods, M. (1981). *Casework: A psychosocial therapy*. New York: Random House.

Kadushin, A. (1972). *The social work interview.* New York: Columbia University Press.

Logan, S., McRoy, R., Freeman, E. (1989). *Social work practice with Black families: A cultural specific perspective.* New York: Longman Press.

Lucas, A. (1972). *Giving and taking help.* Chapel Hill, N.C.: University of North Carolina Press.

Lyndon, B. (1948). Development and use. In *Transference in casework.* New York: Family Service Association of America.

McCarthy, P. R. (1977). Follow-up evaluation of helping skills training. *Counselor Education and Supervision, 17*: 1, 29–35.

McGoldrick, M., Pearce, J., & Giordano, J. (1982). *Ethnicity and family therapy.* New York: Guilford Press.

McGoldrick, M. (1989). Ethnicity and the family life cycle. In B. Carter and M. McGoldrick (Eds.). *The changing family life cycle,* 69–90. Boston: Allyn & Bacon.

Pinderhughes, E. (1989). *Understanding race, ethnicity and power.* New York: Free Press.

Reid, W., & Shyne, A. (1969). *Brief and extended casework.* New York: Columbia University Press.

Reynolds, B. (1942). *Learning and teaching in the practice of social work.* New York: Rinehart.

Satir, V. (1983). *Conjoint family therapy.* Palo Alto: Science and Behavior Books.

Shulman, L. (1979). *The skills of helping individuals and groups.* Itasca, Ill.: Peacock Press.

Truaxx, C. B., & Carkhuff, R. R. (1967). *Toward effective counseling and psychotherapy.* Chicago: Aldine.

Watzlawick, P., Weakland, J. H., & Fisch, R. (1974). *Change.* New York: Norton.

CHAPTER ✆ SEVEN

An intellectual process is set in operation through which feeling may be objectified if the student is not too involved emotionally to be free to think.

—*Charlotte Towle*

PRACTITIONER OBSERVATION: THE SELF MONITORING OF PRACTICE

"Oh no, my client, Lennie is having a relapse of her bulimia, now taking 10 laxatives a day, I am worried that she is endangering herself! Having struggled so when my daughter gorged food, I hope I can be helpful for this client."

Social work practice addresses the intimate and universal issues of living and dying, love, sexuality, self-worth, growing up, and growing old. Social workers often examine clients' relationships with significant others, or lack thereof—including relationships with parents, children, siblings, lovers, spouses, friends, colleagues, and employers. Embracing the significant along with the petty and trivial, the subject matter of social work is the infinite array of problems encountered in living one's life. With no ready solutions for their clients, social workers themselves live with these same day-to-day troubles.

Such universality of life events requires social workers to differentiate their own personal experiences from their clients' situations. But this kind of separation is impossible unless practitioners are conscious of their own feelings and reactions to clients and to the problems clients present. Only then can they plan how to use themselves effectively in their work with clients. In this chapter we discuss the concept of *practitioner observation,* the capacity of social workers to develop an observer stance on themselves as individuals and to utilize those observations in their professional decisions.

Practitioner observation enables social workers to keep their lives separate and distinct from the lives of their clients and to build intervention not on what *they* might need in the same situation, but on what clients need.

When social workers utilize this component, they are able to integrate professional knowledge and skills with their own values and abilities and provide help that is truly useful to clients. In the first case we will examine, the social worker, Pat, has to focus on her client, Lennie, and the problems Lennie is facing with bulimia. Bulimia is an eating disorder in which the person gorges on food and then forces elimination through vomiting or laxatives. Pat *can* use Lennie's similarity to Pat's own daughter and her personal experience with bulimia to help her be an effective social worker. She will be unable, however, to practice effective social work unless she brings to conscious awareness her personal reactions to Lennie.

As we examine practitioner observation, we must again stress that social work practice is not linear. Components do not follow each other in some logical sequence, but rather impact on and shape each other in a complex amalgamation. As we saw in Chapter 5, assessment is the phase of practice where social workers formulate an understanding of events in the client's life and plan a means of responding. Shaped by the assessment, intervention, covered in Chapter 8, spells out the things social workers do to create change. Without practitioner observation, however, the case theory of the assessment may be constructed around the social workers' biases. Likewise, unless social workers distinguish their own preferences from the clients' wishes, the intervention may be based on social workers' desires for their own lives rather than on what is best for the clients.

Moreover, the professional relationship, as reviewed in Chapter 4, is a bonding between the social worker and client. Here again practitioner observation requires that social workers distinguish between their personal and professional relationships so that they can relate to clients as the uniquely individual people they are. And, finally, in terms of the technology of practice, or communication, presented in Chapter 6, practitioner observation prevents the inappropriate influence of social workers' own mores and cultural backgrounds on their interaction, enabling them to use a communication style and vocabulary appropriate to each client.

Later in this chapter, we define practitioner observation and study social workers in practice with clients. Situations are explored in which social workers *identify their thoughts, feelings, and biases about clients; reflect on the impact of their own cultural background and life experience on their practice; intervene with clients who remind them of family and friends; and address client problems similar to their own.* We see there are no ready prescriptions for curing Lennie's bulimia or for helping a woman deal with the effects of infertility on her sexuality, or for working with an aging man who is deciding whether to give up his house and move into a nursing home. We also examine the *relationship between practitioner observation and social science investigation. Social workers* are presented *as evolving organisms who are from particular ethnic and cultural backgrounds, are of a gender and sexual preference, belong to racial and religious groups, and come from a social and economic class.* Practitioner observation is framed as *utilization and integration of self-awareness with the profession's knowledge and skills* and is discussed in relation to case situations involving schizophrenia, child welfare, and domestic violence. First we offer a review of the historical treatment and development of this concept in the social work literature.

Practitioner Observation in the Social Work Literature

Though the term *practitioner observation* is introduced in this book, the analogous concepts of *self-awareness* and *use of self* have long been part of social work practice lore. Only when they are framed within context of the profession's roots, however, can the importance of these terms be understood. Social work began from a "doing" base. Providing charity relief to the poor and indigent and assisting in the settlement of immigrants were the initial tasks of early social workers. With no theories to guide their work, the tools they employed—the only tools available—were themselves. Since the "self" was the primary instrument for enactment of the social work practice, social workers had to become "self-aware" so that they didn't confuse their own problems with their clients'. At the same time, they had to think consciously about their behaviors with clients, to "use" themselves as professionals. Overall, the goal was to make the primary implement of practice, the self, an objective and effective tool.

Self-awareness and use of self can be traced back to the two oldest social work theories, the diagnostic approach and the functional school. As we discussed in earlier chapters, in 1917 Mary Richmond wrote the first book on social casework, *Social Diagnosis*, and became established as the founder of the diagnostic approach. Identifying the worker's insight into the client as a critical component of the social work practice, Richmond later stated: "By direct and indirect action upon the minds of clients, their social relations can be improved and their personalities developed" (1922, p. 255).

Today's readers must keep in mind that effecting change in the minds of clients through the minds of workers was a very novel idea for Richmond's time. Increasingly, the diagnostic school of thought became heavily influenced by Freudian theory, which further developed this radical notion that change within a person could be effected by another person through the process of talking.

Virginia Robinson formulated the social work skills necessary for practicing functional social work. Founded in the 1930s, this school was in part a reaction against what had come to be seen by some as the "illness model" of the diagnostic approach. Important for the functionalists was the professional relationship and the social work agency as it shaped the social work process. Robinson (1936) introduced the concept that social workers have both professional and personal selves and are responsible for developing both.

During the 1940s, Gordon Hamilton further developed the concept of the professional self. In referring to self-awareness, she stated: "Only if we understand to some extent our own motivation can we leave the client free to establish himself securely first with us and thus again with others. . . . [The caseworker] . . . can never be helpful if he exploits his interest in . . . a desire to manage people, or in a need to have them love him for what he does for them. . . . Each individual must make his own solution . . . because his goals and life objectives are *unique for him*" (1946, p. 32).

Distinctions between the professional and personal selves of social workers was further emphasized by Bertha Reynolds, who referred to the professional self as the possession of

> relative mastery, in which one can both understand and control one's own activity in the art which is learned. . . . The person can think of himself in a new way—objectively. He can see himself working as he might see another person in the situation working. He can criticize and change his approach as the situation demands something different. He has become professional in that he can apply knowledge to the solving of practical problems, using himself as instrument, with all his acquired skills and his emotional responses disciplined and integrated to the professional purpose. (1942, p. 81)

In the 1950s, an increasing emphasis on self-examination began to seem like a therapeutic process for social workers. Much time was spent in analysis of the social worker's feelings and thoughts without making the necessary connections to practice behaviors. The following statement is a typical example of this trend:

> The worker may at times be emotionally aware of the client's feelings when anxiety does not permit him to become fully enough aware to deal with them. The worker's ego boundary at the time is such that he is not ready to recapture an earlier ego state of his own—a state his client is at present experiencing. Not being able to recapture the early feeling, he cannot develop empathy with the client. . . . If the supervisor tries to be too convincing and puts too much effort into making the worker understand the client's real emotions, it may constitute an attack on the worker's defensive mechanisms. (Feldman, 1963, p. 299)

Even though the initial purpose of self-understanding was for social workers to increase their ability to control and improve practice with clients, this goal gradually became overshadowed by an emphasis on examination of their own intrapsychic issues.

By the 1970s, concern for self-knowledge was replaced with a new trend—standardization of practice methods. Counseling and psychology dominated the literature with prepackaged scales and training procedures.

The personal traits of a good helper had been reduced to a single quality, being "empathic," and an empathic helper had the qualities of "warmth, empathy and congruence," all of which could be measured on standardized tests. Concepts such as self-awareness and use of self were considered "soft" and difficult to measure, and as such received little attention.

This trend to downplay self-awareness and use of self continues. Even though these concepts are still accepted by practitioners as central parts of their professional culture, recent theorists have not been able to clarify them further. Treatment in the social work literature has been too general or philosophical, with no practical basis, or too concrete, with inadequate conceptual development. Compton and Galaway, in their popular "generalist practice" text, comment only briefly on the capacity to observe self, "which really means to be sensitive to one's own internal workings, to be involved with oneself and one's needs, thoughts, commitments, and values, yet to stand back enough from oneself to question the meaning of what is going on. This means that the helping person must take a helping attitude toward oneself as well as toward others" (1979, p. 185). Although this is a helpful statement, it lacks force and is not elaborated.

Providing one of the more thoughtful conceptions of self-awareness, Max Siporin states:

> Helping in terms of moral responsibilities and obligations calls for a great deal of 'self-awareness.' This is an accurate perception of one's own actions and feelings, and of the effects of one's behavior on others. It means a third ear and a third eye, which one can use to view oneself in action and also to view the innermost recesses of oneself. This is a central value and also a practice principle in that the helper is required continuously to carry on a process of conscious reflection, and of self-reflection on what one is doing, so that one can show what one is doing while performing helping actions. (1975, p. 78)

In order to be useful, however, examples illustrating these concepts as they are put into practice by social workers are needed along with the definition. Without this specificity, it is difficult to relate Siporin's formulation to practice behaviors.

On the other hand, Hepworth and Larsen have offered specificity without theoretical development. In discussing practice with an angry client, they state: "How then should you respond to aggressive and provocative behavior? First it is vital to master your natural tendency to respond defensively. Recognizing that the client's hostility may be displaced from other sources can assist you 'not to personalize verbal attacks or sullen behavior,' thus freeing you from feeling threatened and enabling you to respond facilitatively" (Hepworth & Larsen, 1986, p. 56). Here a theoretical context is lacking in which to understand and consider the advice.

Framing the social worker as somehow different from other persons,

Hollis and Woods have addressed these concepts: "The worker's perception of the client is not that of the average person; attitudinal response to the perception is different" (1981, p. 289). Social workers, however, just like other people, have feeling reactions to clients. The task for social workers is to make use of their reactions with planning and deliberation.

Famous for her social work practice with families, Virginia Satir coedited *The Use of Self,* a thoughtful compilation of essays discussing the self of the helper in relation to the helping process (Satir & Baldwin, 1987). Offering astute insights and pointers about the development of a professional self, Satir does not focus solely on social workers but on all those involved in a "therapeutic" relationship. In a narrower range than the social work field of practice, the examples are helpful though somewhat limited.

Transference and Countertransference

Frequently used in the social work literature, the terms *transference* and *countertransference* are borrowed from the field of psychiatry. As we discussed in Chapter 4, for Freud, transference was an integral part of the psychoanalytic process. Patients were to transfer onto the psychiatrist feelings out of their unconscious that were associated with important persons from early in their life. Insight into these feelings was a major goal of the therapeutic relationship. Concurrently, countertransference was transference by psychiatrists, responses to or projections on their patients stemming from early development that were outside their conscious awareness. Analysis was recommended as training for therapists to inhibit their countertransference reactions.

Recent trends in psychoanalytic theory have altered the conception of countertransference from a focus on repetitive patterns based on early history to include the sum of the clinician's responses to the client. Additionally, countertransference is no longer considered a hindrance and is now recognized as an important aspect of the therapist's understanding and capacity (Sandler, 1976). In social work, similarly, a shift has occurred from framing the worker's countertransference as a personality problem to "one of the most useful tools in diagnosis and treatment, but only if they are recognized and so used" (Wood, 1971, p. 105). Some authors have discussed certain problems and categories, such as depression and character disorder, which elicit countertransference reactions (MacKinnon and Michels, 1971; Pollak, 1961; Austin, 1976). Others, like Strean (1978), urge social workers to discover the ways in which they are susceptible to their clients.

The social work profession has embraced countertransference, a concept integral to another professional discipline, without reflection about its applicability and fit with social work principles. Though the concept has been broadened, it remains a somewhat narrow term, primarily focusing on therapists' negative reactions to clients. Concern with countertransference has fostered an overindulgence in introspection and has not allowed for an examination of practitioners' utilization of their reactions in effective client intervention. Viewed in this limited way, countertransference is something to overcome, a weakness in the social worker's personality that conforms to the medical model of framing treatment in sickness/cure terms.

In contrast to the limitations of the countertransference notion, case material from social workers and their clients support the following definition of practitioner observation. Development of the concept draws on the social work precepts of self-awareness and use of self, processes that are natural and basic to social work practice. Practitioner observation is considered a practice component that can be developed and strengthened, not something to overcome.

PRACTITIONER OBSERVATION DEFINED

Practitioner observation is a concept introduced in this book and is defined as

 The self-examination and articulation by social workers of their personal reactions to clients and the intentional use of this awareness in practice decisions and behaviors. The self-awareness is attention to oneself; to one's thoughts, feelings, biases, values; to one's ethnic, racial, and class background and religious traditions; to the totality of one's life experiences. Feelings of wanting to relate with clients as if they are friends or family members are acknowledged. Distinctions are made between problems the social worker has experienced and those of the client. Self-awareness is utilized and integrated with the profession's knowledge and skills in a professional use of self that is unique and responsive to each case situation.

Practitioner observers are social work professionals actively and continuously engaging in a process of examination, articulation, clarification, description, analysis, revision, and evaluation of their professional practice behaviors. Recognizing that they are partially culture bound and limited by personality attributes, they accept the necessity of ongoing observation of their practice.

Maintaining this distinction between personal issues and client troubles permits social workers to be objective. Only by observing, monitoring, and utilizing their own reactions can social workers contruct an objective assessment, develop a helping professional relationship, communicate clearly and directly, and plan an intervention based on client needs and capacities.

Among the case studies presented later in the chapter we observe social workers who are White and Black, young and old, male and female, politically left and conservative, rural and urban, gregarious and shy. Regardless of ethnic heritage or level of sophistication, each confronts situations over which they anguish and suffer, situations that arouse them profoundly. For example, one of the social workers we discuss in this chapter is a Black woman, married to a lawyer, who enjoys a high income. She grew up on welfare in an abusive family and, working in child protective services, confronts many of the problems she herself experienced as a child. Avowing her blackness and her abusive background as well as her glamorous appearance and her quick intelligence, she has to acknowledge her own unique environmental background and particular inherited gene pool. Her looks, prior experiences, current upper middle-class life style, the attributes of her culture, and her personality all help define who she is as both an individual and a social worker.

Also important in practitioner observation is the relationship formed between the social worker and the client. Social workers often become intimately and deeply involved with their work. Depending on the nature of the interaction, they may become part of an intense emotional dyad with their clients. Clients often view the social worker as a central person in their lives; likewise, social workers can become attached to their clients. After all, they are talking together about very intimate matters, some of which may never be shared with anyone else. These emotional reactions must be monitored by workers as they engage in their practice of social work.

Initially external consultants to whom the client has turned for help, social workers become part of the client's environment during the process of helping. Although they are the outside expert, at the same time they are working with the client from the inside to create change and become active participants in the change process. This dynamic and interactive process of being intellectually *external to* and *a participant in* the work with clients especially requires that social workers be practitioner observers of their own processes.

Functioning as social science researchers, social workers conduct research on their own practice. As they collect data and intervene, social workers are participating in the client's life space. Because they are the measurement tool, the "instruments" through which the social work practice is carried out, they must avoid any contamination from their own biases and function as sharp and insightful practitioners.

Participant Observation and Social Science Investigation

Participant observation, a term associated with the fields of sociology and anthropology, refers to an investigator's study of persons in their natural environment "in the field." Through unstructured interviewing, in which the investigator is able to question, look, and listen, *rich* information is gathered to be used in a *qualitative analysis*. The information is called rich because it is highly descriptive and cannot be analyzed through more traditional quantitative means (Lincoln and Guba, 1985). Investigators participate in the environment of those they study in order to better understand the complete context. Investigators' experiences are taken into account only as they help illuminate the persons being studied (Lofland & Lofland, 1984).

Similarities exist between the social work practitioner and the "naturalistic inquirer" in sociology and anthropology. Work is conducted in the field, people are studied in their natural environments. By asking questions and looking and listening, both develop a sense of the persons they are studying and their surroundings. And the tools for carrying out the inquiry are the investigators themselves.

The differences between these two concepts, however, are significant. First, the target of study is not the same. Participant observation is looking *out* to those being studied, while practitioner observation is looking *in* at the person doing the study. The purpose of study is also dissimilar. Participant observation is intended to research and better understand the people being observed; investigators themselves are not required to change or influence what is being examined. Practitioner observers, on the other hand, must make changes in themselves in order for the real work to be done—which is to produce change in the lives of their clients.

We now examine excerpts from sessions between social workers and clients to illustrate the process of practitioner observation in action. Social workers talk about who they are and the factors that shaped them as social workers, and they discuss the relationship of their personal reactions to their decision making and interventions.

Practitioner observation is the examination and articulation of one's own thoughts, feelings, biases, and values about clients and their situations.

Biases and personal feelings are natural responses to clients and their situations; they are a consequence of working with close and intimate matters. Guilt about having these feelings is unnecessary and unproductive. Responsible practice involves awareness of their presence and attention to any effects they may have on practice decisions. The following case is an example of a situation in which the social worker is uneasy about the condition and problem the client is presenting. *Valuing* youth and independence, *she is biased against elderly clients*, especially those who are needy and ill.

Sandy was a White first-year M.S.W. student in placement at a family service agency. Presenting as highly self-assured and opinionated, she was in her late twenties, returning to graduate school after being successful in the personnel office of a large corporation. Sandy was raised in an affluent Midwestern suburb, where her father was a dentist with a yearly income of over $75,000. Wanting to practice therapy with middle-class, middle-aged, educated clients, Sandy got into social work because it seemed a quick route to becoming a therapist.

Her first interview with Phil, an 80-year-old male who was also White, began this way:

SANDY: What's the problem?

PHIL: It's been getting harder for me in the last few weeks to manage by myself.

SANDY: What do you mean, you've been living alone for years!

PHIL: My neighbor, John, we used to visit together during the week, play cards, take a walk. He could still drive, and we would go get groceries. He had a heart attack and died last month. There's nobody else.

SANDY: Oh, no problem, we can arrange for a volunteer to take you to the grocery store once a week.

PHIL: *(barely audible)* I don't think you understand. It's more than that. My arthritis is bothering me. On some days I have trouble just getting up and getting dressed.

SANDY: Oh, I think you can manage. So it will take you a little longer—you have nothing else to do.

PHIL: I don't think I can live here by myself anymore. *(said very softly and with hopelessness)* Things just don't feel right.

SANDY: I don't see what the problem is.

Sandy later reported to her supervisor:

....

Phil's apartment was a mess. He was complaining about things. I don't know what his problem is, he seems to have it pretty easy. I don't think he needs a worker assigned, and I don't really want to go out there again.

....

Through the supervisory process, as the field instructor reviewed Sandy's practice with Phil, they identified her bias against aging and elderly people as well as her confusion about the social work role. Because she believed that people were responsible for their life choices, Sandy was impatient with someone like Phil, who appeared depressed and seemed to have no idea about how to change his situation. Stating that she wasn't interested in working with the elderly and didn't want to analyze how she had handled the interaction, Sandy shared with her supervisor that she had come into social work to practice with educated clients who would be highly motivated to change. Wanting to do "therapy," she didn't see any value in looking at her practice with Phil.

Sandy had to learn that "therapy" is only one of the many things social workers do and that roles like advocacy, case management, and the provision of concrete services are valuable and important. Moreover, even in the therapeutic process itself it is not possible to control the kinds of problems clients bring in for help. Clients encompass a wide range of social problems, across economic classes and from diverse backgrounds and cultures. To be a social worker, Sandy had to practice with clients representing different age groups, possessing varying resources and capacities, and requiring a range of services. Moreover, working with people who were poor, socially isolated, and hurting, is a particular mission of social work practice.

As Sandy stated:

....

I went through a gradual process of learning to understand where I was coming from. Realizing that I started out wanting to be a therapist, it seemed somehow glamorous. I was not committed to social work and to its mission of outreach to the poor and oppressed. I saw myself helping articulate and attractive clients to better understand themselves. There was nothing glamorous about Phil or his situation. In fact, as I continued to talk about it with my supervisor, I began to realize that I was actually uncomfortable with Phil being old. My real feeling was, "He looks so pathetic, almost ugly." I just didn't want to work with such a case.

....

Once Sandy examined her practice with Phil, she recognized her bias and discomfort with the elderly. She was then able to acknowledge her own indifference to the client's comments, her inability to respond to his need to discuss alternative living arrangements. Her discomfort had made it impossible for her to hear what Phil was needing from her and, initially, for her to receive her supervisor's feedback. She learned that she had been an ineffective therapist and a poor social worker.

To put her practitioner observation to use, Sandy would have to understand that though she might not want to make the elderly her specialty, she could not avoid dealing with aging issues. She would be unable to exercise complete control over the kinds of clients who would come to her for help, and even some of her younger clients might have problems with aging parents. Pushed by her field instructor, Sandy learned that to obtain a social work degree she would have to broaden her conception of social work practice to include more than therapy with articulate clients.

Forced to reexamine her values and ideas about people with whom she had had minimal or no previous contact, Sandy ultimately provided Phil effective social work help. Acknowledging his increasing disorientation and isolation, she helped him join a support group offered through her agency. As he made friends, he had more means of getting out of his apartment and became increasingly less dejected.

Practitioner observation is attention to oneself; to one's ethnic, racial, and class background and religious traditions, to the totality of one's life experiences.

Sometimes the social worker is not biased against a client but may have very strong emotional feelings about the client's circumstances. In the next case, June, a White social work student, describes her experience with Suanna, a 4-year-old Black female. June, nearing her fiftieth birthday, had been an elementary school teacher for almost twenty-five years. Though she liked working with young children, kindergarten through grade two, she wanted to make a career change and work with children individually, focusing on emotional rather than intellectual development. She had considered becoming a social worker for some time, and now that her children were grown and out of the home, June was able to enter a graduate program.

June's first-year field placement was a school-based program that provided intensive therapeutic and educational intervention for emotionally and behaviorally disturbed children, ages 4 to 11. Based on a medical model, this program had children attend intensively staffed classes for six hours a day and receive individual play therapy. These children often came from backgrounds of severe emotional and/or physical abuse.

At the age of 8 months, Suanna was removed from a house where several adults and children under the age of 3 were living in conditions of extreme poverty and neglect. Found unclothed with evidence of malnourishment, sexual abuse, and elevated lead levels, Suanna along with her sisters was placed in foster care under the custody of Children and Youth Services. When Suanna displayed physically aggressive behavior, the foster mother asked to have her removed from the home. Suanna's mother, a 14-year-old, was reported to have been a victim of sexual abuse by her father. She too was placed in foster care with a different family.

June had to confront the very difficult life that Suanna and the other children had experienced. When she compared their lives to the warmth and security her own children had experienced, she felt deeply saddened:

....

I recognized that these children may never have the security of adequate material possessions. Feelings of abandonment, fear, and loneliness could be a permanent part of their lives. I think of my own kids, ages 28, 25, and 12, and sometimes I'm almost overwhelmed by the enormity of the disparity. When I first began the placement, I had to brace myself each time I entered the building. When I saw some of the children, I would feel like crying. There were times I had to go to the bathroom and compose myself.

My field instructor helped me get through those early weeks. She validated that my feelings weren't strange and affirmed that I could have strong feelings

and also be an effective practitioner. Over time I didn't get overwhelmed by my feelings. I could acknowledge their presence and handle the children with more comfort.

....

It is *not* strange to feel emotional in practicing social work. What would be strange is to remain untouched by the life events clients confront. Students, or experienced social workers beginning with a new client population, go through a period of acclimation. They are not simply acquiring knowledge about social work in this setting, but they must learn to accommodate their emotional reactions while also addressing the value dilemmas the work raises for them. Usually, the intensity of feelings abates after the initial period of adjustment.

Social workers must be able to engage in a continual process, enacted with field instructors, supervisors, and peers, in which they acknowledge and discuss their feelings. Perspective is gained in this type of supportive environment. Feelings can then be integrated with available knowledge, out of which evolves a reasonable approach to treatment and intervention.

After her first wrenching weeks with Suanna, June began working on limit setting, with one of the goals being for Suanna to call June by name.

....

I decided on this day to identify myself in the first person in play. I talk about June playing with Suanna. Suanna has not had any consistent limit setting by adults she can trust. I knew how to do limit setting in my role as teacher, but in the play therapy it's different. I have to be very patient and be prepared to go over the same issue for many weeks, repeating my expectations over and over again. We had been working with turning on water from the bathroom faucet to wash hands and had been practicing the following sequence for about a month.

....

JUNE: Before you turn the water on, what do you have to remember?

SUANNA: *(continues to run water)*

JUNE: Before you turn the water on, what do you have to remember? Here, let June do it for you. *(runs water and then turns it off)*

SUANNA: *(turns on water and then turns it off, looking at June and softly saying)* Okay, June, isn't that right, Junie?

....

I was so thrilled, I could hardly believe it. She continued during the rest of that session to call me June. She seemed to want to please me and was herself pleased with her accomplishment. Prior to the water faucet we had played house where Suanna had me be the baby and she played the mommy. She was gentle, covering me with a blanket and asking me if I wanted anything to eat. Just before she called me June, I had again set a limit which she ignored and I then turned off the water myself. I re-explained the limit, she complied and then said those magic words, "Okay, June."

Then I started to feel guilty. Here I've been working so hard for her to learn my name, and I'll be leaving in May, when my placement ends. I question myself whether this is fair. Is it right for me to build a trusting relationship with someone when I know I will be leaving in a specified period of time? I'll be having the Christmas break in a few weeks. Not only will these children not be blessed with many material gifts, but I feel guilty about leaving them when we are just beginning to form a bonding.

....

These feelings of guilt and responsibility are very normal reactions to the deprivations and impoverishment of clients. Again, through supervisory and peer support, social workers can develop clarity about their responsibilities to clients. In the case of Suanna, it is not June's responsibility to provide Suanna with a home. It is also not her responsibility to spend her Christmas break at the treatment facility. By asking for help from her field instructor, June identified and discussed her feelings. After engaging in this process, she was able to develop creative interventions that would be of help to her clients. Skilled practice is hampered by feelings of guilt and undue responsibility.

....

Once I began to feel less guilty, I began to tell my children at the setting that I would be gone for a few weeks. Because they are developmentally delayed, I knew they might have trouble comprehending the length of my absence. I xeroxed a calendar page of the month and put a picture of me and my house at the top. At the time we usually meet, one of the staff will meet with the child and read or play and have the picture. I also circled in red the day that I would be returning. I felt so good after I went through that with my clients. I really need this break and will now be able to take it guilt free.

....

We should also take notice of the practice behaviors in the play therapy that June used so effectively in bonding with Suanna. She exhibited extraordinary patience, reviewing an inordinate number of times the steps to work the faucet. Her voice tone demonstrated at once calmness, gentleness, and strength. She did not talk overly sweetly or in a patronizing way, but rather was definitive in her limit setting about Suanna's behaviors and about her own role as the helper. June appreciated Suanna's small gains and saw them as building blocks for a continual shaping of the practice goals and objectives.

June's spiritual life was also a source of comfort and support for her. She was able to turn to that resource when the harshness of the children's lives began to overwhelm her. Raised in a home where tolerance for others, including those of different racial and religious backgrounds, was not only taught but expected, June did not see a different skin color, but a child who had been denied basic support and love. While physical needs were met in June's childhood home, where her father was a minister and her mother a social worker, material things were not overly valued. What concerned June about Suanna was not her lack of a middle-class lifestyle, but her loss of a more fundamental sense of security.

Social workers are, at times during their practice, reminded about other people they know, often a close friend or family member. Again, this is a natural consequence of developing close relationships with clients and talking with them about intimate topics. As we discussed in the literature review, this effect his been called countertransference.

 Practitioner observation requires recognition of feelings in wanting to relate with clients as if they are friends or family members.

Consider our earlier example, when Pat, the social worker, recognized and acknowledged her motherly feelings toward her client, Lennie; she was "self-aware" of the feelings aroused in her by this client. A tall and very attractive woman in her forties, Pat was White and dressed with dramatic flair in the lastest fashion. Pat had waited to complete the M.S.W. degree until her children were all in school. Now that her daughter and two sons were in their twenties, she was enrolled in a social work Ph.D. program. After employment in a family service agency, Pat had been seeing clients in a private practice she shared with another social worker and a psychologist. Divorced, and in the process of her own personal growth as an independent and autonomous woman, she had been questioning about what works in helping people change. Pat commented:

....

I believe in dialogue as a healing component between people. I've dealt with two major losses in my own life, the death of my closest friend when I was 13 and my divorce. When my friend died, no one talked to me about it. It was really a massive loss, and not being able to process it with anyone made it much harder for me. By the time of my divorce, I already knew about the value of processing and dialoguing with others. I spend a lot of time talking with my client and having her talk with me. In my interaction with Lennie, a lot of her talking is about the ordinary, everyday things of life. Her workday, the way she schedules her time, her friendships are all part of the picture of her gorging on food.

When I first met Lennie, I wanted to take care of her. She is young, attractive, has so much going for her and doesn't know it. When she went back on the laxatives, it really set me off. My own daughter has had eating problems and Lennie looks so much like her. Lennie gets close to me—I have very powerful feelings about her.

My greatest challenge in this work is for me to be attuned to what is going on inside of me, and to somehow put limits on it. To be good at this work one has to give attention to the internal processes, be aware of one's own feelings.

....

Pat then had to plan how to use herself as a professional social worker, to make a "conscious use of self." As Pat recounted:

....

Almost at the same time I went into a head mode—a defense against my own emotions. I had to constantly monitor not to indulge myself, she has a right to self-delineate, to be her own person. I thought about how I learned to self-delineate. It was having a significant other person give me support and permission. I knew she was not needing me to be her mother. I had to figure out how to use the nurturing feelings I had for this client to help her learn to nurture herself.

....

In the following interaction Pat employed her nurturing feelings about Lennie in a way that was useful in the client's progress. In her early twenties and also White, Lennie was tall, slim, and strikingly beautiful.

PAT: Sounds like you're very precious to your husband, Ray. Do you have any pressure issues with him?

LENNIE: He is very loving and caring. *(pause)* He sometimes gets *Playboy* magazine. This bothers me, and I think it contributes some to my problem with my weight.

PAT: Let's look at that. What bothers you about it?

LENNIE: He must like to look at skinny girls. I worry if I get heavy he won't find me attractive.

PAT: Have you talked with Ray about your feelings?

LENNIE: He says that he loves me and that his love is more than just the way I look. I know that, but when I start getting panicky I get worried.

*1 PAT: Lennie, it's clear that you suffer with this issue. What part hurts you the most?

LENNIE: What hurts me the most *(choked up)* is that I see him as so special, and I don't see myself as special. I'm surprised that he chose me as his wife. *(crying)*

*2 PAT: I want to slow you down a bit. It sounds like you're taking a lot of responsibility for this issue in terms of your own shortcomings. I want to comfort you. This issue can be confusing for many women. Let's take it out and look at it.

LENNIE: He says it's nothing to do with me, but I can't separate it.

PAT: It's hard for you to separate it.

LENNIE: When I discovered one of the magazines, it really upset me, brought my illness to a head. It shattered my image of our marriage. I love him. I don't want to be worrying about it constantly and have it destroy my life.

*3 PAT: Lennie, I'd like to credit you. You have had the courage to
*4   talk about this with your husband. My own bias is that there are big differences between men and women. One of the issues for feminists is that holding up these pictures as yardsticks for women is not fair. The men I have talked with say they are visually oriented and take pleasure in looking at the centerfold. I want to give you credit for letting him know where you stand. *(pause)* One of the pieces I heard that I want to ask you about is that it seems in the discovery of these magazines your sense of the sanctity of this marriage was shaken and on one level you're worried that this man may betray you. I'm wondering how you see yourself? What do you see when you look in the mirror?

LENNIE: *(long pause, very quietly)* I see myself as barely average, not very smart. Everything I do is middle of the road. I don't have any special qualities. I think my husband could find somebody who excels in an area. The thing is, I know he loves me *(crying)* for what I do, what I am.

PAT: You have suffered so much along the way. It sounds like it is undemanding, he loves you and you don't have to do anything for it.

LENNIE: Sometimes I think I'm not worth that. Sometimes I cook up a storm because I think I need to do something to earn that. *(heavy crying and sobbing)* He doesn't demand anything from me.

PAT: Would it help you if he did?

LENNIE: I don't know. Part of why that bothers me is that I had so many demands growing up, to be a responsible person, I had to work, to do well in school, to do my chores. I didn't want to marry someone like my father, who was so demanding. Now that I have my husband, it sometimes bothers me. Maybe I don't know what I want.

*5   PAT: What I'm hearing is that you had become comfortable with
                  a certain level of striving for goals. Now you're in a
                  relationship where there are seemingly no expectations.
                  That is a little bit uncomfortable for you, which I think is a
                  normal reaction. This is different for you. What ways does
                  your husband have to let you know that he wants some-
                  thing for himself?

Throughout this exchange Pat showed interest in and concern for Lennie. Comforting Lennie with comments such as "I'd like to credit you," *3,
and supporting by acknowledging her as courageous, *4, Pat explored the
issues raised and stayed with the feelings, *1 and *2. Backing up and picking
up on something Lennie had said earlier, Pat ably helped her begin to
connect the need to be thin with her insecurities about her marriage and
relationship with her father, *5.

Practitioner observation allowed for effective social work practice between Pat and Lennie. Just like their clients, social workers are not responsible for their feelings, but rather for their behavior and for their use of
feelings as they interact with clients. Pat could only maintain a focus on
Lennie's issues with bulimia if she stayed self-aware about her own feelings.
While her motherly feelings were *not* a necessary condition for practice, her
acknowledgement of them was. In observing that she had special feelings
for Lennie, Pat could engage in decision making about how to utilize these
feelings in their work together. Rather than becoming overwhelmed with
her sadness and longing for her daughter, Pat was supportive of Lennie,
providing a safe environment to talk about these very painful and intimate
matters.

In this case the client was similar in age and appearance to Pat's daughter, but clients can also set off feelings in social workers with mannerisms or
other subtle features that are reminiscent of a parent or other close relative
or friend. Prerequisite to effective social work intervention is acknowledgement and rational decision making about how to use personal reactions in
the practice. Awareness of her own reactions to bulimia, and her tendency
to want to mother this client, enabled Pat to exercise control over the social
work practice. Without this recognition, Pat's practice decisions could be
ruled heavily by her emotions. Good social work practice is based on
rational and knowledge-based decisions in which feelings and emotions are
considered and utilized in ways deemed helpful to the client.

The purpose of social work, improving social functioning, covers a very
broad spectrum. Social workers, just like their clients, struggle and suffer as
they interact with their environments. Often social workers are dealing
with, or have experienced, problems similar to their clients.

 *Distinctions are made between problems the social workers have experienced
and those of their clients.*

Jill, Black and in her late thirties, was working with a client, Nancy, also Black, in her late twenties. After years of unsuccessful infertility counseling, Jill and her husband adopted a child. Jill described how she dealt with her own reactions to hearing that her client had had an experience similar to her own:

....

When I first heard Nancy say that she had infertility counseling, I thought to myself, "Oh, no, I know what that's like, that's a bitch. That process puts a strain on any marriage, no matter how good. I wonder how they came out of it?" I then immediately filed away my thoughts. I needed to put that piece together with all the other pieces. I didn't know how big a part it played. It was possible that it didn't play any part. I would, though, have had trouble believing that. I knew it had wreaked havoc with my own marriage for a period of time. I also had a whole lot of theoretical information about this field and knowledge about which strategies are most effective.

Nancy shared this information during my initial assessment phase. It was sometime during the first few sessions. At that point I wouldn't have known whether it was a prominent piece of what was bothering her. I had to wait and see.

I always have my own thoughts, but I keep a boundary around my thoughts and what is going on with clients. I don't want to bother the client with the minutiae of my life. I do want to make use of my own knowledge of what a particular experience is like, if I assess that it may be helpful to the client.

....

On first hearing this client's problem, Jill felt a bit thrown off balance because her own marriage was still recovering from the same issue. As she gathered more information to build an accurate assessment, Jill would consider whether her feelings about infertility were applicable to Nancy. In this way evidence from the client is used to validate whether the feelings of the social worker are those also experienced by the client. Although the situations may be similar, their feelings and reactions may be quite different.

After about two months, Jill had the following exchange with Nancy:

NANCY: As I've told you before, we go through such long stretches of no sex. The other night, after coming back from having dinner, I suggested having sex. Usually we opt for just watching television, but that night we did. It was mildly satisfying, nothing special. Since our trying to get pregnant, it just doesn't seem the same.

JILL: It takes a while to bounce back from that kind of intrusion into your normal rhythms and lovemaking routines.

NANCY: What do you mean?

JILL: It's hard to have sex on some other person's schedule in order to get pregnant. One loses touch with what pleases one's body, with what is arousing and evocative. My husband and I went through infertility counseling several years ago. I remember being told on which days to have sex. It took us at least a year to regain our sexual excitement. I felt as though my body betrayed me.

NANCY: *(crying heavily)* Betrayed, that's what I feel like. My body forsakes me.

Being a practitioner observer, distinguishing the client's reactions from what Jill knew was her own response to infertility counseling, enabled Jill to use personal experience in a planful and highly effective way. Determining, through the assessment process, that the infertility counseling might have resulted in similarly negative consequences for the client, Jill could quickly be sensitive to the subject. Yet even though the client's experiences were similar to those of the social worker, it still took some two months for Jill to decide that her initial reactions were valid for this client and that sharing them would prove beneficial. The client's time frames will not always match those of the social worker, so patience in social work is an important tool.

 Practitioner observation involves utilization and integration of self-awareness with knowledge and skills in a professional use of self that is unique and responsive to each case situation.

The social worker has a range of theories available to understand the client and to plan interventions. As discussed in Chapter 5, the social worker selects specific interventive strategies based on the case theory that has been developed. Social workers' utilization of theories, knowledge, and skills is influenced as well by their own biases and life experiences. At the same time that social workers choose established theories to buttress their case theory, they are attracted to particular frameworks that they feel comfortable with. There is a complex interaction between social workers' thinking about the case, their feelings and preferences, and the theories and skills that they make use of.

In the following three cases we explore the relationship between practitioner observation and the theories, knowledge, and skills applicable to three areas: schizophrenia, domestic violence, and child welfare.

Practitioner Observation and a Client with Schizophrenia

About 40 years old, Dave had been practicing social work for about fifteen years and was employed at a mental health center in the Midwest. Considered a character by his friends and colleagues, he could be described as a middle-aged hippie of the 1960s. Adept at working with clients others found "difficult," he was known to be creative and, at times, unorthodox, in his work. Shaped at an early age by parents who were left of center and politically involved, Dave believed his family background significantly influenced his attitudes as a social worker. Especially compelling was their conviction that a good citizen should not only be concerned about others, but was obligated to create change, to engage in a struggle to redress injustices.

In her middle 20s, the client, Mary, was stocky and not always neatly dressed, with a diagnosis of schizophrenia. Mary's mother initially brought her in to see Dave, reporting that after having had an abortion two years before, Mary had barely talked. Dave commented:

....

At the beginning I felt challenged. This was, after all, a tough case, someone who has not talked for two years! My initial reaction was that I would be able to get this client moving. I felt positive and a sense of energy. After a while, extreme frustration set in for me. I had so much trouble getting a response from her. She appeared to me as (*1) short, fat, and zombielike. One has to watch it at this point in a relationship. I know the facts about schizophrenia, and the difficulty some of these folk have in building relationships. It would have been easy to start (*2) relating to Mary as a schizophrenic, treating her as someone who is "crazy," someone who is scary, and who is not to be held accountable for what she does and who she is. If I did that, I would have lost her for sure. After a long time, probably over a year, I forged a way of relating to Mary. I (*3) shared fantasies about her living a very different life, some of which were quite fantastic. I got her to smile, and then she began talking with me.

....

Befitting Dave's unconventional approach to his work with clients, the two theorists he most relied on were Thomas Szasz and Carl Whitaker. Viewing mental illness as a myth, Szasz (1961) compared psychiatry to astrology, with its disregard for method and a foundation based on false substantives, and posited that mental illness and health do not exist, that they are not real conditions. Believing that troubles begin for people in their communication with each other and in their "learning to learn" about the world, Szasz asserted that therapy should address language and its meaning to patients. For Szasz, the terms *treatment* and *cure* are without meaning and result in harm to both patients and therapists.

One of the most nonconformist of practicing therapists is Carl Whitaker, who, like Szasz, is critical of traditional psychiatric practice (1977, 1988). Advocating that therapists use their own subjective experiences to engage with clients, he will explore fantasies and borrow language from clients in developing an intimate and highly personal relationship. Considered eccentric and even bizarre by more traditional therapists, Whitaker's (1977) case studies provide convincing accounts of his work in helping clients to change.

As we see in Dave's opening remarks and the following exchange with Mary, his own thinking and practice with clients reflected the contributions of these two theorists. When at *1, above, in comments about his own subjective reaction to Mary, Whitaker's counsel is evident, as is the use of fantasies, at *3. Meanwhile, at *2, concerns about the term *schizophrenia* and the impact it might have on him and Mary were shaped by Szasz's work.

At the time of the following exchange Dave had been seeing Mary for over two years. Several months before, Dave had changed Mary's treatment to include weekly group meetings, with a decrease in the individual sessions to every other week. Dave, who was beginning to have angry feelings toward his client, discussed his work:

....

Several months after starting the group she went into a period of frozenness. Starting her in the group because she had been doing well, talking more, I thought she was ready. She seemed to slip back, staring, not saying anything. Aware of feeling furious with her again, I spent long periods of silence with her, myself staring off with my fantasies. Now, I wanted to hit her. I had to talk to myself, "Cut that out, I'm here to help, not to hurt." I figured that whatever was going on with her was hard enough as it is.

....

Dave had the following exchange with Mary:

DAVE: What happened to you on Thursday night in group, do you have any idea?

MARY: I don't know. I'm not sure. I think I was feeling frightened. Afterwards I had a headache. I felt people were attacking me. I was thinking of a circle, when you can't break the motion. If I talk, these people are going to take away all that I have. But, sometimes, I really do want to say something.

DAVE: Sounds pretty awful.

MARY: Well, I didn't like it.

DAVE: I didn't think so. The group is like a movie screen. People's problems get reflected from what they say and do, and what they don't say and don't do. I think the other members were wanting you to come out and play with them, and you refused. My clue for this is that I was aware of being furious with you.

MARY: I know you were.

DAVE: I realize I see you as a group elder. I want you to be a group leader. What do you think about that?

MARY: I have fantasies about that. The leader part isn't a big thing for me, but I'd like to be open. There are things I'd like to say to the group, but then I get scared. I want to be more open. Maybe I can turn some of this around. When I get frozen I think, no, I can't do this. I couldn't do it on Thursday, I just couldn't.

Concerned about the use of labels, especially psychiatric terms, Dave resonated to an opinion piece in the journal *Social Work* in which a former client poignantly shared her own hurtful experiences with a label of "chronic schizophrenic–undifferentiated type" (Anonymous, 1990). Though still employing labels like schizophrenia, Dave was acutely sensitive to some of the problems they invoked.

More than the selection of particular theoretical frameworks was at issue, however, in Dave's practice with Mary. Just like the social workers presented earlier, to be able to utilize his feelings to work with Mary on her issues Dave had to first recognize and analyze his angry feelings toward her. Self-awareness and use of self enabled him not to act inappropriately on his anger and to share his feelings with the client in a helpful way. Helping Mary to acknowledge frustration with herself and to reaffirm the goals she had for her role in the group was respectful and effective social work practice. Szasz and Whitaker provided Dave with a framework in which he could place his practice. Selecting two theories with which he was comfortable, he continued to be informed and shaped by their assumptions.

Practitioner Observation and Child Welfare

Employed with the child welfare office in a large urban city for over ten years, Tania, Black and in her late thirties, had reason to be proud of her accomplishments. Sexual abuse by an uncle when she was 7, no father in the home, and her mother's lack of employment skills and dependence on welfare payments strongly instilled in Tania a commitment to live a better life and to help others rise above such desperate surroundings. A good student, she was encouraged by her mother, who would tell her to "keep her drawers up and her dress down" (Bray, 1992). Not ending up pregnant, as many of her friends had, she believed her mother that she had better things to do. Granted a full scholarship to an area college, several years later she was sent for her M.S.W. by the state welfare department.

Tall and very attractive, she was married to a lawyer and had two children in their early teens. Enjoying a combined income with her husband of over $100,000 a year, Tania had a lifestyle that as a child she could not even imagine. She was contemplative about her roots and how she succeeded. While her mother had only a third-grade education in the segregated Mississippi school system, she encouraged Tania to see education as "the ticket out and away from the life we lived" (Bray, 1992, p. 39).

Even with the strong hand of her mother, backed up by a fourth-grade teacher who also supported and pushed, Tania was very aware that luck was an element in her good fortune. Sensitive to the scarcity of these ingredients in the lives of others, she tried to instill a sense of confidence and self-respect in her clients. Yet despite her background and her many years of experience, there were occasions when, as she put it:

....

I can get caught into blaming clients where I feel no compassion for them. Happening for me specifically with children and abuse, I face a life-long task of building objectivity for women who permit sexual abuse of their children. And, of course, I am constantly working with this in my caseload. Probably my most wrenching case is Bonita and her family.

....

Typical of Tania's complex and terribly demanding caseload, 13-year-old Bonita Miller had been moved back and forth between the home of her mother and foster homes for most of her life. When Bonita was 4 years old, the youngest of four children, investigations of sexual abuse on her 8-year-old sister—who told a friend's mother that her father had put his hands in her panties—led to knowledge that Bonita was also being fondled by him. In conjunction with physical abuse by the mother—welts from a belt buckle on their arms and backs—foster care placement was initiated for Bonita, her sister, and two brothers. Counseling and drug abstinence by the parents moved Bonita and her siblings back in with them within six months. Continued abuse by the father, however, returned the children to their foster parents, the Simpsons, for over two years. After allegations of abuse at the foster home, the Miller children were placed in a residential treatment facility, and at this time the following summary was placed in welfare department records:

....

Recently placed in this agency, the Miller children have experienced instability of residence and reports of abuse by both their natural and foster parents.

It appears from statements by the children that they were locked in their room by the foster mother, Mrs. Simpson, as her means of discipline, who kept Bonita in there for hours at a stretch. After pleading to use the bathroom but refused, Bonita would soil herself and would then be reprimanded for such behavior. Telling her neighbors to ignore Bonita's screams, Mrs. Simpson would refer to Bonita as the "bad one." Encouraging Bonita's siblings to share in the disciplining, she would force them to clean up after Bonita's soiling.

Mrs. Simpson consistently berated the parents, contaminating any gifts or cards they sent by referring to them as junk; calling the mother ugly, dirty and a drug addict; and overall creating an atmosphere in which the children were forced to suppress any positive feelings towards their parents.

When confronted with this information, Mrs. Simpson indicated that she had trouble getting Bonita to listen and follow rules and that Bonita's high level of activity often necessitated locking her in a room. While occasionally Bonita has smeared her feces on the walls, this has not happened recently. Reacting to the level of turmoil and confusion following any contacts with the parents, Mrs. Simpson felt it was in the best interests of the children to limit their activity with them.

It is strongly advised that the Simpson home not be used for further foster placements until these allegations can be substantiated. Bonita shows some evidence of developmental problems. As the children are in need of stability, it is recommended that they reside in this facility until a suitable permanent arrangement can be made for them.

....

After living for several years in the residential treatment facility, following a divorce by the parents these children were returned to their natural mother, Mrs. Miller. Tania was assigned as the social worker to this family, now consisting of Mrs. Miller, age 33, her boyfriend Tom, age 49, the oldest daughter, Ginnie, age 17, the two boys, 15 and 13, and Bonita, age 9.

Knowledge of the literature in the child welfare field, including permanency planning and intensive supportive services for at-risk families, offered Tania many models to choose from as she mapped out her work with the Millers. While in agreement with Fanshel (1982) and Katz (1990) that the major problem in foster care was "achieving early permanency for children," the cases she got, like the Millers, had already been in the foster care system for too long. Also agreeing that the presence of social supports was critical for families at risk of disruption through placement (Stehno, 1986; Jenson & Whittaker, 1987), Tania also knew that most of her families, like the Millers, had very few supports available to them.

Ability to make the best choices of a theoretical framework on which to support interventions with Bonita required Tania to confront her own bias to keep families together. Based on the sexual abuse she received from her uncle, Tania knew that she could have been removed from her mother's home. In spite of the trauma from that abuse and the fears and insecurities from the years of poverty, Tania deeply loved her mother and believed that much of her strength of spirit was instilled by her mother's strong teachings. At the same time, Tania was well aware that keeping children with the natural parent was not always the best choice for their safety and benefit.

Participation in several workshops had hooked Tania on Virginia Satir's humanistic approach to family therapy—that people possess the capacity to realize their potential as human beings and that it is the task of the social worker to help release that potential. Furthermore, Tania felt comfortable with Satir's warm and nurturing style and the way she connected early family history to current interactions. Obtaining a Family Life Chronology (Satir, 1964) for the Miller family, Tania acquired information not previously known. While the thrust of the chronology is to help the family get in touch with earlier times that were hopefully happier, it became clear to all of the Millers that they never had good times. Not mothered herself, at the age of 6 Mrs. Miller and her siblings had been abandoned and raised by a succession of people who knew their mother. Providing shelter and, occasionally, food, these people had instilled in the children no sense of family. Sexually abused by some of the men who passed through these homes, they had never learned the exact identity of their father. With no knowledge of whether her mother was alive or dead, Mrs. Miller hoped she was dead, because "if she is alive, why wouldn't she try to find her kids?" (Mezzacappa, 1992, p. A18). Never really thinking about herself or her future, she became pregnant with Ginnie, her first child, when she was only 16. It was not until a relative of her boyfriend talked with her that Mrs. Miller had learned about birth control.

Relying on Satir's style of nurturing, Tania acknowledged with this family their strengths and creativity, emphasizing Bonita's recent interest in drawing and their renewed attempt at a family life. Satir's tolerance and respect for others and her belief that people have capacities for growth and change provided support for Tania to relate with Mrs. Miller in a way that was nonblaming and accepting (Satir & Baldwin, 1983). Likewise, the history gathering provided a context to understand the family's inability to function as a unit.

Moreover, based on Tracy's network model (1990), Tania conducted a comprehensive social support assessment that revealed that the problem was not in the numbers of people the Millers knew or "the network size," but rather in the "perceived availability of social support." Members of the Millers' social support network gave them no concrete emotional or informational support. From these results, Tania determined that new friends for Mrs. Miller were imperative if she was going to be able to provide a more stable and nurturing environment for the children. Referring Mrs. Miller to a support group for adult female survivors of child sexual abuse, Tania believed help would be available for her childhood traumas while also providing a support network (Knight, 1990).

Again, just as with Dave in the previous case situation, Tania's selection of theoretical frameworks was influenced by her family background and history. Tania's self-awareness and use of self was necessary for effective decisions. In order for Tania to plan appropriately for Bonita, she had to be able to recognize and articulate the mixture of bitterness and satisfaction she felt about her own family life as a child. Once she acknowledged her deep wish to see the Millers happy as a family unit, she could make rational decisions based on the facts and could draw upon the literature to provide effective social work help to Bonita and the rest of the family.

The works of Satir, Tracy, and Knight provided Tania a framework through which she planned her practice. Selecting literature she was comfortable with, Tania found that her thinking and behavior were informed and shaped by what she read and learned.

There were times when Tania felt great anger toward the early child welfare workers assigned to the Miller family—the situation should not have gotten this bad; the children should not have experienced abuse with their mother, in the foster home, and then again when they were returned to the mother—but just as she had to learn to do with Mrs. Miller, she didn't dwell on the past. Just blaming the system, she learned, is ineffectual—like kicking sand. Tania made sure that she functioned energetically and with integrity as a social worker. Not allowing inefficiency or lethargy to go unnoticed, she worked to make the services of her agency humane and responsive and competent. Consequently, besides providing direct services to clients, Tania was committed to improving child welfare services and was involved in advocating for increased funding allocations—as discussed in Chapter 2, the organizational and policy aspects of the person-and-environment social work perspective.

Practitioner Observation and Domestic Violence

Recently placed with family services for her second-year field practicum, Wendy had over five years of volunteer experience in domestic violence. As a high school science teacher, she volunteered at a local shelter for women. After surviving breast cancer, she decided to switch to social work, wanting to be directly involved with creating change in the lives of people.

Residing in a large urban area on the west coast, Wendy was married to a college professor of English who earned about $45,000 yearly. They were in their mid-thirties, White, and had no children. With a strong grounding in feminism, Wendy entered social work with the goal of administering her own shelter for women. Expecting to gain further experience in working with mothers and their children, she was surprised to receive as her first client a male who had been court-ordered to counseling for abuse of his wife.

Wendy had the following exchange with her supervisor, Ellen, who was Black and in her late thirties:

WENDY: I'm feeling very surprised, almost shocked. I just never expected this type of case. I thought family violence victims and perpetrators went to family violence programs.

ELLEN: We provide services to persons dealing with a wide range of problems—domestic violence is one of them.

WENDY: What can I possibly offer to this man? I just can't perceive myself talking to him.
>   *(long pause)*
>   *(somewhat angrily)* Don't you know where I have been these past years?

ELLEN: I do know that you have had experience with women and children who have been abused. You will find working with Mr. K an important opportunity to broaden your exposure. You won't be able to practice social work without having contact with men who have done things which have been harmful and abusive to others. I am here to help you learn how to intervene with these clients.

WENDY: *(less anxiously than before)* I'm not comfortable with this assignment.

ELLEN: I know you are not. There are still many clients I start out with where I feel very uncomfortable. Usually I feel better over time. And remember, I will help you.

WENDY: *(long pause)* I'm not sure. Can I meet with you tomorrow? I need to do more thinking about this.

ELLEN: Sure, how about we meet mid-morning?

Overnight, Wendy did some serious thinking and had a long talk with her husband. Having grown up in a home in which her mother and she were both physically abused by her father, Wendy had not seen herself offering help to men who were abusive to their families. Throughout her years of volunteer work, she had done a lot of thinking about her mother's experiences but had never thought much about her father's feelings. Often in the role of protecting her mother, she had not considered her father as a person. With support from her husband, Wendy decided that Ellen was probably right—she would not be able to avoid contact indefinitely with this population. An excerpt from an Adrienne Rich essay resonated for her:

> In every life there are experiences . . . which by their very intensity throw a sudden floodlight on the ways we have been living . . . the *hypocrisies* that have allowed us to collaborate with those forces. . . . Some people allow such illuminations only the brevity of a flash of sheet-lightning, that throws a whole landscape into sharp relief, after which the darkness closes in again. For others, these clarifications provide a motive and impulse toward a more enduring lucidity, a search for greater honesty. (1979, p. 215)

Seeing a means of reconciling her feminism with both an enhancement of her own life and a commitment to the social work mission of services to all populations, she decided to share with Ellen the personal nature of her concerns.

WENDY: I know you are right that working with Mr. K as a client will probably be important for me. The problem is—I am personally very uncomfortable working with him. You see *(long pause)* my father was abusive to my mother.

ELLEN: *(softly)* I realize this is hard for you. Often in this work we directly have to confront issues with clients that are a significant part of our own lives. I can help you with the specifics of working with Mr. K, suggest things to read, and review your process recordings with you. In terms of your personal issues, you may find it helpful to talk with a professional helper.

WENDY: I've thought of going into therapy, on and off over the years. Do you think I need help?

ELLEN: Not necessarily. You will be the best judge about how you are doing. Our thrust in here is on your social work practice— how you behave with clients. I can provide you with feedback about that. Your feelings about your father, your role in your family—those things you may want to further process with someone you have asked to perform in that role.

Wendy decided to consider further whether to begin a therapeutic process for herself and began her sessions with Mr. K:

....

It was so odd. He didn't look anything like I anticipated. A Black man, in his early thirties, he had a kindly face and a gentle demeanor. Soft spoken, he took his hat off when I entered the room.

Yet, at the very first session, I already had assumptions about his responses—that he was using denial, blaming his partner for the abuse and being manipulative. Bringing my preconceived ideas about how he would respond, I never asked how things felt for him.

Gosh, I was so angry at having to help someone who has been hurtful to others.

In my work at the domestic violence shelter the policy was clear cut. I just never responded to calls from the perpetrator, believing that it would jeopardize the trust of the women.

In this case, I was not only insecure about working with Mr. K, I was also inexperienced.

....

Wendy had several means of support available, including her supervisor, peers, and the literature. Deciding to check in with her former colleagues at the women's shelter, she received conflicting advice. Several reinforced her negative reaction, telling her that she would be forgetting about the victim if she met with the perpetrator. A few, however, supported and encouraged her work with Mr. K.

Fellow students were equally divided in their reactions. When Wendy complained to them that she was overwhelmed and couldn't believe what was happening to her, some suggested refusing the case or asking for a change in the placement while others simply said that they knew she could handle the situation.

The literature was also confusing. Agreeing with Frank and Golden (1992) that women should not be blamed for staying in the abusive relationship, she could also partly understand Bagarozzi and Giddings (1983) when they state that the victim has some responsibility for breaking the cycle of mutual coercion. While she had often questioned why her mother continued to stay in the marital relationship with her father, she realized that other options were just not a possibility. Whatever it was for her mother, perhaps low self-esteem or depression, she got stuck in a bad situation and didn't know she could get out of it. To call her mother codependent with her father (a term first used to describe spouses of substance abusers) was placing unfair responsibility on her mother for the husband's battering behavior.

Having taken a course some summers back with a disciple of Albert Ellis on rational-emotive therapy, Wendy was familiar with that theoretical model, finding comfort in its emphasis on rational decision making (Ellis, 1974). Based on a socially oriented set of assumptions, cognitive theory asserts that an individual's society shapes thinking that, in turn, determines emotions and behavior. As a reaction to feelings of threat or frustration, aggressive behavior can be changed by teaching an individual alternative ways of thinking (Werner, 1979). The notion that if clients could be shown the illogical nature of their internal sentences they would then modify their behavior by controlling their emotions felt empowering to Wendy.

And empowerment was a compelling issue for her. Agreeing with Gutierrez (1990) that it was especially critical to frame her thinking from an empowerment perspective when working with women of color, she believed that also applied to Black men. Boyd-Franklin's (1989) comments on therapists' use of self with Black families and Logan, McRoy, and Freeman's (1989) book on social work practice with Black families both became useful in planning for her practice with Mr. K. These authors not only fit with her feminist orientation, but they offered some specific strategies to address the racial difference between herself and Mr. K and to engage with him in the development of a professional relationship. Cautioning against being overly self-deprecating or allowing anxiety to interfere with the belief bonding, they suggested direct dialogue about the racial difference.

Boyd-Franklin stressed the need for therapists to explore their own perceptions and values—to engage in a process of self-exploration around cultural differences. One of the courses Wendy was required to take in her M.S.W. program dealt with racial and ethnic diversity. Students were forced to confront their own biases and Wendy was able to use course feedback to help frame areas for the continued personal growth stressed in the literature. Moreover, as a White woman receiving supervision from a Black supervisor, Wendy had the opportunity to acquire additional strategies for addressing racial differences during her supervision.

Since Mr. K. was only coming to see her because of the court order—he had not even contracted to work on the abuse—Wendy found additional support from Goldstein's (1984) work on the hard-to-reach client. Starting where the client is, understanding the world from the client's perspective, and avoiding categorization all seemed basic to the mission and values of social work.

The following dialogue came from Wendy's second session with Mr. K:

WENDY: You've indicated that you became very familiar with violence at an early age. What did you mean?

MR. K: When I was 13, my brother, he was two years older than me, got shot *(said slowly and with a pause)* by the police—they were White. Me and my brother were close. The reason for the shooting never got clear.

*1   WENDY: That must have been a terribly difficult time for you. Were you ever angry that the policemen were White?

MR. K: Look, that's the state of things today. White people make the rules.

*2   WENDY: How is it for you working with me as a White woman? Also, you were ordered to come here by a White judge. How are you dealing with this forced treatment?

Following some of the suggestions in the literature, Wendy directly commented on the issue of race, *1, the difference in their race, and the involuntary nature of Mr. K's treatment, *2. Through this kind of dialogue, she allowed for an open discussion about race and the forcible basis of the treatment, began where the client was, and tried to understand the world from his perspective.

Comfortable with the tenets of the cognitive model, especially its emphasis on choice and individual control over one's actions, Wendy utilized a theory she felt attracted to. As with Dave and Tania, her choice of theoretical framework was shaped by her personal preferences. At the same time, awareness of her own angry feelings about abuse and ability for use of self were prerequisites for Wendy to intervene effectively with Mr. K. Finding that she continued to feel much frustration, anger, guilt, and sadness in her work with Mr. K., after several sessions with him Wendy decided to pursue therapy for herself. An article by Miller (1990), presenting the author's journey in understanding interpersonal violence, spurred on Wendy's search for her own greater self-knowledge. She commented:

....

I was feeling so guilty with my anger at Mr. K. I was driven at an early age to help people, and this difficulty in responding to Mr. K's pain was creating great turmoil for me. Emigrating to this country from Italy just shortly before I was born, both of my parents spoke broken English, and my mother barely left the house. As soon as I was old enough, I became the one they relied upon, especially my mother. I was her helper, her link to the outside world.

Living in a neighborhood where everyone looked the same, our family never fit in. Along with this sense of isolation, I also felt protection for people who are different from others.

These early experiences helped shape me as a politically aware person—my stereotype of social workers was an activist one—I felt compelled as a young person to help others feel more valued as individuals. My first career was as a high school teacher, and it wasn't until my bout with breast cancer that I became interested in becoming a social worker.

What a shock for me that in my work with Mr. K I could not relate to his hurt as a person. When I learned about his own traumatic loss of his brother, his difficulties in finding good employment and earning an adequate salary, I recognized that he, just as my mother, is stuck in a bad situation and needs to consider other options for himself. But I was aware that I could not translate what I understood to what I felt, that I needed professional help in making this transition.

....

Awareness of her feelings and acknowledgement of her own background and experiences prompted Wendy to enter therapy. Not wanting herself to be a victim, she took the opportunity to rise above the things that had happened to her. Therapy was not a requirement to practice good social work, just as supervision was not a substitute for therapy. For Wendy, therapy was the option she chose because of the uncomfortable feelings she had about abuse in her home and about working with men who were abusive. Having always taken pride in her passion for relating to others, she became aware that she needed help in handling her emotions.

While cognitive therapy provided her with a theoretical framework she could draw from, she was also aware that abuse in the home was a highly complex issue and the cognitive approach alone might not be effective (Eisikovits et al., 1991). Just like Dave and Tania, Wendy used literature that she felt comfortable with, while her practice and thinking were, in turn, influenced by the theories she read.

ADDITIONAL NOTES

Concluding this chapter, we distinguish between therapy and social work supervision and discuss biases in social work practice.

Social Work Supervision and Therapy

Frequently, the field instructor becomes a highly significant influence on the student social worker. Discussing the intimate matters that are the basis of the work between you and your clients often raises personal issues of your own. While it is essential to utilize supervision to process feelings and reactions to clients and their situations, it is, at the same time, necessary to maintain a distinction between supervision and personal therapy.

Field instructors are available for advice, suggestions, and information about client problems and may offer strategies for intervention. The thrust of the time between you is on your work with the client. While you may reflect together about your own feelings, they are only relevant for the field supervision in terms of how they impact on your social work practice.

You will experience much personal change and growth during your field placement. An in-depth examination of your own personal development, however, should be reserved for outside the supervisory process. Your field instructor should prove a useful resource in helping you focus your supervision on your practice effectiveness.

Biases in Social Work Practice

Social workers are no different than the rest of the human race in having prejudices and biases. Each of us is raised in distinctive cultural milieus and, as such, we are products of particular environments. Our responsibility is to be aware of and attend to our own backgrounds and traditions so that our professional decisions are not unduly influenced by our own preferences.

Recall what we covered in Chapter 3: social work *is* a value-laden profession. Social workers have belief systems and are employed in agencies representing philosophical orientations and value positions. At the same time, clients have their own beliefs, values, and traditions and the practice between social workers and clients addresses ethical and cultural issues. We witness this clearly in the following example, in which it is tempting for the social worker to respond with a positive or negative reaction to the client.

On her first visit to the social worker, a 32-year-old White female reported:

I am in such a quandary. I've been offered an incredible job—a top executive with one of the big advertising firms in New York. I would be the only woman under 35. But my husband is dead set against this. He says the boys are only 5 and 7, and are too young to handle a move closer into the city. I could commute from out here and come home on the weekends—it's a three-hour commute, but he's threatening divorce if I do that. I've been looking for a good job since we moved here to the suburbs three years ago. This is a once-in-a-lifetime opportunity. I need your advice.

A "traditional" response might be: "I can't believe her! How can she even consider this job when her children need her at home?" or "It's good that her husband is being strong, she doesn't deserve him or the children." "It sounds to me like she is considering abandoning her children—how awful!" A more "feminist" position, in contrast, would sound like this: "She needs to self-actualize. Of course she should take the job." "She needs to do what is best for her career—that is the most important thing."

Social workers are not *responsible* for having these reactions. Being human and having feelings does not end when one enters the social work profession. When interacting with the client, however, the social worker should address the following kinds of concerns: What is it the *client* wants to do? If the client does not yet know what she wants, what does she need to assist her in the decision making? What consequences follow from each of the options? Clients can only make informed decisions, based on the facts and *their* values, after considering a range of alternatives and the possible consequences.

Though the practice of social work cannot be value free, you can become self-aware about your values in order to use them appropriately with clients. The extent of social workers' self-awareness about their own beliefs and values will be directly related to their capacity to attend to "who" the client is and "what" the client wants.

You must also work to assure that your views about racial and ethnic groups, class, and cultural traditions will not transfer onto specific clients. While it may not be possible to eliminate general prejudices, decisions made with individual clients in the practice must be free of bias.

SUMMARY

Self-awareness and use of self are deeply rooted concepts in the social work profession. Lack of quantitative tools, such as medications or X-rays, have placed a heavy burden on social work practitioners to be objective and sharp as the primary "instruments" of their discipline.

In this chapter, the concept of practitioner observation is presented as an incorporation of the early constructs of self-awareness and use of self and is defined as

 The self-examination and articulation by social workers of their personal reactions to clients and the intentional use of this awareness in practice

decisions and behaviors. The self-awareness is attention to oneself; to one's thoughts, feelings, biases, values; to one's ethnic, racial, and class background and religious traditions; to the totality of one's life experiences. Feelings of wanting to relate with clients as if they are friends or family members are acknowledged. Distinctions are made between problems the social worker has experienced and those of the client. Self-awareness is utilized and integrated with the profession's knowledge and skills in a professional use of self that is unique and responsive to each case situation.

The social workers in this chapter recognize that they are piecing together pictures of their clients each drawn through a particular prism, which allows some things in and filters out others. Acknowledgement of the particular lens utilized to frame the picture, accompanied by commitment to incorporate new means of depicting the client's life space, can help make social work practice successful. A complicated combination of social workers' experiences and background with the theories and knowledge of the profession supports and shapes practice interventions. Decisions for practice are informed by self-awareness and enacted through a professional use of self, which is crafted through knowledge of the literature and facilitated by the supervisory process.

Making things different for people is a noble and just undertaking, and it is the essence of the social work profession. The object of change in utilizing practitioner observation is to make the social worker's own behaviors different so that they relate to the needs of the client without unduly reflecting the needs of the social worker.

The following statement by Mary Richmond is a fitting way to end this chapter:

> There was real teaching in the world long before there was a science or art of teaching; there was social case work long before social workers began, not so many years ago, to formulate its principles and methods. Almost as soon as human beings discovered that their relations to one another had ceased to be primitive and simple, they must have found among their fellows a few who had a special gift for smoothing out the tangles in such relations. . . . The skill of the social caseworker who is able to effect better adjustment between the individual and his environment seems to many of us . . . to come by nature. . . . How much is being done in social work to develop a native gift through training and specialized experience? (1922, pp. 6–7)

It is through practitioner observation that social workers identify their own uniqueness as practitioners and further their ongoing development as effective helpers.

BIBLIOGRAPHY

Anonymous. (1990). My name is legion, for we are many: Diagnostics and the psychiatric client. *Social Work, 35* (September) 391.

Austin, L. (1976). Dynamics and treatment of the client with anxiety hysteria. In F. S. Turner (Ed.), *Differential diagnosis and treatment in social work,* 274. New York: Free Press.

Bagarozzi, D., & Giddings, C. (1983). Conjugal violence: A critical review of current research and clinical practices. *American Journal of Family Therapy, 11,* 3–15.

Boyd-Franklin, N. (1989). *Black families in therapy.* New York: Guilford Press.

Bray, R. (1992, November 8). So how did I get here? *New York Times Magazine,* 35–42.

Cohen, J. (1983). Insight Development. In A. Rosenblatt & D. Waldfogel (Eds.), *Handbook of clinical social work,* 252–265. San Francisco: Jossey Bass.

Compton, B., & Galaway, B. (1979). *Social work processes.* Homewood, Ill.: Dorsey Press.

Eisikovits, J., Edleson, J., Guttmann, E., & Sela-Amit, M. (1991). Cognitive styles and socialized attitudes of men who batter: Where should we intervene? *Family Relations, 40:* 72–77.

Ellis, A. (1974). *Humanistic psychotherapy: The rational-emotive approach.* New York: McGraw-Hill.

Fanshel, D. (1982). *On the road to permanency: An expanded data base for service to children in foster care.* New York: Child Welfare League of America.

Feldman, Y. (1963). Understanding ego involvement in casework training. In H. Parad and R. Miller (Eds.), *Ego-oriented casework,* 292–306. New York: Family Service Association of America.

Frank, P., & Golden, G. (1992). Blaming by naming: Battered women and the epidemic of codependence. *Social Work, 37:* (January 1993), 5–6.

Goldstein, H. (Ed.). (1984). *Creative change: A cognitive-humanistic approach to social work practice.* New York: Tavistock.

Gutierrez, L. (1990). Working with women of color: An empowerment perspective. *Social Work* (March): 149–153.

Hamilton, G. (1946). *Social casework.* New York: Columbia University Press.

Hepworth, D., & Larsen, J. (1986). *Direct social work practice.* New York: Dorsey Press.

Hollis, F., & Woods, M. (1981). *Casework: A psychosocial approach.* New York: Random House.

Jenson, J. M., & Whittaker, J. K. (1987). Parental involvement in children's residential treatment. *Children and Youth Services Review, 8,* 323–347.

Katz, L. (1990). Effective permanency planning for children in foster care. *Social Work, 35:* 3, 220–226.

Knight, C. (1990). Use of support groups with adult female survivors of child sexual abuse. *Social Work, 35:* 3, 202–206.

Lincoln, Y., & Guba, E. (1985). *Naturalistic inquiry.* Beverly Hills, Calif.: Sage Press.

Lofland, J., & Lofland, L. (1984). *Analyzing social settings.* Belmont, Calif.: Wadsworth.

Logan, S., McRoy, R., & Freeman, E. (1989). *Social work practice with Black families: A cultural specific perspective.* New York: Longman Press.

MacKinnon, R., & Michels, R. (1971). *The psychiatric interview in clinical practice,* 28, 141–146, 252, 266, 334. Philadelphia: W. B. Saunders.

Mezzacappa, D. (1992, November 8). Struggling toward a diploma. *Philadelphia Inquirer,* A1, A18.

Miller, D. (1990, July). The trauma of interpersonal violence. Paper presented at the Helen Pinkus Memorial Lecture, Smith College School for Social Work, Northampton, Mass.

Orr, D. W. (1954). Transference and countertransference: A historical survey. *Journal of the American Psychoanalytic Association, 2,* 621–670.

Pollak, O. (1961). Treatment of character disorders: A dilemma in casework culture. *Social Services Review, 35,* 133.

Reynolds, B. (1970, 1942). *Learning and teaching in the practice of social work.* New York: Russell and Russell.

Rich, A. (1979). *On lies, secrets, and silence.* New York: W. W. Norton.

Richmond, M. (1922). *What is social casework? An introductory description.* New York: Russell Sage Foundation.

Robinson, V. (1936). *Supervision in social casework.* Chapel Hill, N.C.: University of North Carolina.

Sandler, J. (1976). Countertransference and role-responsiveness. *International Review of Psychoanalysis, 3,* 43–47.

Satir, V. (1964). *Conjoint family therapy.* Palo Alto, Calif.: Science and Behavior Books.

Satir, V., & Baldwin, M. (1987). *The use of self in therapy.* New York: Haworth Press.

Satir, V., & Baldwin, V. (1983). *Satir step by step.* Palo Alto, Calif.: Science and Behavior Books.

Siporin, M. (1975). *Introduction to social work practice.* New York: Macmillan.

Stehno, S. (1986). Family-centered child welfare services: New life for an historic idea. *Child Welfare, 65,* 231–240.

Strean, H. (1978). *Clinical social work.* New York: Free Press.

Szasz, T. S. (1961). *The myth of mental illness.* New York: Dell.

Towle, C. (1954). *The learner in education for the professions.* Chicago: University of Chicago Press.

Tracy, E. (1990). Identifying social support resources of at-risk families. *Social Work, 35:* 3, 252–258.

Wallerstein, J. (1990). Transference and countertransference in clinical intervention with divorcing families. *American Journal of Orthopsychiatry, 60,* 3, 337–345.

Werner, H. (1979). Cognitive theory. In F. Turner (Ed.), *Social work treatment: Interlocking theoretical approaches,* 243–272. New York: Free Press.

Whitaker, C., & Keith, D. (1977). The divorce labyrinth, Follow-up to the divorce labyrinth. In P. Papp (Ed.), *Family therapy: Full length case studies,* 117–142. New York: Gardner Press.

Whitaker, C. A., & Bumberry, W. M. (1988). *Dancing with the family: A symbolic-experiential approach.* New York: Brunner/Mazel.

Wood, K. (1971). The contribution of psychoanalysis and ego psychology to social casework. In H. F. Strean (Ed.), *Social casework: Theories in action,* 105. Metuchen, N.J.: Scarecrow Press.

CHAPTER ⟨⟩ EIGHT

Our own world as we find it, our own world as we know it, is
the only possible gateway to a better future.

—Mary Richmond

INTERVENTION: PLANNING
CONTRACTING, EVALUATION

In this final chapter we examine the process of intervention, including the
specific steps social workers plan and initiate to create change in the client's
situation. To serve as a review, discussion about all the practice components
is incorporated into the case analyses. Literature relevant to each of the case
studies is presented and considered by the social workers who inquire into
their practice.

We examine the *intervention plan, which includes a problem statement, goal
setting, contracting, a mode of evaluation, and guiding theories. We explore what is
uniquely social work in the intervention that distinguishes it from other helping
interventions.* The specifics of what social workers do as they intervene with a
case are studied in terms of the *social work mission and values, development of
the relationship, and utilization of communication methods and skills.* Special
emphasis is placed on theoretical frameworks, which are viewed within the
context of *social work assessment and practitioner observation.* We explore *how
social workers decide which theoretical framework will guide their work, whether
different theories are utilized for each client, or whether a particular theoretical
perspective is adopted that shapes all of their practice.* As in all the component
chapters, we end with Additional Notes, presenting a sample plan of intervention.

As we have emphasized throughout this book, social work practice is
not linear; it is a complex and interactive process. We do not begin practice
with relationship and then move into assessment, delaying intervention
until after the assessment and relationship are "completed." Like the other
practice components, intervention commences at the first moment of contact
with the client or the case and evolves continuously through the different

stages of work, responding to changes in the client and reflecting new data and modifications in the assessment. The capacity to understand social work practice as this interactive process is central to effective functioning in the profession.

First we provide a definition of intervention:

INTERVENTION DEFINED

Intervention is defined in this book as

 The mode of procedure used by the social worker to create change in the life of the client. Emerging from the goals and based on the case theory, a plan of treatment states the problem, outlines a strategy of the specific steps in the social work practice, and includes a means of evaluation. Both short- and long-term objectives are identified to establish definitive end points. Contracting between the social worker and the client produces a mutual engagement in the process. Intervention is guided by theories and assumptions about human behavior and the process of change, by the presenting problem, by the agency's mission and social work role, and by the ethics and values of the profession. Encompassing the components of social work practice, the intervention is a reflection of the relationship, shaped by the case theory, and employs communication methods and skills and practitioner observation.

Intervention is shaped by the assessment, which has also drawn on theories of human behavior and treatment. The case theory, the theoretical knowledge, and the intervention must fit together. If these three parts are inconsistent, the intervention is considered to be irrational. Understanding the relationship of these concepts, the ways in which "what" the social worker does is related to "why" it is done, provides the rationale to support practice decisions.

Plan of Intervention

Growing out of the goal setting and related to the case theory, the social worker develops a game *plan* or *strategy*, the approach to working with and changing the client's situation. Often the course of action is implicit in the practice but is not clearly stated. Making explicit the means for ameliorating or resolving the problem will increase clarity about goals and tighten the connections between the case theory, or the worker's understanding of the case, and the means undertaken for problem resolution.

Siporin defines strategy as "a plan for the employment of a set of related methods, resources, and procedures in an assertion of influence, to exchange resources and attain objectives. Generally the practitioner operates from a 'working plan,' which is geared to the attainment of immediate objectives, and on the basis of which successive new objectives and tasks are formulated and agreed upon" (1975, p. 253). Intervention plans contain a problem statement, the established objectives, the specifics of the contract including frequency and length of sessions and the modality of treatment, as well as the evaluation process and guiding knowledge and theories.

Problem Statement

Serving to direct the practice, the *problem statement* provides focus to the intervention and identifies for the social worker and the client the substance of what the intervention is to address. Expanding on the presenting problem, the social worker identifies a larger conception of the problem situation.

Agencies differ in the duration of services they provide to clients. Where there has been time to complete an assessment report, the case theory from that initial assessment period is reformulated into a statement of the problem and placed in the plan of intervention. When time-limited treatment is the preferred course, there will usually be no case theory to draw from, a situation that requires the social worker to conceive a problem statement and combine the assessment report and the intervention plan into one presentation. Examples of both situations—initiating a problem statement and developing one based on the case theory of the assessment—are illustrated in the case studies reported later in this chapter.

The problem statement, which is less developed than the case theory, should include a brief identification of the client and center on the social worker's understanding of the nature of the client's situation. Where services are provided for several months, an intervention plan serves as an important follow-up to the assessment report. With the opportunity to consider new information acquired and additional developments in the client's life, a reformulation of the case theory can help forge a strong and effective treatment plan. Rather than starting from scratch with the development of a problem statement, the social worker modifies and evaluates the initial case theory. This approach to practice should improve both the predictability of the outcome and the actual result.

Short- and Long-Term Objectives

Much criticism has been leveled against social work practice for failure to arrive at clear outcome goals (Compton & Galaway, 1989). With the push for greater accountability in times of decreasing funding, social workers are under pressure to prove that they can accomplish what they set out to do. And without specified objectives, social workers cannot document that they have been effective in their work.

Usually social work intervention involves both immediate action and long-term planning. The severity and crisis nature of the presenting problem and the agency function will determine the direction and intensity of the initial goal setting. In the first case study we will examine, for example, resolution of the school phobia precedes establishment of long-term goals. These may evolve after the solution of the most pressing problem, or the clients may feel satisfied and terminate the practice. In this family service agency there is flexibility for both short- and long-term services to families and individuals.

The goals relevant to the case theory should be feasible, that is, capable of being achieved. And as Egan (1986) has emphasized, the social worker and the client must have the resources and be capable of accomplishing what they have set out to do. With some clients and agencies, an initial goal is the development of an assessment report. For example, a long-term inpatient psychiatric facility might rely on the Bowenian approach to family therapy, in which extensive background information is an integral component of treatment. Several weeks can be spent on completion of a lengthy genogram, which can take even longer if the families are large.

Other agencies strive for behaviorally oriented goals that are capable of precise measurement. These settings may require the use of data collection instruments at admission and discharge, either developed by the agency or available from commercial packets like Hudson (1982), Beck (1961), and Berndit and Petzel (1980). With problems that can be so specified, use of scales can help provide clarity to goals and objectives. A combination of one or more scales with other stated objectives can provide an individualized means of measurement. For example, objectives geared to a student who presents with symptoms of depression and failing grades could include a change on the Beck Scale of Depression along with an improvement in grades to an average level of "B."

Contracting

Simply framed, the *contract* incorporates three main questions: Where does the social worker want to be in a specified period of time? Where does the client seem to be heading? Is there somewhere they can go together? Expressing the commitment of the social worker and the client to their respective roles and responsibilities, the contract is central in carrying out the intervention. While a formal, written contract is not always a necessity, social workers are responsible to make clear the expectations for themselves and their clients, articulating precisely what they each will need to do in order to achieve those goals. The contract should directly reflect the objectives and state the strategy—who will be seen and frequency and expected number of sessions—along with the modality—individual, group, or family.

Maluccio and Marlow have written what is probably still the best definition of the social work contract: "For the purposes of social work, the contract may be defined as the explicit agreement between the worker and the client concerning the target problems, the goals, and the strategies of social work intervention, and the roles and tasks of the participants. Its major features are mutual agreement, differential participation in the intervention process, reciprocal accountability, and explicitness" (1974, p. 30).

Seabury points to the real difficulties in negotiating contracts with clients. Discussing problematic situations and the involuntary client, he cautions against "corrupt" contracts where the social worker has a hidden agenda that is not stated out of fear of generating conflict with the client. Seabury states: "Conflict should not be avoided, differences must be teased out and negotiated, and the sooner differences are revealed the better it is for the service process" (1979, p. 36).

While mutuality is present in the contract process—clients and social workers agree to the nature of their work together and are answerable to each other about the responsibilities they have undertaken—there are also different sets of obligations. Clients may be given "homework tasks" to work on certain issues they have raised during the sessions, and social workers have to follow through with provision of treatment that is helpful to the client during the change process.

Mode of Evaluation   While objectives represent the specific goals the social worker wants to accomplish, the *evaluation* reports the degree to which these goals have been achieved and identifies what has contributed to the results. Knowledge of the variables responsible for the change is particularly important in replicating the process, if successful, or modifying it, if the desired results have not been achieved. Client changes as well as behaviors of the social worker can be addressed in an evaluation of the practice. Responding to pressures within the profession—from outside funding sources as well as clients and insurance companies who pay the bills—social workers and social service agencies must incorporate means of evaluating effectiveness.

Single-subject designs have become an increasingly popular technique, and some advocate for their general application. Others acknowledge the difficulties in breaking down social work practice into the specific behaviors required for this type of research design. (Several good sources that address this debate include Videka-Sherman & Reid, 1990; Corcoran, 1985; Blythe & Tripodi, 1989; Nelson, 1984.) Requiring a baseline (the *A period*) in which the problematic behavior is recorded with no treatment, the *B period* reports the effects of the treatment on the target behavior. Charting is a device common with this means of practice evaluation. Not only must objectives be measurable, however, they must yield quantitative data that is valid and reliable (Grinnell, 1993; Yegidis and Weinbach, 1991; Marlow, 1993).

Whatever research design is utilized, it is necessary to include a means to determine and articulate the effects resulting from the social work intervention. Adherence to the components developed through these chapters, including a detailed assessment report and follow-up plan of intervention, provides the material with which to clearly articulate and document the contributions of the social work practice.

In this chapter's case studies the social workers utilize several means of evaluation, including scales and measurement instruments, records of behavioral changes, logs for monitoring feelings, process recordings, critique of the theoretical framework, thorough examination of the enactment of each of the practice components, and surveys of clients' satisfaction.

Achieving prompt results is critical as the profession strives for strength and viability during a period of shrinking resources while facing increased competition from other professional groups such as counselors, marriage and family therapists, and nonsocial work case managers. The term *managed care* has emerged from the current trends to provide time-limited services in health and mental health using fewer resources with greater effectiveness (Fitzpatrick & Feldman, 1992). Consequently, attention to the pace of intervention is also important. While some may be too slow in "zeroing in" on a specific course of action, others may too quickly narrow options. A decision for comprehensive information gathering as the form early intervention should take is often valid and needs to be supported by a rationale based on the social worker's knowledge and the client's dysfunctions and presenting problem.

Often, though, social workers delay specific steps until they formulate a whole picture of the situation. As we discussed in Chapter 5, however, the notion of achieving complete knowledge is illusory. It is important in practicing social work to move forward as quickly as possible. Social work is not concerned with only studying phenomena; it is the provision of services to real people who are often handling severe crises in their lives. Coming to the social worker for help in changing their situation, clients are not only interested in understanding themselves better but want to have things "different." While an increase in understanding can be one of the goals of an intervention, it should not be the only one for more than a specified period of time. Increase of understanding is more fitting for an academic enterprise than for a process of change and is difficult to measure in terms of differences in behavior.

Knowledge and Theories

There are a plethora of treatment methods, from the behavioral approach to psychoanalytic theory, including reality therapy, cognitive therapy, transactional analysis, and gestalt. Also available are such specifically social work theories as the problem-solving, crisis-oriented, and psychosocial approaches. Over a dozen approaches focus specifically on treating families. Some theories, such as Erikson's life cycles (1963) and Piaget's work on cognition (1963), solely offer explanations of human behavior and development Others, like psychoanalysis (Freud, 1923) and behaviorism (Wolpe, 1969), offer both generalizations about human behavior and principles for treatment. Still others focus on understanding human behavior and form the basis for new approaches to treatment.

A good example of this last type of theoretical development is James Framo's "family of origin" approach to treating families (1981), which was based on the human development theory of object relations. It was first formulated in 1954 by Fairbairn, who postulated that an individual's need for a satisfying object relationship (not the gratification of instinctual drives which had been proposed by Freud) was the primary human motivation (Fairbairn, 1954). In 1967, Dicks expanded Fairbairn's work, believing that interactions between husband and wife reflected needs for satisfying object relations (Dicks, 1967). Developing the marital work of Dicks, Framo focused on the behavior of families across several generations, advocating that clients' families of origin be included in therapy sessions. A focus on understanding individuals was altered to include an interaction between couples, which then evolved into a family approach for the therapy of individuals.

Treatment theories include implicit assumptions about how people change. For example, psychoanalytic theory assumes that to function with intact egos in their adult years, individuals need to process, through an analysis, issues from their early childhood years. However, the "talking through," understanding, and greater insight of psychoanalytic theory are not parts of the change process in behavioral theory, which views insight as irrelevant and unnecessary to the change process. Behaviorism, rather, assumes that people need to be given specific instructions about what and how to change.

The selection of theoretical approach is determined by the assessment— the case theory about the nature of the problem and the kinds of resources (physical, emotional, social) available to the client. While theory guides the practice, the social worker must make decisions about which framework to utilize both for understanding the client and for carrying out the intervention.

Other factors may impact on the choice of a theory. Preferences that reflect social workers' educational preparation and intellectual and emotional biases must be recognized (as discussed in Chapter 7) so that practitioner biases do not inappropriately influence the theories utilized. Employment in agencies advocating a specialized framework may also impact on the choice of theory. For example, social workers at the Philadelphia Child Guidance Clinic will prefer the structural approach as their theoretical framework in family therapy, whereas social workers at the Menninger Foundation will draw on psychoanalytic theory. Yet the evidence from some of these social workers' case examples demonstrates nonetheless the wide range of theoretical approaches utilized in their interventions. With no universally applicable intervention, social workers must be eclectic—discriminating, capable of choosing from a variety of theoretical sources, and not attempting to rely upon a generalized theory for all their cases. Being savvy about the latest research and up to date with the current literature enables social workers to base their decisions firmly on professional knowledge.

How do social workers decide which theoretical framework will guide their work? Should they use different theories for each client, or should they adopt a particular theoretical perspective that shapes all of the practice? We consider these overarching questions in the discussion of the following case material.

CASE 1: SUSAN AND THE HOWARDS

The first case study concerns an adolescent who developed a school phobia. On a Wednesday morning, a call was made from a physician's office to a community mental health center requesting an appointment for a mother and her 14-year-old daughter, Lisa. The center provided short- and long-term counseling to individuals and families. At noon that day, the worker on call at the center, Susan, was buzzed by the secretary and greeted the clients in the waiting room. Exuding confidence and strength, Susan was a petite woman who dressed elegantly. Shaking hands with the mother, she introduced herself—"Hi, I'm Susan"—and asked the mother, Karen Howard, to introduce her daughter. As she saw that Lisa did not offer her hand, she commented matter-of-factly and with a smile, "Maybe you're not quite ready to visit here yet." Susan asked them to walk with her to her office, making small talk about whether they had trouble finding the center.

The office was comfortable, furnished like a family room in a home. There was coffee and Kool Aid, stuffed animals, and toys (for the younger clients). The chairs ranged from stiff backed, for those who didn't quite want to "let down," to low and heavily cushioned for those who want to be "taken care of."

Susan began by asking the mother what she was distressed about and what the physician said to her. The mother revealed that Lisa had been refusing to attend school since the previous Friday, had been sleeping in the same bed as her mother, and refused to go out of the house or see her friends. Having been urged by the family physician to contact the center, Karen made the referral call from her office. The Howard family included the parents, David and Karen, each 46; and three children, Paul, 19; Sally, 18; and Lisa, 14. The parents were both professionals—David was a college professor and Karen was a lawyer. Paul and Sally attended college, in their sophomore and freshman years, respectively.

After about 15 minutes, Susan asked to meet with Lisa alone.

Leaning forward, Susan commented to Lisa that it sounded like she was having some tough problems and told her to describe what had been happening. Lisa was silent for a long while, probably two or three minutes, and then told Susan that her sister, Sally, had left for college a few weeks before. At that time Lisa heard her mother say, "I can't wait until I have all of the kids out of the house. It will be a financial and time pressure relief." Lisa talked about feeling like she was being left all alone, and that nobody cared about her.

Susan asked Lisa to list five to ten ideas and fears that made her feel sad and lonely. Lisa's list included the following: (1) if my parents leave or die, (2) if they don't care or don't want to listen to me, (3) being alone and by myself, (4) not having any friends, (5) not having a sister or brother to do things with, or to talk to, (6) if nobody cares about me.

Susan thanked Lisa for sharing this list with her and scheduled a time for the following day to have a more lengthy appointment with the parents and Lisa. She obtained their written permission to talk with the school counselor and the family physician and, to quicken the process, asked them to advise these offices that she would be contacting them later that day for information.

By 3:30 that same day, Susan called Lisa's school counselor and learned that Lisa had been a good student, with no particular psychological problems or unusual number of school absences and that she had a moderate number of extracurricular involvements. The family was oriented to high achievement and academic success, and both siblings had done well in academics and athletics. The counselor had recently become concerned by Lisa's frequent contacts with her office, where she had been talking about feeling depressed and worthless. A close friend of hers recently moved away, and another was rejecting her. In checking back with the physician's office, Susan learned that there had been no particular problems with Lisa's health.

On the following day Susan met with the parents for an hour and with Lisa for an hour. The parents shared that they had been working with a counselor and were considering divorce. They did not know how much Lisa knew about their marital problems.

Susan spent some time doing a genogram, a tool used to develop a family picture across time (McGoldrick and Gerson, 1985). From the extensive background information about this family she drew a family tree indicating ages, employment, marriages, deaths, and any other significant facts about all members of both Karen's and David's families. The genogram revealed that both Karen and David were the middle of three children, and in each family the third child had been dysfunctional, continuing to live home with their mothers. The fathers were both deceased.

The parents reported that a few weeks before, just shortly before the two siblings left for college, Lisa failed to make the tryouts for the volleyball team. After then starting the cross-country team just this past Friday, Lisa told the coach she would not be participating. She spent the weekend home in the house, basically in her room. She ate minimally and insisted on sleeping in bed with her mother.

The following exchange took place between Susan and Lisa:

SUSAN: Of the six things you listed for me yesterday, which one feels most important to work on today?

LISA: I think the thing about friends. I had this friend—Janie. She was my next best friend. She moved August 15. We had a surprise breakfast for her before she moved. I have this other best friend, Laura, who was my best friend, and it seems like I've lost her.

SUSAN: How is that?

LISA: During volleyball tryouts, the week of August 25, I had called her a lot the week before, and she didn't call back. She's in the real popular group now. She began to get in it last year.

SUSAN: When did she call you last?

LISA: Sometime in the middle of August she had called. It seems like I don't fit in with any group. There are these certain groups, and they say "hi" to me, but it seems like after they say that they walk off. And if I'm standing there, it's like they exclude me from the gossip. I act like I don't care. But then when I'm in class, I feel like crying, and I just can't stop; so I leave the class and go to the bathroom or to the counselor's office.

SUSAN: And then what happens?

LISA: Well, the counselor listens a while. But then she says, "Well, you have to go back to class now." I just don't want to sit in a class and cry.

Susan encouraged Lisa to talk on another 10 minutes in more detail about the groups at school, who was in them, and her relationships with each person. Then she shared with Lisa some of her thinking:

SUSAN: Okay. Now let's talk a bit about what we are going to do. You have a lot of difficult and complicated things going on. We'll want to take lots of time to explore in detail what is going on with you and the kids at school. In addition, you have a lot of stress from the loss of one friend moving and another friend you can't count on now. You have the loss of your sister going away to college, so that now you are the only kid at home. Your folks are real busy with their lives and work now, and are trying to work out the problems in their relationship.

You're having a lot of doubts now about yourself—how you're doing things and how you want to do them. This is something most people your age are working real hard on. It isn't that we all don't have problems like these to deal with. But you're having them all at once, and at a time when you don't have a friend you feel you can trust to talk to. So what you have is a great deal of stress coming down on you. One of the things we know about lots of stress is that it interferes with your ability to think clearly, and that makes it even harder for you to figure out your problems.

There are some things we can do to help reduce stress, and one of the most important ones is exercise. Are you getting any exercise? Is there some kind of exercise that you like to do?

LISA: I like to run. I'm thinking about going out for track.

SUSAN: Excellent! How often do you run?

LISA: Well, I'm planning to run every day or almost every day.

SUSAN: Great. That will help a lot. Also, what about your diet and sleeping?

LISA: I'm not very hungry, but I'm eating okay. I am having some trouble getting to sleep, and I'm waking up some.

SUSAN: Okay. We'll need to do some more talking about sleep next time to give you some help with that. By the way, I think it would be pretty nice if you could talk to your sister on the phone some. Can you do that?

LISA: Yes, I think I can. I'd like to do that.

SUSAN: Now, let's talk about school. One of the things we know is that the longer you stay out of school, the harder it is to go back. So we need to find a way for you to go back right away that will feel O.K. to you. Let's see. *(pause, thinking)* Suppose we work it out like this; and we'll have to get your folks' approval, and see if they'll be able to do it. We'll have them take you to school in the morning, and at the end of each hour, one of them will call the school counselor, and see if you need them to come get you. If you do, they will come and talk to you or take you out for an hour. But, at the end of the hour it's very important that you go to your next class. Your responsibility will be to go by the counselor's office at the end of each hour and tell the counselor whether you need your parent to come by. So that the most you would have to be at school at a time is one hour. What do you think? Can you manage that?

LISA: I think that sounds okay.

SUSAN: Okay. Shall we talk with your parents about it now?

LISA: Okay.

Susan invited the parents into the office and shared the following with them:

SUSAN: Lisa is under a lot of stress right now. She and I will want to do a lot of talking and work on the things that are bothering her. I've explained to her that it's important for her to get back into school right away, but she will need your help. *(explains the plan)*
        Would you all be able to work out a schedule so that one of you was available to call the school at the end of each hour? You'd also need to be near enough to the school so you could go by and pick Lisa up for an hour, or just talk to her a while there, if she prefers.

KAREN: I think we can do that. Maybe one of us can do mornings and the other afternoons.

DAVID: Yes, I think that will work.

KAREN: *(to David)* Why don't you take the morning, and I'll take the afternoon?

DAVID: Okay.

SUSAN: *(to Lisa)* Remember that if you leave the school, you need to be back for the beginning of the next hour. Since this is Thursday, how about if we set up a meeting for Monday? You can let me know how our plan is going, and Lisa and I will continue working on her problems with her friends. I'll call the counselor and explain our plan before tomorrow morning.

KAREN: Monday is okay.

SUSAN: Okay. The secretary will set it up for you. I'll see you all on Monday. We'll spend a little while all together, and then Lisa and I will meet to continue her work.

Saturday: Lisa traveled to her sister's college and spent Saturday night with her.

Monday: Susan learned that Lisa went to school both Friday and Monday. Her parents called school hourly, and Lisa asked a parent to come by only once on Friday. The school counselor did not require Lisa to go by her office at the end of each hour, but told the parents they weren't needed if Lisa had not come by. Susan decided not to insist that Lisa go by the office as regularly as they had initially agreed.

Lisa suggested she might like some medication for her anxiety. Susan asked her to think about it and let her know the following day, if she was still feeling that way, Susan would arrange an appointment with the psychiatrist to talk about medication. (Lisa did not call back for medication.)

Tuesday: In a parent conference, Lisa's mother asked if Lisa was being manipulative because she had asked to be taken to school every day and for the parents to call school each hour, but she had gone through all of Monday and today without needing them. She also took the car, forgot to ask permission, and visited a friend yesterday. She then got angry at her parents for being angry at her about taking the car. In addition, she refused to sleep with her mother last night and slept in her own bed. Susan asked about sleeping history and learned that Lisa had slept with her sister about three-fourths of the time until the sister left for school and had slept with the mother for the past two weeks.

Susan encouraged the parents to respond "normally" to Lisa as a kid who had broken the rules about car use. She advised that for now they continue to meet her needs for contact with them, as she asked for it. Susan pointed out that the behaviors she was exhibiting are usual adolescent behaviors (anger at parents, refusing to sleep with parents, visiting a friend, forgetting to ask when using the car) and represented a move in the right direction.

Thursday: A week after the initial intake, the father, David, reported that for the last two days Lisa had told him to call only at noon. Lisa was in school on a regular basis, was interacting socially with friends, was exercising regularly, and had no problems with eating or sleeping.

The remarkable success in this example of a social work intervention may not be typical for its prompt results. All of the activity we just reviewed took place during the first two sessions, in less than a week! Such dramatic change does not often occur in such a brief period of time. Change resulting from social work practice, however, can be quicker than we may expect. Let us now examine Susan's intervention.

Susan's Plan of Intervention

Problem Statement

Because of the short time period in this intervention, Susan coalesced the intake and intervention plan into one report—the plan of intervention. Her problem statement was that *the school phobia was Lisa's way of dealing with an increasing sense of isolation from family and friends. The school phobia was in a very early stage of development, with absence from school being the primary problem. Other components of the problem included a possible depression; Lisa's overly close relationship with her family and perceived lack of friends; dropping out of school activities; and changes in diet, exercise, and sleep patterns. These would need to be further assessed over the course of treatment.* The case theory Susan evolved over several sessions will be discussed more fully in the section on the unique social work aspects of the intervention.

Short- and Long-Term Objectives

Susan had both immediate and long-range goals in her practice with the Howards. Believing that it was critical to develop an intervention that would work quickly on getting Lisa back to school, she stated:

....

My most immediate goal was to get Lisa back in school. In fact, I think at the very first visit that was probably everybody's goal. Other immediate goals included greater social involvement for Lisa, developing a means for Lisa to continue her relationship with her sister, and better eating and sleeping habits, with more physical exercise.

At that early point, the long-term goals would not yet have been clearly formulated. I was thinking along the lines of the need for less emotional intensity in the family and that Lisa negotiate the separation from her parents with less trauma. I knew I would never get to these if I didn't help with some resolution of the school attendance problem.

Further assessment of the situation might be necessary—such as whether Lisa is depressed—depending upon attainment of these other goals.

....

New and more long-range tasks emerged after attainment of the immediate objectives. Long-term tasks for Lisa included the formulation of a more complete assessment of her mental functioning and an increase in her skills to navigate the rest of her adolescent years more smoothly—to balance the needs for her parents (decrease) and those for peers and school activities (stabilize).

Other goals evolved for the mother. After about a month of seeing Lisa and only brief visits with the parents, Susan added individual sessions with the mother. Focusing on the mother's parenting of Lisa and relationship with her own mother (the maternal grandmother), these sessions lasted for about four months. The objective was to improve Karen's parenting through enhancing her understanding of the parenting she had received from her mother, identifying some changes she might like to make.

Previous experience with school phobia had convinced Susan that if the short-term objective was successfully resolved—that is, getting the child back in school—the long-term objective of altering family interaction patterns might not need attention. Moreover, the family's willingness to follow her advice supported Susan's belief that they could get Lisa back in school.

In this case, Susan was right on target from the very beginning. She was able to initiate immediate action on the short-range goals and then, probably partly because of that success, was also able to take action on the long-range objectives.

Contracting

Though Susan and the Howards did not negotiate a formal written contract, they were in agreement about the nature of their work together and their respective roles and responsibilities. Just as is usually the case, each person brought personal objectives into the practice session. The parents wanted Lisa to be back in school and to behave in a less depressed fashion. Lisa wanted more friends and not to feel so alone and isolated. Susan's first concerns were around Lisa's school attendance and withdrawn behavior. The task for Susan and the Howards was to reach an agreement so that some of every family member's objectives received attention.

Susan explained clearly what she would be doing—that she would meet individually with Lisa and separately with the parents. When she met with Lisa, they focused on Lisa's list of priorities as well as Susan's concerns about Lisa's diet, exercise, and sleeping routines. At the same time, Lisa was given specific instructions to follow about school attendance and about asking for help from her parents to maintain her school attendance. With the parents, Susan enabled them to help Lisa with these changes, guiding them with clear directions about what they are to provide for Lisa. Everyone was responsible for his or her own tasks.

Connecting her goals of getting Lisa back in school with the case theory of a school phobia related to a growing isolation from family and friends, Susan explained her planning strategy, including whom she would be seeing and how frequently:

. . . .

Concerned that there were larger family issues impacting upon Lisa's refusal to attend school, I decided to redirect energy to a solvable problem, away from the issue of school attendance, and not yet on the family relationships. My strategy was to reframe the problem as one dealing with school friends and general body care. I wanted to convey the message that we needed to get this school thing dealt with so that we could deal with the more serious problems. The reason for "minimizing" the school phobia is that it has often proven an effective strategy in getting it resolved.

. . . .

Information from the literature about school phobia informed Susan's strategy and will be covered in more detail shortly when we look at the case theory. Also shaped by the literature was Susan's decision to separate work with the parents from the treatment with Lisa. Instead of seeing the whole family for treatment, she saw Lisa on an individual basis and focused the work with the parents on empowering them to help Lisa, with the use of frequent phone calls for backup during the first week of treatment.

Administration of the *Beck Depression Inventory* (1961, 1979) would provide further assessment data about the extent of Lisa's depression. Collaboration with school officials added to the development of a fuller profile about Lisa's capacities. Acting quickly on the immediate presenting problem, Susan included an ongoing assessment in negotiating her work with the Howards.

Mode of Evaluation

With the definition of the problem including Lisa's absence from school, her return to classes provided a simple behavioral measure of change. In earlier clients with school phobia, Susan utilized a single-subject design, charting the students' attendance (or days absent from school). While some clients enjoyed participating in graphing the behavioral changes, Susan found that even where results were not obtained lack of change could also be made very visible for both her and the client. With the Howards, the level of activity was so high, and such a multitude of issues was all addressed at once, that it was difficult to begin with a chart of school absence.

A firm believer in evaluating her effectiveness, Susan considered larger questions of her intervention strategy. As she had hypothesized, Lisa did not test high on the depression scale, providing support for the approach taken. Susan attributed the prompt results to her use of reframing the school attendance problem into one of diet and exercise and her support of Lisa's need for increased parental involvement (from "paradoxical" approach to change put forward by Watzlawick, Weakland, & Fisch, 1974). Preferring the combination of paradox and Bowen (1978), Susan stated that the latter offered the Howards different ways of treating each other based on learning a new understanding of themselves as a system.

Documenting all of her interventions with school phobia, Susan recorded the theoretical framework she utilized. Of the fifteen families she saw with school phobia, with twelve she relied on the combination of paradoxical theory and the Bowenian model and had quick results similar to that with the Howards. For the other three families, she relied on a structural approach (Minuchin, 1974) with two and, for the third, utilized only the Bowenian model. She was not successful with structural family therapy and the phobia, losing both of those families to treatment after three sessions. On the other hand, the Bowenian emphasis on understanding the family over time was useful in helping the third family alter their interactions but took too long in returning the child to school.

Adherence to the components of social work (reviewed later) provided coherence to Susan's social work intervention. Susan acknowledged that she formulated her interventions while actively considering each of the social work components. While sometimes she might emphasize relationship building, at other times communicating in just the right way became more significant. Assessment was what unified and held together everything else she did, and with the Howards she quickly formed an understanding of their situation.

Some social workers may feel more comfortable going more slowly than Susan when they first meet with a client. Depending on one's experience and knowledge about the presenting problem, more time might be spent developing the assessment before deciding on a particular intervention. This process might involve gathering more background information, examining the literature, and checking with other social workers and a supervisor. An intervention is still taking place as these activities go on; what may not yet be set in motion are long-term objectives and a focused strategy for problem resolution. When a decision is made to develop a more thorough assessment, that process can become the intervention for a specified period of time. In this type of situation, the strategy, goals, and contracting of the intervention include gathering more information to increase understanding of the problem situation for both the client and the social worker.

Yet what did Susan do to get such prompt results? Based on her extensive experience and practice with this type of problem and population, Susan very quickly began her strategy of action. At the moment she met the clients, at noon on that Wednesday, she was forging an understanding of the case and negotiating a contract while she also continued to construct a more complete understanding of the client. Drawing on her more than fifteen years of experience as a social worker and her extensive experience with children, adolescents, and families and school phobia, Susan was comfortable proceeding at a quick pace.

Guiding Theories
When Susan was asked if she practiced with a theoretical perspective, she responded:

....

There are several frameworks which I use. Developmental theories, psychodynamic, systems, and intergenerational are all useful to me in helping me understand what is going on with my clients, how they got to where they are, what it is that is missing in their lives. The brief therapy models, behavioral, transactional analysis, hypnotic, and Whitaker's existential have all provided me with very useful ways to do the work with the clients, to bring about change, to help me decide what it is I need to do.

I use them all. I use several different ones all at once. I pay attention to how they all work and I decide which door to open, based on what I assess the client is needing. *In the case of the Howards, from intergenerational theory (Bowen, 1978) I used a genogram (McGoldrick & Gerson, 1985) and learned that the third child in each parent's family of origin was dysfunctional, resulting in their remaining in the home to care for the parents. I decided to use a genogram because I wanted to test my hypothesis that some of Lisa's behavior was carrying out a family tradition. From systems theory (Goldenberg & Goldenberg, 1991), I tried to understand the relationships of these three people. My assumption was that the daughter felt angry with each parent but was not communicating this feeling. The mother and daughter were very close, maybe too close, since the daughter was sleeping with the mother during the school phobic period. I knew that the mother was using the daughter's problems to complain to the father that he wasn't meeting the daughter's needs. I was hypothesizing a systems imbalance, probably the parents communicating to each other through the daughter. The paradoxical approach (Watzlawick, Weakland, & Fisch, 1974) provided an intriguing means of helping to reframe the family interaction. Prescribing to the family that they get more involved with Lisa's day resulted in Lisa's reaction to move in the opposite direction.*

....

Like the more than twenty experienced social work practitioners interviewed for this book, Susan decided on a theory to use *based on what she assessed that the client needed.* Theory guided her intervention with the Howards only after she had done some thinking about what was most applicable for their particular situation.

In this case, partly because of her experience and high level of skill, Susan was able to draw on a very rich range of theories that nicely complemented each other and produced prompt change in the Howards.

The Intervention as Uniquely Social Work

As we discussed in Chapter 1 and reviewed in many of the case discussions, the purpose of social work is to improve social functioning. The locus of attention for social workers is person and environment, and social caseworkers strive for individual change while also attending to organizational service delivery, issues of policy, and the client's community. Professional ethics guide social work interventions, which also comprise the components of relationship, assessment, communication methods and skills, and practitioner observation. A process of practice evaluation must also be enacted.

Let us now analyze Susan's intervention with attention to each of the earlier chapters.

Relationship to Social Work Mission, Values, and Ethics

Susan's practice with the Howards is an excellent demonstration of a social work intervention. With *simultaneous attention to the individual,* Lisa, *and to* Lisa's *environment,* Susan addressed the school, family, and friends as well as the smaller systems of siblings and parents, focusing on Lisa's social functioning.

One of the first things Susan did was to *collaborate* with staff from other agencies (see Chapter 2). By calling the school counselor and the physician's office, she acquired information about Lisa's physical, psychological, and social situations. Knowledge about the client's medical history, academic record, any special psychological testing, and her social adjustment is necessary for an effective intervention. For example, if Susan had learned that long periods of school absenteeism were part of Lisa's school record or that she had a learning disability, she might have initiated a different approach.

Lisa was treated with respect, as a *self-determining* individual. Asking Lisa what she wanted from the therapeutic process, Susan *began where the client was*. Susan also abided by the ethic of *confidentiality*, asking for the consent of the family in obtaining information from the school and physician (Chapter 3).

This family service agency was structured for prompt response to crisis, with the opportunity for frequent contacts with clients when necessary. Susan was available to meet with the family within hours of their call to the agency and scheduled several meetings with the family and Lisa during the first week.

Encompassing the Components of Social Work Practice

Susan practiced using all the basic components of social work practice, including *establishing a relationship* (Chapter 4) with Lisa and the parents, *utilizing communication methods* (Chapter 6), *formulating her case assessment* (Chapter 5), and *observing herself as a practitioner* (Chapter 7).

Susan's straightforward and respectful manner of talking and clear set of directions conveyed her belief in the client's worth and capacity to change. At the same time, Susan's belief in her own competence was evident. Her strong sense of confidence and "take-charge" attitude assisted in the establishment of a *belief bonding*. There was a mutual belief that the client was worthwhile and capable of change and the social worker was capable of helping the client.

Susan used the *communication* methods of *exploration, validation, confrontation*, and *reflection*. She started out *exploring* with Lisa and then *validated* Lisa's worth and *reflected* what she heard Lisa to be saying. She *explored* with the parents and also used *confrontation* in helping them see Lisa as an adolescent dealing with the normal problems of growing up and separating from them. Susan also employed general communication skills. She *gave information* to both Lisa and the parents, *sustained the dialogue, used silence* with Lisa, and both *focused and summarized* for Lisa and her parents.

Remember that there is a direct relationship between the *intervention* and the *assessment*. Susan's *case theory* centered on her hypothesis that Lisa's school phobia was, in part, her way of dealing with an increasing sense of isolation from family and friends. Developmental theory (Mahler, 1963) informed Susan that some of Lisa's feeling was a natural component in the separation process adolescents must experience as they grow up. This process, however, was exacerbated for Lisa, with both siblings leaving the home and the parents' marital troubles.

While Susan recognized the larger picture of Lisa's family situation in her case theory, the plan of intervention had to zero in on a particular piece of the client's life—in this case, absence from school.

Susan explained her case theory:

....

I sensed that the mother might be tired of parenting and might be giving mixed messages to the daugher, both being tired of her and wanting to hold on to her. The consequences of the behaviors exhibited by Lisa was a greater holding on between her mother and herself. She was able both to please the mother and also "get back at her," by being overly needy and by "messing up" the family image. I felt it was important for Lisa to have renewed opportunity for relationships outside the family, to both reduce the emotional intensity of the family and to increase her own sense of self.

Lisa was also reacting to the stress she perceived her parents were experiencing in their marriage. She was responding to them as a unit and probably fearful of the dissolution a divorce could bring. She may even have been experiencing some feelings of abandonment.

There were alternative ways of thinking about this case. I could have been more concerned with Lisa's relationship with both her parents, with the hostility evident in her manipulation of them. There was also the mother's hostility to her husband and how that might be the central factor contributing to Lisa's disruptive behavior. If I assessed these to be the main issues, I would have planned a different intervention.

....

As discussed in Chapter 5, the social worker begins to formulate hypotheses almost immediately while striving to understand what is happening and considering how to bring about change. Prior experience and knowledge about children with school phobia enabled Susan to develop her hypotheses quickly and decide which theories she would draw from, both for her assessment and her intervention.

Susan's hypothesis that the critical problem to address first was Lisa's school phobia determined the literature she turned to and shaped the intervention plan she developed. When she looked at the literature on school phobia, data supported that school-phobic children have a strong element of fear and need to experience security and safety (Lassers, Nordan, & Bladholm, 1973). Considering how to address Lisa's fear of loss, Susan chose a behavioral, not cognitive approach, believing it would offer quicker results. This decision further impacted on the theories she used to understand the case and to carry out the intervention.

In Chapter 7 we stressed the importance of self-awareness to one's own reactions to clients in order to be planful and deliberate in decisions and behaviors. Susan commented about her observation of herself as a practitioner:

....

I come across as very self-assured. It is always important for me to attend to each client and the problem being presented, so if necessary, I can change my presentation. With Lisa's current issues—loss of self-control, feeling vulnerable to the world—I wanted to soften my self-presentation. I needed to come across as nurturing and caring, maintaining my presentation of competence but including more of a gentleness. I'm very comfortable working with people from different backgrounds, and a range of ages and problem areas. I consider it my responsibility to present myself in such a way that the client can relate to me and accept my help.

I have a daughter who has recently been a teenager, and the Howards are professional and upper middle class, as is my family. However, this particular case did not pull on my issues. The family was close friends with the executive director of the agency, but that didn't arouse anxiety for me, I am comfortable that the director respects my work.

....

Of the same race (White) and social class (upper middle) as the Howards, and the parent of a daughter, Susan had to be sure that she did not respond to the Howards as she would to family or friends, or assume that their problems were analogous to her own. Though she had worked with many other similar cases, her interaction with the Howards and Lisa was geared specifically to who they were and how they were functioning. Open to drawing from different theoretical models, she documented the results, thereby providing the means to base her future decisions on past outcomes. Aware of her own biases and feelings, she was articulate about use of herself as a professional social worker.

Case 2: Sheila and the Georgios

We will now consider another case study, the Georgios and their 4-year-old daughter who was born with brain damage. At 10:00 A.M. on Tuesday Rick and Lynn Georgio, in their late twenties, arrived for their weekly appointment with Sheila Anderson, the social worker. A construction worker, Rick earned about $25,000 a year. Previously employed as an office clerk, Lynn was now home taking care of their 8-month-old son, Peter. After three months of regular sessions, a feeling of comfort had developed. The Georgios knew and trusted Sheila and were clear about the expectations for their work together. Having kept the use of last names, they shook hands, said hello, and sat down to begin work. Seated at her desk, Sheila could turn her large swivel chair to face the couple, who were seated together on a small couch with firm pillows.

In her late thirties, Sheila was married to a schoolteacher. They had a daughter, age 11 and a son, age 14, who attended parochial school. As Catholics, they regularly attended church but also practiced birth control. With short blond hair, Sheila dressed comfortably in slacks and a sweater, making it easy on herself when she sat on the floor with some of her young clients.

Katie, the Georgio's 4-year-old daughter, attended the Easter Seal Pre-school, where Sheila had been the social worker for over ten years. The school provided small classes for disabled children up to the age of 12 concurrent to services for their families. Born two months premature be-cause of complications in the pregnancy, Katie suffered a Class IV brain hemorrhage when she was two days old, resulting in cerebral palsy primari-ly affecting the left side of her body. On that same day she suffered the first of four grand mal seizures and was currently medicated with Tegretol to control the seizure activity.

Over the past eight months significant progress had been made in the development of Katie's language skills, eating, and ambulation. Functioning at 25 percent of the cognitive level for a 4-year-old, Katie could, with assistance, pull herself to standing, though she usually crawled. Still in diapers, she was being weaned from junior baby foods and was beginning to develop self-feeding skills. Responsive to certain commands, she ex-pressed a limited number of phrases. Affectionate, with beautiful long brown hair and blue eyes, Katie enjoyed music. While her full potential was uncertain, educational and developmental goals for Katie emphazied basic life skills.

A week before, Sheila and the Georgios had discussed Katie's educa-tional goals and the development of her individualized education program (IEP). At that time Rick suddenly began to describe the kinds of goals he wished they could have written. During that session Sheila was visiting the Georgios in their home, where they had coffee and seated themselves around the kitchen table. Small and neat, the house was not far from a large car plant, one of the big employers in the area. Some of the houses were in satisfactory shape and others were rundown. Rick's repair skills were evi-dent in the good condition of their home. In this office visit, Sheila returns to what Rick had previously raised:

SHEILA: The last time we were together we were talking about Katie's IEP goals, and Rick, you said you wished we could be writing goals for her to be running, talking, and playing soccer by the end of the year.

RICK: *(soft, contemplative smile)* Yeah.

SHEILA: Lynn, what kinds of things do you wish for Katie?

LYNN: *(looking down, defeated)* That she'll be able to play with other kids her age, do the things they do, grow up, get married, have kids.

SHEILA: *(directed to both)* Please describe the kinds of feelings that come up for you when you think about those wishes.

RICK: *(looking sad)* Well, we know we have to be realistic. I'm already prepared that Katie might be at home with us for the rest of our lives. That's fine, just as long as she is happy.

SHEILA: How is it for you when . . . how do you feel when you think about the difference between those realistic goals for her and your dreams for her?

LYNN: *(looking at Sheila as Rick looks at her)* You feel sad. . . . Just the other day, I was in Toys 'R Us picking out a Halloween costume for her. There were other mothers there with their daughters and the children were saying "Mommy, I want this and that." And I thought, "Poor Katie, she doesn't even know what I am getting for her. She can't even tell me what she wants."

SHEILA: What do you do with those feelings . . . when your heart is right here? *(touching her throat)*

LYNN: Cry.

SHEILA: *(long pause)* And then what?

LYNN: Then I get myself back together and go on. And I think, I'm glad for what we have—that she's this good.

SHEILA: Rick, are you able to cry?

RICK: No. I get angry instead. Before I hurt my shoulder, I used to lift weights. That's sort of how I got my anger out.

SHEILA: Well, anger is an important outlet, too. It's just a bad deal that men are taught not to cry.

RICK: *(looking at Lynn)* It's just that, if we're at the hospital with Katie and she's crying *(referring to Lynn)*, I feel I can't or we'll both be a mess.

SHEILA: You know, there were times when my son was undergoing procedures for his kidney condition and he took a turn for the worse, that my husband cried. It made me feel closer to him—that we were getting through it together. I still knew he cared deeply when he wasn't crying, but I felt less alone when he cried, too.

LYNN: *(looking at Sheila intently and nodding)* Yeah . . . you don't feel like you're the only one going crazy.

SHEILA: How much do you talk together about how you each are feeling?

LYNN: We rarely talk together like this about Katie. There's really not much time.

RICK: And it's not going to change anything.

SHEILA: How does this feel to you now—talking to me about these things? Is it really uncomfortable for you, or is it okay? Is it so tough that you would rather not do it?

LYNN: *(softly)* I like talking like this.

RICK: *(laughing)* Yeah, get this lady out of my hair.

SHEILA: That's okay.

RICK: No seriously, We're saying more things with you here than we usually say to each other.

SHEILA: Good, and aren't you saying that while you are getting something positive out of this, you also are uncomfortable doing it?

RICK: Yes, it's hard for me when Lynn is feeling bad.

SHEILA: *(pause)* You know one of the difficulties we have identified is that you Rick, get impatient when Lynn starts expressing her feelings, that you feel powerless to help her.

And that you, Lynn, hold back and don't express yourself for fear of upsetting Rick.

I'd like to just talk a few moments here with Lynn, and if you, Rick, would sit here.

(turning to face only Lynn) I was wondering if you have imagined, from time to time, what your relationship with Katie would be like now. Are there things that you think about . . . that you wish you could be doing together?

LYNN: *(sadly)* Yes, there are lots of things . . .

SHEILA: *(softly and cautiously)* What kinds of things do you think about?

LYNN: Well . . . that we could take walks together . . . *(eyes filling with tears)*, that she would let me do her hair.

SHEILA: She gets upset . . .

LYNN: Yeah . . . she gets upset when I try to do her hair. . . . And I'd like to dress her up in pretty dresses . . . *(voice is cracking, she is crying)*

> I would love to . . . you know . . . just take her out for a
> fun day . . . just hold a conversation with her.

SHEILA: *(places a hand on Lynn's shoulder and looks reassuringly at Rick.
They all sit together for a few minutes)*

Unlike the case study of Susan's work with the Howards, here there
would be no quick resolution of a pressing problem. While progress had
been made, promptly and effectively, the issues were subtle and would
need longer-term attention. We now turn to Sheila's intervention.

Sheila's Plan of Intervention

Problem Statement

Following the standard procedure at this setting, when Katie was admitted
to the school program the Georgios were assigned to Sheila for an intake/
assessment report. Three months after the first session another summary,
the plan of intervention, was developed. Drawing from her case theory
formulated in that initial report, Sheila made the problem statement in her
intervention plan that *the Georgios had unresolved grief about their daughter's
handicap, which was making it difficult for them to function in some of their other life
roles. Requesting assistance in coordinating the medical and educational services
provided by the setting, they also expressed an interest in talking about their
marriage and their relationship with each of their children. Chronic or recurrent
sorrow (Trout, 1983) was stressing the marriage and interfering with their parenting
of both Peter and Katie.*

Short- and Long-Term Objectives

Short-term objectives included developing both clarity about the educational
plan for Katie and understanding of her medical condition and prognosis.
The Georgios would need knowledge about Katie's educational goals and
her cognitive and physical capacities as well as building confidence in their
capacity to coordinate her care.

Feeling less grief and loss over Katie were longer-term goals identified
by the Georgios and Sheila. In talking about their sorrow, Lynn shared that
she spent a good portion of her day either crying or feeling like crying, while
Rick had periods of extreme frustration and even anger.

Improvement of marital communication was another longer-term goal.
Married only two years prior to Katie's birth, they had both commented on
the change in their relationship. They didn't enjoy sex as much and they
didn't talk and have fun together the way they used to. Finally, each of them
desired greater comfort with their roles as parents, both to Katie and to
Peter.

These goals were feasible, were directly related to the problem statement, and contained some means of measurement.

Contracting

Devoting a session to the development of a written contract, the Georgios discussed their goals and Sheila presented her understanding of their situation with recommendations for treatment. They reached an agreement to have weekly sessions alternately at the school and home. During the school visits, they would structure some time to meet with Katie's teachers and medical staff, while at home Peter would join them for part of the time. Often, the home visits elicited important information. Standard tests would be administered to Katie and results shared with the Georgios. Grief work would occur as they allowed some time in each session to discuss their feelings about Katie's incapacities. Reviewing what it was like when she was born, they would also talk about their current interactions with her. While most of the sessions would be joint, there might be occasions where Sheila met individually with Lynn or Rick.

Presenting her strategy, Sheila discusses some of the literature on unresolved grief and shattered dreams (Tomko, 1983), focusing specifically on Trout's research on parents with handicapped children (1983). Explaining that she believed that they had been holding themselves back from acknowledging their very strong feelings about Katie's condition, she offered them the opportunity to express these feelings over the next six months. They agreed to renegotiate the contract at the end of that time.

Based on the objectives, the contract provided specificity about the number and duration of sessions, who would participate, and the substance of the work.

Mode of Evaluation

Specifically developing measurable objectives, Sheila reviewed each of them as she evaluated her practice effectiveness. She evaluated the Georgios' knowledge about Katie's medical condition and educational capacities after six weeks by their ability to identify and access the different reports about Katie, and their scheduling of monthly meetings with the medical staff and primary teacher. Her evaluation was based on changes in the Georgios' behavior—increased assertiveness in managing Katie's case—not merely on their statements of increased comfort.

Sheila's examination of her theoretical choices convinced her of the success of the psychosocial and educational approaches she utilized. At the same time that she provided support and increased the Georgios' comfort, she taught them the specifics of agency procedures and scheduled the initial meetings with the other staff until they became familiar with the process.

Agreeing with the literature that supports extended grief for parents of children with handicaps (Moses, 1987), Sheila set a one-year time period for a decrease in the amount of Lynn's crying. On the other hand, she looked to see a change in Rick from anger to feelings of sadness after four weeks. Drawing on Worden (1982), Sheila believed that Rick must experience his grief and that there were tasks he could be assigned to help him move through the process. When Sheila asked Rick to maintain a log in which he was to enter his feelings each day, at the end of the month he reported almost no anger, with periods of sadness several times per week. Log recording was a tool Sheila regularly utilized to assist clients in becoming aware of their feelings and she was pleased that it had again been effective.

A believer in homework assignments for her clients, Sheila asked the Georgios to spend four hours a week together doing something they enjoyed before having children. In reviewing the period prior to Katie's birth, they recalled how much fun they had dancing and signed up for dancing lessons at the local high school. A combination of psychosocial casework (Hollis, 1981) and Satir's family therapy (1964) provided the Georgios a means of recapturing some of the romance in their relationship. Sheila always found such client tasks useful in helping clients to change.

The Georgios reported comfort with their parenting roles after six months. Closely related to achievement of the other objectives, Sheila process-recorded or videotaped her sessions with the Georgios to assure that each time they met their work addressed parenting issues. Intensive review of her own interactions with clients provided Sheila with the means to keep improving her effectiveness. Having decided that parenting roles was an overarching concern and knowing how easy it was to get sidetracked, Sheila used process recordings to check her work to assure that parenting issues got included each time.

Guiding Theories

While familiar with the work of Kübler-Ross on the stages of grief (1969) and Tatelbaum's later work on grief stages (1980), Sheila resonated to a letter written by Freud to a friend whose son died: "We find a place for what we lose. Although we know that after such a loss the acute stage of mourning will subside, we also know that we shall remain inconsolable and will never find a substitute. No matter what may fill the gap, even if it be filled completely, it nevertheless remains something else" (Freud, 1961, p. 386).

Personal and professional experience had convinced Sheila that life is not lived in rigid stages, problems are not always resolved, and respect for clients' feelings enables clients to accept these feelings as well. Instead of viewing grief as a life event that must be resolved or passed through, Sheila drew on Trout's work on chronic sorrow:

> Many parents in our study seemed to be grieving for a lost child even as they stared at their living—but handicapped—newborn. . . . The loss is made worse by the fact that the deceased cannot be seen and held, then concretely released and grieved. . . . The feelings of grief are complicated by the very real demands of the new baby, and by the guilt that often accompanies the yearning for the lost perfect child while the living and defective child beckons. (1983, pp. 338–339)

Accepting the permanence of their very real loss, and not trying to hide or block those feelings from their consciousness or from each other, would, according to Sheila's thinking, enable the Georgios to incorporate the sadness into their lives. Explaining that true grief symptomatology continually resurfaced for parents of handicapped children, Trout argued that:

> For some parents, the overpowering sense of loss recurs at milestones in the life of the fantasized child [the normal one who was never born]. The day the "child we didn't have" would have waved good-bye and hopped on the bus for the first day of school becomes, instead, just another day of endless care for the multiply impaired child. (1983, p. 341)

Work on dream dissolution, the loss of the fantasy of what might have been, by Tomko (1983) supports Trout's position that this type of grief is highly intense. Similar is Moses's (1987) concept of the "shattered dream," which states that the fantasied normal child is continually grieved yet intangible, a being only the parent knows. Davis (1987) concurs with Tomko that lost fantasies as well as lost realities must be addressed and suggests that the mourning for a disabled child is cyclic and not always resolvable.

Kratochvil and Devereux have conducted research with parents of older disabled children. Though they are well adjusted, with solid employment and stable home environments, these parents continue to experience grief. The mother of a 21-year-old cried "every now and again. Maybe it doesn't come out where tears are actually shed, but inside you cry that she's not capable of doing things the way the other children are" (1988, p. 422). Sheila particularly appreciated Kratochvil and Devereux's (1988) advice to social workers for continued follow-up with these families and their suggestion that consultative services be made available to parent associations who provide group support to these parents.

Finally, Sheila also utilized Satir's emphasis on reacquainting families with happier times to provide them with a means of balancing their grief with a strong marital union (Satir, 1964). As we see in Sheila's discussion in practitioner observation, her personal and professional experiences shaped her decision to utilize these particular theories and strategies.

The Intervention as Uniquely Social Work

Relationship to Mission, Values, and Ethics

The social work thrust on *social functioning* is manifest as Sheila considers the *individual* pain of Lynn and Rick within context of the *environment* of their marital relationship, Katie's condition, and their interaction with their son, Peter. *Coordination with agency* medical and educational staff is an important component of their work. County and state funds supported Katie's educational and medical treatment, and these *policies* provided Katie with excellent education and medical care. With a decrease in the availability of long-term services, the *agency's mission* of extended care to children with handicaps met an important need in the community. Sheila had to be familiar with eligibility requirements and had to complete the necessary forms, including a thorough intake report and follow-up treatment plan. When Katie nears the age of 12, the social worker will need knowledge about other *community resources* to make appropriate referrals for her further care.

Respecting the Georgios as *self-determining*, Sheila reviewed with them the range of options for Katie's care. And applying the principle of *informed consent*, she directly discussed the strengths and limitations of the many treatment options. Based on this knowledge, the Georgios needed to make the decision they believed was best for their family and for Katie.

Encompassing the Components of Social Work Practice

Building a *belief bonding*, Sheila demonstrated belief in the Georgios' worth and capacity to change while also conveying her belief in her own ability to help them. She made use of *exploration, validation,* and *reflection* as well as the *communication skills* of *using silence, focusing,* and *providing information*. Based on her case theory that the Georgios needed to permit themselves to grieve, Sheila relied heavily on the tool of *validation*, in which she offered support for their feelings. She also *explored* their feelings with them and *reflected* back what she heard them saying. *Providing knowledge* from the literature and from the agency staff was an important component in their work together.

Chronic or recurrent sorrow (Trout, 1983) was the thrust of Sheila's *case theory*. As she explained:

....

This concept suggests what a profound loss of relationship is felt by the parents. While the Georgios are very affectionate, loving, and interactive with Katie, there are still many aspects of their parent-child interaction with Katie which are lost. My focus on Lynn's feelings in the earlier session was based on my belief that the couple's marital problems partly resulted from Lynn's difficulties in expressing her feelings to Rick and his difficulty in hearing her. Modeling for Rick, I was patient in letting Lynn express herself. I also wanted him to see that she could show grief, even cry, and then get herself back together. Though Rick has expressed some feelings of loss, he struggles with his inclination to comply with male sex stereotyping and maintenance of control.

....

Since the Georgios might always confront this chronic sorrow, it was important, according to Sheila's hypothesis, that they find a place for it in their lives, yet not allow themselves to be paralyzed by their grief. Also drawing on Worden (1982) and Tatelbaum (1980), who believe that people need to experience grief, she was teaching Rick that expressing his feelings could be more helpful than "bottling them up."

Aware that they love Katie and were still reeling from the unfairness of what has happened to them and their child, Sheila recognized that the Georgios would need to consider her limitations realistically in their future planning for her.

While acknowledging their terrible loss, Sheila utilized exercises from Tomko's work (1983) on shattered dreams to help them process their feelings. As with Susan's development of a case theory, the theory Sheila turned to helps shape formulation of her case theory, impacting further on her utilization of other theories for strategies of the intervention.

Also, like Jill in Chapter 7, Sheila had to decide about the use of self-disclosure. Acknowledgement of the difficulties she experienced with her child's kidney condition was used only to help Mr. Georgio generalize his difficulty with sad feelings to other males. Placing his behavior within the context of learned male attitudes suggested that there were alternative ways of handling such feelings, the crying of Sheila's husband being offered as one such option.

Nonetheless, this seemingly simple intervention required Sheila to do a great deal of processing. Discussing her feelings in supervision and immersing herself in the literature, Sheila felt comfortable that she was maintaining a distinction between her own issues as a parent of a disabled child and those of the Georgios, and that the example could be helpful to her client. Still, it was her own recurrent sorrow that prompted her to draw on the particular theorists she utilized. As she says:

....

Though my son is now 14 and can lead a relatively normal life, dialysis will always be part of his experience as will a vulnerability to poor health. Not a day passes where I don't have sadness that he cannot live a more "normal" life. He will never be able to confront the same choices of other people, and I will never get over the unfairness of what happened to all of us.

....

At the same time Sheila has to acknowledge and articulate her own feelings, she attends to the best use of herself as the Georgios' social worker. Whether the approach and theories that made sense to her would also be most applicable to them Sheila determined by becoming familiar with a range of the literature and effectively using supervision and consultation with peers. Sheila and the Georgios shared the same religion—the Catholic faith (the Georgios are of Italian descent)—and she had to decide whether to bring spirituality into the sessions. Learning that the Georgios regularly attended church, and cognizant of the debate within the profession about whether there was a place for spirituality in the practice of social workers (Canda, 1989), Sheila decided that spiritual counseling was already available to her clients and did not incorporate issues of faith into her practice with them. Through a continual process of self-awareness she could make informed decisions and function as a professional social worker, focusing on the needs of the Georgios rather than her own issues.

Case 4: Catalina and the Wrights

The final case study comes from a hospice setting, where a child confronted the death of a parent. During the social worker Catalina's fourth visit to Bill, he requested help in preparing for a visit from his 12-year-old daughter, Polly, who would be arriving the next day for a week. Dying from AIDS, Bill, divorced five years previously, was a successful lawyer in his midforties. Insistent that Polly not be told the nature of his disease, he had told her he had cancer (which he did, as a consequence of the HIV virus).

Since her parents' divorce, Polly spent Christmas and summer vacations with Bill on the west coast. He had not seen her for several months, during which time his health had deteriorated. Bill was now emaciated and had daily visits from homemaking services and one hot meal delivery from Meals on Wheels.

Assigned to the unit providing services to the dying patient, Catalina knew there might be only limited time to work with Bill. Concerned about his adamant wish to keep the AIDS diagnosis a secret from Polly, she asked if he would be willing to discuss this further with her. Also in her forties, Catalina had a lively manner, with great ease at talking about many topics. Even after working with hospice for almost five years, however, she still had to fortify herself when visiting dying patients in their homes. Believing that it was important to maintain boundaries, she always made sure to bring a chair into the room so that the patient would not have to share the bed.

Catalina shared with Bill her respect for him and the courage with which he was addressing his death (getting papers and legal work in order and talking quite openly with his doctors about the time frame for his expected death). Yet, at the same time, she confronted him with her worry for Polly if he forbade Hospice workers and family members to discuss the nature of his disease with her. Drawing on the literature about children grieving the death of a parent, which advocates for open and honest discussion about the death, she advised him that his wish could hinder Polly's later adjustment (Woelfelt, 1990; Rando, 1984). At the same time, she shared with him that a frank discussion with Polly could be very upsetting for both of them; intense anger and sadness were possible. Her confrontation led them into a discussion about the stigma attached to AIDS and his worries about Polly once she knew that her father was gay. Their session ended with Bill's agreeing to reconsider his decision.

Called to the home two days after Polly left, Catalina got there an hour before Bill's death. He was in a coma, however, and never regained consciousness. When Polly returned for the funeral services, Catalina got to spend some time with her. They found a private place to talk, and Catalina gave her a hug.

POLLY: What was it like when my father died?

CATALINA: I was called by the spiritual counselor, who was requested by your dad. When I got there he was in a coma. Though he couldn't respond, I talked with him and told him I valued him and respected his courage. I sat there with him until he died.

POLLY: *(crying)* I didn't get a chance to say goodbye. . . . I meant to call him that night before, but I was so busy and forgot.

CATALINA: You know, Polly, your dad would not have been able to talk with you anyway. He was in a coma. I think he knew when he said goodbye to you a few days ago that it would be his last conversation with you.

POLLY: Why didn't he tell me so that I could say goodbye?

CATALINA: I don't know. I believe you can still do that, in a way. Think of what you would like to tell him. We can arrange to have that conversation together later today and I can help you. It will also be important for you to have people who you can talk with later, after you return home. I can contact people like me in your state to get in touch with you. Will you be able to talk with your mom, or aunt?

POLLY: Yes, I can talk with my mom. You know, my dad and I talked about a lot of things when I was with him. I finally felt close to him again. He told me that he has had several close friends since his separation from my mother, and that some of them have been men.

CATALINA: How are you feeling about that?

POLLY: I'm just feeling so scared. Sounds like my dad was different from how I knew him, and now he's dead and I can't talk with him anymore. *(long pause)* Dead sounds so scary.

CATALINA: What seems scary to you?

POLLY: I don't know. *(long pause)* Just seeing someone die.

CATALINA: What do you think happens when someone dies?

POLLY: They roll around and make a lot of noise, then they stop breathing and their eyes roll back into their heads.

CATALINA: I've never seen that happen. Usually breathing changes, it gets very shallow and they breathe sort of like this. *(illustrates by taking short breaths)* Sometimes there is a sigh as they take their last breath and other times they stop breathing without a sound. Most often they look peaceful when it is over. *(long pause)* That is how your Dad looked.

Catalina's Plan of Intervention

Problem Statement

Because of the time-limited nature of hospice services—in some situations there are only one or two visits—Catalina integrated her assessment report and plan of intervention. Dual concerns were addressed in the problem statement—the immediate issue of Bill's dying and the longer-term matter of Polly's adjustment to her father's death. Catalina believed that *Bill's capacity to confront his imminent death was being complicated by the unease he was experiencing about his homosexuality and concerns about his daughter's image of him. In addition, the daughter, Polly would have initial feelings to confront around the death of her father.*

Short- and Long-Term Objectives

While Catalina's objectives would be short term, long-range concerns could be identified and discussed with the family for follow-up work. Brought in because of Bill's terminal illness, her primary objective was to assist him in facing his death, with a reduction of some of the fear and anxiety. Providing his daughter, Polly, with an opportunity to talk about her feelings after his death, and assessing her need for longer-term follow-up, was the other objective they each identified.

Contracting

In her initial session with Bill, she responded to his request for hospice services by explaining that her work was to be responsive to his needs as he was facing his impending death. Yet at the same time, she told him, she might raise concerns or questions for him. They agreed to meet twice a week and that she would be available to receive phone calls from him and, if necessary, to schedule more frequent visits.

When Catalina also clarified that there were other hospice services available to family members after his death, Bill agreed that he would like his daughter, Polly, to have the opportunity to discuss her feelings with someone, preferably Catalina.

Mode of Evaluation

Process records of her sessions with clients provided Catalina with a means of assuring that she did focus the sessions on the issues of dying—which was what brought them together. Though objectives and contract are always clear in these cases, Catalina stated that she was continually surprised at how easy it was to get sidetracked.

....

Even though I have been doing this work for some time it is easy for me to slip into avoiding the central issue—the death. I have noticed that clients will accommodate that because they are sensitive to the discomfort people have in talking with them about their dying. But usually, they want and are in need of that very conversation. They are busy taking care of other people's feelings, and they should not have to do that with the hospice worker!

....

Regular review of her process recordings in supervision and occasional use of audio tapes helped Catalina monitor the amount of time she spent addressing the topic of death in each of her client sessions. Increases in clients' requests for sessions with her, and their positive comments in a survey about the usefulness of the treatment that they had been helped in feeling less anxious, also provided support for her services.

Harder to evaluate was the effectiveness of follow-up services to family members. While Catalina got Polly started on her grief process, Polly resided in another part of the country, making it difficult for Catalina to check back with her at a later date about her adjustment. The bigger problem was that large-scale studies have not been conducted comparing the adjustment to death by people who have received hospice services versus those who have not. Design and implementation of such a study would be very difficult, not the least of which would be the definition of a good adjustment to death! As we saw with the Georgios, there are many views in the literature about normalcy in the grieving process.

In Catalina's agency, questionnaires were completed by family members providing their feedback about hospice services. Some information was obtained that evaluated overall agency service provision (availability and flexibility of services and other administrative matters) as well as the social worker's individual treatment (did the social worker listen, appear interested in them, seem competent and knowledgeable?).

Guiding Theories

Unlike Sheila in the previous case study, Catalina relied on the work of Kübler-Ross (1969) to understand the grieving process. Helping clients to experience each of the five stages was a central part of her intervention.

Developing phases of grief through observations in her work with the dying, Kübler-Ross posited that initially persons experienced *shock, denial,* and *isolation,* thinking, "This can't be true." *Anger* is the second stage, which may be projected or displaced onto the environment and other persons. *Bargaining* follows, where the individual tries to strike a deal promising good behavior for a cancellation of the impending death. The fourth stage is *depression,* in which the dying experience the sadness of their situation. And finally comes *acceptance,* in which if the individual "has had enough time . . . and has been given some help in working through the previously described stages, he will reach a stage during which he is neither depressed nor angry" (1969, p. 112).

Also informing Catalina's intervention was Jewett's work on grieving in children, which suggests that treatment is necessary for children coping with parent deaths: "Because every major loss disrupts the development of self-esteem, the smooth progression of life, and the sense that events are predictable and meaningful, recovery from such a loss requires that damaged self-esteem be repaired, continuity be reestablished and a sense of meaning be restored" (1982, p. 129).

Implicit in the theories that view grieving as a series of stages that must be experienced is the assumption that grief was resolvable—experiencing the stages of grief resulted in a process of resolution. Simos supports this perspective in her discussion of grief as part of the life cycle: "The adolescent on the way to maturity faces a number of losses. He must relinquish and mourn the infantile body, the infantile identity and role, and the childhood image of his parents. The failure to work through these losses results in a person who has achieved chronological but not emotional maturity" (1979, p. 16).

Catalina also drew on children's books that address the death of parents, including Boulden, 1989; Buscaglia, 1982; and Viorst, 1971. The stories provided an entry into discussing the grieving, especially when the child had trouble in talking with her.

The Intervention as Uniquely Social Work

Relationship to Mission, Values, and Ethics

Based on a holistic view, hospice care addresses the needs of dying *individuals* within the immediate *environments* of their homes. Attention is also paid to the family members and to the available resources for health care and ongoing maintenance needs of the client. Knowledge is necessary about *policies* regulating funding for the needed services and euthanasia. Catalina's intervention was shaped by the time-limited nature of her agency's services. With services to the dying patient the main focus of her unit, *referrals* to other hospice departments and to other community settings was a basic component of Catalina's work with clients. Reflecting the multiple social work perspective of person and environment, attention is given to the *community*, the *agency*, and *policies* and *regulations*.

While respecting Bill as a *self-determining* individual and the *confidentiality* of their work together, Catalina also structured the practice so that he could make decisions with *informed consent*. Advising him that "coming out" with Polly could be very difficult for her, she also shared from the literature that working through grief is facilitated by prior honest discussion with the dying person.

Encompassing the Components of Social Work Practice

Facile in establishing the professional *relationship*, Catalina developed a belief bonding with both Bill and Polly. Viewing Catalina as the last link with her father, Polly quickly turned to her for *information* and *support*. Responding to cues from Polly, Catalina physically reached out to touch her with a hug. In other uses of *communication*, Catalina *validated* both Bill and Polly—she stayed with each of them in respecting where they were, putting no pressure on them to feel or think differently. Also utilizing *exploration*, Catalina "reached for" them to describe their current experience, *using silence* effectively in not rushing to answer difficult questions for them. *Confrontation* was an important method in assisting Bill to consider alternative ways of handling his final contacts with Polly.

Catalina's *case theory* was that the difficult process of confronting death is exacerbated for Bill by his reluctance to discuss his homosexuality with his daughter, Polly. Yet for Bill to reach the stage of acceptance posited by Kübler-Ross, he needed to clear his conscience of this unresolved issue. Similarly for Polly, an honest and emotion-laden final meeting with her father would facilitate her acceptance of his death.

As Catalina stated:

....

It is the job of hospice social workers to help children understand that death and dying are part of the life cycle; that we experience feelings and emotions about these losses which need not only to be expressed but also heard by another human being, that we find ways to reconcile our feelings into a new and different life. Helping children to participate in the lives of dying parents, encouraging open communication about their concerns and feelings, and being there with them in their sadness and tears while allowing them to continue to be a child produces positive outcomes.

....

Gestalt therapy's "empty chair" technique (Perls, 1969) provided a vehicle for Polly to complete the "goodbye" conversation with her father. Catalina found a quiet spot in which Polly and she could talk and, placing a chair in front of Polly, helped her engage in the conversation that she could not have with her dead father.

Agreeing with Christ and colleagues (1991) from the Sloan-Kettering Memorial Cancer Center in New York that it is optimal for children to work through the death at least six months before its occurrence, Catalina was concerned that Polly did not have that opportunity. Greenberg also emphasized that the child's successful adjustment to the death experience is dependent on "intra-familial communication and shared expression of feelings" (1975, p. 396).

Rando's work with the mourning of young children also shaped Catalina's thinking:

> The fact that children do not continuously evidence grief in overtly visible ways erroneously leads some to believe that they do not understand the loss or recognize its implications, or else that they are not grieved by it. Nevertheless, children do mourn, even when it is not clearly evident. (1984, p. 154)

Strongly believing that it was critical for Polly's future that she address and work through her feelings with a professional, Catalina relied on some of Woelfelt's (1990) suggestions about helping the child identify a support system and coping mechanisms.

Of Hispanic background, Catalina found comfort from her Catholic religion, as did Sheila in the previous case study. She believed in an afterlife and did not approach dying patients with the discomfort she observed in her co-workers. She needed to recognize this difference, however, in her interventions with clients, many of whom did not share these views. While her calm could bring solace to some of her clients, others might find it a lack of interest or attention. Practitioner observation is an important ingredient in Catalina's successful work with dying patients and their families.

Although she had been a social worker for over fifteen years, with five at the hospice, Catalina continued to find her work challenging and, usually, rewarding. Never quite knowing what to expect, especially on home visits (which made her uneasy), she relished the opportunity to get a different slant on things she thought she already knew. This is the engrossing and unpredictable nature of social work—everyone's story is simultaneously different and yet the same.

The constant presence of death provided Catalina with a different perspective on life:

....

Hospice work with death and dying has really more to do with living than with dying. It has made me acutely aware of the finiteness of life and the importance of creating meaning and worth in the limited time we all have. I try to see that when death arrives it is peaceful, nothing to be feared, and that with losses we gain new insights and new hope.

....

ADDITIONAL NOTES

We conclude this chapter with a sample plan of intervention. Remember that in Chapter 5 we discussed the format of the assessment report, which focuses on background information and the nature of the presenting problem formulated during initial sessions with the client. As the thrust of this summary, the social worker's case theory provides a comprehensive analysis of the situation and a detailed statement and understanding of the problem. Also included is a beginning treatment plan and prognosis. After an interim period of not more than three months, the intake summary should be followed up with a plan of intervention. Development of this treatment plan includes a review of the adequacy of those initial formulations along with a consideration of what has transpired in the work with the client up to that time. The thrust shifts from an understanding of what the client is presenting to a strategy for change.

In the following sample plan of intervention the client was Lester, a 28-year-old White male. Single, he had been underemployed since his graduation from an ivy league university several years before. Raymond and Beth, the social workers, both had Ph.Ds and were employed with a Veteran's Administration hospital in the Midwest. Beth's special training was in family therapy, while Raymond worked primarily with individuals and groups, both inpatient and outpatient. Lester was referred by the alcohol treatment program to Raymond and Beth, who functioned as a team in outpatient psychiatry. When Lester had been a patient for two months in their day treatment program, they requested outpatient treatment concurrent to their weekly group support meetings. His attendance at the daily group meeting had been sporadic for the previous two weeks.

Plan of Intervention

Problem Statement

It is a good idea to begin the plan of intervention by reviewing, and perhaps reformulating, the case theory you developed in the assessment report. After these intervening weeks you should be better able to form a clear and concise presentation of your understanding of the client's problem.

If you are in a setting that provides only short-term services, your treatment plan will probably also function as the intake summary. In this type of situation it is important that you develop a clear statement of the problem and include basic background information at the beginning of your treatment plan. The important point is that you need a problem statement to direct the intervention. If you have a case theory from your assessment report, modify it, taking into account new information you have gathered since its development. If there is no previous case theory, formulate a statement of the problem and include some of the basic identifying information you would have presented in the assessment report—how the client came to the agency, what the person requested, and basic demographics. How you understand the problem situation is of central importance and should be stated briefly and clearly.

While a thorough diagnostic summary was available from Lester's two months of treatment with the alcohol unit, Raymond followed up on some of the issues raised in the initial intake report including obesity, substance abuse, and depression. Taking advantage of the services available in a large medical facility, he asked for a thorough physical examination and conducted a mental status review—a standard set of questions utilized by the setting to evaluate suicide and homicide risk and to provide data about any psychotic thinking (similar to the one used by Cara in Chapter 3). The medical exam indicated an unhealthy weight with the presence of an eating disorder—gorging on food. Some suicide risk and chronic depression were evident from the mental status exam. While the physician wanted to recommend antidepressant medication, he refrained because of the substance abuse—the patient reported getting drunk on an average several times per week.

Because a comprehensive case theory was already developed in the initial assessment, Raymond and Beth constructed the following problem statement—briefer than the case theory and emphasizing their own understanding of Lester's problem situation:

....

Lester has experienced depression, including feelings of suicide, worthlessness, and anxiety from the time he was a young child—the client's earliest memory was of not feeling good about himself. Always overweight, he had few friends but was a good student. When he was away in college he was the happiest. While he traveled for several months after graduation, his mother unexpectedly died within the year. Upon her death, Lester was unable to resolve his very close relationship with her.

Moving in with his father and living near his sister, his drinking and eating has increased. He has become isolated from others and dependent upon his family for living needs and all social interaction and emotional support.

While feeling protected by his mother, he also resented her doting behavior and now feels unprepared to deal with the world. He is trying to recreate his earlier family system, behaving as the younger and needy kid brother with the sister, who is a psychologist.

His primary problem is the depression, with the overeating and alcohol as secondary symptoms.

....

Objectives

Discuss with clients what objectives they bring to the treatment and articulate with them those you are identifying, striving to make them concrete and observable. This is not always as easy as it sounds. Often clients come in to see social workers with only very vague goals, such as: I want to feel less anxious, or I want to have a better life. It will be impossible, however, to document adequately whether you are being helpful to the client without clarity of purpose.

Though it is best to have agreement on all objectives, there are situations where the client and social worker acknowledge additional goals without agreeing on them. Raymond, Beth and Lester agree on the following objectives:

....

1. *Stop drinking.*
2. *Reach a medically recommended weight.*
3. *Increase social life by some planned activity with others at least twice a week.*
4. *Feel less depressed.*
5. *Work through feelings and loss of mother.*

Lester did not agree with the following objectives:

6. *Decrease involvement with father and sister.*
7. *Get employment.*

....

While the first three objectives and the seventh were clear, objectives 4, 5, and 6 were not as operational (measurable). Although Lester did not concur that he was overinvolved with his family, Raymond and Beth shared that this was their assessment and that over the course of their sessions with him they would further clarify and strive to include the goal in their work together. Lester was also not interested in getting a job, but again, the social workers stated that this was one of their goals for him and they would return to discuss that in future sessions with him. He did agree to have as an objective a discussion about his concerns with employment.

Contracting

Here you negotiate what you and the client will need to do in order to obtain the objectives, including the strategy for accomplishing the work. Even once you have clear objectives, it may not be self-evident how to get clients from where they are to where they want to be—if it were, they would be able to accomplish all these things without any professional help!

....

We advised Lester that in our experience the twelve-step programs such as Alcoholics Anonymous had the best results with changing compulsive habits like his drinking and overeating. As a Jewish person, however, Lester was not comfortable with the spiritual message that permeates those programs. Instead, we agreed that Lester would attend every day for the next two weeks the group treatment meetings through the hospital. Whenever he felt like having a drink he would call the group leader or crisis hot line.

For the weight loss, Lester agreed to visit with the hospital dietician and craft a diet to meet some of his food tastes but result in a slow weight loss of five pounds per week.

Lester acknowledged that several of the group members got together after meetings for a movie and agreed to join them, just once a week for now.

We also shared our strategy with Lester. Raymond would meet with him for one hour every week and focus on the early relationship with his mother. After the drinking activity ended, a referral would be made to the psychiatrist for antidepressant medication (emerging from objectives 4 and 5). We shared with Lester that the recent literature supports a biological component to depression (Markowitz, 1991), and that his chances of feeling less depressed might be markedly improved if he were able to take one of the antidepressant medications.

Beth would then meet with Lester and his father and sister for a total of four sessions, two hours each. Sessions would be videotaped and might be viewed by the family together or just by Lester. Explaining that she would do a genogram to provide a historical picture of his family through several generations (McGoldrick & Gerson, 1985), Beth told Lester that she and he would meet together with Raymond.

We also advised Lester that the two of us would meet together as a team, and occasionally with the group leader, to plan treatment.

....

Mutuality was evident—all parties had a clear set of responsibilities, demonstrating commitment to the therapeutic process. Number and frequency of sessions were agreed on, with an evaluation session at the end of two months to "take stock" of where things are.

It will not be unusual for you to have goals that you and your clients do not agree on. When this occurs, you may acknowledge with clients what you would like for them to accomplish and contract for a later reconsideration. Or, as Raymond and Beth did, you may reframe the goal to obtain agreement.

Mode of Evaluation

As we discussed earlier, you must be able to document the changes resulting from your intervention and identify what has contributed to the results.

Raymond and Beth maintained logs in which they recorded the problems clients present to them, the treatment applied, and the results. They also process-recorded at least a 5-minute segment of sessions as well as audio or videotaping each session.

....

With the good results of the outpatient treatment program in reducing alcohol abuse, we will ask to have weekly meetings with them and Lester to determine progress on the drinking. Client self-reports and interaction in the group meetings will serve to evaluate alcohol abstinence. After meetings with the dietician, Lester will also report on his weight at these meetings. He will also maintain a social diary, reporting his activities, amount of time spent, and who initiated the contact. The diagnostic criteria for major depressive episode taken from the diagnostic and statistical manual of mental disorders (DSM-III-R) will be administered after one month to measure changes in his level of depression. Another mental status review will also be completed by Lester at that time.

In our log we will make regular entries to track the relationship of our guiding theories with change in the client's behavior.

....

Change process research (Reid, 1990) considers the interaction between the process of each intervention and the outcome variables. Through analyses of process recordings and videotapes Raymond and Beth examined the things they said, including the communication methods and skills, and monitored the development of the belief bonding and their use of practitioner observation.

Guiding Theories

The more than twenty experienced social work practitioners interviewed for this book, and the hundreds of social workers this author has had the good fortune to know in her almost twenty-five years of practice, agree that while theory guides the practice, the social worker alone is responsible for making decisions about which theories to employ with each client. Even those social workers trained in a particular model, such as psychodynamic or structural, do not always so limit themselves—rather, in deciding how to best understand and intervene with a client, they discriminate among the many available theories.

In your plan of intervention, identify the theories you are utilizing for understanding the client and implementing the strategy of change. There may be particular models your agency supports and those you believe help explain the change process.

Raymond believed that object relations offered a relevant perspective through which to understand Lester, while Beth wanted to utilize family systems theory and Bowen. They commented:

....

Lester appears to still be defined by the relationship with his mother. As he describes his childhood, he never adequately separated from her (Mahler, 1963). In his current relationships he seems to continue to evoke the same pathogenic responses from his father and sister where he feels incapable, infantilized and resentful while they feel anger and manipulated by him (Blanck & Blanck, 1979).

While these theories may offer some means of understanding Lester, there is enough evidence available about the physiological basis to depression (Markowitz, 1991), that we need to consider the use of antidepressant medication. Most likely, helping Lester better understand the impact of his early childhood on his current life will not be enough to help him change these current destructive patterns. Therefore, abstinence from the alcohol is the initial goal. Self-help groups have been generally effective in providing support and confrontation in the acquisition of abstinence. Although Lester is not interested in joining Alcoholics Anonymous, he is willing to participate regularly in the group program run through the hospital. Utilizing Shulman's work on phases of the group process (1979), our evaluation of the group's effectiveness has been pretty high. Over the past year, 40 percent (15 males) of those participating regularly have abstained from drinking.

Once his drinking is under control, some family systems work (Bloch, 1973) along with use of the genogram (McGoldrick & Gerson, 1985) can provide Lester with greater understanding of his family with specifics to change some of the patterns of interaction.

....

Additional Thoughts

Just as in the assessment report, it is fine to include a section in which you share some of the thoughts with which you are grappling. Some social workers like to discuss prognosis for success and failure, in which they share their thinking about the likelihood of success for this plan of intervention, identifying the factors that may contribute to success and those that may interfere. Such a process can enable the social worker to foresee potential difficulties and plan around them.

SUMMARY

Social work treatment emerges from the case theory of the assessment, is related to the stated objectives, and encompasses all the components of social work practice that have been developed throughout this book.

Intervention has been defined as

෬   *The mode of procedure used by the social worker to create change in the life of the client. Emerging from the goals and based on the case theory, a plan of treatment states the problem, outlines a strategy of the specific steps in the social work practice, and includes a means of evaluation. Both short- and long-term objectives are identified to establish definitive end points. Contracting between the social worker and the client produces a mutual engagement in the process. Intervention is guided by theories and assumptions about human behavior and the process of change, by the presenting problem, by the agency's mission and social work role, and by the ethics and values of the profession. Encompassing the components of social work practice, the intervention is a reflection of the relationship, shaped by the case theory, and employs communication methods and skills and practitioner observation.*

Donald Schon (1983) has introduced the term *reflection-in-action* to describe professional behavior. Just as for other professionals, much of the knowledge that social workers possess is tacit knowledge. That is to say, the knowledge base for practice behaviors is implicit in the behaviors, an intuitive knowing. This is the art of professional practice; the thinking occurs outside the social worker's awareness. There is first a doing, then an awareness of the thinking behind the doing. While actions are based on knowing, the social worker cannot articulate that foundation unless asked.

Social work practice encompasses both art and science. In the case studies we examined here, social workers have articulated their thinking and provided the basis for their decision making. The continuing articulation of their knowing and doing by practitioners of social work maximizes the technology of the profession's science and enhances the beauty of its art. Just as painters approach a blank canvas each day, so social workers need to start each client contact as a fresh beginning. Easy as it would be to get mired in the gritty details of life, how liberating to believe that one can start anew! Social work cannot be practiced without this deep belief in the continuing possibility for change.

BIBLIOGRAPHY

American Psychiatric Association. (1987). *Diagnostic and statistical manual of mental disorders.* (3rd ed., rev.). Washington, D.C.: APA.

Beck, A. (1961). An inventory for measuring depression. *Archives of General Psychiatry, 4,* 561–571.

Beck, A., Rush, A., Shaw B., & Emery G. (1979). *Cognitive theory of depression.* New York: Guilford Press.

Berndit, D., & Petzel, T. (1980). Development and initial evaluation of a multi-score depression inventory. *Journal of Personality Assessment, 44,* 396–403.

Blanck, G., & Blanck, R. (1979). *Ego psychology II.* New York: Columbia University Press.

Bloch, D. (Ed.). (1973). *Techniques of family psychotherapy: A primer.* New York: Grune & Stratton.

Blythe, B., & Tripodi, T. (1989). *Measurement in direct social work practice: Guidelines for practitioners.* Newbury Park, Calif.: Sage.

Boulden, J. (1989). *Saying good-bye activity book.* Santa Rosa, Calif.: Jim Boulden Publishing.

Bowen, M. (1978). *Family therapy in clinical practice.* New York: Aronson.

Buscaglia, L. (1982). *The fall of Freddie the leaf: A story of life for all ages.* Thorofare, N.J.: Charles Slack.

Canda, E. (1989). Religious content in social work education: A comparative approach. *Journal of Social Work Education, 25:* 1, 36–45.

Christ, G., Siegel, K., Mesagno, F., & Langosch, D. (1991). A preventive intervention program for bereaved children: Problems of implementation. *American Journal of Orthopsychiatry, 61:* 2, 171.

Compton, B., & Galaway, B. (Eds.). (1989). *Social work processes.* Belmont, Calif.: Wadsworth.

Corcoran, K. (1985). Clinical practice with nonbehavioral methods: Strategies for evaluation. *Clinical Social Work Journal, 3,* 78–86.

Davis, B. (1987). Disability and grief. *Social Casework, 68,* 352–357.

Dicks, H. V. (1967). *Marital tensions.* New York: Basic Books.

Egan, G. (1986). *The skilled helper.* 3rd ed. Monterey, Calif.: Brooks/Cole.

Erikson, E. (1963). *Childhood and society.* New York: W. W. Norton.

Fairbairn, W. R. (1954). *An object relations theory of personality.* New York: Basic Books.

Fitzpatrick, R., & Feldman, J. (Eds.). (1992). *Managed mental health care.* Washington, D.C.: American Psychiatric Press.

Framo, J. L. (1981). The integration of marital therapy sessions with family of origin. In A. S. Gurman & D. P. Kniskern (Eds.), *Handbook of family therapy.* New York: Brunner/Mazel.

Freud, E. L. (Ed.) (1961). *Letters of Sigmund Freud.* New York: Basic Books.

Freud, S. (1923). *The ego and the id.* London: Hogarth Press.

Goldenberg, I., & Goldenberg, H. (1991). *Family therapy: An overview.* Monterey, Calif.: Brooks/Cole.

Greenberg, L. (1975). Therapeutic grief work with children. *Social Casework,* (July), 396–403.

Grinnell, R. (1993). *Social work research and evaluation*. Itasca, Ill.: F. E. Peacock.

Hartman, A. (1983). *Family-centered social work practice*. New York: Free Press.

Hollis, F., & Woods, M. (1981). *Casework: A psychosocial therapy*. New York: Random House.

Hudson, W. (1982). *The clinical measurement package*. Homewood, Ill.: Dorsey.

Jewett, C. (1982). Helping children cope with separation and loss. Boston: Harvard Common Press.

Kratochvil, M., & Devereux, S. (1988). Counseling needs of parents of handicapped children. *Social Casework, 69*, 420–426.

Kübler-Ross, E. (1969). *On death and dying*. New York: Macmillan.

Lassers, E., Nordan, R., & Bladholm, S. (1973). Steps in the return to school of children with school phobia. *American Journal of Psychiatry, 130:* 265–268.

McGoldrick, M., & Gerson, R. (1985). *Genograms in family assessment*. New York: W. W. Norton.

Mahler, M. (1963). Thoughts about development and individuation. *The psychoanalytic study of the child*, vol. 18, 307–324. New York: International Universities Press.

Maluccio, A., & Marlow, W. (1974). The case for the contract. *Social Work, 19:* 1, 28–36.

Markowitz, L. (1991). Better therapy through chemistry? *Family Therapy Networker* (May/June) 23–31.

Marlow, C. (1993). *Research methods*. Belmont, Calif.: Brooks/Cole.

Minuchin, S. (1974). *Families and family therapy*. Cambridge, Mass.: Harvard University Press.

Moses, K. (1987). *Lost dreams and growth* [videotape]. Chicago: Resource Networks.

Nelson, J. (1984). Intermediate treatment goals as variables in single-case research. *Social Work Research & Abstracts, 20*, 3–10.

Perls, F. (1969). *Gestalt therapy verbatim*. Lafayette, Calif.: Free People Press.

Piaget, J. (1963). *The origins of intelligence in children*. New York: W. W. Norton.

Rando, T. (1984). *Grief, dying and death: Clinical interventions for care-givers*. Champaign, Ill.: Research Press.

Reid, W. (1990). Change process research: A new paradigm? In L. Videka-Sherman & W. Reid (Eds.), *Advances in clinical social work* 130–148. Silver Spring, Md.: NASW.

Richmond, M. (1922). *What is social casework?* Philadelphia: Russell Sage.

Royse, D. (1991). *Research methods in social work.* Chicago: Nelson-Hall.

Satir, V. (1964). *Conjoint family therapy.* Palo Alto, Calif.: Science and Behavior Books.

Schon, D. (1983). *The reflective practitioner.* New York: Basic Books.

Seabury, B. (1979). Negotiating sound contracts with clients. *Public Welfare, 37:* 2, 33–39.

Shulman, L. (1979). *The skills of helping individuals and groups.* Itasca, Ill.: Peacock.

Simos, B. (1979). *A time to grieve.* New York: Family Service Association of America.

Siporin, M. (1975). *Introduction to social work practice.* New York: Macmillan.

Tatelbaum, J. (1980). *The courage to grieve.* New York: Harper & Row.

Tomko, B. (1983). Mourning the dissolution of a dream. *Social Work, 28,* 391–392.

Trout, M. (1983). Birth of a sick or handicapped infant: Impact on the family. *Child Welfare, 62,* 337–348.

Videka-Sherman, L., & Reid, W. (Eds.). (1990). *Advances in clinical social work research.* Silver Spring, Md.: NASW.

Viorst, J. (1971). *The tenth good thing about Barney.* New York: Macmillan.

Watzlawick, P., Weakland, J., & Fisch, R. (1974). *Change.* New York: W. W. Norton.

Woelfelt, A. (1990). *Helping children cope with grief.* Muncie, Ind.: Accelerated Development.

Wolpe, J. (1969). *The practice of behavior therapy.* New York: Pergamon Press.

Worden, J. (1982). *Grief counseling and grief therapy.* New York: Springer.

Yegidis, B., & Weinbach, R. (1991). *Research methods for social workers.* New York: Longman.

APPENDIX 1

THE SOCIAL WORK CODE OF ETHICS

As adopted by the 1979 NASW Delegate Assembly and revised by the 1990 NASW Delegate Assembly.

Preamble This code is intended to serve as a guide to the everyday conduct of members of the social work profession and as a basis for the adjudication of issues in ethics when the conduct of social workers is alleged to deviate from the standards expressed or implied in this code. It represents standards of ethical behavior for social workers in professional relationships with those served, with colleagues, with employers, with other individuals and professions, and with the community and society as a whole. It also embodies standards of ethical behavior governing individual conduct to the extent that such conduct is associated with an individual's status and identity as a social worker.

This code is based on the fundamental values of the social work profession that include the worth, dignity, and uniqueness of all persons as well as their rights and opportunities. It is also based on the nature of social work, which fosters conditions that promote these values.

In subscribing to and abiding by this code, the social worker is expected to view ethical responsibility in as inclusive a context as each situation demands and within which ethical judgement is required. The social worker is expected to take into consideration all the principles in this code that have a bearing upon any situation in which ethical judgement is to be exercised and professional intervention or conduct is planned. The course of action that the social worker chooses is expected to be consistent with the spirit as well as the letter of this code.

In itself, this code does not represent a set of rules that will prescribe all the behaviors of social workers in all the complexities of professional life. Rather, it offers general principles to guide conduct, and the judicious appraisal of conduct, in situations that have ethical implications. It provides the basis for making judgements about ethical actions before and after they occur. Frequently, the particular situation determines the ethical principles that apply and the manner of their application. In such cases, not only the particular ethical principles are taken into immediate consideration, but also the entire code and its spirit. Specific applications of ethical principles must be judged within the context in which they are being considered. Ethical behavior in a given situation must satisfy not only the judgement of the individual social worker, but also the judgement of an unbiased jury of professional peers.

This code should not be used as an instrument to deprive any social worker of the opportunity or freedom to practice with complete professional integrity; nor should any disciplinary action be taken on the basis of this code without maximum provision for safeguarding the rights of the social worker affected.

The ethical behavior of social workers results not from edict, but from a personal commitment of the individual. This code is offered to affirm the will and zeal of all social workers to be ethical and to act ethically in all that they do as social workers.

The following codified ethical principles should guide social workers in the various roles and relationships and at the various levels of responsibility in which they function professionally. These principles also serve as a basis for the adjudication by the National Association of Social Workers of issues in ethics.

In subscribing to this code, social workers are required to cooperate in its implementation and abide by any disciplinary rulings based on it. They should also take adequate measures to discourage, prevent, expose, and correct the unethical conduct of colleagues. Finally, social workers should be equally ready to defend and assist colleagues unjustly charged with unethical conduct.

Summary of Major Principles

I. **The social worker's conduct and comportment as a social worker**

   A. **Propriety.** The social worker should maintain high standards of personal conduct in the capacity or identity as social worker.

   B. **Competence and professional development.** The social worker should strive to become and remain proficient in professional practice and the performance of professional functions.

   C. **Service.** The social worker should regard as primary the service obligation of the social work profession.

   D. **Integrity.** The social worker should act in accordance with the highest standards of professional integrity.

   E. **Scholarship and research.** The social worker engaged in study and research should be guided by the conventions of scholarly inquiry.

II. **The social worker's ethical responsibility to clients**

   F. **Primacy of clients' interests.** The social worker's primary responsibility is to clients.

   G. **Rights and prerogatives of clients.** The social workers should make every effort to foster maximum self-determination on the part of clients.

  H. Confidentiality and privacy. The social worker should respect the privacy of clients and hold in confidence all information obtained in the course of professional service.

  I. Fees. When setting fees, the social worker should ensure that they are fair, reasonable, considerate, and commensurate with the service performed and with due regard for the clients' ability to pay.

III. **The social worker's ethical responsibility to colleagues**

  J. Respect, fairness, and courtesy. The social worker should treat colleagues with respect, courtesy, fairness, and good faith.

  K. Dealing with colleagues' clients. The social worker has the responsibility to relate to the clients of colleagues with full professional consideration.

IV. **The social worker's ethical responsibility to employers and employing organizations**

  L. Commitments to employing organizations. The social worker should adhere to commitments made to the employing organization.

V. **The social worker's ethical responsibility to the social work profession**

  M. Maintaining the integrity of the profession. The social worker should uphold and advance the values, ethics, knowledge, and mission of the profession.

  N. Community service. The social worker should assist the profession in making social services available to the general public.

  O. Development of knowledge. The social worker should take responsibility for identifying, developing, and fully utilizing knowledge for professional practice.

VI. **The social worker's ethical responsibility to society**

  P. Promoting the general welfare. The social worker should promote the general welfare of society.

APPENDIX 2

RESEARCH METHODOLOGY

1. Literature

After an exhaustive search of the social work practice literature, including historical and contemporary pieces, a substantive outline was formulated with the most frequently cited propositions that had been serving as the theory base of social work practice. Incorporating the competencies into the shape of a grid enabled us to view traditional practice principles alongside major authors, and at the same time attend to fields of service and population groups.

While the important texts are included in the chapter bibliographies, the following sources were particularly important in shaping the author's thinking:

Aptekar, H. (1941). *Basic concepts in social casework*. Chapel Hill, N.C.: University of North Carolina.

Blalock, H. (1969). *Theory construction: From verbal to mathematical formulations*. Englewood Cliffs, N.J.: Prentice-Hall.

Glaser, B., & Strauss, A. (1967). *The discovery of grounded theory: Strategies for qualitative research*. New York: Aldine de Gruyter.

Kasius, C. (1950). *A comparison of diagnostic and functional casework concepts*. New York: Family Service Association.

Lincoln, Y., & Guba, E. (1985). *Naturalistic inquiry*. Beverly Hills, Calif.: Sage.

Lofland, J., & Lofland, L. (1984). *Analyzing social settings*. Belmont, Calif.: Wadsworth.

Perlman, H. H. (1989). *Looking back to see ahead*. Chicago: University of Chicago Press.

Reynolds, B. (1942). *Learning and teaching in the practice of social work*. New York: Russell and Russell.

Richmond, M. (1922). *What is social casework: An introductory description*. New York: Russell Sage Press.

Roberts, R., & Nee, R. (1974). *Theories of social casework*. Chicago: University of Chicago Press.

Siporin, M. (1975). *Introduction to social work practice*. New York: Macmillan.

Yin, R. (1984). *Case study research: Design and methods*. Beverly Hills, Calif.: Sage.

2. Case material

Twenty social workers were selected to be interviewed based on recommendations by peers and colleagues for outstanding practice with clients. While many had experience in supervision and teaching, almost all had at least fifteen or more years of direct practice with individual clients. Personal interviews of about three hours in length were held with each of the social workers. The questionnaire is reported below.

On completion of the practice components, ten social work students were asked a modified set of questions to balance the range of case material and amplify the practice behaviors. Six experienced social workers and social scientists served to pilot the range of questions and reviewed a preliminary draft and chapter outline.

3. Reliability and validity

Tests for reliability and validity are difficult issues for case study research. To address construct validity—whether the case material represents practice cases—multiple sources of evidence were used with review by key informants. The expert social work practitioners represented a range of practice experiences and diverse training. Cases were from different agencies and geographic locations and were studied through process documents, case records, and audio and videotape material.

Internal validity—are the inferences correct?—was managed through the development of lengthy and descriptive explanations about the social work practice transpiring in each case example. These descriptions were offered by the practitioners through structured interviews. Narratives were elicited from the social workers to determine their decision-making process, the actual things they said and did, the conditions under which their behaviors were enacted. The narratives provided logical links between the case material and the propositions from the literature.

For external validity—will the findings generalize beyond the cases analyzed in this research?—analytical generalizations were formulated by the researcher. These generalizations form the basis of the social work theory building, one of the major outcomes of this project. Compared and contrasted with the propositions from the literature, they went through several revisions.

Concerns for reliability were addressed through thorough documentation, with a complete operationalization of the steps undertaken by the researcher. With this multiple case study design, replication logic answers the question, Do the different cases involve the same pattern of practice behaviors?

APPENDIX 3

QUESTIONNAIRE

Interview Guide for Practice Theory Project/P.I. Cynthia Bisman Brownstein

Introduction for practitioners

As we discussed on the phone, and as I indicated in our correspondence, this research is looking at practitioner's thinking about their practice. I want to initiate conversations about, not interrogate. There is not a right or wrong here. I will, hopefully, not be doing much of the talking. In grounded research the theory is developed out of the data. I am not talking with you out of a particular theoretical framework, but will be working at building generalizations out of all the conversations with experienced practitioners.

This particular case situation is offering us a vehicle for you to talk about your practice. It can also be used in the book as an example or model of how a practitioner proceeds. The really useful and important contribution here, is your talking about your thinking about what you are doing. We are not evaluating what you did. It is important for me to hear about your approach. When you work with a client what do you look for in terms of proceeding? What led you to do what you did? What reasons or assumptions or, perhaps, theories prompt or shape your behavior? These are not easy questions, and there may not be ready answers. There is not a specific answer I want or need. I just want to hear you talk about your reasons for what you were doing.

These interviews will be the telling of the story of the *what* and *how* of social work practice. I am asking experienced social work practitioners, like yourself, to talk about how they form a relationship, how they go about understanding the problem and how they decide how to define it (assessment), what they decide to do about it (how they formulate a plan of intervention), what they say and how they interact (communication), what they actually do (intervention), how they know they are doing it or how they monitor what they are doing and how they evaluate what they have done (evaluation). The interviews will be focusing on a session with a particular client.

We have already discussed issues of confidentiality. I will be changing the names of the workers and the clients to assure that confidentiality will not be violated.

Confidentiality Be sure to get worker and agency approval on confidentiality for client, worker and agency.

Brief description of the setting   Get agency brochure to provide basic information about kinds of services. Ask about typical kinds of problems seen, and how the social worker functions at this setting (Save this for the end *or a* follow-up phone call or you will spend too much time on this).

Observe   the surroundings—what is it like to be in the office of the social worker, where does the client sit, and where does the social worker sit?

Brief factual summary of case   Age, gender, type of employment, salary, educational level, ethnicity.

Presenting problem   How did the client get to the worker, self-referred or other (who?), why? How does the client, referral, state the problem?

What role did the referral source play in how you initially proceeded?   How did you use that information with the client?

Review of the previous practice
How many previous sessions have you had with this client?
What are some things you said and did early on when you first met this client?
What do you call this, when you are initially beginning with the client?

Getting Started
What was the nature of your initial contact?
How did you introduce yourself?
How did you talk about what you would be doing together?
How did you physically situate yourselves in the room? Why?
Where do you greet the client?
How did you agree on working together and the details of that? Was there clarity by both of you about what you would be doing, any sort of contract? What did you talk about?

Building a case approach   (this session, from the audio or videotape or process recording)
What were you trying to do in this particular piece of practice? Why? What was going on here?
How does this piece of practice relate to your ongoing work with this client?
How did you decide on this way of proceeding?
Were there alternatives that you considered?

Impact of worker's thoughts and feelings   (this session)
Describe what you were feeling in this session.
Describe what you were thinking during this session.
How did your feelings affect what you were doing?
How did your thinking affect what you were doing?

Relationship

What did you actually do to form the relationship?

Describe the kind of relationship you have with this client.

How is the relationship evident in this piece of practice?

How did who this person is shape the kind of relationship you formed?

How did who you are shape the kind of relationship you formed?

Communication

Describe how you communicate with this client.

Are there particular ways you talk, words you use, ways you posture yourself? Why? Does that vary via the client?

How does the client's bio-psycho-social situation and functioning affect how you communicate?

Evaluation

How do you decide whether you like what you are doing here?

How long will you be continuing what you are doing with this client? Why?

How will you decide to make any changes in what you are doing?

What factors will go into your considerations?

How do changes in the rest of the client's life affect your decision?

What part does the client play in what you do?

How do you decide whether you are effective?

Termination

How do you end your sessions?

Do you try to end in a specific way?

General Perspective on Practice

Assessment

Describe how you shape what is presented to you by the client into your own understanding.

What pieces do you look for in shaping the information into a problem statement?

What is your problem statement for this client?

How is a "person-in-environment" perspective evident in this piece of practice?

How do you obtain information about the client's social functioning?

How important is it for you to get information about the client's social situation?

Influences of training, experience, agency, etc.

How alike was this case to others you have had?

How much did your experience with other cases affect what you did with this case?

How does the agency service delivery shape what you do with the client? How have you used your training and experience in your work with this case?

Discuss things that we have not touched on that impact on your practice with this client (in terms of issues at the setting, personal issues with you, and things about this client).

If you could restructure some features at your setting, what would you do?

Demographics of worker

Age

Years of experience

Type of experience

Education

Training

Ethnicity

Gender

Tenure in agency

Theoretical perspective: Please discuss your theoretical perspectives—your training and models you now prefer.

INDEX

TO THE OWNER OF THIS BOOK:

We hope that you have found *Social Work Practice: Cases and Principles* useful. So that this book can be improved in a future edition, would you take the time to complete this sheet and return it? Thank you.

School and address: _____

Department: _____

Instructor's name: _____

1. What I like most about this book is: _____

_____

2. What I like least about this book is: _____

_____

3. My general reaction to this book is: _____

_____

4. The name of the course in which I used this book is: _____

_____

5. Were all of the chapters of the book assigned for you to read? _____

   If not, which ones weren't? _____

_____

6. In the space below, or on a separate sheet of paper, please write specific suggestions for improving this book and anything else you'd care to share about your experience in using the book.

_____

_____

_____

_____

_____

_____

Optional:

Your name: _____ Date: _____

May Brooks/Cole quote you, either in promotion for *Social Work Practice: Cases and Principles* or in future publishing ventures?

Yes: _____ No: _____

Sincerely,

ATT: Cynthia Bisman
Brooks/Cole Publishing Company
511 Forest Lodge Road
Pacific Grove, California 93950-9968

Brooks/Cole is dedicated to publishing quality publications for education in the human services fields. If you are interested in learning more about our publications, please fill in your name and address and request our latest catalogue.

Name _____

Street Address _____

City, State, and Zip _____

ATT: Human Services Catalogue
Brooks/Cole Publishing Company
511 Forest Lodge Road
Pacific Grove, California 93950-9968